Auke-wingeke-tawso, or,
'Defender of His Country'

The Circumstances & Services of Charles
Michel de Langlade (1729 – 1800)

A.K.A., "The Bravest of the Brave"
Through the French-Indian
& American Revolutionary War Periods

Compiled & Edited
Cody Cole

Auke-wingeke-tawso, or, 'Defender of His Country'
Copyright © 2024 by Cody Cole

All rights reserved. No part of this publication may be reproduced, distributed, or transmitted in any form or by any means, including photocopying, recording, or other electronic or mechanical methods, without the prior written permission of the author, except in the case of brief quotations embodied in critical reviews and certain other non-commercial uses permitted by copyright law.

Tellwell Talent
www.tellwell.ca

ISBN
978-1-77962-148-1 (Hardcover)
978-1-77962-147-4 (Paperback)
978-1-77962-149-8 (eBook)

Adult likeness of Charles Langlade, as illustrated in the "Wisconsin State Journal" (Saturday, June 26th, 1976 edition).

Table of Contents

Illustrations vii
Acknowledgements & Dedication.................................... xi
Introductory Notes by the Compiler & Editor xiii
Prologue xvii

Chapter I: 1668 – 1753: The Ancestral History of Charles Michel de Langlade; His Birth; Early Life and Career..1

Chapter II: 1754 – '60: Charles Langlade & the French & Indian Theatre of the Seven Years' War in North America, A.K.A., "the War of Conquest" 52

Chapter III: 1761-63: The English Occupation of Green Bay to Pontiac's War..289

Chapter IV: 1764 – '81: Charles Langlade, the Brewing Storm & the American Revolutionary War 314

Chapter V: 1782 – 1800: The Later Life & Career of Charles Langlade; His Death, etc.,..357

Epilogue 379
Bibliography..393

Illustrations

Supposed youthful likeness of Charles Langlade, illustrated by Harold Kimberly Lawson (circa. 1900) .... Cover illustration

Adult likeness of Charles Langlade, as illustrated in the "Wisconsin State Journal" (Saturday, June 26th, 1976 edition) iii

"French and Indian War: Map of the Scene of Operations". From "Harper's Encyclopedia of the United States" (circa. 1900) xviii

Circa. 1900 black & white photo of page one of Charles Langlade & Charlotte Bourassa's marriage contract. Dated August 11th, 1754. From "The French Regime in Wisconsin, 1634-1760: 1748-1760", by Reuben Gold Thwaites (1908). Document donated to the Wisconsin Historical Society in 1903 by Charles & Charlotte's descendants, the Grignon family 47

The initial disposition of English General Edward Braddock's army, the French, Canadians and Indigenous warriors at the onset of the Battle of the Monongahela, July 9th, 1755. From "Montcalm and Wolfe", by Francis Parkman (19th century; various editions) 50

The later disposition of English General Edward Braddock's army, the French, Canadians and Indigenous warriors during the Battle of the Monongahela, July 9th, 1755. From "A Half Century of Conflict", by Francis Parkman (19th century; various editions) 51

The pommel of the sword (Neville Public Museum, Green Bay, Wisconsin Photo ID#: L817A) presented to Charles Langlade for his distinguished services rendered to the French cause, leading up to the 1760 campaigning season, by King Louis XV. High quality modern-day photograph courtesy of the Neville Public Museum of Brown County, Green Bay, Wisconsin, who retain the copyright of the photo and possess the weapon. (Image cropped slightly from the left by the compiler/editor.) 191

Charles Langlade's British scarlet red Officer's coat (Neville Public Museum, Green Bay, Wisconsin Photo ID#: L817). Modern-day photograph courtesy of the Neville Public Museum of Brown County, Green Bay, Wisconsin, who retain the copyright of the photo and possess the item 288

The region in which English General John Burgoyne's army campaigned in 1777. From "The American Revolution", by John Fiske (1891) 313

A silver-mounted flint-lock pistol (Wisconsin Historical Society, WHI-164071), owned by Charles Langlade. Modern-day photograph courtesy of the Wisconsin Historical Society, who retain the copyright of the photo and possess the weapon 356

Charles Langlade's letter of July 26th, 1800, to Messrs. Rocheblave and Porlier. From "The French Regime in Wisconsin, 1634-1760: 1748-1760", by Reuben Gold Thwaites (1908) 368

Charles Langlade's colored porcupine quill decorated buckskin travelling sack (Wisconsin Historical Society, WHI-164070). Used to carry weapons, attire, documents and so forth. Modern-day photograph courtesy of the Wisconsin Historical Society, who retain the copyright of the photo and possess the item 377

"The brilliant service and the utter obscurity of this man (Charles Langlade) cause one to almost despair of history."

> *"History of Wisconsin Under the Dominion of France", Stephen Southric Hebberd (1890).*

"For length and variety of service, and for successful leadership of Indians in war, America has never known the equal of Charles de Langlade."

> *"The Northwest Under Three Flags, 1635 – 1796", Charles Moore (1900).*

"(Charles) Langlade was mild and patient (…) He knew how to inspire at once the affection and the respect of his acquaintances. His integrity was proverbial (…)."

"Memoir of Charles de Langlade", Joseph Tasse, Esq. (1855).

Acknowledgements & Dedication

Infinite thanks are due to my publisher, Tellwell Canada, and their representatives, Mitchel Anderson and Alyza Nykhol Alenton, for their boundless patience, sound advice and encouragement over the course of this project, plus Benjam Mosquera and Joseph Apuhin for additional formatting and design. With very special thanks additionally due to; David Driscoll and Lisa Marine of the Wisconsin Historical Society for permission to reproduce modern, high-quality photographs of Charles Langlade's porcupine quill travelling sack and his silver mounted flintlock pistol; and to Daniel Fulwiler and Dennis Rosloniec of the Neville Public Museum of Brown County, Green Bay, Wisconsin, for written permission to use modern, high-quality photos of Charles Langlade's British officer's scarlet red coat and sword.

This work is dedicated to; my family ("Mom"/Catrina; "Dad"/Scott; "Bro"/Kyle, plus my extended family and friends too numerous to name but whom I love and cherish no less); my many former teachers at Ridgewood Public School; Fenelon Falls Secondary School; as well as the Wisconsin Historical Society; the Neville Public Museum of Brown County, Green Bay, Wisconsin, and to the descendants of Charles Langlade, who, to this day, continue to live in Wisconsin, U.S.A., Ontario, Canada, and doubtless elsewhere.

Introductory Notes by the Compiler & Editor

"*Auku-wingeke-tawso, or, 'Defender of His Country': The Circumstances & Services of Charles Michel de Langlade (1729 – 1800), A.K.A., 'The Bravest of the Brave' Through the French-Indian & American Revolutionary War Periods*" was written over the course of nearly three years. Ironically, many hours' worth of research was more-or-less conducted in vain (although not without immense interest to the compiler and editor), as they had been spent attempting to connect Charles Langlade to specific persons, places and events the man was associated with over the course of his life and career. This process was further complicated by the sheer number of incorrect spellings of Charles Langlade's name (particularly his last) which the compiler of this work encountered while conducting research. Among them; "*L'anglade*"; "*L'englade*"; "*Longlade*"; "*Langdale*"; "*Langlead*"; "*Langlad*"; "*Langlake*"; "*Langland*"; and "*Langloid*", with the compiler of this work additionally noting at least one occasion when Charles Langlade was confused with a French-Canadian officer named "*de Langy*", who was stationed in North America during the 1750s.

Every work listed in the "*Bibliography*" provided valuable information, no matter how brief or seemingly inconsequential independently, while most notable persons in this work, at their first introduction by the compiler and editor himself, are accompanied by their exact or approximate birth and death date, if such information could be found. Additionally, words or sentences contained within crescent parentheses/brackets in reproduced documents are original to the document, while squared parentheses/brackets are inserted by the compiler, often enclosing a correction, additional information, potentially offensive language, or three periods — which indicates that unneeded or unrelated text was omitted.

Lastly, the compiler and editor would like to address the act of scalping (the removal of hair-baring skin atop the head), which is referenced several times in historical documents contained withing this work, and which has been historically (negatively) associated with Native North American Indigenous peoples, although the practice itself is recorded in Europe by Herodotus (in 1502) as dating far back as the ancient Scythians (a nomadic Iranian equestrian people) between the 7th to 3rd centuries B.C.E., while other examples of its implementation have been noted in Scandinavian, Visigoth, Frankish and Anglo-Saxon histories.

In the context of post-Columbus (1492) North America, albeit being otherwise largely out of date, Eastern Montana College's 1986 publication, *"Teaching the Indian Child"* (edited by Dr. Jon Reyhner), contains the most concise and informed opinion on scalping that the compiler and editor of this work could yet find:

"Writers made scalping a significant aspect of all Indian life and used this as evidence of 'savagery'. They did not make it clear that the Indians in the New England area were paid bounties for scalps by both the French and the English. They also do not mention that some [European] colonists also made an income collecting bounties for scalps. Children's history books do not tell how the custom of scalping spread with the intensification of intertribal war brought on as Indian tribes were pushed west by European settlers. The emphasis on scalping is just one example of inaccurate stereotypes which falsify the picture of Indian life."

Now, without further ado, the compiler of this work would like to conclude by bidding you, the reader, thanks, for having read thus far, and hopes that the rest of this work will prove worthy your time.

Your most humble and obedient servant,

Cody Cole.

September 22nd, 2023.

P.S., Upon a last minute inclination, the compiler of this work would additionally like to apologize in advance of any possible errors or misrepresentation (no matter how small) which may, inadvertently, be contained within this work. It was in no way the compiler's desire to deliberately mislead and he hopes that any such errors or misrepresentations in this book (should they exist) will not detract from your overall appreciation of this work, detailing the very real, unique and varied life of Charles Langlade, and the turbulent times during which he lived, for it is the compiler's most ardent desire that, above all else, and if nothing else, that this work will serve to foster an appreciation of history in those whom the subject is of minimal interest and foster a deeper appreciation in those already obsessed.

Thank you again for having read thus far, and please forgive me for having been indeed exposed a liar in this late addition to the introduction of this work, as in the previous letter that constitutes in it, I concluded with, "Now, without further ado", but now, well... I have "furthered your ado", as it were.

C.C.

September 29th, 2024.

Prologue

As Washington Irving observed in his *'Astoria; Or, Anecdotes of an Enterprise Beyond the Rocky Mountains'* (1882), *"**Two leading objects of commercial gain [gave] birth to wide and daring enterprise[s] in the early history of the Americas; the precious metals of the south, and the rich peltries of the north. While the fiery and magnificent Spaniard, inflamed with the mania for gold, ha[d] extended his discoveries and conquests over those brilliant countries scorched by the ardent sun of the tropics, the adroit and buoyant Frenchman, and the cool and calculating Brition, [...] pursued the less splendid, but no less lucrative, traffic in furs amidst the hyperborean [wooded] regions of the Canadas, until they ha[d] advanced even within the arctic circle.*"

Indeed, *"It was the fur trade, in fact, which gave early sustenance and vitality to the great Canadian provinces"*, asserts Irving, who goes on to note that, *"a new and anomalous class of men gradually grew out of this trade. These were called [the] 'Coureurs des [or 'de'] bois', rangers [or 'runners'] of the woods; originally men who had accompanied the Indians in their hunting expeditions, and made themselves acquainted with remote tracts and tribes; and who now became, as it were, 'pedlars of the wilderness'. These men would set out from Montreal with canoes well-stocked with goods, with arms and ammunition, and would make their way up the mazy and wandering rivers that interlace the vast forests of the Canadas, costing the most remote lakes, and creating new wants and habitudes among the Natives. Sometimes they sojourned for months among them, assimilating to their tastes and habits with the happy facility of Frenchmen; adopting in some degree the Indian dress, and not unfrequently taking to themselves Indian wives"*, with any offspring they may have, in turn, referred to as "*Bois brulés*" ('*charred*' or '*burnt*' wood), or, more popularly, the "*Métis*".

From "Harper's Encyclopedia of the United States" (19th century; various editions).

Chapter I

1668 – 1753: The Ancestral History of Charles Michel de Langlade; His Birth; Early Life and Career.

Charles Langlade's origins can be traced to the Castelsarrasin commune community, located in the Occitanie region of Southwest France, an area which had suffered greatly during the Hundred Years' War (1337 – 1453), between France and England, and the French Wars of Religion (1562 – 1598 and 1621 – 29), between the Catholics and Protestants. Situated in a fertile plain approximately 34 miles (55 km) Northwest of the city of Toulouse and one mile from the banks of the Garonne River, it was here, in approximately 1639, that Charles Langlade's great grandfather, Pierre Mouet de Maras, was born. Of noble birth, as a young man, attaining the rank of ensign, he joined the Carignan-Saliéres Regiment and was soon en-route to North America.

The Carignan-Saliéres Regiment was the first regiment of regular troops ever sent to the "*New World*" of North America by the French. Raised in Savoy, Italy, by Thomas Francis, the 1st Prince of Carignan (1596 – 1656) in 1644, eight years later, it served with distinction under the great French general, Louis II de Bourbon, the Prince of Condé (1621 – 86) during the Fronde Rebellion (1648 – 53). Following the Treaty of the Pyrenees (November, 1659), unable to maintain the regiment himself, the Prince of Condé, in a word, "donated" it to the King Louis XIV (1638 – 1715), *"The Sun King"* of France, under whom, it was incorporated into the French army.

Five years later, the regiment won further distinction in the Austro-Turkish War (1663-64), in which most of central Europe allied against the Ottoman Empire, after which, in 1665, it was dispatched to North America, under the command of Colonel Henri de Chastelard de Salières (1602 – 80), from which the regiment would derive the latter half of its name.

Along with the regiment came Alexandre de Prouville, Marquis de Tracy (circa. 1600 – 70), a nobleman, whom King Louis XIV had appointed *"Viceroy of America"*, and instructed to proceed to Canada, where, with the aid of the Carignan-Saliéres Regiment, he was to put a stop to the Iroquois raids on New France (Canada + the Mississippi) and to establish unity in the colony's administration, which was to be helmed by Daniel Remy, Sieur de Courcelles (1626 – 98), who was to serve as the colony's new Governor General, replacing Augustin de Saffray, Sieur de Mesy (1598 – 1666), while Jean Talon was appointed the colony's Intendent.

On the 19th of June, 1665, four companies of the Carignan-Saliéres Regiment arrived at Quebec, ahead of the Marquis de Tracy, who arrived eleven days later with four others, in addition to a number of dedicated colonists, marriageable women, artisans and domestic animals, with the remainder of the vessels carrying the Carignan-Saliéres Regiment, as well as new Governor General, de Courcelles, and Intendant, Talon, arriving at Quebec between September 12th and 14th. In total, the regiment consisted of approximately two thousand to twenty-two hundred men, with most of its officers and many of its troops having been from wealthy and/or noble families of France, among them, Charles Langlade's ancestor.

The most pressing issue to be addressed by the newly arrived government and army remained the raids of the Iroquois. As the latter's main incursion route was the Richelieu River, before the year 1665 was over, the French had constructed three forts along said river; one at Sorel, near the mouth of the Richelieu; a second just below the Chambly Rapids; and a third just above the rapids, while an addition fort was constructed along the St. Lawrence River, between the mouth of the Richelieu and Montreal Island.

Subsequently, service-expired officers and troops were gifted grants for land and financial compensation to build homes and clear land for cultivation, a colonial-encouragement measure which indeed encouraged many to settle down and stay in Canada, one such being, Pierre Mouet de Maras, who, by the 1670s, had married a Canadian woman by the name of Marie Teupin, and afterwards, settling at Trois Rivierés — an administrative region outside Quebec, dedicated the remainder of his life helping to raise a family of seven sons; Pierre; Jacques; Réné; Louis; Michel; Joseph; Marie; and two daughters; Madeleine and Thérèsa. The eldest son, born in 1669, and named after his father, was also an ensign in the army, and later married Elizabeth Jutras, with whom he would have eight children; Marie; Francoise; Marie-Josette; Jean-Baptiste; Marie-Marguerite; Didace; Isabelle; and Augustin.

As was common practice at the time, Pierre Mouet (the younger) elected to bestow an ancestral surname upon his son, Augustin. In this case, he chose *"de Langlade"*, which, although as of yet unknown in North America, already carried considerable prestige in France — two de Langlades, Raymond Girard (circa. 1540 – 1600), and later, his grandson, Jean Girard (circa. 1580 – 1650), having served as Mayor of Périgueux (from 1592 – 95 and in 1647, respectively). Both had resided in the Château de la Chalupie, outside Eyliac, France.

Augustin Mouet de Moras, Sieur de Langlade, better known simply as Augustin de Langlade, was born at Trois Riviéres, in September, 1703, to Pierre Mouet (the younger) and Elizabeth Jutras, and while still a youth, became involved in the flourishing fur trade, which brought him into favorable contact with many local Indigenous First Nations. Through these associations, by 1727, he had met and married Domitilde (circa. 1692 – 1782), the widow of Daniel Villeneuve (married 1712; died 1724) and the elder sister of Nissowaquet (circa. 1715 – 97), known to the French as *"La Fourche"* (*"The Fork"*), the influential King (or Chief) of the Ottawa Nation. From this marriage was born several children. The eldest, a daughter named Agate, was born approximately 1722. She was followed by a son, baptized on the 9th of May 1729, and named Charles Michel Mouet de Moras de Langlade.

As a youth, Charles received a dual education, from both the French Jesuit missionaries, namely Father Pierre du Jaunay (1705 – 80), for years based in Michilimackinac, who taught him French, reading and writing, while the extended Indigenous side of his family taught him the language, customs and traditions of the Ottawa people, and in the company of whom, the young Langlade would partake in his first military campaign.

All accounts of Langlade's life and career concur that it was while he was still a youth when he first experienced the trials and tribulations of a military expedition, however few agree on his approximate age at the time at the time — although all agree he was no more than ten or eleven years old at the most. This uncertainty is compounded by the fact that the year of Langlade's birth itself is subject to debate, as while it is a fact that he was *baptized* on May 9th, 1729, no record of his birth, specifically, is known, and baring that in mind, his grandson, Augustin Grignon (1780 – 1860), whose *"Seventy-Two Years' Recollections of Wisconsin"* — assembled from various interviews held between himself and L.C. Draper from May 26th to June 8th, 1857, were the earliest and perhaps (until now) the most comprehensive summary of Langlade's life and career — casually asserts that his ancestor was born in 1724 and was subsequently ten years old at the time of his first military venture, the circumstances of which he recalled thus:

"[…] When he [Langlade] was ten years of age, the Ottawas were engaged in a war against some allied tribe of the English, who aided to interrupt the French communication with Louisiana […]. This village was located on a prairie, protected by such defenses as Indians were able to make; and twice had the Ottawas attacked the place, and twice been discomfited. When urged by the French Commandant […] to make a third attempt upon the enemy's stronghold, they declined; but at length King Nis-so-wa-quet and his brothers, prompted by some superstitious dream, whim, or

prestige, said they would again make the trial, provided, they could be accompanied by their young nephew, Charles de Langlade, and would go on no other condition. The [French] Commandant went to the Sieur Augustin de Langlade, and made known the requirements of the chiefs; and, surprised at the request for such a mere lad to accompany them, and thinking perhaps it was a plan which the youth had formed, and had desired his uncles to put into effect, M. [Augustin] de Langlade went to his son and asked him concerning the matter, when Charles frankly assured his father that it was no plan or wish of his. "Well," said the father, "you must go with your uncles; but never let me hear of your showing any marks of cowardice." Reaching the place, young Charles and some other lads, also taken along, were placed in the rear, in full view, but out of danger of the attack, which was soon made; and after a severe assault, the place was taken. Viewing the conflict, Charles used to relate to me, in his old age, that it then seemed like a ball [game] to him. Ever after, when the Ottawas went on war expeditions, they were invariably accompanied by young Charles de Langlade."

Under the presumption that Charles Langlade was born in 1724 as his grandson, Augustin Grignon, contended, the following document from 1733 relates a renewed Franco-Indigenous military expedition against the Foxes (or "*Renards*") and their then allies, the Sauk (or "*Saki*"), which bares much similarity to the events in which Grignon spoke of his grandfather partaking, and it is worth noting that, at the time of this event, Langlade would have been nine years of age (once again presuming he was born in 1724, as opposed to '29), much to the credit of Grignon's recollections, recorded one hundred and twenty four years later:

"Quebec, November 11th*, 1733.*

Monsiegneur — Monsieur de Beauharnois had the honor by his letter of the first of July last to inform you of the orders that he had given to the Sieur De Villiers whom he had sent back as Commandant at La Baye, and of the manner in which was to act regarding the Renards [Foxes]. The result has not fulfilled our expectations.

The Sieur de Villers, the younger, an Ensign in the troops, who has succeeded to the Command of that post through the death of his Father, has sent one of his brothers [likely Louis Coulon de Villiers] and the Sieur Douville with letters giving us the particulars of what happened in the month of September last at the Post of La Baye.

Monsieur De Villiers, the Commandant of that Post arrived there on the 16th of the said month of September alone in his canoe. He had left at a distance of half a League from there the Sieur De Repentigny, a Lieutenant, who was Commandant at Missilimakinac, together with 200 [Indigenous warriors]; Outawacs [Ottawa], Folles Avoines, and Sauteux, and about 60 French. The Sieur De Villiers had given him orders to be ready to march as soon as he heard the signal of 3 gun-shots and he had also detached his son, the Ensign, with 10 Frenchmen and 50 [Indigenous warriors] to the Petit Cacalin [later known as "Little Kaukauna", Brown County, Wisconsin, approximately ten miles above the modern-day city of Green Bay], a passage by which the Renards might escape.

When Monsieur De Villiers arrived at the French fort, he at once sent for the Saki [Sauk] Chiefs to inform them of their father's Intentions. The chiefs came to him and he explained to them that their father had granted the remnant of the Renards who were with them, their lives; but on the condition that they should submit to his orders and go to Montreal. After a council which lasted some time, as the Sakis Chiefs gave no positive answer, Monsieur De Villiers sent 4 of them back to their fort to tell their tribe that if within a certain time they did not send the Renards to him, he would go and get them himself. When the specified time had elapsed without the Renards appearing, and when Monsieur de Villiers, whom the sieur De Repentigny had joined, saw that the Sakis were not coming back, he resolved to go to their fort in person accompanied by two of his children, by the Sieur Douville, the younger, his son-in-law, and by 7 or 8 French to ask them to deliver up the Renards to Him.

He had just given orders to the Sieur De Repentigny to guard the approaches to the Sakis' fort with the remainder of the French lest the Renards should escape. When Monsieur De Villiers arrived at the door of the fort he asked the Sakis for the Renards. He found there some armed Sakis who told him to withdraw, and when he tried to enter a [warrior] approached him with uplifted Tomahawk and at the same moment three gun-shots were fired, one of which killed one of the Sieur De Villiers' sons at his side. The father and the French discharged their pieces and this was followed by other volleys from the Sakis by which Monsieur de Villiers was killed, and three French were wounded.

Monsieur De Repentigny, who guarded the approaches on the side of the woods, ran up and was killed a moment afterward in a sortie that the Sakis made against him. The Sieur Duplessis, a Cadet in the Troops, and six other French met the same fate. 200 of our (Native warriors) who had remained in the French fort went to the assistance of the others and when the Sakis saw them coming they withdrew into their fort. 3 of them were killed.

Three days after this action the Sakis evacuated their fort during the night and the Ensign, Sieur De Villiers, who had returned from le petit Cacalin, assembled all the French and [Indigenous warriors] — Outawacs [Ottawa], Folles Avoines and Sauteux — and pursued the Sakis and overtook them about 4 o'clock in the evening 8 Leagues from the post. He attacked them and fought them until night. 20 Sakis and 6 Renards were killed in this last fight; 9 were mortally wounded besides others who were wounded and whose number is not known. On the side of the Sieur De Villiers, his brother, a Cadet with aiguillettes, received a gun-shot wound in the arm; The Sieurs Daillebout, the des Musseaux brothers, and 8 other French were also wounded while two others were killed.

The Outawacs [Ottawa] lost 9 men, the grand Chief of the nation being among the number; the Folles Avoines 6; the Sauteux 2 and 4 wounded in all.

Monsieur De Beauharnois will at once give the necessary orders to attack the Sakis and the remainder of the Renards to avenge the blood of the French that has been shed, and he will concert with Monsieur Hocquart regarding the expense that will have to be incurred. He has the honor to submit to you by a private netter the Names of the officers who are to replace those who have been killed. We unite with him in asking you for their promotion which they deserve, and a pension for Madame De Villiers, to provide for her subsistence and that of her numerous family, since she is a widow with 10 children. The Sieur De Villiers who was wounded and the Sieur Douville, the younger, arrived this evening from Montreal. Fortunately, the Vessel Le Saint Joseph of L'Isle Royale which sailed this morning, had been compelled to put back in consequence of a leak. It will sail tomorrow at daybreak and we have barely time to write you this letter.

We remain with very profound respect, Monseigneur, Your very humble and very obedient servants,

Beauharnois.
Hocquart."

Indeed, *"My grandfather told me he was in the battle with the Sauks (for the Sauks and Foxes were allies)"*, explicitly recalls Augustin Grignon, later on in his *"Recollections"*, with his description of the settlement in his narrative as being located "on a prairie" consistent with a January 15th, 1731 report, addressed to the French Ministry by Giles Hocquart (1694 – 1783), the Intendant of New France at the time, in which he describes the Foxes (also known as the *"Renards"*) as having been located *"in a Plain situated between [the] River Wabache [Wabash] and the River of the Illinois, about 60 leagues to the south of the extremity or foot of Lake Michigan, to the east south east of Le Rocher in the Illinois County"*.

Nonetheless, for the remainder of this work, the compiler of this work will assume that Charles Langlade was born the year of his baptism — 1729, as opposed to 1724, while acknowledging that Augustin Grignon may indeed be correct, and additionally, that Langlade could possibly still have accompanied the expedition as related above from 1733, but as a four-year-old instead — an occurrence that most certainly would not have been out of place during the period, however, while granting credence to the possibility that the events of 1733 are entirely unrelated to Langlade, and that the events his grandson recalls him partaking as a youth occurred elsewhere and at a later date.

With that in mind, Augustin Grignon's (1857) account bares much similarity to that of an elder north-western storyteller only referred to as *"Old Pierre"* (whom may have been a Grignon descendant - there were many), and whom, in either 1880 or '81, was interviewed **"*in the village of Ste. Anne, on the Ottawa [River], one beautiful evening in the month of July*"**, and whose entire tale was subsequently published under the title, *"The Couriers of the West"* in George Bryce's book, *"Manitoba"* (1882):

*"**My grandfather was a voyageur, and lived to be of great age**,"* recalled "Old" Pierre, "***and [he] told me the stories of the wild Indians of those days, and our brave French Canadians who were a match for them. There was a great man of whom he used to speak much, Monsieur de Langlade. […] My grandfather told me that when Langlade was a child about seven years of age, there was a war raging between the Ottawas, many of whom lived at Michilimackinac, and another tribe allied to the English. Twice the young men of the Ottawas had gone forth to attack a village of the enemy, and each time had they been driven back. The French officer at the fort urged them to make the attack again. The Ottawas were not willing. At last, their chief said that he had had a dream; that in the dream he saw a fight; that the young Langlade was there; and that in his dream the Ottawas seemed to win the day. The dream gave the young men courage on its being told them. They must be accompanied by the child Langlade, and they would go upon the war-path once more. The father Langlade, at first unwilling, at last agreed, but only on a pledge given by the boy that he would never disgrace his father by being a coward. The Ottawas were now ready to go forth; they advanced with the terrible***

war-cries of the [Natives]; inspired by the recollection of the dream and the presence of the boy, they gained the day [...]. The young Langlade was now held in great honor; they said he was no doubt preserved by a mighty Manitou ["Great Spirit"]."

"*About 1745, the Sieur Augustin de Langlade and his son, Charles, left Mackinaw, and migrated to Green Bay [then invariably known as La Baye ("The Bay")]; or, La Baie des Puants — "The Bay of Stinking Waters", where they became the principal proprietors of the soil,*" continues Augustin Grignon's "*Recollections*". And whether coincidence or not, in a letter dated September 22nd, 1746, and addressed to the French Ministry, jointly, from the Governor-General of New France, the Marquis de Beauharnois (1671 – 1749), and the colony's Intendent, Giles Hocquart, the following extract can be found:

"**We endeavored to find a farmer for the post of La Baye [Green Bay] but without success. [...] Nevertheless, Monsieur de la Corne, the Commandant at Michilimackinac, provided for the safety and indifferently for the trade of the said Post, by allowing two private individuals to fits themselves out at Michilimackinac for said place of La Baye, on condition that they pay 1,000 livres each.**"

Augustin and Charles Langlade "**settled on the east side of the Fox River, near its mouth [...],**" notes Augustin Grignon in his "*Recollections*", and there they were shortly thereafter joined by "*a few settlers, beyond their own family. M Souligny, the son-in-law of Sieur [Augustin] de Langlade, with his wife [Agate, Charles' older sister];*" as well as "*Monsieur Carron, who had been many years engaged in the Indian trade, and had fully twenty years before been among the Menomonees [...].*" Grignon goes on to state that, although others many had come as well, he could not recall whom and when, but asserts that "**probably no more than eight persons formed the little colony who commenced the permanent settlement of Wisconsin.**"

"**That their reception by the Indians inhabiting Green Bay was pleasant, was distinctly told me by my grandfather**", Grignon continues, "*but the band of Te-pak-e-ne-nee, or "The Night-Man",* *living about two miles up the Menomonee River, at their village of Min-nekau-nee, or Pleasant Town, where Marinette or Menomonee City is now located, used to come down, and make their threats that they would take by force Indian goods from Augustin de Langlade's store, or the Government stores in [the] charge of Charles de Langlade, calculating to intimidate, in order to get credit for goods, or have some given to them; but Charles de Langlade would pleasantly say to them, "Well, my friends, if you have come here to fight, we can cross to the prairie on the other side of the river, and have a little fun." But [the band of Te-pak-e-ne-nee] knew too well [Charles'] reputation as a soldier even from his boyhood, and declined his invitation, and he had no more difficulty from them."*

Around the same time "*a blacksmith of the name of Lammiot [...] located himself at Green Bay,*" continues Grignon, and "*an Indian, named Ish-qua-ke-ta, left an axe with him to be repaired. At length the Indian came for his axe, and threw down a skin [pelt of fur] as the price for the work, and took his property.*" However, as Grignon notes, the blacksmith, whose temper ran as hot as his kiln, and whose memory frequently as dull as the blades he mended, "*replied that it was not his [Ish-qua-ke-ta's] axe — that he had none, and bid him off. High words followed, and Lammoit seized the Indian by the neck with his hot tongs, both burning and choking him, when Ish-qua-ke-ta struck Lammoit a heavy blow over the head with the axe, and knocked him down senseless. The Indian hastened to Charles de Langlade, and frankly said, "I have killed the blacksmith." "What did you do that for?" [asked Langlade.] "Why!" [replied] the Indian, "Look here — see how he choaked and burnt me; I had to do it in self defense." De Langlade went and found Lammoit, carried him to his bed, and employed an Indian doctress to take care of him. When nearly recovered, and elder brother of Te-pak-e-ne-nee called, and asked to see the blacksmith, as he wanted to see how he was getting along. Upon entering the room, and walking up to the bed, he stabbed him with a knife, and killed him instantly. When asked by the attendant (doctress) why he had killed Lammoit, he [the elder brother of Te-pak-e-ne-nee] said he pitied the blacksmith, and wished to put an end to his sufferings.*" Augustin Grignon concluded this anecdote from Charles Langlade's early life by stating that, "***The murdered fled to some distant region, and remained till the excitement against him had cooled down, when he returned, and thus escaped a merited punishment. But he was not long after killed by an Indian in a drunken brawl.***" And it is worth noting that, once again, Grignon's "*Recollections*" bare much similarity to that of "*Old Pierre*", who recalled the same story thus, over twenty years after Grignon had originally:

"**Ah! Messieurs, my grandfather would get warm as he told us of the attacks, […] war-deeds and bloodshed of those wild times**," Old Pierre mused. "**He used to tell a terrible tale about a man of French origin, who came to Baie Verte to work at his trade, that of a blacksmith. An Indian had one day given the blacksmith, Amiot, an axe to mend. He came a few days afterwards, offering as pay for mending of the axe, a pelt, as was the custom. The blacksmith, forgetting all about the Indian having left the axe, denied there was such a thing of his there. The [Indian] replied warmly, and claimed his hatchet, with loud exclamations. Out of patience at last, Amiot seized the Indian by the neck, and burnt him terribly with the red-hot tongs. The Indian, mad with rage, delt in return such a blow with his axe, that the blacksmith was struck senseless to the earth. The [Indian] came to Langlade, told him what he had done, and that he had done it in self-defense, langlade went to the aid of the wounded man, who had recovered his senses, but was found to have a frightful gash in his head. Like a good Samaritan, he [Langlade] had him [Amiot, the blacksmith] taken to a neighboring house, where an Indian girl waited on him. But the worse is still to tell. One day, when Amiot had got past danger, a brother of the cruel chief, Tepakeneni, asked permission to see the blacksmith. No sooner had he entered the house, than he fell upon the half-recovered man, and delt him a fatal blow with his knife. The Indian girl asked the murdered why he had so acted, when he replied with a jest, that he had taken pity on the sick man, and wished to put him out of pain.**"

"*The [...] Foxes were at this time located at the Little Butte des Morts ["Little Mound of the Dead"], on the western bank of the Fox River, [...] some thirty-seven miles above Green Bay,*" continues Augustin Grignon's "*Recollections*", and "*as the details of the war which eventuated in the expulsion of the Sauks and Foxes from the Fox River Valley in 1746, are of much interest, I shall give them as fully as I have learned them from the lips of my grandfather, Charles de Langlade, who took an active part in some of the occurrences narrated, and from other ancient settlers and Indians.*"

From their principal village upon the Little Butte des Morts, as Grignon recalled, the Foxes "*made it a point, whenever a trader's boat approached, to place a torch upon the bank [of the Fox River], as a signal for the traders to come ashore, and pay the customary tribute, which they extracted from all. To refuse this tribute was sure to incur the displeasure of the Foxes, and robbery would be the mildest punishment inflicted. This haughty, imperious conduct of the Foxes was a source of no little annoyance to the traders, who made their complaints to the [French] Commandants of the western posts, and in due time, these grievances reached the ears of the Governor of Canada.*" However, as it quickly became apparent that neither the French Commandants, nor the Governor-General himself were predisposed to take any immediate action to address these grievances, one of the traders directly affected decided to take matters into his own hands. That man was Pierre Paul Marin, a.k.a., "*La Perriere*" Marin, or, simply, the "*Sieur Marin*", born in 1692, and whom, in local Green Bay tradition, is frequently referred to as "*Pierre Paul*", or "*Captain Morand*":

"*Capt. Morand, [...] a prominent trader among the Sauks, and the Indians on the Mississippi, had a place of deposit on the bank of the Mississippi, I think on the eastern bank of the river, and about eight or nine miles below the mouth of the Wisconsin [River], called Fort Morand*", recalled Augustin Grignon. "*[And] he had another depot nine miles west of Mackinaw, also known as Fort Morand [where] the repeated extractions of the Foxes in the shape of tribute, while [he] prosecuted [his] trade between Mackinaw and the Mississippi, through Green Bay and [the] Fox River, so vexed Morand, that he resolved on driving them from their position; and raising a small volunteer force at Mackinaw, increased doubtless at Green Bay, and by the friendly Indians, and though I have heard my grandfather repeatedly speak of this expedition both with others in whose day it had occurred, and to his family, yet I cannot positively say that he accompanied Morand — but judging from his military character, the numerous services of the kind in which he participated, and his familiarity with the details of this war, I doubt not he was of the party, and served in all of Morand's expeditions."*

After amassing men, munitions and canoes, *"**Morand's force was deemed sufficient**"*, resumes Grignon's narrative, *"**and his fleet of canoes started from Green Bay up the river** — each canoe having a full complement of men, well armed, and an oil-cloth covering large enough to envelope the whole canoe, as was used by the traders to shield their goods from the effects of the weather. Near the Grand Chute, some three miles below the Little Buttes de Morts ["Little Hill of the Dead"], and not yet within view of the latter, Morand divided his party, one part disembarking, and going by land to surround the village, and to attack the place when Morand and his water division should open their fire in front. The soldiers in the canoes, with their guns all ready for use, were concealed by the oil-cloth coverings, and only two men were in view to row each canoe, thus presenting the appearance of a trader's fleet.*

In due time the Foxes discovered their approach, [...] placed out their torch, and squatted themselves thickly along the bank as usual, [...] patiently await[ing] the landing of the canoes, and the customary tribute offering. [However] when sufficiently near to be effective, the oil-cloth coverings [of the canoes] were suddenly thrown off, and a deadly volley from a swivel-gun [small caliber mounted cannon], loaded with grape and cannister shot, [plus] the musketry of the soldiers, scattered death and dismay among the unsuspecting Foxes; [with] this severe fire [...] almost instantly seconded by the land party in the rear, [which was] quickly repeated by both divisions, so that a large number of the devoted Foxes were slain, [while] the survivors escaped by rapid flight up the river."

They "*next took post about three miles above the Great Buttes des Morts, on the southern or opposite bank of the river, on a high sandy point of land, with a marsh on its eastern border*", recalled Augustin Grignon. And here, "*Morand, the same season, followed them, but of course could not have resorted to his old ruse, and must have approached the town in the night, or just before daybreak; [in any event,] according to the general statement given me by my grandfather and aged Indians, another severe battle ensued, and many Foxes were killed, though not so many as at the Little Buttes des Morts, and again, they [the Foxes] were forced to fly. [...] The surviving Foxes located themselves on the northern bank of the Wisconsin [River], twenty-one miles above its mouth, and some little distance below the mouth of (the) Kickapoo River; when I first passed there, in 1795, I saw some crude remains of this village. As soon as the enterprising Morand heard of the new locality of his determined enemies, who still seemed bent on obstructing his great trading thorough-fare, he concluded it would be unsafe for him to suffer them to remain there, and consequently lost no time, even though winter had commenced, to collect his tried and trusty band of French and Indians, and make a distant, winter expedition against the Foxes. Perhaps he thought, as he had once defeated them by stratagem, and them by the usual mode of Indian warfare, that it would now be policy to push his fortunes by a winter campaign, and fall upon his inveterate (stubborn) foes, and strike a fatal blow, when they would least expect it.*

Captain Morand pursued on foot with his troops up [the] Fox River and down the Wisconsin, taking with them snowshoes to meet the exigencies [demands] of the season, and [on which they pursued the Foxes] for [...] two hundred miles. The Foxes were taken completely by surprise, for Morand's men found them engaged in the amusement of "jeu de paille", or, [a] game of straw[s]; and surrounding the place, and failing suddenly upon them, killed some, and captured the others. So well planned was

Morand's attack, and so complete was the surprise, that not one of the Foxes escaped. Only twenty Fox warriors were taken, with a large number of women and children. […]

I have been told that Capt. Morand, having fully conquered the Foxes, and having the last remnant of them in his power, concluded to give them their freedom, but probably required them to retire over the Mississippi; and that he liberated them at their town where he took them. […].

Of Capt. Morand, I know nothing further", admits Augustin Grignon in his "*Recollections*". However, "***Captain de Velie was at this time Commandant of the small garrison at Green Bay. He was relieved by the arrival of a new officer […], and the new Commandant brought with him demands for the Sauks of the village opposite the fort, who had hitherto demeaned themselves well, to deliver up the few Foxes living amongst them, in consequence of intermarriages or otherwise. All were readily given up, except a Fox boy, who had been adopted by a Sauk woman. De Velie and his successor were dining together, and becoming somewhat influenced by wine, some sharp words passed between them relative to the tardiness of the Sauks in surrendering the Fox boy; when De Velie arose, and taking his gun and a negro servant, crossed the river to the Sauk village, which was surrounded by palisades or pickets. He found the Sauks in council, and was met by the Sauk chief, of whom he demanded the immediate surrender of the remaining [Fox boy]. The chief said he and his principal men had just been in council about the matter, and though the adopted mother of the youth was loath [or reluctant] to part with him, […] they hoped to prevail upon her peaceably to do so. The chief proceeded to visit the old woman […] three times […] to prevail upon her to give up the [Fox] boy, [but] returning each time without success, [assured] De Velie that if he would be a little patient, he was certain the old [woman] would yet comply with his demands, as she seemed to be relenting. [However] in his warm blood [intoxicated state], the Frenchman was in no mood to exercise patience, when he at length drew up his gun and shot the chief dead. Some of young Sauks were for taking instant***

revenge, but the older and wiser men [...] begged them to be cool, and refrain from inflicting injury on their French Father, as they had provoked him to commit the act. [But] De Velie, whose anger was yet unappeased, had got his gun reloaded by his servant, and wantonly shot down another chief, and then a third one; when a young Sauk, only twelve years of age, named Ma-kau-ta-pe-na-se, or "the Black Bird", shot the enraged Frenchman dead."

As warranted as de Velie's death may have been, the French were nonetheless compelled to avenge it, however, as Grignon again notes in his *"Recollections"*, *"**The [French] garrison [of Green Bay] was too weak to attempt the chastisement of the Sauks [on their own], but upon the arrival of a reinforcement, joined by [...] French settlers, Charles de Langlade among them, the Sauks were attacked at their village, [where] a severe battle occurred, in which several were killed on both sides, and the Sauks finally driven away. In this battle two of my father's uncles were among the slain on the part of the French. The Sauks now retired to the Wisconsin River, and located themselves [on the] Sauk Prairie [...].**"* Grignon goes on to observe that the former's *"severe chastisement of the Foxes, had the effect to keep the Wisconsin tribes on friendly terms with the whites for many years."*

In volume one of William Rudolph Smith's *"The History of Wisconsin in Three Parts"* (1854), a similar account of the expedition against the Foxes is preserved, with its source being a Michael Brisbois, who was born in 1760, and whom, in 1781, settled in the Wisconsin village of Prairie du Chien, where he lived until his death in 1837.

In 1785, Brisbois married an Indigenous Winnebago woman, with whom he would have three children, after which, in 1796, he remarried to Domitelle Gautier de Verville (1781 – 1847), the daughter of Claude-Charles Gautier de Verville (circa. 1738 – 1803), the son of Charles Langlade's half-sister and whose name will become recognizable later in this work, as a frequent collaborator of Charles Langlade's. According to Brisbois' testimony:

"*A detachment of a considerable number of men, under the command of Monsieur Morand, was sent from Mackinac in a boat, in all respects resembling a traders' boat, which ascended the Fox River from Green Bay. The soldiers were concealed in the boat by a covering of skins, and they cautiously proceeded undiscovered, in this manner, up the river as far as the Great Butte des Morts, since so called, at which place was the great village of the Ottagamies [another name of the Foxes]. On their arrival here, the Foxes, as usual, appeared in full force on the banks of the river, in order to stop the boat, and extract from the supposed traders the customary payment of tribute. Capt. Morand had with him in the boat a swivel gun, well charged with canister and grape [shot]; the signal was given; the covering of the boat was immediately thrown off, and a volley from the concealed soldiers, together with a discharge from the swivel [gun], did murderous execution on the thickly crowded Ottagamies [or Foxes]. Scarcely had they time to recover from their first surprise, when a repetition of discharges from the musketry and the cannon nearly annihilated the whole tribe [;] the remainder of the band of Foxes soon after left this part of the country, and moved west of the Mississippi.*"

However, as period historian, W.R. Smith himself notes of Michael Brisbois' testimony, "**There is certainly a confusion of dates, or blending of incidents, in these accounts.**" And this confusion is perhaps most obvious in the similarities between the events of 1733, as earlier recorded (perhaps young Charles Langlade's first experience of war), in which Captain de Villiers was killed, and those attributed to 1746 by Augustin Grignon, in which a "Captain de Velie" was similarly killed. It is also obvious in the fact that a campaign of Pierre Paul Marin, waged against the Foxes in the year 1730, is recorded as having possessed the exact same circumstances of those which Augustin Grignon attributes to 1746 — that of oil-cloth covered canoes, concealing armed men and a swivel cannon, dividing into two separate forces, which ambush the Foxes, riverside. But it is worth noting that although Charles Langlade would only have been one year old in 1730, were he born in 1729, as generally accepted, were he born in 1724 instead — as his grandson later contended, he'd have been perhaps just old enough to accompany Marin's early 1730s expeditions.

Nonetheless, by 1746-47, Marin, or "*Morand*" as he was locally known, had assumed command of the French outpost of St. Joseph, Wisconsin, from where, later in that year, he reported on the dismal state of Indigenous affairs, which the sitting Governor-General of New France, Roland-Michel Barrin, the Marquis de la Galissonière (1693 – 1756) and the colony's Intendent, Giles Hocquart, noted, amongst other proceedings, in an official journal of events for the year 1747, which were subsequently transmitted to the French Ministry:

"*We are in receipt, also, of news from the River St. Joseph*", continues the lengthy journal, after detailing events pertaining to several other French outposts. "*Sieur Laperrière Marin, commanding at that post, writes us on the 5th and 30th of July last. It appears that the English are endeavoring to debauch the Nations belonging to that post, as well as all the others […].*" And indeed, within the same official journal of events of the year 1747, the Governor-General and Intendant acknowledge having received word of an Indigenous uprising that same month in the following terms:

"*July 20th. We are in receipt of letters both from Montreal and Detroit; those from Detroit are very interesting. Chevalier de Longueuil, commanding that post, writes us, on the 23rd June, that some Hurons [or more accurately, Wyandot or Wendat] of Detroit, belonging to the tribe of the war chief Nicholas, who, some years since, had settled at Sandoské [Sandusky Bay, Lake Erie], have killed five Frenchmen who were on their return from the post at the White River, and stolen their furs; that all the Indians of the neighborhood, except the Illinois, had formed the design to destroy all the French of Detroit on one of the holidays of Pentecost, and afterwards to go to the fort and subject all to fire and sword; that some Hurons, having struck too soon, the plot had been discovered by a Huron [woman] who came to give Chevalier de Longueuil notice of it; that this conspiracy is the fruit of the [wampum] belts the English have had distributed among all the* tribes by the Iroquois [...]; that on this notification he caused all the settlers to retire within the fort in order to be prepared for any new treachery."

A far more detailed account of what was called *"Nicholas' Conspiracy"*, however, based upon official period documents, can be found within the 1871 first published edition of the *"Journal of Captain William Trent"* (1752), which was penned by Trent (1715 – 78) while the event was still a recent memory, and its inclusion, the compiler of this work deems absolutely necessary, on account of the fact that one of Nicholas' co-conspirators, the Miamis, would later earn the distinction of being on the receiving end of the first verifiable military campaign in which a young Charles Langlade commanded, a campaign which had as its objective; the quelling of Miamis' ongoing revolt, post-Nicholas' Conspiracy; and the scaring away of the English trader-instigators. As per Trent's *"Journal"*:

"In 1745, a large party of Huron Indians belonging to the tribes of the war chief Nicholas removed from the Detroit River to lands on the north side of Sandusky Bay. They were a powerful body of men; active, energetic, and unscrupulous. They had in some manner been offended by the French at Detroit, which affords the reason of their change of habitation. Nicholas, their principal chief, was a wily fellow, full of savage cunning, whose enmity, when once aroused, was greatly to be feared.

Late in the same year a party of English traders from Pennsylvania visited the village of Nicholas, and were received with marked attention. Nicholas had become an implacable enemy of the French, and was therefore ready to make a treaty of amity and good will with the English. He accordingly permitted the erection of a large block house at his principal town on the bay, and suffered the traders to remain and dispose of their stock of goods. Once located, the English established themselves at the place, and, according to French accounts, acquired great influence with Nicholas and his tribe. This influence was always exercised to the injury of the French.

On the 23rd of June, 1747, five Frenchmen, with peltries, arrived at the Sandusky town from the White River, a small stream falling into the Wabash nearly opposite the present town of Mt. Carmel, Illinois. These Frenchmen, being wholly unaware of the presence of English among the Hurons, were unsuspicious of danger, and counted upon the hospitality and friendship of the Indians. Their presence, however, inspired anything but tokens of goodwill. Nicholas was greatly irritated at the audacity of the French in coming into his towns without his consent. The English traders noticing this feeling urged the chief to seize the Frenchmen and their peltries. This was accomplished on the afternoon of the day of their arrival. The fate of the poor Frenchmen was soon determined. Nicholas condemned them to death, and they were tomahawked in cold blood. Their stock of peltries were disposed of to the English, and by them sold to a party of Seneca Indians.

The news of these outrages created much feeling among the French at Detroit, and especially so among the traders in the Ohio country. As soon as the Sandusky murders came to the information of the governor of Canada, he ordered M. de Longueuil, commandant at Detroit, to send a messenger to Nicholas demanding the surrender of the murderers of the five Frenchmen. The demand was not complied with.

Three other messengers in turn followed, but were met with the same refusal. M. de Longueuil then sent a peremptory demand, requiring the surrender of the murderers, to be disposed of according to his pleasure; that the Hurons must ally themselves at once with the French, or the latter will become their irreconcilable enemies; that the French were disposed to look upon the recent murders as acts of irresponsible parties, and not of the Huron tribe, and that all English traders must leave the Indian towns forthwith.

The answer returned to these propositions amounted to a defiance, and [so] preparations were made for an expedition against Sandusky.

The crafty Nicholas [however] was not less active than the French. He formed a great conspiracy for the capture of Detroit and the upper French posts, and the massacre of the white inhabitants. How long this conspiracy had been brewing, we have no information; we know that by August, 1747, the Iroquois, Hurons, Outaouagas, Abenaquis, Pous, Ouabash, Sauteurs, Outaouas, Mississagues, Foxes, Sioux, Sacs, Sarastaus, Loups, Pouteouatamis, Chaouenons, and Miamis had entered. into a grand league, having for its object the extermination of French dominion and authority in the West. Every nation of Indians, excepting those in the Illinois country, entered into the plan with zeal and alacrity.

Offensive operations were to commence at once. A party of Detroit Hurons were to sleep in the fort and houses at Detroit, as they had often done before, and each was to kill the people where he lodged. The day set for this massacre was one of the holidays of Pentecost. A band of Pouteouatamis were commissioned to destroy the French mission and villages on Bois Blanc Island; the Miamis, to seize the French traders in their country; the Iroquois, to destroy the French village at the junction of the Miami and St. Joseph; the Foxes, to destroy the village at Green Bay; the Sioux, Sacs, and Sarastaus, to reduce Michilimackinac, while the other tribes were to destroy the French trading- posts in their respective countries, seize the traders, and put them to death.

This great conspiracy, so skillfully planned and arranged, would have been attended with a frightful loss of life, and the utter annihilation of French power, but for its accidental yet timely discovery.

It seems that a party of Detroit Hurons had struck before the other tribes were ready, by the murder of a Frenchman in the forest a few leagues from Detroit. This act was unauthorized by the Huron chiefs, who had made their arrangements for occupying the houses at Detroit, and were only waiting for the appointed time, to strike the fatal blow. So fearful were the chiefs that their object would be detected since the murder, that a council was held in one of the houses, which had been obtained for the purpose, to determine whether any change of operations was necessary. While they were in council, one of their [women], going into the garret of the house in search of Indian corn, overheard the details of the conspiracy. She at once hastened to a Jesuit priest, and revealed the plans of the [Natives]. The priest lost no time in communicating with M. de Longueuil, the French commandant, who ordered out the troops, aroused the people, and gave the Indians to understand that their plans had been discovered, and would be discomfited. With great alacrity messengers were dispatched to the forts and trading-posts, which put the people on their guard, and caused them to retire to places of safety. All the settlers in the vicinity of Detroit were notified to enter the fort; the post at Miami was abandoned, and relief asked for from Quebec.

When the Hurons at Detroit found they had been detected, they sullenly withdrew, the commandant being unwilling to open actual hostilities by detaining them. Soon after this the Indian operations began, though confined to a small scale, on account of the vigilance of M. de Longueuil in apprising his countrymen of their danger. The latter part of August, 1747, a number of Frenchmen were killed at Chibarnani; eight traders were seized in the Miami country; a man named Martineau was killed near Detroit; the Sauteurs attacked a convoy of French canoes on Lake St. Clair, captured one and plundered the goods; the Outaouas killed a number of French traders residing in their country; the Foxes murdered several traders at Green Bay; a French trader was killed on the Miami; a party of Hurons attacked the inhabitants of Bois Blanc Island, and wounded three men. Five of the Hurons were captured, taken to Detroit, and heavily ironed. One was soon after killed by the people, and another committed suicide. Other murders were committed, and trading-houses destroyed, but the conspiracy had been pretty effectually broken up by its timely discovery. Soon after hostilities had commenced numbers of those who had entered the league deserted it, and craved the pardon and favor of the French. First among these were the Outaouagas, and Pouteouatamis, the latter having agreed to destroy the Bois Blanc villages. Thus weakened, the plans and efforts of Nicholas were in a measure paralyzed.

On the 22nd of September, a large number of boats, containing one hundred and fifty regular soldiers, arrived at Detroit from Montreal. Upon hearing of this, Nicholas abandoned all his plans, and was ready to make peace on the best terms he could obtain. He knew that certain destruction awaited his villages, unless pardon was obtained, for the French commandant was already meditating a punishment for him and his people, for the murder of the five traders the June previous. During the summer two chiefs of the Detroit Hurons, Sastaredzy and Taychatin, had visited Detroit on a professed mission of friendship. They were seized and sent to Quebec to answer for the murders committed by the Sandusky Hurons. Sastaredzy died at Quebec on the 4th of August; Taychatin was released when peace was made. Nicholas secured the pardon of himself and the Sandusky Hurons upon the most favorable terms, that of maintaining peace in the future. The French abandoned their demand for the murderers of the five traders, and made no conditions as to the Indian trade with the English. Even during the winter that followed, 1747-8, Nicholas received at the Sandusky villages, on two occasions, a party of Englishmen from Philadelphia, and allowed his people to trade with them. Soon after this, Nicholas received belts and other tokens of friendship from the English. These things came to the ear of M. de Longueuil, and he lost no time in asking instructions from Quebec.

On the 14th of January, 1748, Nicholas sent fourteen of his warriors to Detroit to ask for the release of the three remaining Indians captured at Bois Blanc Island. M. de Longueuil wishing to secure Nicholas as an ally, granted his request, and the prisoners were released.

In February, 1748, French soldiers rebuilt and again occupied the post on the Miami. The same month, La Jonquire, Governor of Canada, ordered M. de Longueuil to give Nicholas notice that no English traders would be allowed among his people, or in the Western country, and if any were found, they should receive notice *to quit forthwith. Agreeable to these instructions, a French officer was sent to Sandusky, who notified Nicholas of the wishes of the governor of Canada. Finding several English at the towns, the officer commanded them to leave the country, which they promised to do.*

Finding himself deserted by nearly all of his allies, his power for mischief gone, and the activity and determination of the French to suffer encroachments from the English no longer, Nicholas finally resolved to abandon his towns on Sandusky Bay, and seek a home farther west. On the 7th of April, 1748, he destroyed the villages and fort, and on the following day, at the head of one hundred and nineteen warriors, and their families, left for the White River in Indiana. Soon after he moved with his people to the Illinois country, locating on the Ohio, near the Indiana line, where he died, in the fall of 1748."

The year following year, a result of the growing friction between the French and English as to the actual territorial limits of their domains, the former's desire to maintain their monopoly on Indigenous trade and the latter's most recent instigation of Indigenous revolt against French rule (via. Nicholas' Conspiracy), King Louis XV (1710 – 74) of France decreed that all Englishmen be expelled from French North America, with the Governor-General of New France, the Marquis de la Galissonière, ultimately selecting Pierre-Joseph Céloron de Blainville to undertake the task of expelling them.

Céloron was born in Montreal on December 29th, 1693, and at an early age entered the military. In 1734, he is noted as serving as the Commandant of Michilimackinac, a role he would hold until the end of the decade, after which, he was appointed the Commandant of Detroit, a role he is documented as already possessing by July of 1742. That same year he is also noted as having been promoted a Chevalier of the Military Order of St. Louis, and a Captain in the *"Troupes de la Marine"*. In November, 1747, in a report on Indigenous affairs by Charles Deschamps de Boishébert (1727 – 97) can be found the following extract:

"Good officers are stationed at the frontier posts where we keep garrisons. As, for example, at Fort St. Frederic […]. Mr. de Celeron is Commandant there; an officer of great capacity, who has commanded with distinction in several posts, at Michilimackinac, where he persevered good order amongst the Indians, who are all around, and the French, making himself loved, by both the one and the other. He was sent thence to the Chickasaws in 1739, and was the only officer commanding the party that went with the Canadians and Indians to that village. He came down to Quebec, was ordered the next year to go command at Michilimackinac, and to make the establishment there such as the General desired; thence he went to command at Detroit. He came here [Montreal]; war broke out; was sent to Niagara, where he remained two years; returned to Montreal; was sent by the General to Fort St. Frederic, where he has been during the last six months. He has acquired the esteem of everybody; deserves promotion, being one of the best officers we have, and even one of the oldest Captains."

Evidently, the Governor-General of New France, the Marquis de la Galissonière, had made a wise choice in selecting the experienced and well-liked Céloron to lead the upcoming expedition, which was not of a military nature, however, but rather, a diplomatic one, which had the additional goal of reestablishing aimable French-Indigenous relations, which had become tenuous and uncertain since Nicholas' Conspiracy.

The expedition commenced on the 15th of June, 1749, and would ultimately last until the 10th of November, during which time, Céloron and his force, consisting of approximately two hundred and sixteen French-Canadians and fifty-five French-aligned Indigenous representatives (perhaps including a young Charles Langlade), visited numerous Indigenous settlements along the Ohio River, belonging to various Nations, tribes and bands, and in each of which, Céloron himself would deliver speeches promising friendship and gifting wampum (decorative and/or ceremonial beaded) belts, with the hope of inducing those who received them into confirming allegiance to the French and denouncing the English. Some of the Nations, tribes, bands and the settlements they inhabited were more receptive than others, with none more ominous and foreboding than those of the Miami under Chief Memeskia (circa. 1695 – 1752), better known to the English as "*Old Britain*", for his firm attachment to them, and to the French as "*La Demoiselle*" ("*The Lady*" or "*The Woman*" — the circumstances surrounding this moniker unknown), and whose replies to Céloron's speeches were vague and non-committal. Granted, that that chief's sentiment in regards to the French is best illustrated by his actions during Nicholas' Conspiracy, which were noted in the previously referenced official journal of events of the year 1747, which was jointly penned by the Governor-General, the Marquis de la Galissonière, and the colony's Intendant, Giles Hocquart:

*"**Sieur Douville states that he has had bad news from the Miamis […].***

***He has assurances that the Senecas had given an English [wampum] belt to La Demoiselle, chief of a portion of the Miamis, allies of the English, to procure his, Sieur Douville's, assassination, with a reward to whomsoever should carry his head to the English Governor. The same course has been pursued towards Mr. de Longueuil.*"* (However, Nicholas' Conspiracy terminated before this arrangement could be fulfilled.)

La Demoiselle's settlement was located near the confluence of the Miami River with Loramie Creek and was known as "*Pickawillany.*" It was here, through late August into mid-September, 1749, that Céloron endeavored to win over the Miami under La Demoiselle to the French cause, but meeting with no definitive success, on the 20th of September, he and his men departed. Six days later, the following extract can be found within Céloron's official journal of the expedition:

*"**The 26th [of September]. I had called to me, Cold Foot, chief of the Miamis established at Quiskakou, and some others of note, to whom I repeated, in presence of M. de Raimond and the officers of my detachment, what I had said at the village of the Demoiselle and the answers I got from them. After listening with much attention, he rose and said to me: "I hope I am deceived, but I am sufficiently***

attached to the interests of the French to say that the Demoiselle is a liar. It is a source of all my grief to be the only one who loves you, and to see all the nations of the south let loose against the French."

And let loose they would. And in short order too. For it was no sooner than Céloron had left the Ohio River in November to return to Montreal, that English traders returned to trade amongst the Natives, with many simultaneously encouraging the most hostile of them to resume their previously aborted revolt against the French, among the most willing of these being the Miami under La Demoiselle, based out of Pickawillany, and who wasted no time in arranging a repeat of Nicholas' Conspiracy, knowledge of which promptly came to the ears of the French Commandant of Fort Miami (Fort Wayne, Indiana), Charles de Raymond (1722 – 1805), who then promptly forwarded them to his subordinates in a letter dated January 5th, 1750. However, a clearer picture of the plot came to Raymond's attention the following month, courtesy of the French Commandant of the Illinois, Jean-Baptiste Benoiest (or, simply, "Benoit") de St. Cler ("Clair"; circa. 1700 – 57), and is as such:

"Feb. 11, 1750.

Monsieur — I have the honor to give you notice of a Conspiracy which is being planned against us since last summer at the instigation of the English [...] who is making use of La Demoiselle, chief of the Miamis, who have withdrawn to La Riviere à la Roche. He has given messages to have us attacked both by the Nations of Ouabache [Wabash], and by those who are domiciled with us. This is what I discovered a few days ago:

The rebel [La Demoiselle] had a collar [gorget — neck shield/ armor] given by the Ouyatanons to one named 'Pedagogue', and an English flag to his brother who is of the family of the Rouansas, the first Chiefs of the Ylinois [Illinois]. That message was received and sent to the Kaoskias, who agreed to it. It was also sent to the Peorias. The answer has not yet come. La Mouche Noire, who is a Pianguichias chief, is expected here this spring. He is to bring a collar as a last message to carry out the Conspiracy, according to what I have been told. La Demoiselle is to come with his people, and those of Ceniôteaux to take, in passing, the Miamis, the Ouyatanons, and the Pianguichias, that they may all join [with our domiciled [natives]] to attack us. [There is a rumor also that our domiciled [natives] are inducing the Missouris and Osages to unite with them. We have only two not very large bands [of natives] who do not consent to this, but they will be compelled by force to declare themselves.] When the blow is struck they are to go and get the English and bring them here. La Demoiselle has given them to understand that they will get goods cheap.

I beg you, Monsieur, to give me notice if you see that the [Indigenous] Nations of your section are in motion, so that I may be able to parry the blow and do you keep on your guard. On my part, I will have recourse to surprise. [...] We are having much trouble in our territories. I know not what the result will be, but I hope to avert everything.

I have the honor to be entirely, monsieur, Your very humble and very obedient servant,

Benoiest de St. Cler.

At Fort de Chartre, the 11th of February, 1750."

However, in the fall of 1750, Charles de Raymond was relieved of command of the Miami fort, on account of his reports concerning the conspiracy of La Demoiselle and his Miamis being considered alarmist, in addition to his outspoken criticisms of the Governorship of New France and the corruption of its administrators, while Benoiest de St. Cler (or "Clair") was shortly thereafter reassigned to French Louisiana. This would have serious consequences, for without de Raymond, St. Cler and their well-informed spies amongst the Miamis, details concerning La Demoiselle's plot, and the continual efforts that highly influential chief was undertaking to bring them to fruition, became vague and intermittent. However, in a letter to the French Ministry, and dated September 20th, 1750, the new

Governor-General of New France, Jacques-Pierre de Taffanel de la Jonquière (1685 – 1752), who had succeeded the Marquis de la Galissonière to the role in late 1749, nonetheless admitted that the state of Indigenous affairs remained bleak, despite the efforts of his predecessor to improve them:

"You will also see, Monseigneur, by my letter of the first of August last, that the mission of the Sieur de Cèloron to la Belle Rivière [the Ohio River] has had quite a different effect from that expected by [the late] Monsieur the Comte de la Galissonière; that, on the contrary, the [Indigenous] nations have gathered together in that region, that they are in greater numbers and more angry than ever against the French; and that, although he [Céloron] summoned the English to withdraw and forbade them to come back, they nevertheless continue their trade with those nations and even urge them to attack the French."

Indeed, the following year, in a letter addressed to the American-born English Governor of New York, George Clinton (1739 – 1812), de la Jonquière found occasion to accuse four specific English traders of this very intention, between dismissing a previous accusation of French trespassing onto English domain by Clinton, and assuming a position of moral superiority over the latter:

"Montreal, 10th August, 1751.

Sir: I did not receive, until the 3rd of this month, the despatch your Excellency did me the honor to write to me by Mr. Cornelius Cuyler on the 12th of June last.

You cannot complain, Sir, of the post I have caused to be erected at the foot of the Niagara carrying place, much less pretend that it is an usurpation on the lands of the subjects of the King, your Master.

Your Excellency might as well have said that I have invaded the territories of the King of Great Britain, for if it were true that the Iroquois of the Five [actually Six] Nations are his subjects, their lands would incontestably belong to his Britannic Majesty.

This, nevertheless, Sir, is the foundation you have wished to give to your complaint.

You, very unadvisedly, and in opposition to your own understanding, call the Five Nations subjects of the King, your Master. They are no such thing, and you would be very careful not to put forth such a pretension in their presence. You treat them with much more circumspection; and it is yet to be established that they have regarded the English in any other light than as their brothers. This is an evident proof that so far from acknowledging them as their Masters, they declare themselves, on the contrary, in every respect, independent of them; and they even do not conceal that the English hold directly from them the posts they have in their territory, and that they will oblige them to surrender these whenever they shall think proper.

If the Five Nations were to subject themselves to any Crown, they could not help acknowledging the dominion of the King, my Master, and their neutral inclination would lead them to do so.

In fact, Sir, you are not ignorant, and ancient and modern history bear testimony, that the French are the first white men that appeared on the territory of the Five Nations. It is with them that they first formed an alliance of friendship. It is from them they have received their first assistance; accordingly from that very moment did they call the French their 'Father'.

It is unquestionable, then, that the French were the first to penetrate into the territories of the Iroquois; from that very moment they have taken possession of it, and this possession has been uninterrupted.

Now, were these lands susceptible of any dispute between the Kings, our Masters, and the question had been discussed at the time of the Treaty of Utrecht and Aix la Chapelle, it could not, in fair justice, but be decided in favor of France.

But the Iroquois wish to be the sole masters of their lands; they cease not to say that it is God who gave them to them, and that they acknowledged him alone for Master and Sovereign. This they have signified by authentic documents to the English and to the French.

I add, that the French, after having conquered their lands in the wars they had with them, gave those back to them and restored them to their rights by solemn treaties.

From all which it must be concluded that your Excellency has had no authority to object against the post I have caused to be established. It has been erected with the perfect knowledge of the Iroquois of the Five Nations, who alone are competent to complain of it. They did not oppose it; they consented to it, and have acknowledge that it would contribute as much to their advantage as to that of the French. It is only a house of refuge (hospice), an entrepot of provisions, and a halting place for French voyageurs from the upper country.

I never should have thought that you would have claimed the four Englishmen who have been arrested, inasmuch as they have stated that they had a license from the Governor of Philadelphia, and none of them having exhibited it to me, they are considered as vagabonds and bush rangers.

But as your Excellency takes their part, and as nothing less than that is necessary to persuade me that you authorize and approve their conduct, I will consent to explain the reasons which caused their capture.

You are not ignorant, Sir, of the expedition M. de Celoron made in the year 1749 to the Beautiful [Ohio] River by order of the Marquis de la Galissonnière; that he renewed for, and in the name of the King, my Master, the possession which his Majesty always held of those lands; that he summoned all the English traders there at the time to retire; that he wrote to the Governor of Philadelphia to inform him that he had fulfilled his mission, and to warn him that if any English traders should thereafter again make their appearance on the Beautiful River, they would be treated without any delicacy.

I had the honor to write you myself on the 7th of March, 1750, on that subject, and to request your Excellency to issue an order forbidding all the subjects of New England to go and trade on the territory of the King, my Master. In the same letter I had the honor to express to you my just sensibility at all the secret movements of the English to induce the Indians, who, from all time, have been our closest allies, to destroy the French.

Although you did not honor me with any answer, I flattered myself, notwithstanding, that you would adopt strict measures to arrest the course of all these seductions, and maintain, on your side, the union that ought to subsist between us. But the result has undeceived me. The English, far from confining themselves within the limits of the King of Great Britain's possessions, not satisfied with multiplying themselves more and more on Rock River (Riviere a la Roche), with having houses and open stores there, have, more than that, proceeded, within sight of Detroit, even unto the fort of the Miamis.

This proceeding, following so many unneighborly acts, the evil consequences whereof we but too sensibly feel, have placed M. de Celeron, the commandant at Detroit, under the necessity of ordering these Englishmen to be arrested.

Three of them were first arrested at Ayonontout, the place selected in 1747, by Nicolas, the Rebel Huron Chief, as his stronghold, near the little lake of Otsanderket, that is to say within ten leagues of the town of Detroit. The names of these three Englishmen are Luke Arowin, an Irishman by birth, an inhabitant of Pensilvania, Joseph Fortiner, an inhabitant of the town of Gergé, and Thomas Broke, an inhabitant of Linguester. Lastly the fourth Englishman, named John Pathin, an inhabitant of Willenstown, has been arrested in the French fort of the Miamis, by M. de Villiers, commandant of that post.

The capture of these four English ought not surprise you: 'tis certain, Sir, that they did not risk coming to say, under his M. C. Majesty's cannon, except with sinister views.

Here is proof of it.

1st. None of these Englishmen were ignorant of M. de Celoron's interdiction to the English traders in 1749; that interdiction is public throughout every place in New England, and consequently they are in the wrong when they do not confine themselves there.

2nd. *It cannot be said that they were at Ayonontout to trade with the Indians, because they had nothing but presents to distribute among them.*

3rd. *It is so evident that they wish to hold a Council with the Indians in every respect fatal to the French, that they encamped in a place selected by Nicolas, a Huron chief, a rebel to the French, for his stronghold; they doubtless wished to persuade the Indians to entertain the same feelings as Nicolas, and to attach the most influential to them, in order to resuscitate that chief, who is dead, and to put in execution his nefarious project.*

4th. *What is remarkable and conclusive is, that the leader of these three Englishmen, Luke Arrowin by name, speaks all the Indian languages, is accustomed to the Upper Countries, and is very capable of making them subscribe to whatever he wishes.*

This is so complete a proof, that it is unanswerable. As for John Pathin, he entered the fort of the Miamis to persuade the Indians who remained there, to unite with those who have fled to the Beautiful [Ohio] river [...].

The little property that was taken belonging to these prisoners, has been claimed by the Indians as plunder. They have not been ill treated. Mr. Cuyler saw three of them in this town, who have their liberty, and want nothing. John Pathin could enjoy the same freedom, but he is so mutinous, and uttered so many threats, that I have been obliged to imprison him at Quebec.

You perceive, Sir, that the English traders observe no longer any discretion, that nothing can restrain them, and that they are redoubling their efforts to excite the Indian Nations against the French. 'Tis time to correct this, and you cannot do it too promptly. If any Frenchman was wicked enough to do anything prejudicial to the English, I would have him punished most severely, and if any are so venturesome as to go on the King if Great Brittain's lands, I disavow them from this moment, and consent that you secure their persons.

> Mr. Cuyler will have the honor to report to you all the regard I have had for him, and that I granted him my authority for all the business he had to transact in this Colony, although the French have nothing directly or indirectly to do with it.
>
> He will be able also to tell you how sincerely I desire to reestablish the most perfect intelligence between the subjects of our Governments; to this I shall direct all my attention, and as soon as your Excellency will unite your efforts to mine, we shall have no difficulty in succeeding.
>
> I must not conceal from you, Sir, that your Deputy, Mr. Cuyler, has brought hither with him his brother, Mr. John Cuyler, who is not mentioned in his passport. It has been reported to me that this John Cuyler, who is a merchant, was trading with the French, and even with the Indians, and was constantly conferring with them in the house in which he lodged in this town, all which is highly improper.
>
> I have the honor to advise your Excellency, that I issue my orders to have all the English sent back to New England, who will come to this Colony unprovided with a passport from their governor. I shall await impatiently your answer.
>
> I have the honor to be respectfully, Sir,
> Your most humble and most obedient servant,
>
> La Jonquière."

Jonquière died in March, 1752 with his role as Governor-General being temporarily assumed by Charles Le Moyne, Baron de Longueuil (1687 – 1755), brother to Paul Joseph, the Chevalier de Longueuil (1701 – 78), the French Commandant of Detroit, until de la Jonquière's actual successor from France, Michel-Ange de Menneville, the Marquise du Quesne (or "Duquesne") [circa. 1700 – 78] could arrive, which eventually occurred in August.

In the meantime, the temporary Governor-General, the Baron de Longueuil, wrote the French Ministry on the ever-deteriorating state of Indigenous affairs, in which La Demoiselle and his band of

Miamis played an increasingly prominent role. This letter reads, in part:

"*April 21, 1752.*

My Lord — The late Marquis de la Jonquière had the honor to report to you in his letter of the 13th 7ber, the ill success of the orders he had given in a secret instruction to Mr. de Celoron; that the band of La Demoiselle and other Indians of the Beautiful [Ohio] river had pushed their rebellion to excess, had adopted the English and had openly declared themselves the sworn enemies of the French.

In the same letter that general had the honor to inform you that he had adopted wise measures to secure the conquest of La Demoiselle's fort, to expel the English from the Beautiful river, to punish the Indian nations and to make them feel the King's power.

I doubt not, my Lord, but that letter had at first created great hopes of the execution of the expedition which was projected and concerted in the best possible manner by the late M. de la Jonquière.

But the dispatch which that General had the honor to write you on the 29th of October on the subject of Mr. de Belestre's voyage, and of the scalps taken by the Nipissings, will only create an apprehension in your mind that his orders and purest intentions would be fruitless.

In fact, my Lord, the orders which Mr. de la Jonquière dispatched last spring to Mr. de Celoron, and repeated in his letter to him of the first of October, were not executed any more than those he had given him as far back as 1750, before his departure for Detroit. I cannot actually fathom the reasons which prevented that officer obeying them, as he makes no mention thereof in the letter he has written to the late Mr. de la Jonquière on the twenty-sixth day of January last.

[…] Mr. de Celoron's letter is accompanied by one that Mr. Desligneris wrote to the late Mr. de la Jonquière on the 4th of

January. 'Tis from this last letter that I learned more particularly the unfortunate state of our affairs.

From the accounts which Mr. de Celoron transmitted to the late Mr. de la Jonquière subsequent to those, a detail of which that General had the honor to give you, and previous to Mr. Celoron's being able to receive his last orders, sent in his letter of the first of October, it appears that it will be out of his power to make any movement.

He observes, first, that after the arrival of the Militia men under the command of Lieutenant de Longueuil, and twenty days' consultation among the [allied Native] nations, the latter had concluded, our force being insufficient to attack La Demoiselle and his allies, to keep the hatchet to use it when complete success would be certain, and to wait until the spring; that the delay these Indians demand, put it out of his power to execute anything with the few Frenchmen he has; that it is easy to perceive by the maneuver of the Indians, that they cannot be induced to follow the French unless the latter are in strong force; that he has notified the Commandants of the River St. Joseph and of the Ouyatanons of the resolution these Indians had adopted, and that, should their Indians be of the same mind, nothing can probably be effected, and they must confine themselves to putting their post in a secure state.

[…] Mr. de Joncaire writes, on the 30th of August [1751], that he had just learned that a meeting of the Illinois, Ouyas, Pianguichas, Miamis, Delawares, Chaouanons and the Five Iroquois Nations, was to be had this year at La Demoiselle's, and that the whole tends, in his opinion, to a general revolt.

[…] To so many circumstances equally critical, are superadded the scarcity of provisions, and great appearance of famine at our Southern posts.

[…] The crops have also failed at the Beautiful [Ohio] river. Mr. de Joncaire and the other Frenchmen have been reduced to a couple of handfuls of Indian corn a day; neither meat, nor grease, nor salt.

Famine is not the whole scourge we experience; the smallpox commits ravages; it begins to reach Detroit. One woman has died of it at the Huron village.

This disease prevails also at the Beautiful [Ohio] river.

[...] You perceive, my Lord, the sorrowful condition of the entire[ty] of that Upper Country.

[...] I am with most profound respect, My Lord,
Your most humble and most obedient servant,

Longueuil."

Indeed, with "*so many circumstances equally critical*" occurring simultaneously, one might expect that nothing less than a miracle would be required to avert the total collapse of French dominion in North America, in light of so many calamities amalgamating at once, and fortunately for the French, one such miracle occurred, two months to the day following the Baron de Longueuil's letter, on June 21st, 1752, the circumstances of which, the recently arrived new Governor-General, the Marquis Duquesne, later transmitted in a letter to the French Ministry, dated late October:

"*Monseigneur — I have the honor to send you the Journal of the Sieur de Langlade [unfortunately lost] who has won much glory through the blow he struck the Band of La Demoiselle and who brought me five Englishmen who were in the Miamis' fort. I am sending them to Monsieur de L'abbady, Commissioner at la Rochelle so that he may put them in prison pending your orders. I trust that this blow, added to the complete pillage suffered by the English on this occasion, will discourage them from trading on our lands.*

It is so rare, Monseigneur, that a war with [Natives] can bring about a very stable peace that I should not be surprised if, at the instigation of the English, the Miamis were to ask their allies for help. Nevertheless, I have had no news of it, and I hope that my action in the Belle Rivière [Ohio] country will awe all the Nations.

> *As the Sieur de Langlade is not in the service and has married a [Native] woman, I will content myself with asking you, Monseigneur, for a yearly pension of 200 livres wherewith he will be highly pleased. He is acknowledged here to be very brave, to have much influence on the minds of the [Natives], and to be very zealous when ordered to do anything. It seems to me, Monseigneur, that such a reward would have a very good effect in the country.*
>
> *I remain with profound respect, Monseigneur, your very humble and very obedient servant,*
>
> *Duquesne.*
>
> Quebec, October 25, 1752."

The events to which this letter speaks had originated in the spring of that year, 1752, and had commenced so soon as the rivers had thawed enough to be traversed by canoe. After rendezvousing at Michilimackinac, an assembled force of between one hundred and seventy and two hundred and forty Ottawa and Chippewa warriors, led by Charles Langlade departed on a vast, thousand mile, combined river-overland military expedition, to reduce, perhaps, the biggest threat to both the French monopoly on trade and their lines of communication between the Upper Country (Canada) and the lower Mississippi: The band of Miamis under Grand Chief Memeskia, better known as "La Demoiselle" to the French or "Old Britian" to the English, based out of Pickawillany.

In the spring of 1752, Charles Langlade was not yet twenty-four-years of age (per the year of his baptism) yet already possessed upwards of a decade of warring experience, having during that time (March 28th, 1750 specifically, as noted in the Michilimackinac Register; contrary to the Marquis Duquesne's statement of his being "not in the service") attained the rank of Cadet in the French *Troupes de la Marine*, while remaining active, alongside his father, Augustin, in trade. He had also, during this period, begun a relationship with an Ottawa woman, with whom, he would have one son, the self-styled,

Charles de Langlade Jr., who would later go onto serve with distinction in the War of 1812.

At about 9 o'clock in the morning, on the 21st of June, 1752, the Ottawa and Chippewa expeditionary force, led by Charles Langlade, came in sight of Pickawillany. The women working in the cornfields observed them first, carrying alarm back to the town, which was largely unoccupied on account of the spring hunt — its population having dwindled from approximately four hundred Indigenous families to few more than La Demoiselle, his inner circle, plus nine English traders, the latter of whom utilized the settlement as a base of operations, and whom were scattered amongst their individual residences about the settlement.

So precipitous was the arrival of Charles Langlade's force that they seized upon many women and children, whom they detained as captives to ensure compliance from the Miamis, while the English traders present were forced to fight their way to the perceived safety of the settlement fort. And while five eventually managed to enter the stockade, the remaining three were forced to shut themselves up in a barricaded home, where, hopelessly surrounded, outnumbered and ill-equipped, they soon surrendered, with one, whom had been injured during the struggle, subsequently put to death. Meanwhile, Miami Grand Chief, La Demoiselle and his inner circle met their end in full view of the Miamis fort, the brutality of the former's death in particular perpetrated by Charles Langlade's force specifically to send a message to those who bore witness to it. Yet, a deputation sent to the Miamis fort by Langlade shortly thereafter made it clear to those shut up within that they would be spared any further violence, and the women and children taken captive released, if the Miamis handed over the English traders whom Langlade's force knew were being harbored within. Needless to say, that after a brief period of consultation and deliberation, the remaining Miamis, wisely considering their desperate position; without sufficient food; munitions or personnel to withstand an extended siege, agreed.

Thus, did Charles Langlade accomplish, with apparent ease, via ruthless efficiency, that which Céloron had failed to even attempt in the two-and-a-half years since his initial 1749 expedition upon the Ohio River — despite being ordered to do so on at least three occasions, and that which was a goal of three consecutive French-Canadian Governor-Generals; suppress competing English trade(rs) to the fullest extent; and subjugate the Indigenous Nations, tribes or bands of which had continued in open rebellion against the French since the days of Nicholas' Conspiracy, several years previous, chief among these being the band of Miamis of the late La Demoiselle, whose years of open plotting and intrigues against the French were suddenly no more.

However, the remaining Miamis didn't entirely betray the English. As Langlade's force knew not the exact number of English traders present in Pickawillany, the morning of their attack, the sly Miamis were able to deliver up only six of the actual nine traders (the seventh deceased), claiming that that was all of them, while they hid the remaining two — perhaps the two with the most influence or best personal connections, those two being Thomas Burney and Andrew McBryer.

In his letter of October 25th, 1752, in which he belatedly transmitted the success of Langlade's expedition against Pickawillany to the French Ministry, the Marquis Duquesne admitted that he would not be surprised to learn that the band of Miamis of the late La Demoiselle had asked the English for help, and indeed, such was the case, later the very day of Langlade's attack no less — in a letter dated June 21st, penned immediately following the departure of Langlade and his men, upon their receiving of the English traders demanded in exchange for peace, which was then promptly delivered to the English Governor of Virginia, Robert Dinwiddie (1692 – 1770):

"From the Twightwee Town, June ye 21st, 1752.
Our good Brother of Virginia:
This comes by our Brother, Thomas Burney, who was with in the last unhappy battle we had with our enemies, the French and French Indians, who engaged our Fort at a time when all our warriors and briskest men were out a hunting. They had two hundred and forty fighting men, [who] appeared suddenly and

took us by surprise, when they had sent us wampum and a fine French coat in token of peace and good will, just to deceive and draw our people out a hunting, and then fall upon us, as a more weak and defenseless part, being only twenty men able to bear arms, nine of [whom] were our brothers, the English, who helped us much; but their stores and houses being on the outside of the fort, our enemies plundered them, and took six of our brothers, the English's goods, and to our great loss, their [gun] powder and lead, and kill'd one of them English, and scalped him. They killed our great Pianckosha King, whom we call'd Old Britain, for his great love [of] his brothers, the English. Brother [the Governor of Virginia], we send you by our brother Burney one scalp and a belt of wampum, to let you know we are more concern'd for the loss of our King, and our brothers that were taken and kill's than for ourselves, altho' in great distress for want of arms (weapons) and ammunition, for we must look upon ourselves as lost, if our brothers, the English, do not stand by us, and give us [gun] powder and lead and arms. To confirm what we say and to assure you that we will ever continue true friends and allies to our brothers, the English, we send you this scalp and belt of wampum.

P.S. — There were but two Frenchmen [who] appear'd among the Indians in the time of battle, altho' we understood there were thirty Frenchmen within two miles of us, all the time of action, who were ready to receive their share of the plunder."

And considerable was that plunder, which period historian, C.W. Butterfield (1824 – 99) assessed to be of approximately £3,000 in value (a vast some in those days), in furs and sterling.

Subsequently, on February 2nd, 1753, five of the English traders who were captured by Charles Langlade's Ottawa and Chippewa force at Pickawillany gave the following testimony of their ordeal, which read, in part:

"[We] were trading […] with the Five [actually Six] Nations on the River Ohio […] when [we] were met on the 22nd of June 1752, by a party of one hundred and seventy Canada-French and some

Indians, having a French officer at their head named Langlade, who took these declarants prisoners."

Notably, however, the Marquis Duquesne's letter of October 25th, 1752, concerning the defeat of Pickawillany, contains two discrepancies in regards to Charles Langlade; firstly, and already addressed, that Langlade was "***not in the service***", for as previously stated, within the Michilimackinac Register, under the date of March, 28th, 1750, Langlade was noted as having already achieved the rank of Cadet; and secondly, that Charles was already married, as no additional documentation exists to support that claim (to the compiler's knowledge anyways), in contrast to his subsequent marriage, which occurred in August, 1754.

On that day, Michilimackinac was host to one of the Great Lakes Region's most celebrated unions, between Charles Langlade, and Charlotte Bourassa, a young, well-educated and refined French woman, noted for her uncommon graces of person and amiability of character. She was the daughter of retired *voyageur*, Sieur Réné Bourassa (circa. 1688 – 1778), with the official marriage contract between her and Charles, dated August 11th, 1754, reading as follows:

"Before the Undersigned Royal notary Residing at the post of Michilimackinac, and the undermentioned witnesses, came and appeared Charles Moras, Esquire, Sieur Langlade the younger, for himself and on his own behalf — of the one part; [And Demoiselle Charlotte Enbroise Bourassa — of the others part.]

The said parties, acting of their own free will and inclination, in the presence and with the advice and consent of their relatives and friends hereinafter mentioned, to-wit:

On behalf of Sieur Langlade: — Sier Augustin Moras, Esquire Sieur Langlade, and Domitilde, his father and mother; Sieur Blondeau and Demoiselle Nanette Villeneuve, his brother-in-law and sister; Sieur Nicolas Vollan, cousin; Demoiselle Anne Villeneuve, his sister, Monsieur Herbin, Captain of Infantry, Commandant for the King; Sieur Mantet, friend; Sieur Lamy Hubert, friend; Charles Gautier, nephew.

And on behalf of the said Demoiselle Charlotte Enbroise Bourassa: — Sieur Réné Bourassa and Dame Lerigé Laplante, her father and mother; Sieur Réné Bourassa, the younger, her brother; Sieur Gonneville, the younger, cousin; Réné Bourassa, nephew; Demoiselle Nanette Chevalier, sister-in-law; Monsieur Delaunay Detisné, Esquire, Sieur Dailleboust, friend; Monsieur Marin, an officer of infantry, friend; Monsieur The Chevalier de Repentigny, Lieutenant of Infantry, friend; Réné de Couange, the younger, friend; Louis Biscornay, friend, and Sieur Herbin, the younger, friend.

Which said parties have Acknowledged and Admitted that they have stipulated and agreed Together in good father to the matrimonial promises and Covenant hererin contained regarding the marriage to be shortly Celebrated Between the said Charles Langlade and Demoiselle Charlotte Enbroise Bourassa who have mutually promised and do promise to take One another for Husband and Wife under the law and name of marriage, the same to have Celebrated and solemnized before our mother the Holy Catholic, apostolic and Roman Church as soon as possible and as shall be advised and decided Between Them, their relatives, and friends.

The said future Consorts shall Be One and common as to Property for all Moveable and Immovable Acquisitions they may have and acquire together during their future marriage under the Coutume de Paris, in force in this country.

The survivor of the said future Consorts shall have and take his or her portion apart and from the Property of the said Community to the amount of the sum of Fifteen Hundred Livres according to the valuation to be made of the same, and without Confusion, or one half the said sum in cash at the choice of the said survivor.

And in the event of the dissolution of the said future marriage, it shall be lawful for the said future Wife to take or accept the said Community or to Renounce the same; and in the event of Renunciation of the said Community, she may take back, free and clear of all charges, whatever she may have brought with her or may have come to her by inheritance, gift or otherwise with her dower as aforesaid without being liable for any debts or obligations incurred or given during the said Community, although she may have obliged herself of have been Condemned thereto, wherefrom she shall be freed and wherefor she shall be indemnified out of the property of her sad Husband or by his heirs, and for which reprise and indemnity are given. She shall have her claim from this day upon each and every the present and future Properties of the said future Husband.

The said parties have constituted and do constitute the bearer of these presents as their general and special attorney, giving Him all powers for obtaining the authentication thereof. All that is above contained and stipulated has been said, covenanted and agreed upon between the Appearing and Contracting parties in executing these presents — Which, otherwise and without the Clauses and Covenants therein Contained, would not have been executed.

For thus, promising, obliging and renouncing, etc.

Done and executed in the office of the said Notary in the year one thousand, seven hundred and fifty-four, on the eleventh of August, in the afternoon, in the presence of the Sieurs [Repetition of names, omitted].

In view and Contemplation Of the said future marriage and on account of the affection the said Husband has for the said future Wife, he has given and by these presents he gives irrevocably to the said future Wife, her heirs and Assigns, there of accepting, each and every the properties that may belong to him after his death, provided that at the time of such death there be no child Living issue of the said future marriage, For, in the Event of there being any such child, the said Gift shall be null and void As if it had never existed.

In return for the above, the said future Wife Gives the future Husband the enjoyment of all her properties, both her own proper and the Acquisitions and Goods that may belong to her after her death, provided there be no child issue of the said marriage; For, in the event of there being such a child, the said Gift shall be null *and void as if it had never existed. The said Gift of the enjoyment for life of the property granted to the said future Husband during his lifetime to be subject to the Obligation of keeping the houses and hereditaments in good order; of making the usual repairs thereto that are required of an usufructuary during his life-time; of delivering the same over in good Order when the usufruct Constituted by the said Gift ends, and of having the said present Gift registered where ever the same may be necessary.*

The said parties have constituted and do constitute the bearer of these presents their General and Special Attorney, giving Him all powers.

For thus, promising, obliging, Renouncing, etc.

Done and executed, after this contract was duly Read in the presence of the parties, their relatives and friends who signed the original of the same with the said Notary, after it was Read according to the ordinance.

[Signed,] Cardin.
Royal Notary.

Auke-wingeke-tawso, or, 'Defender of His Country'

MARRIAGE CONTRACT BETWEEN CHARLES LANGLADE AND
CHARLOTTE BOURASSA

Circa. 1900 black & white photo of page 1 of Charles Langlade & Charlotte Bourassa's marriage contract. Dated August 11th, 1754. From "The French Regime in Wisconsin, 1634-1760: 1748-1760", by Reuben Gold Thwaites (1908). Document donated to the Wisconsin Historical Society in 1903 by Charles & Charlotte's descendants, the Grignon family.

Notable witnesses to the marriage of Charles Langlade and Charlotte Bourassa, which was officiated by missionary, Father Le Franc, include; Frenchman, Sieur Louis Herbin (1711 – circa. 1784), Captain of Infantry and Commandant at Michilimackinac from 1754-57; his son, Sieur Herbin the Younger, Lieutenant of Infantry and former Commandant at Fort Chambly; Joseph, Sieur Marin the Younger (1719 – circa. 1767), son of the late Pierre Paul Marin (1692 – 1753), in whose early campaigns Langlade may have served, described as a "friend" of the bride, no less; and Chevalier Louis Repentigny (1727 – 86), Lieutenant of Infantry, Commandant on the Sault and frequently present at Michilimackinac.

However, as period historian, Francis Parkman (1823 – 93) later observed, "*his honeymoon was hardly over*" when Charles Langlade was once again called upon to lead an allied Indigenous force on the war path, as the tenuous peace which existed between the French and English domains in North America began to irreversibly crumble.

Since the Treaty of Aix-la-Chapelle, which had ended the last full-scale North American war, while the French had sought to cement control over the Great Lakes Region and the Mississippi River, by a network of forts along the banks of the Ohio River, and with the objective to hem in the English colonies along the coast, the English had been likewise been eyeing the Ohio River Valley, but as the most logical region for the expansion of Virginia's tobacco cultivation, as the soil was fertile, and the colony's own land was largely exhausted due to incessant cultivation. This, combined with the two-fold goal of establishing more permanent trading ties with the local First Nations, led to the formation of the Ohio Company, based in London, England. Supported by wealthy businessmen and politicians alike, among them, the Governor of Virginia, it received a grant from the British government for six hundred thousand acres of land in the Ohio River Valley, and soon thereafter sent representatives to claim the location of the said grant and to establish a friendly rapport with any local First Nations. However, on receiving news of the English representatives' intrigues, the

Governor-General of New France called upon them, and any other English planter or trader who occupied the region, to retire from what he asserted was rightfully His French Majesty's dominion, lest they be seized upon as trespassers. But the English were defiant.

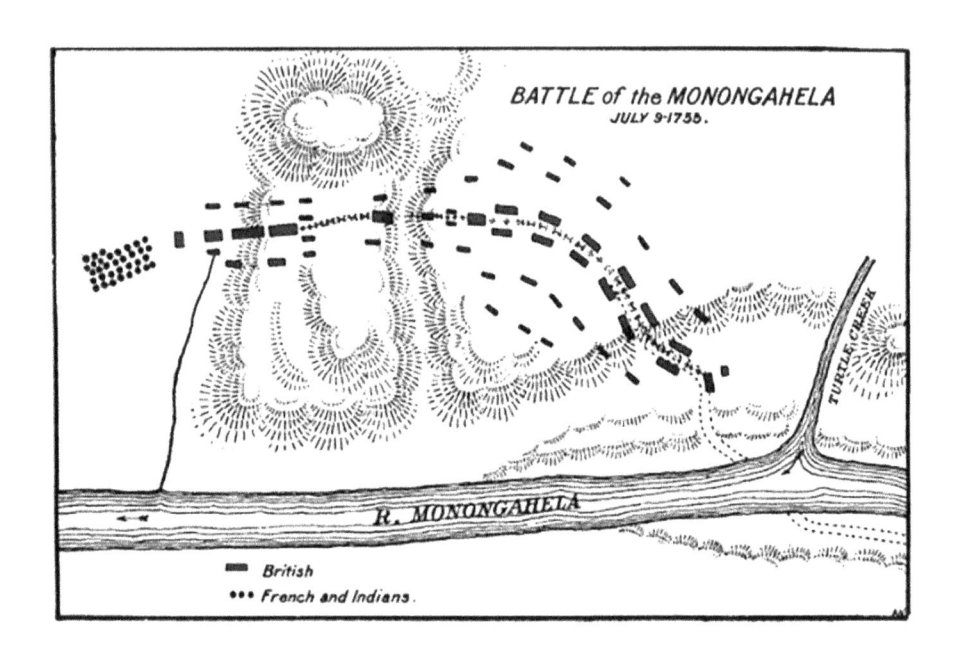

(1 of 2) The initial disposition of English General Edward Braddock's army, the French, Canadians and Indigenous warriors at the onset of the Battle of the Monongahela, July 9th, 1755. From "Montcalm and Wolfe", by Francis Parkman (19th century; various editions).

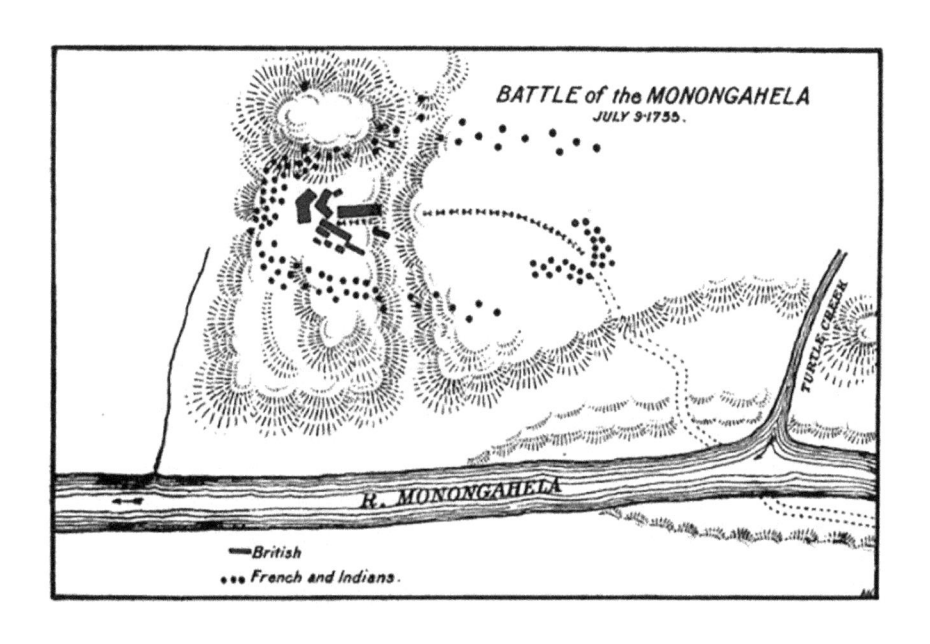

(2 of 2) The later disposition of English General Edward Braddock's army, the French, Canadians and Indigenous warriors during the Battle of the Monongahela, July 9th, 1755. From "A Half Century of Conflict", by Francis Parkman (19th century; various editions).

Chapter II

1754 – '60: Charles Langlade & the French & Indian Theatre of the Seven Years' War in North America, A.K.A., "the War of Conquest"

In the spring of 1753, to solidify their claim to the Ohio River Valley, the French-Canadian government dispatched Pierre Paul, Sieur Marin, in command of a two thousand-man strong *Troupes de la Marine* and allied Indigenous force to construct a series of forts from which they could enforce their regional claims more aggressively. Marin's force first constructed Fort Presque Isle, located on the south shore of Lake Erie, in the vicinity of modern-day Erie, Pennsylvania. This was followed soon thereafter by Fort Le Boeuf, which was built to guard the strategic headwaters of Le Boeuf Creek, near modern-day Waterford, Pennsylvania.

Alarmed by the rapid progress of Marin's French allied force, and the fact that, as an investor in the Ohio Company, he personally stood to lose considerable sums of money if the Ohio could not be retained, Virginian Governor Dinwiddie commissioned Major George Washington (1732 – 99), then twenty-one-years-of-age, and whose brother was also an investor in the Ohio Company, to intercept Marin's force, and order them to depart.

In the meantime, on October 29th, 1753, French Commandant at Michilimackinac and patron of Charles Langlade, Pierre Paul, Sieur Marin died suddenly at the age of sixty-one after a brief illness and was succeeded in his command on the Ohio by Jacques Legardeur de St. Pierre (1701 – 55). Saint-Pierre, whom Washington would later describe in his journal as having "**much the air of a solider**" received the young Virginian, after a long journey, courteously, on December 11th, 1753, at Fort Le Boeuf (modern-day Waterford Pennsylvania), even inviting him to dine with himself and a few other French officers in the fort. Washington accepted, and afterwards presented St. Pierre with the formal complaint he had been commissioned to deliver by Virginian Governor Dinwiddie.

St. Pierre, however, dismissed the Virginian Governor's grievances out of hand. Polite, yet firm, he made it clear to Washington that by virtue of France's 17th century exploration of the region, it was theirs, and they would not be leaving. And to Governor Dinwiddie, whom Washington had been the commissioned messenger of, he addressed the following letter, which he sent with Washington back to Virginia at the former's departure, approximately a week after having arrived:

"*Sir,*

As I have the honor of commanding here in chief, Mr. Washington delivered to me the letter, which you wrote to the commander of the French troops. I should have been glad that you had given him orders, or that he had been inclined, to proceed to Canada to see our General, to whom it better belongs, than to me, to set forth the evidence and the reality of the rights of the King, my master, to the lands situate along the River Ohio, and to contest the pretensions of the King of Great Britain thereto. I shall transmit your letter to the Marquis du Quesne. His answer will be a law to me. And if he shall order me to communicate it to you, Sir, you may be assured I shall not fail to dispatch it forthwith to you. As to the summons you send me to retire, I do not think myself obliged to obey it. Whatever may be your instructions I am here by virtue of the orders of my General; and I entreat you, Sir, not to doubt one moment but that I am determined to conform myself to them with all the exactness and resolution which can be expected from the best officer. I do not know that in the progress of this campaign anything has passed which can be reputed an act of hostility, or that is contrary to the treaties which subsist between the two Crowns; the continuation whereof interests and pleases us as much as it does the English. Had you been pleased, Sir, to have descended to particularize the facts, which occasioned your complaint, I should have had the honor of answering you in the fullest, and, I am persuaded, the most satisfactory manner, &c.

Legardeur de St. Pierre.

From the Fort on the River au Boeuf, December 15, 1753."

However, undeterred by St. Pierre's rebuff, the English, led by fur trader and merchant William Trent, and under the direction of Governor Dinwiddie, began constructing a fort of their own, Fort Prince George, near the strategic confluence of the Allegheny and Monongahela rivers, to compete with local French dominance. However, before Washington could be redeployed to them with urgently needed reinforcements dispatched from Virginia, and supplemented by allied Mingo warriors, the arrival of overwhelming French forces under the command of Claude Pierre Pecaudy de Contrecoeur (1705 – 75), on April 16th, 1754, from Fort Machault (modern-day Franklin, Pennsylvania; later known as Fort Venango - see "Map of the Scene of Operations".), forced Trent and his group to abandon their works.

French-allied Indigenous scouts then reported back to Contrecoeur that Washington's Virginian-Mingo relief force had been identified, located, and was approaching. In response, the French commander penned a summons for them to retire, and entrusted it to Joseph Coulon de Villiers, the Sieur de Jumonville (1718 – 54), whom, at the head of a French-Canadian and allied Indigenous scouting party, he then ordered to incept Washington's force, and present it to them.

Few, however, could have foreseen the events that would ultimately transpire between Washington's and Jumonville's forces, and fewer still the effects that their meeting would have on the course of history. And as a result, to this day, the subsequent events are subject to much debate and interpretation. What is certain, is that on the morning of May 28th, 1754, over the course of a battle which lasted approximately fifteen minutes, the majority of Jumonville's force was either killed or captured by Washington's, including the French commander himself. But regardless of the circumstances, the repercussions of those fifteen minutes, commonly referred to as the "*Battle of Jumonville Glen*", would be felt far and wide.

In its immediate aftermath, a series of troop mobilizations and counter-mobilizations were undertaken, by both the French and the English. The Thirteen English colonies however, had the apparent upper hand, with by one estimate, possessing twenty times the inhabitants of French Canada and Louisiana, while the English navy additionally continued to dominate the high seas, severely limiting New France's import potential. The result of these set of circumstances was that New France was obliged to incorporate large contingents of Native Indigenous warriors into its ranks to fill the voids. And few men were more capable and willing to lead these warriors into battle than Charles Langlade.

Relished by the French colonial government since his daring, successful raid on the Anglo-Miami trading stronghold of Pickawillany, two years prior, at the breakout of hostilities in the Ohio River Valley in 1754, the twenty-five-year-old, recently married veteran was immediately summoned by the Governor-General to both personally assemble and lead a contingent of allied-Indigenous warriors in defense of New France. And compelled by both his dedication to his professions — trading and warring, his love of service and the rewards and recognition that accompanied them, by the spring of 1755, he had successfully amassed one of the most fearsome and formidable expeditionary forces in central American history, made up of the finest warriors from many of the most enduring and powerful Nations, tribes and bands on the continent.

Among them, according to Charles's grandson, Augustin Grignon, were "***the Ottawas, Chippewas, Menomonees, Winnebagoes, Pottawotamies, Hurons or Wyandots***" and likely many others. While for his personal command structure, he selected his father-in-law, the legendary Ottawa Warrior-King, Nissowaquet, as well as

Pontiac (circa. 1700 – 69), an experienced warrior-commander in his own right, with many years of dedicated service to both the Ottawa Nation and New France to his name. Other notable additions to Langlade's ranks were men whose names are inexplicably linked to the history of Wisconsin — some more recognizable and documented than others. Among them, Charles' "*brother-in-law, Souligny, his brave nephew, Gautier de Verville, Pierre Caree, La Choisie, La Fortune, Amable de Gere, Philip de Rocheblave, Louis Hamline, and Machar*", according to Charles' grandson, Augustin Grignon.

And to supplement his authority in the coming struggle, on March 15th, 1755, the Court of King Louis XV (1710 – 74), issued Langlade the following commission from France:

"From the King.

His Majesty, having chosen Sieur Langlade to serve as Ensign unattached with the troops maintained in Canada, orders the Governor, his Lieutenant-General of New France, to receive and acknowledge him in such capacity of Ensign unattached of all those to whom and as the same may appertain.
Given at Versailles, the 15th March, 1755."

And with their newly promoted leader at their head, Langlade's assembled force repaired at once to the recently completed Fort Duquesne, built upon the spot formerly occupied by the partially built English Fort Prince George, which French commander, Contrecoeur, had forced William Trent and his men to abandon before George Washington and his reinforcements could arrive, the year before.

Situated at the strategic confluence of the Allegheny and Monongahela rivers, where the two unite to form the greater Ohio River, the French fort had only been constructed within the last year and was named in honor of the then Governor-General of New France. However, although the positioning of Fort Duquesne appeared optimal on a map, the reality was much more complex. The site, soft and muddy, was severely prone to inundation, limiting the speed of troop movements, while the fort itself was prone to artillery bombardment from an adjacent flatland high-rise.

Nonetheless, in the first week of July 1755, Ensign Langlade, at the head of a force between eight hundred and fifteen hundred strong, arrived outside the walls of Fort Duquesne, where they encamped for as far as the eye could see, and mingled with the throngs of warriors from every corner of Canada which had already arrived, many of which would later integrate themselves into service under Langlade, on account of his methodical and enthusiastic leadership, further ballooning his force's numbers as the war subsequently dragged on.

Meanwhile, the English were no less active in their counter-preparations, with Major-General Edward Braddock (born circa. 1695) — A veteran of nearly fifty years active service, being appointed to the command of a retaliatory Anglo-American expeditionary force on September 27th, 1754, on the personal recommendation of the Duke of Cumberland (1721 – 65), the third and youngest son of King George II (1683 – 1760), with the former afterwards proceeding directly from London to Cork, Ireland, from whence, after much delay, his army ultimately set sail from, on January 14th, 1755, arriving on the coast of Virginia between February 20th and March 2nd.

On April 15th, the recently arrived General took part in the Council or Congress of Alexandria with the governors of five English colonies; Robert Dinwiddie of Virginia; Horatio Sharpe (1718 – 90) of Maryland; Robert Hunter Morris (1700 – 64) of Pennsylvania; William Shirley (1694 – 1771) of Massachusetts; and James De Lancey (1703 – 60) of New York, at the house of John Carlyle (1720 – 80), with the meeting's most significant outcome being the adoption of a four-pronged plan of attack against New France, with General Braddock's army — the main push — to be directed against Fort Duquesne, at the confluence of the Allegheny and Monongahela rivers, while the Governor of Massachusetts, William Shirley, was to lay siege to Fort Niagara, Sir William Johnson (1715 – 74) was to move against Fort St. Frederick on Crown Point, New York, and Lieutenant-Colonel Robert Monckton (1726 – 82) marched on Fort Beausejour, between Nova Scotia and Acadia.

That decided, on April 20th, General Braddock's army left Alexandria and proceeded to Fredericktown, Maryland, where it was joined by George Washington, who was appointed one of Braddock's aid-de-camps on the coming expedition, and where the General was greatly disappointed to find that the army's promised transportation of horse-drawn wagons with drivers were virtually non-existent. However, after speaking to the Postmaster-General, one Benjamin Franklin (1705 – 90), Braddock's needs were soon taken care of, with the latter securing Braddock's army one hundred and fifty wagons, horses to pull them and drivers to man them, among those, future legendary American pioneer-frontiersman, Daniel Boone (1734 – 1820), who was twenty-one at the time.

From Maryland, General Braddock's army pressed onto Fort Cumberland, which was to be its last stop before entering French and allied Indigenous-contested wilderness. Here, by May 19th, the entire army had amassed. It consisted of the 44th and 48th Regiments of Foot, the former commanded by Sir Peter Halkett (1695 – 1755) and the latter by Colonel Thomas Dunbar (died 1767), with each numbering approximately seven hundred men; thirty sailors; one thousand two hundred Colonials; by some accounts with perhaps as many as one hundred and fifty Indigenous allies, supplemented by the one hundred and fifty wagons, two thousand horses, and their drivers, which had been requisitioned for the expedition by Benjamin Franklin.

On June 7th, General Braddock's army commenced its march against Fort Duquesne with Sir Peter Halkett's 44th Regiment, followed by the remainder of the army on the 8th. However, almost immediately, it was beset by delays occasioned by the thickly wooded, stream and river laden, rocky terrain. So much so that over the course of ten days, General Braddock's army had scarcely marched thirty miles, the result of which was the decision to divide the army in two, with Braddock leading approximately twelve hundred selected men, including Sir Peter Halkett, Lieutenant Thomas Gage (1718/19 – 87) ahead, while the slower second half of the army, including the horse-drawn artillery and baggage carts followed as rapidly as possible, albeit at a distance.

And while the army was on the march, English Governor Shirley of Massachusetts penned a letter to Secretary Thomas Robinson, the 1st Baron Grantham (circa. 1695 – 1770), detailing the commencement of the campaign:

"Boston, New England, June 20th, 1755.

Sir: I had the honour to acquaint you in my last that Major General Braddock had informed me by letter from Williamsburg soon after his arrival in America, of the plan of operations he propos'd this year [:] the attack of the French Forts upon the Ohio with the two British regiments, two of the New York Independent Companies and the Provincial troops of Virginia Maryland and North Carolina, amounting all of them to about 2400 men, under his own command; and the reduction of the French Forts at the Strait of Niagara with the two American new rais'd regiments, which service he purposed to put under my command. The measures for removing the French from their incroachments upon the Isthmus of Nova Scotia and St John's River were as I had before acquainted you Sir, concerted, and the expedition against the French incroachments at Crown point form'd, before the General's arrival.

The business of my own Government (the General Court being sitting when I received his Excellency's letter) and in particular the disposition & orders relative to the two last mention'd expeditions, which were requisite to be settled before I left the Province in order to keep all the preparations going on in my absence, for carrying them into execution in case the General should approve of them at my interview with him, necessarily detained me from setting out from Boston untill the 30th of March. On the twelfth day of April I arrived at the Camp at Alexandria in Virginia, about 565 miles distance from this place, where I had the honour of meeting the General and the same day, after consulting with Commodore Keppell and myself, His Excellency determin'd upon the whole plan which consisted of the before mention'd operations upon the

Ohio, at Niagara, in Nova Scotia, and Crown Point, to be executed as near as might be about the same time. The first part of the plan indeed, was in effect concluded upon, and several steps taken in it (the whole corps of the British Regiments, except two Companies, being march'd with their baggage and greatest part of the train of artillery for Winchester in their way to Wills's Creek) before my arrival. The attempt to remove the French from their incroachments in Nova Scotia and at Crown Point were, upon my communicating the propos'd schemes for effecting them, to the General, both intirely approv'd of by him; and an express was thereupon sent the same day, with his directions for Colonel Lawrence immediately to proceed in the former, according to the place concerted between him and me, without staying till the regiments in Nova Scotia should be compleated to 1000 men each for which he had lately received orders. The attempt of the reduction of the French Forts at Niagara with mine and Sir William Pepperrell's regiments (as His Excellency had propos'd in his letter) was at the same time determin'd upon by him, and in order to secure the important pass there in the most effectual manner, it was agreed to have some vessels forthwith built to command the navigation of the Lake Ontario; the care of doing which the Commodore hath committed to me.

According to this plan the French will be attack'd almost at the same time in all their incroachments in North America; and if it should be successfully executed in every part, it seems highly probable that all points in dispute there with them may be adjusted this year, and in case of a sudden rupture between the two Crowns the way pav'd for the reduction of Canada, whenever it shall be His Majesty's pleasure to order it

After I parted with the General, I found from the deficiency of Sir William Pepperrell's levies, that there was no prospect of his raising more than 600 men by the time, that the troops destin'd for Niagara must begin their march, and as two of the Companies of his regiment were order'd to be posted at Oswego upon an expectation that the French would attack it which will reduce them to 1400 men, and that force would in the general opinion as well as my own be too weak an one to secure the pass at Niagara; in my return thro' the Government of New Jerseys, I apply'd to the Assembly there, which was then sitting to permit the Regiment of 500 men, which they had lately voted to raise for the expedition against Crown Point, to join their forces under my command in the reduction of Niagara, and prevail'd with them and Gov. Belcher to pass an Act for that purpose, by which means my troops were augmented to 1900. As the diversion which must be occasioned to the French Forces in Canada by the attack of Niagara, must make a less force sufficient for the reduction of the French Fort at Crown Point than was at first determin'd to have been employ'd in it; before the attempt on Niagara was projected, I thought this regiment might be spar'd from the service at Crown Point; and the General hath since approv'd of this augmentation of the Niagara forces.

It being generally apprehended that the troops under my command would be still too weak for the service at Niagara, as with that pass the French must lose the only practicable communication they have be[twe]en Canada and the Mississippi (that lying across the Lake Ontario from thence over the Strait of Niagara to Lake Erie, and over that into the River Ohio which falls into the Mississippi) & consequently all hopes of establishing themselves in the rich country behind the Apalachian Mountains, or of maintaining their extensive fur trade there, without both which Canada can be of but small value to them; so that it must be expected they will use their utmost efforts to defend it: this I say, Sir, being the general apprehension, at my return to Boston, the Assembly of my own Government pass'd a vote enabling me to employ as many of the troops rais'd within this Province for the service at Crown Point, as I should think proper in that agst [against] Niagara; leaving 3700 in the whole for Crown Point, and provided the men were willing to go with me and the other Governm[ent]'s concern'd consented to it. Since which I have obtained the consent of all the other Governments, but one.

With this reinforcement I shall not have an opportunity of acquainting the General in time to receive his approbation, before I set out for Niagara. But as 3700 men, in conjunction with 300 Indians which we have reason to depend upon being engag'd in the expedition against Crown Point, is doubtless a much more adequate force now for the reduction of the French Fort there, than 5000 the utmost that was proposed before would have been when the whole strength that is left in Canada would have been muster'd at Crown Point to defend it against our attack; and are certainly a much more sufficient force for that service than 2400 (the whole of my troops, if they should be increased with 500 more) will be for gaining and securing the pass at Niagara, upon which depends the Southern Dominion now in dispute between us and the French, which is of infinitely more value than the Fort at Crown Point; I think there can be no doubt of his approving it.

In addition to these reinforcements I am in hopes of procuring a number of Indians to join with me at Schenectady and Oswego, which are necessary in the service for scouts, outguards in marches thro' narrow defiles, and to guard the battoes [boats] in their passage thro' the narrow parts of rivers and creeks, and gaining intelligence; and as the General could not spare me any part of his train of artillery, I have, with the pieces I have taken from Castle William in this Province, others which I have borrow'd of Governor De Lancy from New York, and some pieces of ordnance which I have caused to be cast within my own Government, collected a proper train for the service.

In my passage back to Boston thro' the several Governments concern'd in the expedition against Crown Point, I had an opportunity of settling several points among them which retarded their movements in it; and I hope the troops destin'd for that service will be fitted out in proper time; they are most or all of them upon their march for Albany the place of rendezvous, and many of them arrived there and on the point of proceeding from thence towards Lake Champlain.

My own regiment began 13 days ago to march in divisions from hence to Providence in Rhode Island government where they were all imbark'd and sail'd five days since with a fair wind for Albany, thro' which they will directly march for Schenectady, without making any halt; and I hope by this time their transports may have enter'd Hudson's River. The New Jersey regiment arriv'd at Schenectady some days ago, as I have reason to hope all the heavy pieces of artillery did, which I have order'd to be immediately put on board the battoes prepar'd there for them, & transported with other military stores and part of the provisions to Oswego with that Regiment before the waters grow low. The two Companies of Sir William Pepperell's regiment and one of the Independent Companies of New York have been some weeks at that Fort & employ'd in strengthening it & making it as defensible as the very weak state of it will admit in so short a time. Two other Companies of Pepperell's have been several days detach'd to the Great Carrying Place near the Wood Creek in the way to Oswego, with orders to clear it of any French Indians which may be sent to obstruct the passage of the Creek by falling great trees across it, to guard the battoes as they pass through it, mend the roads for the more easy conveyance of the artillery, stores, and battoes over the Carrying Place, and making the passage of the battoes thro' the narrow parts of the Creek more practicable in the difficult places.

The battoes for transporting the forces have been all made and ready at Schenectady some time, together with the stores procur'd at New York and those purchas'd here, and the builders and workmen whom I have hir'd for building the vessells and boats to be employ'd on the Lake Ontario, [...] must be built at Oswego, have been sent there several weeks ago, and at work upon them; so that I hope to get them upon the Lake before I leave Oswego, which I look upon to be a point of great importance. I have procured seamen to. navigate them, and the Officers appointed by the Commodore to command them are arriv'd from Virginia, and are gone with the stores for Oswego to have them rigg'd & fitted out with the utmost expedition. Part of my Regim. is order'd to proceed with their baggage in battoes as soon as may be from Schenectady to Oswego, and having now set the forces for Crown Point in motion and settled the affairs of my government as much as I can before I go, I shall set out the 24th instant for Providence and imbark on board the Province Sloop for New York, from whence I shall proceed in 24 hours after my arrival for Albany up Hudson's River with the remainder of Sir William Pepperrell's regiment now at New York and some levies of my own, which are to join me there; & having settled everything which remains to be determin'd between me and Colonel Johnson concerning the expedition to Crown Point under his command, & the forces to be employ'd in it, I shall pass on to Schenectady and proceed directly from thence to Oswego, with the remainder of the forces destin'd for that service; and having seen the vessells and boats to be employ'd on the Lake Ontario or at least some of them fitted out, or very near it, and gain'd what intelligence I can and the time will allow, of the situation of the French at Niagara, I shall proceed with all the forces artillery and stores there, as soon as may be.

 The New England troops rais'd for the service at Nova Scotia were ordered, before I left Boston to repair thither on the 7th of April, in order to sail for the Bay of Funda, and about 2000 of them accordingly appeared there, & were imbark'd by the 221 of that month, and waited for the arms from England, which did not arrive at Boston until the 17th of May, being the day before my return thither from Virginia; the vessel in which they were sent happening to have a long passage of about ten weeks; so that the troops did not sail until the 23rd of May. Their stay the last month gave me uneasiness; had I been upon the spot as there were 1000 stands of arms at Annapolis Royal and 800 might have been had here, tho' not so good as those sent from England, I should have chosen to have sent them away before; but I have reason to hope that they will succeed as it is. I have receiv'd an account, dated 15th instant [this month] from Col. Lawrence, of their arrival at Scheignecto on the 2nd and that he concluded from not having received any news from thence, that they were by that time masters *of the Isthmus, and was of opinion the reduction of the French Fort at St Johns River would after that be an easy task, if the two French 34 Gun Frigates, which we had intelligence were in the Bay of Funda, for the protection as he supposed of that River, should not be too hard for our sea force there, which consisted of three twenty gun ships only, and a sloop of war. The news I received here four days ago of a French squadrons being spoken with off Bank Vert near Newfoundland, full of soldiers standing for Louisbourg, gave me no small concern for the success of the expedition to Nova Scotia; but it was reliev'd in two hours by an account of Admiral's Boscawen & Mostyn with eleven sail of the line being spoken with off St Johns River at Newfoundland nine days ago, close at the heels of the French, and having sent a letter to Cap Aldrick the Commandant there, acquainting him that they were going to cruise off Louisbourg; otherwise the stay of the New England troops here the last month, might have ruin'd the attempt for recovering the Isthmus, if not occasion'd the loss of the whole Province.*

The Acts pass'd lately in the several Colonies to prevent the exportation of provisions to Louisbourg, together with the embargo in Ireland, have greatly distress'd the French at Louisbourg and the effects must be soon felt in all their settlements in North America.

A few days ago I had a letter from the General dated 20 of May from Fort Cumberland at Wills's Creek in which he complains that the inexpressible disappoints he hath met with, hath retarded his march a month beyond the time he at first intended; but by the advices I have since received from Gov. Morris and Gov. Dinwiddie, I hear he hath surmounted his difficulties, and it was judg'd would proceed the beginning of this month from Fort Cumberland for the French Fort called Fort Du Quesne upon the Ohio, which is computed to be from 90 to 110 miles distance from Wills's Creek, where very possibly he may be arriv'd by this time & begun his attack, in which I have little or no doubt in my own opinion of his succeeding, tho' it is pretty certain the French have sent a reinforcement of 900 men (100 of them regular troops) and stores, very lately either to the Ohio or Niagara, and many of their battoes have pass'd by in sight of Oswego. When I had the honor of conferring with His Excellency at Alexandria, he purpos'd to build some vessels at Presque Isle for securing the navigation of the Lake Erie; which if effected must, together with those designed for Lake Ontario, make us masters of the Great Lakes and Ohio and the country there, until the French can get a superior force upon those Lakes, which it seems very difficult if not impracticable for 'em to do, when our vessels shall be cruising upon them. I hear from Gov. Morris that at the General's request he hath establish'd a magazine of Provisions in the back parts of Pennsylvania, from whence he will be easily supply'd by a new road, whivh he, Mr. Morris, is making thro' the mountains to the waters of the Ohio, and which the General proposes to him to extend to Veningo and Niagara; all when, if executed, must be of infinite use for marching the troops to & subsisting them upon the Ohio and at Niagara from a Colony more abounding with provisions than any at present in North America.

The General's presence and activity hath infus'd spirit into the Colonies concern'd in the attempt against Crown Point, and by the Commission which he hath given to Colonel Johnson for taking upon him the management of the Indian Affairs, and the ready money he hath most opportunely advanc'd to him for engaging 'em in the English Interest, he has greatly promoted that service. The expedition to Niagara this year is wholly owing to His Excellency's proposal of it.

I am now to acknowledge, Sir, the receipt of your letters dated the 23rd and 24th of Jan., and 10th of February the contents of which are answer'd in the foregoing part of this letter, except that I beg leave to observe that in the last mentioned you seem to think that the soldiers in New England are enlisted for His Majesty's service in general terms, whereas it is at present impracticable to raise any number of them without acquainting them with the place of their immediate destination, nor will any born in these Colonies inlist to go to the Southward of Niagara, at furthest. The command under which they are to act, is likewise another very material point with them.

I beg leave further to observe Sir, that the common fund, which you seem to suppose to be provided by the several Governments in the Colonies for the support of His Majesty's service will never be agreed upon by the Assemblies among themselves, tho' acknowledg'd to be necessary to all; that, and a plan of Union must be establish'd by an authority from home or neither of them will be effected; & this you will perceive by the inclos'd extract of the minutes of Council at Alexandria, is the opinion of the other Governors who were present there as well as my own. And if I might presume, Sir, to suggest my opinion further in this matter, nothing would be a firmer cement of His Majesty's colonies, or go further towards consolidating them in the support of his service & government there, and the defense of their common interests against a foreign power, than the establishment of such a fund and a plan of Union among 'em; nor do I think they would be difficultly reed by them from the Parliament.

You will perceive, Sir, by the inclosed copies of my message to the Assembly of my own government and their message in answer to it, upon the subject of their finding provisions for mine and Sir William Pepperrell's regiments, according to the directions of Gen. Braddock's inclos'd letter, and paying their Quota of the levy money for the raising of them, that they refuse to do it.

I beg leave to assure you, Sir, that I shall consult [...] as much as may be consistent with His Majesty's service in the expense of the expedition under my command. I omitted to observe to you before that the reason of my being the Colonel of the two New England Regiments gone to Nova Scotia was principally for the sake of encouraging the inlistments and saving the expense of the pay of two Colonels, having no expectation of any allowance or pay to myself in it.

I hope Sir, consideration will be had of an allowance for my necessary suite in the expedition under my command, & as the execution of the command will be attended with an extraordinary *charge to myself, especially in the rank to which I have lately had the honour to be promoted in His Majesty's army, I hope His Majesty will be pleas'd to order me a proper support in it during the time of the service. The expense of my travelling charges out of my own pocket in my journey to Alexandria and back (being about 1250 miles) tho' I made use of my own horses half the way and my servants the whole, and had some horses found for me in two of the governments, exceeded £200 sterling, which is near double the income of my Government to me for the time I was absent from Boston.*

The inclos'd copy of the General's instructions will show you, Sir, the extent of my command.

My desire of laying before you a particular state of the Colonies with regard to the operations carrying on there against the French, and the very little appearance there is of their forming a plan of Union among themselves, as recommended by His Majesty, in one view, hath drawn this letter into a greater length than I design'd, which I hope you will be pleas'd to excuse on that account. I am with the greatest regard,

   Sir,

      Your most humble, and most obedient servant,

W. Shirley."

After an exhaustive march, on the 8th of July, 1755, as they neared their objective, General Braddock's army pitched camp for the night, approximately two miles from the Monongahela and Allegheny rivers, in the vicinity of a rivulet known as *"Crooked Run"*. He was now within two brisk marches of Fort Duquesne, with only the Monongahela River itself between them. Overnight, Braddock concluded his arrangements for crossing it, with the intention of reaching the fort itself by the morning of the 10th, the same day which the Governor-General of New Frace, the Marquis de Vaudreuil, penned a letter to French foreign Minister, Jean-Baptiste de Machault d'Arnouville (1701 – 94), in which he relayed intel of the English's plans and movements, as well as his counter measures:

"Quebec, 10th of July, 1755.

My Lord: I had the honor to inform you, in my letter of the 2nd instant, that the English were sending a number of people towards Chouaguin, where they had built sloops carrying 10 guns, and two sorts of little galleys; that a force of 3000 men were assembling also at Fort Necessity, within about 40 leagues of Fort Duquesne, where the van-guard, consisting of 700 men, had already arrived.

We had confirmation of this intelligence from some reliable Indians belonging to different villages, who had given us pretty strong assurances of it, not admitting of a doubt. They have also added, as a very sure thing, that 4000 men were going to Choueguin; that the 5 Nations would form the wings of this army; that the English were desirous of seeing Niagara and Fort Frontenac, and that 600 bateaux had, moreover, been built at Orange, where they were busy constructing a great many others; that 5000 men were encamped outside Orange, covering two leagues of country; that this army was to march against Fort St. Frederic, and afterwards advance on our settlements on this Continent. I am about sending, my Lord, some reinforcements to the latter fort, but this diver ion will not cause me to make any change in my Lake Ontario project, which I had the honor to communicate to you. The preservation of Niagara is what interests us the most. Were our enemies masters of it, and to retain Choueguin, the Upper countries would be lost to us, and we should have no further communication with the river Oyo [Ohio].

I had the honor to inform you that I should order 400 men whom I would take from Presqu'isle, to fall back on Niagara, but the danger to which Fort Duquesne is exposed has caused me to change my mind, and they will proceed to the latter post.

I will confess to you, my Lord, that I find myself much embarrassed, and that I think any other person in my place would be equally so. I arrive in a country where, I am assured, everything is peaceable; I find, in consequence, no store of provisions laid in, no carriages built, and I must oppose the enemy's attacks on all sides in less than six weeks. The necessary preparations are hastening forward, and notwithstanding M. Bigot's activity, I doubt if he will be able to put me in a condition to carry out my plans completely.

You will learn this autumn, my Lord, the success of my projected operations, and the event alone will enable me to decide as to the demands I shall have to make on you.

I start to-morrow for Montreal, where my presence is necessary both for the dispatch of the troops and the levy of militia. I have the honor to be, with the most profound respect,
My Lord,
    Your most humble and
    Most obedient servant,

            Vaudreuil."

  Meanwhile, a proposition by Sir John St. Clair (died 1767) to General Braddock, to force march the very night of the 8th of July with a large contingent of men to envelop Fort Duquesne in a pre-dawn raid was abandoned, likely on account of the men's fatigue. However, at a little before three o'clock in the morning on the 9th, Colonel Thomas Gage, with an advance party of approximately four hundred men, was dispatched from Braddock's main body to secure a traversable ford across the Monongahela River for the rest of the army. An hour later, St. Clair, leading the corps of engineers who were to lay roads for the wagons and artillery followed, with General Braddock himself beginning to march at six. On the way, he received word from Gage's advance party that although the latter and his men had encountered a handful of French-Indigenous scouts on the opposite side of the first ford, they had retired without incident, and by eleven o'clock, the army had reached the second ford, successfully crossing it by two in the afternoon.

Not doubting the fact that he and his men were under practically continuous surveillance whilst they conducted themselves across the Monongahela River, the size, discipline and appearance of his army not only assured Braddock himself of success in the upcoming conclusion to his campaign, but he hoped would deter any feeble attempts at resistance outright. In his later life, George Washington would later reflect that he could scarcely recall a more resplendent sight than Braddock's army that very morning. The glimmer of the men's muskets, the cleanliness of their bright red attire, and their undaunted dedication to their duty which animated all. Every man was dressed in his best uniform, so that they appeared as if on parade, with pipers pipping, drummers beating, and flags hoisted high.

For approximately three-quarters of a mile below the mouth of what was then the adjacent Turtle Creek (*"Tulpewi Sipu"* to the local Lenape), the Monongahela River was uncharacteristically shallow, and could easily be forded. And it was here that much of the subsequent catastrophe which ultimately befell Braddock and his men would play out. However, up until that morning, the French-Indigenous chain of command at Fort Duquesne had been wholly indecisive. As late as the 7th of July, overall fort commander, Claude Pierre Pecaudy de Contrecoeur had not committed himself to a course of action in advance of Braddock's army's arrival. There is little reason to doubt that he either intended to abandon the flawed position altogether, or submit to an honorable capitulation, both of which were common practices in pre-nineteenth century, North American frontier warfare, and either of which would have been advisable in this specific situation, considering the unknown size of Braddock's force, which, at the time, may have been rumored to be larger than its actual size.

The most detailed account of subsequent event states, that on the 8th of July, one of Contrecoeur's captains, Daniel Liénard de Beaujeu (1711 – 55), a popular figure with New France's Indigenous allies who had adapted the use of traditional upper body war paint to inspire confidence, proposed to the commander that he be granted permission to assemble a band of men which would ambush Braddock's men as they forded the Monongahela. Contrecoeur initially accepted, but declined to assign specific men to the task, and instead, requested Beaujeu issue a call of volunteers, which was allegedly answered by the entirety of the fort's garrison, which Contrecoeur disliked, and so he requested Beaujeu instead appeal to the throngs of assembled Indigenous warriors, invariably led by Charles Langlade, to assist him. He called them to a council in which he laid out his designs to them, however, evidently having been misled as to the actual size of Braddock's approaching force, which in reality numbered approximately two thousand six hundred and fifty men, a spokesman for the assembled warriors allegedly replied *"How, my father, are you so bent upon death that you would also sacrifice us? With our eight hundred men do you ask us to attack four thousand English?"* However, he concluded by adding *"But we will lay up [sleep on] what we have heard, and tomorrow you shall know our thoughts."*

Early the next day, the morning of July 9th, while the Indigenous warriors under Langlade were preparing to conclusively decline Captain Beaujeu's request for assistance in an ambuscade against Braddock's force of a rumored four thousand men, an Indigenous front-line runner from the Monongahela appeared at the reassembled Fort Duquesne council, and perhaps bringing with him a more accurate assessment of Braddock's army's numbers, excited the energy of all those who were gathered, who resolved at once to march against Braddock's significantly smaller than previously believed force. Approximately nine hundred men, an estimated six or seven hundred of which were Indigenous, one hundred and fifty were Canadians, and seventy French, then prepared for battle, applied body paints, stocked up on ammunition, and at length set off from the fort, with Captain Beaujeu (officially) and Charles Langlade (unofficially) leading, with Jean-Daniel Dumas (1721 – 94), and François-Marie Le Marchand de Lignery (1703 – 59) acting as official subordinates.

But although Braddock's force had perhaps been revealed to have been smaller than previously believed, the objective of the approximately nine hundred men who marched from Fort Duquesne under Beaujeu and Langlade's command was not got to toe-to-toe with what was still a very formidable army, but simply delay and harass them as them as they marched to their objective — the fort. Their strategy going into battle was informed by the fact that Braddock's army would have to traverse a narrow ford within the steep confines of the Monongahela River's banks. It was their intention therefore to dispute Braddock's men while they attempted to exit the river bed before falling back to take up positions on a set of local, highly advantageous ravines, located a short distance between their side of the river and the fort. However, belatedly arriving on the scene, the music of Braddock's pipers and drummers, interspersed with the crashing of felled trees convinced them that the former's army had already crossed the river, but on the contrary, they had only just begun to do so.

The arrangement of Braddock's army as it left the riverbank was documented as follows; the engineers, who felled trees; their guides, perhaps some guarding foot soldiers; as well as six light horsemen, who proceeded in advance of Colonel Gage's approximately four hundred-man strong contingent, which itself was followed by the road working crew under the command of Sir John St. Clair, which was protected by two six-pounders (cannons), with parties of eight militiamen patrolling their respective flanks. They were followed by yet another light horse brigade, which was divided into four squads, and intended for extreme flanking maneuvers. Behind them was a group of seamen, brought all the way from the coast, followed a subaltern officer with a company of grenadiers and a twelve-pounder (cannon).

Hastening in the direction of all the ruckus that Braddock's men were producing, the approximately nine hundred men under Captain Beaujeu and Charles de Langlade first encountered the engineers at the head of Colonel Gage's advance party. Among these, engineer, Robert "Harry" Gordon was allegedly the first to spot the approaching French-Indigenous forces, whom at their head was Beaujeu, attired and painted in a Native American fashion. In the same moment, realizing he was in the midst of Braddock's army, Beaujeu abruptly halted and waved his hat, which was the signal for the Indigenous warriors under Langlade to disperse themselves to the left and right of his position, which they did, posting themselves behind trees, deadfall, rocks, and other forms of natural shelter, from which, they promptly levelled a most devastating volley of musketry upon the English. However, Colonel Gage quickly rallied the men under his command from their confused stupor to return fire, though, as would be characteristic of the developing engagement, so well concealed were the French, Canadian and Indigenous warriors before them, that few Englishmen could sufficiently see, let alone hit them.

Sir John St. Clair's road working crew then came up to reinforce Gage, and encouraged by their bolstered numbers, he ordered them to advance against what he perceived as the center of the French, Canadian and Indigenous line. As they did so, they were struck by another withering musket volley, which cut down many a man, however, they answered with a volley of their own, supplemented by cannon grapeshot, which killed all the French, Canadians and Indigenous warriors who were not immediately sheltered, including Captain Beaujeu, but animated, zealous encouragement from Charles Langlade, Jean-Daniel Dumas, and Marchand de Lignery restabilized the line, saving it from the verge of total collapse. For a period thereafter, the contest entered a stalemate, as the French, Canadian and Indigenous forces suffered few additional casualties, on account of their sheltered positions, while the English continued to bring up reinforcements to replace those who had fallen. However, as the battle wore on, it soon became apparent that sheltered precision was gaining the upper hand over traditional military order, discipline and reinforcements, for although similarly encouraged on by their superior officers, the redcoats not only made easy targets on account of their bright and vibrant attire, but lacked the advantageous benefit of cover their French-Indigenous foe had so carefully selected.

Nonetheless, in the meantime, General Braddock himself, and who's portion of the army hadn't yet left the confines of the river bank, upon hearing the opening volleys of musket fire, promptly ordered Lieutenant Colonel Ralph Burton (died 1768) forward with approximately eight hundred men of the main army to reinforce the line, while approximately four hundred men were held back to protect the baggage train. However, before Burton could arrive on the scene with his reinforcements, Colonel Gage's advance party was irreversibly put to rout after suffering mounting losses in the open. The two parties collided with each other in a confused whirl of friendly fire, exasperated by deliberate sharp shooting of their commanding officers by the French, Canadian and Indigenous forces.

At last, Braddock himself arrived on the scene, and endeavored in vain to restore morale and some semblance of traditional military order amongst his shattered ranks, however, unaccustomed to the perils of Indigenous, guerilla-style warfare, the European troops, alarmed by the losses they had hitherto suffered and by the incessant firing of a largely unseen enemy, which poured down upon them from every conceivable angle, simply could not be induced to reform and reengage, while the few local militia, which were better adapted to this exact mode of warfare, were expressly barred from partaking in it, and indeed, ridiculed and chastised personally by Braddock as cowards for attempting to do so.

"The Enemy kept behind trees and logs of wood, and cut down our troops as fast as they cou'd advance", later recalled one, unnamed English witness to the spectacle. **"The soldiers then insisted much to be allowed to take to the trees, which the General denied and stormed much [against], calling them cowards, and even went so far as to strike them with his own sword for attempting [to take shelter behind] the trees."**

Meanwhile, despite their successful opening volleys which had struck down French Captain Beaujeu, amongst others, at the commencement of the battle, the English use of artillery in the engagement had been of little consequence, as most of the French, Canadian and Indigenous warriors present had either long since sought some form of cover amongst the thick woods or had shot down the English cannon crews where they stood. Colonel George Washington and Captain Thomas Waggoner (circa. 1715 – 70) of the Virginia Militia briefly rallied a band of approximately eighty men in a desperate counterattack, taking up positions behind a fallen tree, however, they themselves were then swiftly counterattacked, resulting in approximately fifty killed outright, with numerous others injured, while those who were able retreated once more. At long last, sensing victory, the dreaded *"Indian war whoop"* was sounded by members of the French, Canadian and Indigenous forces, who then bounded forward and charged the disintegrating English lines.

"The yell of the Indians is fresh on my ear, and the terrific sound will haunt me until the hour of my dissolution", recalled a *"Captain Leslie"* (perhaps Matthew Lesley, of General Braddock's staff, whose last name is indeed occasionally recorded as "Leslie" and whom is documented as having survived the ordeal), another English witness to the event. **"I cannot describe the horrors of that scene. No pencil could do it, or no painter delineate it so as to convey to you with accuracy our unhappy situation."**

However, the decisive moment of the engagement came approximately three hours after it had commenced, when Braddock himself, in the midst of giving orders, was hit by a musket ball, which passed through his right arm, knocking him off his fifth horse of the battle and lodged itself in a lung. As what remained of his army's discipline dissolved around him and took to flight, the mortally wounded General was nearly abandoned on the field of battle, but for the intercession of Robert Orme (circa. 1725 – '81 or '90), one of Braddock's aide-de-camps on the expedition, and one of only two (the other being George Washington) that had miraculously survived the Monongahela ordeal. Although the General himself had initially demanded that he be left to his melancholy fate where he fell, Orme disregarded this demand, and instead induced Captain Robin Stewart (1729 – 1809) of the light-horse Virginian Militia and another unnamed American officer, to assist him in conveying the General to safety.

It was approximately five o'clock in the evening when Braddock's army finally abandoned the battlefield, and although the sickly Colonel George Washington, General Braddock's local guide and adviser on the expedition, and whom was at the time of the battle recovering from a debilitating fever, was able to muster a handful of Virginian militiamen into a best attempt at a rear-guard to cover the rest of the army's retreat, there could be no disguising the fact that Braddock's Expedition had been a catastrophic disaster for the English, which had dispelled any notion of quick and easy war in America, and had awaken the nation to the grim fact that many more would have to die before any tangible progress against the French, Canadian and Indigenous forces of New France was to be made. Of the approximately two thousand, six hundred and fifty men that General Braddock had led into battle that morning of July 9th, between four and five hundred were slain outright, with approximately four of five hundred more wounded, with sixty-three of eighty-nine commissioned officers among those dead or wounded. The French, Canadian and Indigenous casualties on the other hand, numbered less than fifty killed, and less than sixty wounded, out of approximately nine hundred men.

With their mortally wounded commander in tow, what remained of General Braddock's army continued to retreat through the night of the 9th into the morning of the 10th of July, whence they arrived at the plantation of Christopher Gist (1706 – 59), another of Braddock's local guides on the ill-fated expedition, where a brief halt was made. However, fearing pursuit by the French, Canadian and Indigenous forces, the retreat was resumed on the 12th, in the direction of Will's Creek. Before departing, however, anything of value which could not be transported was burned or otherwise ruined to prevent its falling into the enemy's hands. This included several cannons, which were disabled, while an estimated fifty thousand pounds (22679.6 kg) of unused gun powder were emptied.

The next day, Sunday, July 13th saw the steep decline of General Braddock's condition. He spent his final hours in tortured agony over his wound and army's defeat, overheard to repeat to himself *"**Who would have thought it?**"* under his dying breath. Among his final acts was to bestow upon George Washington several of his most treasured possessions before uttering his final words, spoken to aide-de-camp, Robert Orme, who had rescued him from the battlefield: "*We shall better know how to deal with them another time*," he is alleged to have said, before dying around eight, with the devastated remains of his army resuming their retreat the following morning, leaving the entire frontier virtually unopposed to French, Canadian and Indigenous, incursions.

Meanwhile, wholly satisfied with their unexpected victory, the primarily Indigenous, French and Canadian force had in fact totally abandoned their pursuit of Braddock's decimated army, and returned to the site of the battle to plunder the fallen and the contents of their baggage train, which contained gold, silver, quality guns and ammunition, as well as General Braddock's personal papers, which included his letters and instruction from the King's Court, which were at once conveyed to the Governor General of New France, and made it plain to see that the English were fully committed to war.

Charles Langlade's first act following the victory over Braddock's army was to issue a decree that all liquors discovered be destroyed to avoid consumption, which resulted in a reported "great quantity" being disposed of, depriving himself, his allies, family and friends alike of a toast to a victory, described by Pierre Pouchot (1712 – 69), a French military engineer serving in New France at the time, as "*the fiercest and most glorious in which [Natives] ever engaged.*" Indeed, so prevalent had his leadership on the battlefield been that day, that Langlade was jointly proclaimed "*Ake-wauge-ketausa*", or "*Military Conqueror*", by his Indigenous brethren, with the literal translation of his title meaning "*He Who is Fierce for the Land*", although an alternative spelling of "*Auke-winge-ketaw-so*", meaning "*Defender of his Country*" is also recorded. However, to the Menomonee (Folles Avoines) specifically, he was simply known henceforth as the "*Bravest of the Brave.*"

News of General Braddock's defeat spreadv quickly. Captain John Rutherford (1737 – 1804), who was a member of the Council of New York and had commanded one of the New York battalions in Braddock's army, wrote of their defeat in an unaddressed and undated letter:

"*I have delayed writing this week past out of vexation at our proceedings here, but now a retreat is ordered and the blow struck to our shame and the glory of the Indians, who, with a very few Canadians amongst them, have entirely defeated our General and the division of our troops which he carried along with him, and what is worst of all, our train of artillery is left in their hands, which ruins all hopes of doing anything this way. Sir Peter Halkett was killed in the field, regretted by all mankind, [though] his son[s], Lieut. Halkett [and] Major Halkett came off unwounded with a few officers more, [but] all the rest [were] killed or wounded, many dangerously, amongst whom are the General and Sir John St. Clair. Capt. [Horatio] Gates has a slight wound. [Gates] with 50 of his men, having marched with the first division, my company and [that of] Capt. Demires with the remainder [...] under Lieut. Spearing, marched in the second division, except a few of our men who had gone up to the first division with a convoy of provisions; the slaughter on our side is surprising, considering General Braddock had fifteen hundred (men) and I don't believe the Indians had three hundred, but they chose a very advantageous ground within nine miles of Fort Duquesne. The General told us he would never be five miles from us, so that the one division might support the other whenever attacked; what made him change his resolution and order Col. Dunbar to keep us behind with provisions and tired wagon horses, God knows [...].*"

While nine days after the defeat, George Washington, who miraculously survived the carnage and was keen to ease a worried mind, while also downplay unfortunate events, wrote his mother:

"*To. Mrs. Mary Washington, near Fredericksburg.*

Fort Cumberland, 18th July, 1755.

Honored Madam,
As I doubt not but you have heard of our defeat, and perhaps, had it represented in a worse light, if possible, than it deserves, I have taken this earliest opportunity to give you some account of the

engagement as it happened, within ten miles of the French fort, on Wednesday the 9th instant.

We marched to that place, without any considerable loss, having only now and then a straggler picked up by the French and scouting Indians. When we came there, we were attacked by a party of French and Indians, whose number, I am persuaded, did not exceed three hundred men [it did]; while ours consisted of about one thousand three hundred well-armed troops, chiefly regular soldiers, who were struck with such panic, that they behaved with more cowardice than it is possible to conceive. The officers behaved gallantly, in order to encourage their men, for which they suffered greatly, there being near sixty killed and wounded; a large portion of the number we had.

The Virginia troops showed a good deal of bravery, and were nearly all killed; for I believe, out of three companies that were there, scarcely thirty men are left alive. Captain Peyrouny, and all his officers down to a corporal, were killed. Captain Polson had nearly as hard a fate, for only one of his was left. In short, the dastardly behavior of those they call regulars exposed all others, that were inclined to do their duty, to almost certain death; and, at last, in despite of all the efforts of the officers to the contrary, they ran, as sheep pursued by dogs, and it was impossible to rally them.

The General was wounded, of which he died three days after. Sir Peter Halket was killed in the field, where died many other brave officers. I luckily escaped without a wound, though I had four bullets through my coat and two horses shot under me. Captains Orme and Morris, two of the aids-de-camp, were wounded early in the engagement, which rendered the duty harder upon me, as I was the only person then left to distribute the General's orders, which I was scarcely able to do, as I was not half recovered from a violent illness that had confined me to my bed and a wagon for above ten days. I am still in a weak and feeble condition, which induces me to halt here two or three days in the hope of recovering a little strength, to enable me to proceed homewards; from whence, I fear, I shall not be able to stir till towards September; so that I shall not *have the pleasure of seeing you till then, unless it be in Fairfax. Please give my love to Mr. Lewis and my sister; and compliments to Mr. Jackson, and all other friends that inquire after me.*

I am, honored Madam, your most dutiful son."

Other period Anglo-American narratives of General Braddock's defeat are as follows;

The first is commonly referred to as *"A Seaman's Journal"*, which was allegedly penned by one of the few seamen who had accompanied General Braddock's army to the Monongahela, although a nineteenth century reevaluation concluded that the "Seaman's Journal" was actually written by one of Braddock's army's engineers, Robert "Harry" Gordon, who was attached to the 48th Regiment, and whom, according to legend, was the first man of Braddock's army to see the French, Canadian and Indigenous warriors coming in the moments before the battle erupted. The journal, in total, runs twenty-three pages, beginning on April 10th, three months before the defeat on the Monongahela, and concludes with the embarkation of remaining seamen and troops aboard ship off the coast of Virgina, over a month after the defeat, on August 18th. The most consequential entry of the journal is (of course) in reference to the battle, and is as follows:

"On the 9th. July. The advance party of four hundred men march'd about seven o'clock. Some Indians rush'd out of the bushes, but did no execution. The party [of four hundred men] went on and secured both passes of the river, and at eleven, the main body began to cross with colours [flags] flying, drums beating, and fifes playing the 'Grenadiers March', and soon formed, when they thought that the French would not attack them, as they might have done [...] with such advantages in crossing the Monongahela. The advanc'd party was a quarter of a mile before the main body, the rear of which was just over the river, when the front was attack'd. The two Grenadier companies formed the flank, the piquets, with the rest of the men, were sustaining the carpenters while they were cutting the roads. The first fire the enemy gave was in the front, and

they likewise gaul'd the piquets in flank, so that in a few minutes, the Grenadiers were nearly cut to pieces and drove into the greatest confusion, as was Capt. Polson's company of carpenters. As soon as the main body heard that the front was attack'd, they instantly advanced to secure them but found them retreating, upon which, the General ordered the artillery to draw up and the battalion to form, [but] by this time, the enemy had attack'd the main body, which faced to the right and left and engaged them, but could not see whom they fired at. It was in an open road that the main body were drawn up but the trees were excessive[ly] thick [a]round them and the enemy had possession of a hill to the right, which consequently was a great advantage to them. Many officers declare that they never saw above five of the enemy at one time during the whole action. Our soldiers were encouraged to make many attempts by the officers (who behaved gloriously) to take the hill, but they had been so intimidated before by seeing their comrades [...] falling, that as they advanced up towards the hill and [with their] officer's being pic[ked] off, which was generally the case; they turn'd [...] about and retired [back] down the hill. When the General perceived [this, he was] convinced that the soldiers would not fight in a regular manner without officers [and so] he divided them into small parties and endeavor'd to surround the enemy, but by this time the major part of the officers were either kill'd or wounded, and in short, the soldiers were totally deaf to the commands and persuasions of the few officers that were left unhurt. The General had four horses shot under him before he was wounded, which was towards the latter part of the action, when he was put into a wagon with great difficulty as he was very solicitous for being left in the field. The retreat now became general, and it was the opinion of many people that had we had greater numbers, it [the result] would have been just the same [...], as our advanc'd party never regained the ground they were first attack'd upon. It was extremely lucky [that] they pursued [us] no further than the first crossing of the river. But they kill'd and scalp'd everyone they met with. The army march'd all night and join'd Colonel Dunbar the next day, fifty miles distant from the field of battle, when the General order'd Colonel Dunbar to prepare for a [further] retreat, [...] for which, they were obliged to destroy great quantities of stores and provisions, to furnish the wounded officers and soldiers with wagons. The General's pain increased hourly, and on the 12th of July, he died, greatly lamented by the whole army [and] was decently though privately buried the next morning.

The numbers kill'd, wounded and left in the field, as appeared by the returns of the different companies, were eight hundred and ninety-six, besides officers. The two companies of the Grenadiers and carpenters suffered most. Colonel Dunbar's Grenadiers were seventy-nine complete, out of which [only] nine returned untouch'd. Sir Peter Halket's were sixty-nine, [of which] only thirteen came out of (the) field. Every Grenadier officer was either kill'd or wounded. The seamen had eleven kill'd or wounded out of thirty-three. It was impossible to tell the exact numbers of the enemy, but it was premised by the continual smart fire [that was] kept [up] during the whole action [...]. Mr. Engineer Gordon [evidently speaking of himself in the third person] was the first man that saw the enemy, being in the front of the carpenters, making and picketing the roads for them, and he declared [when] he first discover'd them, that they were on the run [forwards], which plainly [shows that] they [had] just come from Fort Duquesne and that their principal intention was to secure the pass of [the] Monongahela River, but [that] the officer who was their leader, dressed like an Indian, with a gorget [neck/throat armor/shield], waved his hat, by way of signal to [the Indigenous warriors and Canadian militia to] disperse to [his] right and left, forming a half moon [shape around Braddock's stretched-out army]. Colonel Dunbar continued his retreat and arrived with the with the remains of the army at Fort Cumberland [on] the 20th [of] July, and on the 21st, the wounded officers and soldiers were brought in."

The newspapers of the time, naturally, ran wild with the story, as oral eyewitness accounts, written reports, diaries and journals were circulated, privately and publicly. In late August, 1755, the London publication, *"Gentleman's Magazine"* published the following article, which referenced initial reporting by the *"Pittsburg Gazette"*, and attempted to summarize the entirety of Braddock's failed enterprise thus:

"Of the expeditions set on foot against the French in America, mentioned in our last, the issue of one only was then known, the capture of fort Beausejour, by Gen. Monkton, who commanded the expedition to Fundy. We have received the following accounts of Gen. Braddock, who was destined to the Ohio.

It was said by letters from Virginia, dated June 22nd, that on the 12th, Gen. Braddock, with 2,000 regular troops, had passed the Allegheny mountains, and was within 5 days march of Du Quesne, a French fort on the Monongahela River, which runs into the Ohio. Sir John St. Clair having advanced near enough to view it, and consider the adjacent ground, remarked a small eminence that was within cannon shot; and the fort being built of wood, and garrisoned with 1,000 men, it was proposed to erect a battery on this eminence, and set fire to the place, by throwing into it a great number of red hot balls.

Letters from Philadelphia, dated June 25th, gave an account, that the General had been long detained at Will's Creek, and greatly distressed for the want of forage and provisions. Landing the troops at Virginia is said to have been a most unfortunate error, as neither forage, provisions, nor carriages were there to be had, and that if they had landed in Pennsylvania it would have saved £40,000 sterling, and shortened the march six weeks. He was, however, promised 150 wagons, and 300 horses, with a large quantity of forage and provisions, to be furnished from the back settlements of Pennsylvania; but after tedious and anxious expectation of these succours, he received instead of 150 wagons, only 15; and instead of 300 horses only 100. This disappointment, however great, was much aggravated when the wagons were unloaded, for the provisions stunk so intolerably, that he must have suffered very greatly from hunger, who could eat it. While he was in this distress, he received an unexpected supply of £500, in provisions and wine, from Philadelphia, which was sent him by the hands of Mr. [Benjamin] Franklin. The General accepted this present, with great joy, and urged Mr. Franklin to use his interest to procure farther assistance. Mr. Franklin observed that General St. Clair's dress was of the Hussar kind, and this gave him a hint which he immediately improved. He caused a report to be propagated among the Germans, that except 150 wagons could be got ready, and sent to the general within a certain time, St. Clair, who was a Hussar, would come among them, and take away what he found by force: The Germans having formerly lived under despotic power, knew the Hussars too well to doubt their serving themselves, and believing that Gen. St. Clair was indeed a Hussar, they provided instead of 150, 200 wagons, and sent them within the time that Mr. Franklin had limited.

The Pennsylvanians also advanced a farther sum above the King's bounty, and sent him 190 wagons more, laden each with a ton of corn and oats, four wagons with provisions and wine for the officers, and 60 head of fine cattle for the army.

The General, as soon as he had received these supplies, pursued his march, having received from time to time various and contradictory accounts of the strength and motions of the enemy: Fort Du Quesne was sometimes said to be garrisoned by its full compliment, 1,000 men; sometimes he was assured by French deserters, that the garrison did not consist of more than 200, and that there were but 500 at (Fort) Venango and [Fort] Presq'Isle, on the banks of Lake Erie, distant from Du Quesne about 90 miles. He received also frequent intelligence of French parties in motion, particularly of a considerable number that were seen in batteaux [boats], on Lake Ontario, as we supposed on their way to the Ohio, and of 600 that had passed the lake in 120 canoes and batteaux, and were going to Niagara. It was now expect[ed] that the next advices would give an account of the siege, if not of the capture of fort Du Quesne, as everyone had been taught to believe, that our force in this part of the world was so much superior to the French, that to march and take possession was the same thing; but in the midst of this impatience and confidence, we were alarmed with the report that Gen. Braddock had been defeated, and soon after the following article appeared in the [Pittsburg] Gazette.

'Whitehall, Aug. 26th, 1755.

By his Majesty's ship the Sea-Horse, from Virginia, advice has been received, that Major General Braddock, having advanced with two thousand men, and all the stores and provisions, to the Little Meadows (about 20 miles beyond Fort Cumberland at Will's Creek) found it necessary to leave the greatest part of his wagons, &c, at that place, under the command of Col. Dunbar, with a detachment of eight hundred men, ordering him to follow as fast as the nature of the service would admit. The General having by this means lessened his line of march, proceeded with great expedition, his corps then consisting of about twelve hundred men, and 12 pieces of artillery, together with the necessary ammunition, stores, and provisions. On the 8th of July he encamped within 10 miles of Fort Du Quesne; and on the 9th, on his march through the woods towards that fort, was attacked by a body of French and Indians, who made a sudden fire from the woods, which put the troops into great confusion, and occasioned their retiring with great precipitation, notwithstanding all the endeavors of the General and his officers, many of whom were killed whilst they were using all possible means to rally the men. The General, who exerted himself as much as man could do, after having five horses killed under him, was shot through the arm and the lungs; of which he died the fourth day. Sir Peter Halket was killed on the spot. Two of the General's aids de camps, (Capt. Orme and Capt. Morris) were wounded. His secretary, (son to Governor Shirley) was killed. Sir John St. Clair, quarter-master-general, and his assistant, Mr. Leslie, both wounded. It is reckoned there were about 200 killed, and 400 wounded; the latter are mostly collected at Will's Creek, to which place Col. Dunbar, with the remainder of the troops, has retired; from whom a more particular account is expected.

The following list has been received of the officers killed and wounded on the occasion:

'Staff:

- *Major General Braddock } - died of his wounds*
- *Robert Orme, Esq., Aid de Camp } - wounded*
- *Roger Morris, Esq., Aid de Camp } - wounded*
- *William Shirley, Esq., Secretary } - killed*
- *Sir John St. Clair, Dep. Quar. Master Gen. } - wounded*
- *Matthew Lesely, Gent., his assistant } - wounded*

Late Sir Peter Halket's Regiment:

- *Sir P. Halket, Col., } - K*
- *Lieut. Col., Gage } - W*
- *Captain Tatton } - K*
- *Capt. Gethins } - W*

[Sir Peter Halket's Regiment's] Subalterns:

- *Lieut. Littleler } - W*
- *Lieut. Dunbar } - W*
- *Lieut. Halket [Sir John's son] } - K*
- *Lieut. Treeby } - W*
- *Lieut. Allen } - K*
- *Lieut. Simpson } - W*
- *Lieut. Lock } - W*
- *Lieut. Disney } - W*
- *Lieut. Kennedy } - W*
- *Lieut. Townsend } - K*
- *Lieut. Nartlow } - K*
- *Lieut. Pennington } - W*

Colonel Dunbar's Regiment:

- *Lieut. Col. Burton } - W*
- *Major Sparkes } - W*
- *Captain Cholmley } - K*
- *Captain Rowyer } - W*
- *Captain Ross } - W*

[Colonel Dunbar's Regiment's] Subalterns:

- *Barbut } - W*
- *Walsham } - W*
- *Crimble } - K*
- *Wideman } - K*
- *Hanfard } - K*
- *Glandwin } - W*
- *Edmeston } - W*
- *Brereton } - K*
- *Hart } - K*
- *Montresuer } - W*
- *MacMullen } - W*
- *Crow } - W*
- *Sterling } - W*

Artillery:

- *Capt. Lieut. Smith } - K*
- *Lieut. Buchanan } - W*
- *Lieut. McCloud } - W*
- *Lieut. McCollar } - W*

Engineers:

- *Peter McKeller, Esq. } - W*
- *Robert Gordon, Esq. [according to legend the first member of Braddock's army to encounter the French, Canadians and Indigenous warriors on the Monongahela River] } - W*
- *Williams, Esq. } - W*

Detachment of Sailors:

- *Lieut. Spendelow } - K*
- *Mr. Talbot, Midshipman } - K*
- *Capt. Stone, of Gen. Lascelie's Reg. } - W*
- *Capt. Floyer, of Gen. Warburton's Reg. } - W*

Independant Companies of New York:

- *Capt. Gates } - W*
- *Lieut. Sumain } - K*
- *Lieut. Howarth } - W*
- *Lieut. Gray } - W*

Virginia Troops:

- *Capt. Stephens } - W*
- *Capt. Poulston } - K*
- *Capt. Peronie } - K*

[Virginia] Subalturns:

- *Hamilton } - K*
- *Wright } - K*
- *Splitdorff } - K*
- *Stuart } - W*
- *Wagoner } - K'*

Several other accounts of this action, and lists of the dead and wounded have appeared in the papers, and are said to be taken from private letters. By the [Pittsburg] Gazette account, General Braddock seems to have been attacked by an ambuscade of French and Indians, on his march through the woods, before he came within sight of the enemy; by the other accounts, he seems to have reached an advanced party of the French, before the action began. They are to this effect.

The French, who were posted at fort Du Quesne, and on the Ohio, consisted of 1,500 regular, and 600 irregular troops [both numbers vastly exaggerated – editor's note], who had with them a considerable number of Indians in their interest [this, however, is accurate]. These forces, having gained very particular intelligence of Gen. Braddock's design, of the number and condition of his forces, and the route they were to take, no sooner found that he was advancing after having received his last supply of provisions, than they also advanced towards him, and having chosen a very advantageous piece of ground, and intrenched themselves in a masterly manner, having about six miles south of their fort, they formed a camp a thick wood on each side of them, which extended along the route the General was to take. When he was come within three miles of their intrenchments, they drew out of their lines, placing their 600 irregulars in front, as a forlorn hope, and their 1,500 regulars behind to support them; they also stationed a great number of their Indians in the wood, on each side, who effectually concealed themselves behind trees and bushes.

Soon after this fatal disposition was made, General Braddock appeared with his troops in the following order.

- *Colonel Gage and Burton of Halket's Regiment.*
- *The General with Dunbar's Regiment.*
- *The troops from Virginia, Maryland and Carolina.*

As soon as the whole army was got between the two ambuscades, the men were alarmed by the Indians, who fired singly at the

General, and other particular officers; upon this they pushed forward, as the enemy was in sight, though not within musket-shot, and as soon as they came near enough, the attack was begun by the Colonels Gage and Burton. This was a signal to the Indians to ambush, who immediately gave the war whoop, and raising from the thickets, discovered themselves on both sides, flanking out men in volleys, which did incredible execution.

The advanced guard, being now between three fires, immediately gave way; but being rallied with much difficulty by the officers, they gave one fire, and then returned in the utmost confusion, and threw Dunbar's Regiment, which was behind them, into the same disorder: They were with unspeakable difficulty and trouble once more rallied by their officers, and stood one fire from the enemy, but then without returning it, both the regiments fled, with the utmost terror and precipitation, deserting their officers, who though alone kept their ground till of 60 only 5 remained that were not either killed or wounded. — The Virginians who formed the rear still stood unbroken, and continued the engagement on very unequal terms near three hours, but were then compelled to retire. These letters give the same account of the General as that in the Gazette, but add that all our baggage, provisions, and even military chest, [has] fallen into the enemy's hands [they did]. Other letters, however, contradict this particular, and say that the artillery, baggage and military chest [is] safe [it was not], being two days behind the army.

There is indeed some reason to hope that this is true, from the account published by authority [however, the authority had cause down to downplay events], for it is there said, that the General left the baggage, &c, behind him twenty miles, that he might march with the greater expedition [speed]; the very reason for his leaving them behind seems to prove, that he went forward without halting, and that it was with impossible the men with the baggage should keep near him; so that they must have been considerably behind him when the action happened, it is probable the broken troops joined them in their retreat, and proceeded safely with the baggage to Will's Creek."

The Gentleman's Gazette's article, detailing General Braddock's defeat, concludes; *"On the other hand, it is alleged, the defeat is owing more to presumption and want of conduct in the officers, than the cowardice in the private man [the soldiers]; that a retreat ought to have been resolved upon the moment they found themselves surprised by an ambuscade; and that they were told by the men, when they refused to return the charge, that if they could see their enemy they would fight him, but that they would not waste their ammunition against trees and bushes, nor stand exposed to invisible assailants, the French and Indian rangers, who are excellent marksmen, and in such a situation would inevitably destroy any number of the best troops in the world."*

One of the most detailed analysis of Braddock's defeat published immediately following its disastrous conclusion was penned the day before the Pittsburg Gazette's article was written, by clergyman, Charles Chauncy (1705 – 1787) under the alias *"T.W.",* on August 25th, 1755, and published later that same year in Boston, under the (abridged) title of *"A Letter to a Friend; Giving a Concise, but just Account, According to the Advices hitherto received, of the Ohio Defeat."*

"Sir," it begins.

"As you live at a distance from the seat of news, and may know nothing of the Ohio-Defeat but from hearsay reports, which, having passed thro' a variety of hands before they have reached you, must be very uncertain, and mixed with a great deal that is not true, I have been at the pains, for your gratification, to put together, from the best accounts, the whole of what may be depended on for fact, in relation to this interesting affair to all the British American Governments: And if I should hereupon add a few thoughts, tending to point out to you wherein this defeat, however inglorious in itself, is yet naturally and powerfully adapted to serve these Colonies in the end, it may give some relief to your anxious mind, and dispose

you to wait, with a becoming submission, the issue of those military operations which are but just begun.

The first news of this defeat was bro't us in a letter from Col. Innes, dated July 11th, in these words, 'I have this moment received the melancholy news of the defeat of our troops, the General killed and numbers of our officers, our whole artillery taken. In short, the account I have received is so very bad, that, as please God, I intend to make a stand here. It's highly necessary to raise the militia everywhere to defend the Frontiers.' It at once appeared to everyone, from the general air and strain of this letter, that the aged Colonel was under the influence of a strong panic when he wrote it, for which reason we were disposed to hope, that matters were not so bad as he had suggested; and by after contradictory accounts we were encouraged in this hope, till the second of this instant [this month — August], when, upon the arrival of the western post, it was put beyond all doubt, by a variety of letters, that the Ohio: re[e]ncounter was, on our side, every way as disadvantageous as we were at first led to conceive it to be.

By comparing the accounts we have hitherto received, it appears, 'that the General proceeded from the little meadows with about 1300 men, mostly British, besides the necessary artillery, ammunition, and provisions, leaving the main body of the convoy under the care of Col. Dunbar, with orders to join him as soon as possible; that on the 9th of July the Monongahela was passed first by 300 men, then by 200, then by the General himself, with the column of artillery, baggage, and main body of the army, about one o'clock; that immediately upon this a quick and heavy fire was heard from the front; that the detachments of the 2[00] and 300 men gave way, and fell back in great consternation upon the main body, who were hastening to sustain them; that this struck the men with such a panic, and bro't on such confusion as could not, by any expedients, be afterwards remedied; and that in consequence of this, notwithstanding the courage and resolution of the officers, the enemy obtained a complete victory, killing and wounding a great many (at the lowest computation, between 6 and 700 soldiers, officers and private men, were killed, wounded, besides pioneers, waggoners, servants, &c.) and obliging the rest to quit the ground [battlefield], leaving behind them the artillery, ammunition, provisions and whole baggage.'

The number of the enemy remains still somewhat uncertain. One of the officers writes, 'it was impossible by the disposition of the French and Indians to judge of their number.' Another is pretty certain, 'that they did not exceed above 3 or 400.' A Gentleman from Philadelphia of good intelligence says, 'by the best accounts there were about 400 Indians and 80 French.' I am inclined to think, they were not much more numerous [they were]; for if they had, they would probably have cut off the whole army, as they had so great an advantage against them, and fired, not in the European way, but by taking aim, in which method of firing the Canadians, as well as Indians, are very dexterous.

But whether their number was great, or small, they made [...] havoc [on] our men. Perhaps, all circumstances considered, history will scarce[ly] furnish an instance of such a dreadful carnage. To be sure, the like was never before seen in North-America: Nor could it have happened, humanly speaking, without great misconduct, either in the officers, or soldiers, or both. Some are pleased to lay the blame on the soldiers; speaking of them as cowards, and as leaving their officers to fall a sacrifice to the enemy. Others seem to think, the chief commander was rather principally faulty in not using due caution, and a prudent forecast, to guard the men against the surprise which involv'd them in destruction.

It does not come within my present design to enter upon an enquiry into the blamable source of this mischief; tho' you will unavoidably perceive my opinion about it, by reading what I have to offer with respect to the tendency of it finally to serve the interest of even all the British American Colonies.

I readily own, this defeat, in many respects, is a terrible evil. Great dishonor has been reflected on the British arms; the Indians will be more strongly attached to the French than ever; the French are inspir'd with greater courage and resolution, while, at the same time, their strength is very much increased by the artillery, ammunition, and stores bro't by us, within 7 miles of their fort, at an immense expense of labour and money: Besides all which, our southern colonies are thrown into perplexity and confusion, and lie doubly exposed to the depredations of the [Natives] of the wilderness."* The author goes on to observe that, *"Had General Braddock been opposed by French Regulars only, he would probably have met with little interruption in his progress; but, as he had to do with the Canadians and Indians, who fought in a way he was an entire stranger to, he soon fell a prey into their hands: Nor would numbers have served him; they would only have given, occasion for a more horrible slaughter of men. The plain truth is, Regular troops, in this Wilderness-country, are just the fame that irregular ones would be in Flanders. American irregulars would easily be confounded by regular troops in the open fields of Europe; and regular troops would be as easily reduced to the like confusion by American irregulars in the woods here.*

I would not be understood to mean by what I here say, as tho' we did not need regular troops, or could not make use of them to good purpose. For, as France has fent over a considerable number of their regulars, it is highly proper there should be regulars to oppose them; and, in laying siege to their fortifications, regulars are the fittest to be employed: But, as there is no way of marching to the French fortresses, or to their regulars, either in, or out of them, but thro' the American woods and thickets, the best regular troops that could be sent us would, without all doubt, be attacked in their march; and should this be the case, they would probably be soon destroyed, or obliged to retreat with loss, not being skilled in the only method of fighting that would be of any, real service to them. General Braddock's defeat is a practical instance that must forever silence all dispute upon this head."

As for the French, their official reports of General Braddock's defeat tended to be more reserved in their detailing of events. The most comprehensive, however, translated from the French is as follows:

> *"Account of the Battle of Monongahela, 9th July, 1755. Depot General de la Guerre, Paris. No. 189 in the Carton marked '1755, Marine.'*

M. de Contrecoeur, Captain of Infantry, Commandant of Fort Duquesne, on the Ohio, having been informed that the English were taking up arms in Virginia for the purpose of coming to attack him, was advised, shortly afterwards, that they were on the march.

He dispatched scouts, who reported to him faithfully their progress. On the 17th instant [this month — July] he was advised that their army, consisting of 3000 regulars from Old England, were within six leagues of this fort. That officer employed the next day in making his arrangements; and on the ninth detached M. de Beaujeu, seconded by Messrs. Dumas and de Lignery, all three Captains, together with four Lieutenants, 6 Ensigns, 20 Cadets, 100 Soldiers, 100 Canadians and 600 Indians, with orders to lie in ambush at a favorable spot, which he had reconnoitered the previous evening.

The detachment, before it could reach its place of destination, found itself in [the] presence of the enemy within three leagues of that fort. M. de Beaujeu, finding his ambush had failed, decided on an attack. This he made with so much vigor as to astonish the enemy, who were waiting for us in the best possible order; but their artillery, loaded with grape [shot], having opened its fire, our men gave way in turn.

The Indians, also, frightened by the report of the cannon rather than by any damage it could inflict [due to the thickness of the woods], began to yield, when M. de Beaujeu was killed. M. Dumas [then] began to encourage his detachment. He ordered the officers in command of the Indians to spread themselves along the wings so as to take the enemy in flank, whilst he, M. de Lignery and the other officers who led the French, were attacking them in front.

This order was executed so promptly that the enemy, who were already shouting their 'Long live the King,' thought now only of defending themselves.

The fight was obstinate on both sides and success long doubtful; but the enemy at last gave way. Efforts were made, in vain, to introduce some sort of order in their retreat. [But] the whoop of the Indians, which echoed through the forest, struck terror into the hearts of the entire enemy. The rout was complete. We remained in possession of the field with six brass twelves and sixes [cannons], four howitzer carriages of 50, 11 small royal grenade mortars, all their ammunition, and, generally, their entire baggage.

Some deserters, who have come in since, have told us that we had been engaged with only 2000 men, the remainder of the army being four leagues further off. These same deserters have informed us that the enemy were retreating to Virginia, and some scouts, sent as far as the height of land, have confirmed this by reporting that the thousand men who were not engaged, had been equally panic-stricken and abandoned both provisions and ammunition on the way.

On this intelligence, a detachment was dispatched after them, which destroyed and burnt everything that could be found. The enemy have left more than 1000 men on the field of battle. They have lost a great portion of the artillery and ammunition, provisions, as also their General, whose name was Mr. Braddock, and almost all their officers. We have had 3 officers killed; 2 officers and 2 cadets wounded. Such a victory, so entirely unexpected, seeing the inequality of the forces, is the fruit of M. Dumas' experience, and of the activity and valor of the officers under his command." One of whom was Charles Langlade.

As noted previously, most of Braddock's army's baggage was abandoned and subsequently carried back to Fort Duquesne. There, a detailed list of all that had been acquired by the French was tallied, and is as follows:

"*Return of the artillery, munitions of war and other effects belonging to the English, found on the field of battle after the action which took place on the 9th of July, 1755, within three leagues of Fort Duquesne, on the River Oyo [Ohio], between a detachment of 250 Canadians and 650 Indians, commanded by Captain de Beaujeu, and a body of 2000 English men under the command of General Braddock, exclusive of the considerable plunder that the Indians took.*

- *4 brass pieces with the arms of England, of the calibre of 11lbs.*
- *4 ditto, of 5-and-a-half lbs.*
- *4 brass mortars or howitzers, of 7-and-a-half inch diameter.*
- *3 other grenade mortars, of 4-and-a-half inch diameter.*
- *175 balls of 11lbs.*
- *57 howitzers of 6-and-three-fourths inch.*
- *17 barrels of powder, 100lbs.*
- *19,740 musket cartridges.*
- *The artifices for the artillery.*
- *The other articles necessary for a siege.*
- *A great quantity of muskets, fit and unfit for service.*
- *A quantity of broken carriages.*
- *4 or 500 horses, some of them killed.*
- *About 100 head of horned cattle.*
- *A greater number of barrels of powder and flour, broken.*
- *About 600 dead, of whom a great number are officers, and wounded in proportion.*
- *20 men or women taken prisoners by the Indians.*
- *Very considerable booty in furniture, clothing and utensils.*
- *A lot of papers which have not been translated for want of time; among others, the plan of Fort Duquesne with its exact proportions.*

Note. - The Indians have plundered a great deal of gold and silver coin."

In addition, all General Braddock's personal letters were also acquired by the French, a fact noted in a letter addressed to French Commissary, Andre Jean Baptiste Doreil (circa. 1715 – 60s) from French Major-General Jean Erdman (or Armand), the Baron de Dieskau (1701 – 67), a former aid-de-camp to the great Marshal, Maurice de Saxe (1696 – 1750), and whom had been imported into North America from Europe by the French on February 20th, 1755:

"*Montreal, 16th August, 1755.*

Sir: I start in a moment for Fort St. Frederic to place myself at the head of a body of about 3000 men, to meet an English force of 4500 men, whose design is to seize Forts St. Frederic, St. John, Chambly, and afterwards to advance as far as Montreal. I shall try, however, to mar their plan. The troops are in the best disposition possible, and panting only for the attack. All I fear is, that the enemy, who imagine all our troops to have gone on the expedition against Chouaguen, will beat a retreat on learning that we are on the march.

The battalions of la Reine and Languedoc are of the party; but Guienne and Bearn had, as you are aware, already arrived at Fort Frontenac when we were apprised of the enemy's movements against the Colony. We are as well acquainted as themselves with all their treacheries, from General Bradock's papers, which have been found on the field of battle near Fort Duquesne. There are some from this General to the British Minister, Mr. Robinson; copy of the latter's answer; also one from the Duke of Newcastle and the Secretary of the Duke of Cumberland. It appears that this last is the prime mover of the whole. Their plan was concluded two years ago, since which time they have not ceased their preparations for its execution this year. To wit, that General Bradok, with a force of 3000 men, should attack Fort Duquesne, and proceed thence to Niagara, which was to be attacked at the same time by the Governor of Baston, at the head of a force of 3000 men; and, in order to cap their treachery, General Johnson was to come with 4500 men and enter the heart of the Colony, It is with this last that I shall have to do. *In regard to the expedition against Niagara, I believe that they will not dare attempt it, inasmuch as there are 1200 men at Fort Frontenac, all ready to march against Chouaguen, in the supposition that the enemy will strip that place in order to attack Niagara, into which we have thrown 300 men.*

The English have, in an intrenched camp at Chouaguen, 2500 men, exclusive of the garrison and a vast number of bateaux, for it was from this fort that they were to proceed against Niagara.

The defeat of the English on the Ohio, and especially the death of General Bradok, who has been killed, must have furiously deranged their plans, and I calculate on deranging them still a trifle more, provided they hold on.

Mr. de Vaudreuil is getting a translation made of all the letters taken on the defeat of the English General on the Ohio. They have had their General and 1500 killed, and all their artillery captured. These letters will be sent to Court on the return of my expedition.

If you find occasion, Sir, to write to France, inform Messrs. the Ministers hereof, and send them this letter. I shall not be able to render them a very positive account until I return from my campaign.

I have the honor to be, &c.,

Baron de Dieskau."

Thus, the hope of the Gentleman's Gazette article previously reproduced — that General Braddock's military chest and personal articles was safe, was in reality, entirely unfounded.

"***In this melancholy manner ended so important an expedition***", noted the "*Complete History of the Present War: From Its Commencement in 1756, to the End of the Campaign, 1760*", one of the earliest attempts to chronical the French and Indian War, published in 1761, scarcely a year after hostilities had ceased. "***This defeat had the worst consequences imaginable; as it as it gave so much spirit and alacrity to our enemies afterwards; and went a great way in keeping the Indians firm to their new allies: so on the contrary, we suffered by the battle, as much as the enemy gained;***

from that time, the Indians in our interest, despised us as not able even to protect ourselves, and much less them; and that in a country where we were so much more numerous than the French.

But the Indians were not the only people terrified by Mr. Braddock's defeat; a universal panic seized on all our colonies, out of which they did not soon recover, and which consequently must have been of the greatest disservice to our cause. Many persons in England have taken great pains to find out by whose ill conduct this battle was lost. But with a very little reflection it will appear plain, that no single person was the reason of it; but a chain of a thousand different accidents, and blunders in the ministers who planned the expedition, and the disaffection of the provincials to the service. The capital mistake of all, was the landing the troops at first in Virginia, whereas they ought certainly to have been landed in Pennsylvania; for Mr. Braddock could get neither provisions nor carriages in Virginia, both of which he might have had in great plenty in Pennsylvania; and what was as material, the shortness of the rout to Fort du Quesne, by way of Pennsylvania, which would have shortened their march at least six weeks, and might have been performed with half the fatigue and expense of that, by way of Virginia. But in every scheme which was planned by the then ministry in England, we find so much short-sightedness and such manifest weakness, that we cannot at all wonder at the ill success which attended their administration."

And "**while the operations we have just detailed were progressing beyond the southern limits of Canada,**" swiftly transitions the 'History of Canada: From the Time of its Discovery till the Union Year', (Vol. 1, 1860), by François-Xavier Garneau (translated by Andrew Bell) - an invaluable source for period history, "**the British forces charged to reduce Forts Niagara and St. Frederick assembled at Albany.**" And because they would not only bring about a drastic change in French North American command, but directly impact the career Charles Langlade, a brief summary of the post-July 9th, General Braddock's defeat, late 1755 campaigning season is in order.

After assembling in New York, the aforementioned British forces, numbering approximately fifty-five hundred men, under the command of General Phineas Lyman (1716 – 74) and Colonel Sir William Johnson, commenced their joint expedition with little difficulty, reaching the portage between the Hudson River and Lake George, where General Lyman then halted with a contingent of men to begin construction on Fort Lyman (renamed *"Fort Edward"* a year later by Colonel Johnson), which was to serve as a base of operation for the British on that frontier, while Colonel Johnson proceeded to the head of Lake George. However, the transactions of the British in the region did not go unnoticed, nor where their objectives a secret to the French.

On September 1st, 1755, French Major-General Jean Erdman (or Armand), Baron de Dieskau, in command of approximately three thousand men, stationed at Fort Frederic, received advanced warning of Colonel Johnson's impending march against him, and at once resolved to counterattack. His resolve to do so informed by the fact that the British Fort Lyman/Edward was not yet complete and could therefore theoretically be conquered.

Leaving half of his army at Carillon/Ticonderoga to act as a rearguard should the half he led against Fort Lyman/Edward be defeated, the Baron proceeded against the latter with approximately two hundred and twenty regulars, six hundred and eighty Canadians — commanded by Lieutenant Louis de Repentigny, and six hundred Indigenous warriors, who were led by Legardeur de St. Pierre (who had met a young George Washington two years prior), officially, and possibly Charles Langlade, unofficially (indeed, Lieutenant de Repentigny, who commanded the Canadians on this occasion, was primarily stationed in the greater Michilimackinac region which Langlade called home and where he assembled his throngs of Indigenous warriors for campaigning).

On September 7th, the Baron's force pitched camp on the Hudson River, within three miles of Fort Lyman/Edward. His intention was to attack the fort the next morning, however, during a Counsel of War that night, the Canadian and Indigenous warriors, which constituted the overwhelming majority of the Baron's corps, upon personally eyeing the Baron's intended target, at once declared their objection, as the fort was well within British territory, however, the camp of Colonel Johnson on the other hand, which had been pitched on French territory near Lake George, they would gladly assail. Begrudgingly, the Baron assented to the change, and the next morning, he ordered his men forward in three columns, hoping to encircle Colonel Johnson's camp, which, unbeknownst to him, outnumbered him, being approximately twenty-five hundred men strong.

Meanwhile, aware that the Baron was advancing in his and Fort Lyman/Edward's general direction, Colonel Johnson dispatched a contingent of approximately twelve hundred militiamen and two hundred allied Indigenous warriors, under the command of a Colonel Williams, to lay in ambush for him in advance of his arrival, however this plan was foiled when an Anglo-American prisoner taken by the Baron informed him of the pending ambush, with the Baron promptly resolving to set a counter-ambush for Williams' men.

He accordingly ordered the Canadian and Indigenous warrior columns of his corps to lay in ambush in the woods to the left and right sides of his main column, which stood in the open center as bait for Colonel Williams' men, who, in short order, appeared from the opposing tree line. The Baron de Diesaku's main column at once exchanged a volley of musket fire with Colonel Williams' men, with the latter, as well as Legardeur de St. Pierre, among the Baron de Diekau's most able subordinates on the campaign, both being killed almost instantly, at which time, the Canadians and Indigenous warriors scattered to the left and right of the Baron's main column, rose up from the woods, fired a volley at the remnants of the late Colonel Williams' men and then charged, with the Anglo-American survivors promptly fleeing the battlefield.

The Baron gave chase with a portion of his men, while a number of Canadians and Indigenous warriors were left behind to tend to the wounded or rest after their exhaustive march through dense and rugged country, not to mention the subsequent battle.

At approximately 11 o'clock in the morning, the Baron, with the portion of his men who had followed him, arrived outside of Colonel Johnson's entrenched camp alongside Lake George, which the Colonel had had barricaded with beached batteaux (boats), horse drawn carts, felled trees, and had mounted with cannons. Undaunted, however, after arranging his men into columns, the Baron commenced the attack.

While the column of regular troops repeatedly charged the barricaded camp, were repulsed, reformed, then recharged, the columns of Canadians and Indigenous warriors flanked the position, and attaining a higher ground to its left, had marginal success pouring musket fire down into Colonel Johnson's intrenchments. However, the Baron's regulars were still unable to penetrate the camp's fortifications, despite their numerous charges, with the last of these including the Baron personally, who led it with sword in hand. And it while he was advancing thus, in the process of issuing orders, that the Baron was struck, almost simultaneously, by three musket balls. His second in command, Pierre-Andre Gohin, the Comte de Montreuil (1722 – 96), who had had his arm crippled by a musket ball, and saw the Baron fall, aided him to nearby tree, where he propped him up and called to two Canadians to aid the Baron from the battlefield.

Upon arriving, one of the Canadians was struck and killed instantly by a musket ball, with his body falling on top of the Baron, while the other was injured. At this juncture, the Baron declined any further efforts to remove him from the battlefield, and instead ordered his second in command, the Comte de Montreuil, to hold the line and keep up the assault, however, after five hours of fierce combat, the Canadians and Indigenous warriors, having suffered one in every fourth man killed or wounded, began to flee the battlefield, with many of the remaining regulars following suit. The Comte de Montreuil vainly attempted to rally them, however, with the majority of the officers, save himself, having been killed over the course of the day, it proved an impossible task for him to restore order so soon.

Thus, the wounded Baron de Dieskau was abandoned on the battlefield, where he was afterward found and taken prisoner by Colonel Johnson's men, leaving the command of the French and their allies in North America vacant.

For the English, the successful defense of Colonel Johnson's camp provided a much needed morale boost, however, there was no disguising the fact that the 1755 campaigning season had been far from the overwhelming success that had been anticipated. The planned expeditions against Fort Duquesne, Fort St. Frederic and Fort Niagara — the latter attempted by General William Shirley with approximately fifteen hundred men, simultaneously to Colonel Johnson's defense of his camp, had all failed, while the Governor-General of New France, the Marquis de Vaudreuil, aware of the importance of maintaining a foothold in the upper Lake Champlain frontier region, following the Baron de Dieskau's defeat, ordered the construction of another fort at Carillon/Ticonderoga, which he had garrisoned.

That fall, the following document, titled a *"**Journal of the Operations of the Army from 22nd July to 30th September, 1755**"*, penned by an unknown diarist and summarizing the year's most significant military operations, was circulated amongst French North American high command, with its first entry dated the week after General Braddock's defeat on the Monongahela (July 9th):

*"**July 16th. We received our orders to march from Quebec to Montreal. The scarcity of bateaux has been the cause of our having proceeded by land. We kept along the bank of the river, which is pretty thickly inhabited; arrived on the 22nd at Three Rivers, a small town with an état-major, and on the 27th at Montreal.***

The regiments, told off by divisions of four or five companies, had marched and partially gone to Fort Frontenac, where we were to form a camp, and to proceed thence to lay siege to Choyen. That project could not be put into execution, having been obliged to make them march to prevent the enemy besieging Fort St. Frederic, and it became necessary to recall the regiment of La Reyne and our first division, which was already far advanced. The enemy had

three armies; one destined for the Beautiful [Ohio] river, where they were defeated. The corps was three thousand strong, under the command of General Brandolk [Braddock], whose intention was to besiege Fort Duquesne; they had considerable artillery, much more than was necessary to besiege forts in this country, most of which are good for nothing, though they have cost the King considerable. M. de Beaujeu, who was in command of that fort, notified of their march, and much embarrassed to prevent the siege with his handful of men, determined to go and meet the enemy.

He proposed it to the Indians who were with him, who at first rejected his advice and said to him: 'No, Father, you want to die and to sacrifice yourself; the English are more than four thousand, and we-we are only eight hundred, and you want to go and attack them. You see clearly that you have no sense. We ask until tomorrow to make up our minds.' They consulted together; they never march without doing so. Next morning M. de Beaujeu left his fort with the few troops he had, and asked the Indians the result of their deliberations. They answered him; They could not march. M. de Beaujeu, who was kind and affable, and possessed sense, said to them: 'I am determined to go and meet the enemy. What! will you allow us to go alone? I am sure of conquering them.' The Indians, thereupon, decided to follow him. This detachment was composed of 72 Regulars, 146 Canadians and 637 Indians. The engagement took place within four leagues of the fort, on the 9th day of July, at one o'clock in the afternoon, and continued until five. M. de Beaujeu was killed at the first fire. The Indians, who greatly loved him, avenged his death with all the bravery imaginable. They forced the enemy to fly with a considerable loss, which is not at all extraordinary. The Indian mode of fighting is entirely different from that of us Europeans, which is good for nothing in this country. The enemy formed themselves into battle array, presented a front to men concealed behind trees, who at each shot brought down one or two, and thus defeated almost the whole of the English, who were for the most part veteran troops that had come over the last winter. The loss of the enemy is computed at

1500 men. M. de Brandolk, their General, and a number of officers have been killed. 13 pieces of artillery, a great quantity of balls and shells, cartridge boxes, powder and flour have been taken; 100 beeves, 400 horses, killed or captured, all their wagons taken or broken. Had not our Indians amused themselves plundering, not a man would have escaped. It is very probable that the English will not make any further attempt in that direction, inasmuch as, in retiring, they have burnt a fort they had erected for their retreat. We have lost three officers, whereof M. de Beaujeu is one, 25 soldiers, Canadians or Indians; about as many wounded. We have not been so fortunate on this side. Let us return to our own operations.

Instead of going up the River St. Lawrence we have ascended the River St. John, on the north bank of which stands Fort St Frederic, about 45 leagues from Montreal. All had reached there on the 1st of September. Our army was composed of the Regiments of La Reine and Languedoc, amounting to about 720 men, 1500 Canadians and 760 Indians, Iroquois, Hurons, Abenaquis and Nipissings. Never was there seen so considerable an army in this Colony. They numbered, in all, three thousand and some odd men, all in the best dispositions to treat the English as well as they had been treated at Fort du Quesne; which would have been the case had not our General been deceived.

As it is very difficult to obtain any news of the enemy, owing to the difficulty of the country, we were ignorant of his strength; for all those who had been sent to scout did not report themselves. We were impatiently expecting a trustworthy man, who finally returned and reported that he had seen a somewhat considerable force building a fort, which, in fact, was true. It was resolved, in consequence, that we should go and occupy the carrying place and passes; that, in fine, we should remain on the defensive; we set out with that view on the 34 to go to a place called Carillon, on the shore of Lake Champlain, quite near the carrying place which is between Lake St. Sacrament and that lake. Whilst proceeding thither, and within six leagues of the fort, there arrived a canoe *of our Indians which had been, likewise, sent on the scout, with orders to take a prisoner; this was accordingly done, bringing, also, back the scalp of another man that had been killed. This prisoner was examined and threatened to be handed over to the Indians to be put to the most cruel death, should he conceal the truth. He may be said to have sacrificed his life for his country. He has deceived M. de Dieskau and assured him that there remained but 500 men at the fort, and that the remainder had returned to Orange. He stated that the camp was left standing to deceive us; that the fort was not finished; in fine, that all the artillery for the siege of St. Frederic, as well as everything that was necessary, had arrived. On the deposition of this prisoner, our General changed the defensive into offensive. It was resolved that the camp of the enemy could be easily overwhelmed and their fort taken with a detachment of 1500 men. There was ordered out, in consequence, from the regiment of Languedoc, which had been augmented to the number of 35 men, two pickets of an equal number, and a like quantity from the regiment of La Reyne, making 216 for the two battalions, 600 Canadians and all the Indians. They left on the 5th. The Indians told M. de Diescaut that it was better to go up Lake Champlain to turn the enemy; that it would be easier to conceal our march from them thus than by going by Lake St. Sacrament by which they were to come, as they had erected their establishment at the head of the latter, and had cut roads for the passage of their artillery. That route was, therefore, decided on, and the men landed after having proceeded about ten leagues on Lake Champlain; left one hundred men of our infantry to guard the bateaux; this was ordered after the departure of the detachment, on reflection that these bateaux might be necessary; they marched during the night to reach them.*

The detachment landed on the 6th within 8 leagues of the enemy; each man, officer and others, then shouldered his knapsack. On the 7th, marched nine leagues, always through woods and over mountains.

On the 8th, made six leagues and arrived quite near the enemy. Our Indians began by killing an officer belonging to the enemy who was going in full speed, on horseback, to notify, of his own accord, the Commandant of our arrival, and that we were to attack him. His despatches were opened and it was then discovered that the prisoner had deceived us; that, exclusive of the 500 men of the fort, the camp was well guarded and intrenched. But instead of following the original plan, which was so much the more natural, since the fort had not been alarmed, it was determined to attack the camp with the remark, that the more there were of them the more will we kill and the men set out.

The 2nd adventure was one of the most damaging for a detachment of 400 of the enemy, which was on its way from the camp to reinforce the fort; it was hacked and cut to pieces; scarcely one third of the party escaped. We continued our route, and met the enemy drawn up in order of battle, outside their fort; marched within musket shot of them without their fire. A sharp volley made them reenter their camp in double quick time. The firing thus continued from noon until three o'clock. They discharged their cannon frequently, but without any effect. The report astonished our Indians, to whom it was unexpected; and, as they do not like it, they retired. A portion of the Canadians, though good soldiers behind trees, followed their example. We were thus left alone with the other portion of the Canadians. M. de Dieskau, who had always continued at the head of the Canadians, came shortly before to us. He calculated and presumed on the good disposition of his remaining two hundred men, to enable him to force the intrenchment and two thousand men behind it. He drew his sword and cried, 'March! Let us force the place.' We had marched as well as possible, and it may be said that our detachments have done wonders. M. Dieskau retired to the left to allow us full scope, and was wounded an instant after by two musket balls. Our right, it was discovered, was exposed, and the enemy were sending people past that point. M. Maron, Second Captain, commanding the grenadiers of La Reine, took upon himself to march against those who would cut him off. They fired a long time whilst retreating; our Indians came, very luckily, to their relief, and forced the enemy to retire;

otherwise, they would have been all killed. The remainder of the retreat was accomplished without any interruption; some in one, others in another direction, and so they gained their bateaux. M. de Dieskau remained on the field of battle. Chevalier de Montreuil, who found himself in command, repaired to him before the retreat, with some grenadiers and his servants, for the purpose of removing him, but he would never consent, and said that he was unable to return, and therefore that the bed on which he then lay, was as good a death-bed as the one they would procure him; that it was useless. The loss of two grenadiers, who were killed at his side, made him repeat that they may go; that he should not alter his resolution, and he forced M. de Montreuil to retire and abandon him on the field of battle. Of our Regulars, we have lost Chevalier de la Furjoniére, who was in command of a picket of the regiment of Languedoc; he has been killed, on the field of battle; M. de Parfoura, who commanded the 2nd picket of that regiment, has been wounded; also an officer of the regiment of La Reine; 26 grenadiers or soldiers killed; 43 wounded. We have lost 120 men, Canadians or Indians, and at least as many wounded. M. Bernier, M. de Dieskau's Aid de Camp, and two Captains of the Colony and one Ensign killed and five wounded.

After this unfortunate adventure, our troops returned, worn out and dying of hunger. We had then got back within five leagues of Carillon. On the 12th we started to come down to Fort St. Frederic, where we have left four hundred Canadians. We fortified ourselves strongly at both places. The two battalions of Béarn and Guienne are quiet in the camp at Frontenac.
FINNIS."

Following the conclusion of the campaigning season, prior to the onset of winter, Charles Langlade was once again presented with the opportunity to enjoy a brief reprieve from warring, and temporarily dismissing the Indigenous Nations and tribes which had accompanied him into battle, returned to his dearly beloved,

Charlotte, who's tender company he had scarcely begun to enjoy following their wedding the previous year.

In many ways, Charlotte was Charles' opposite. Of a slender figure, she was noted for her exceptional beauty, with flowing black hair, reminiscent of her husband's own, however, infinitely more reserved and reportedly of a vastly higher education than Charles, although popular with his family and friends, as well as within the local community, she nonetheless possessed a life-long fear of the more remote Indigenous Nations and bands which her husband and his colleagues theoretically commanded, but who were less inclined to obey, and more inclined to extreme violence, although this fear never once dissuaded her from the rugged frontier life she shared with him.

In her and their family's company, Charles spent the late fall and winter months, certainly happily recounting the glory he had won during the campaigning season for all those who wished to hear it. However, the "off season" of 1755 wasn't entirely spent in leisure by Charles, for in October of the that year, Captain Louis Herbin, Charles's old friend (witness to his and Charlotte's wedding), patron, and long serving French Commandant at Michilimackinac, at once saw the merit in having the young, intelligent and enthusiastic natural leader permanently stationed at the neighboring post of Gabagouache (modern-day Grand Haven), and so issued the following proclamation proclaiming the twenty-six-year-old Commandant of said post, which was located on the Grand River, Michigan:

*"**Louis Herbin, Captain of Infantry, Commandant for the King at the post of Michilimackinac:***

Mr. De Langlade [...]., is ordered to start from this post, as soon as he receives the present order, to go and take the command of the whole of Grand River and dependency, and will locate his establishment at the place named Gabagouache.

First Article of Instruction. We order him to leave Kanamazo [Kalamazoo River] free for all traders who may desire to go there.

Second Article. We very expressly forbid him from going to trade in any or all other places under penalty of punishment reserved to us in this order to him.

Third Article. We direct him to exert all his authority with which we entrust him, that the Indians be not debauched by any [person] under his authority; and also to exert all his power to live in peace, and have a good understanding between them and the Indians, and that they obey in all things commanded them for the good of the service.

Fourth Article. He shall not permit any trader nor hired man to absent himself without permission, and shall not permit any hired men to go off hunting without seeing them when they start. He shall see that they do not carry any goods to interfere with the trade of others; this is on the supposition that the Indians do not bring any provisions themselves for your supply. He will take every precaution necessary to avoid the abuses which creep in; rendering me an account of all such abuses, and punishing by a good fine those who shall commit such frauds.

Fifth Article. Having been further informed that a number of hired men were libertines in their intercourse with the squaws; and being desirous to remedy an abuse so prejudicial, we order Mr. De Langlade to take every care that the master of each hired man give me the names of such guilty ones on their return, in order that a public example may be made of them.

Mr. De Langlade will take all necessary precautions to prevent the Indians of St. Joseph from inducing any portion of our hired men from going to the country of the Ilinois, or other place, which might be prejudicial to our interest, in view of the want which we might have for the men in the spring.

We enjoin him to encourage them [the Indians] to come and listen to my words, which will be the sentiments of their Father Onontio [the Indigenous title of either the Governor-General of Canada, the Marquis de Vaudreuil, or the King of France].

We enjoin him, moreover, to give information to the gentleman in command at St. Joseph, of the difficulties which might arise *between his nation and mine, to give him correct information of such things as he might be ignorant of, or in which he might be deceived by the people in his employ.*

We rely upon the vigilance and exactitude of capacity of Mr. Langlade for the discipline of the men under his command. We give him power to act in the place in matters which I cannot foresee, and in all cases for the good of the service, being always careful to act in such manner that no reproach or complaint be made to me on your account, under penalty of the punishment inflicted by the ordinances.

Made at Michilimackinac, 15th October, 1755."

This appointment gave Langlade sole command not only of the Grand River itself, but of its numerous tributaries and their surrounding wilderness. His new role also afforded him absolute authority over all the local traders and appointed him a judiciary, to which all forms of local disputes were to be brought, considered, and decided. In addition, he was also to serve as the local *"Superintendent of Indian Affairs,"* in the capacity of which, he would strive to ensure harmony, not only between the various local Indigenous Nations, tribes, bands, etc., but most importantly between them and the government, who relied on both their trade and manpower. The latter of these roles — Superintendent of Indian Affairs — Langlade would retain until his death, forty-five years later.

In the meantime, following his appointment to Gabagouache, he established winter quarters on the Grand River, Michigan, where he was joined by members of his family, including his wife, Charlotte, who, in January 1756, gave birth to a daughter, Charlotte Catherine, affectionately known to friends and family as *"Lalotte"*. Father Le Franc, a close friend of the family, made the arduous journey on snowshoes to the isolated settlement to perform the child's baptism (completed on January 29th, per the Michilimackinac Register), and though Charles was subsequently afforded a few months of quality time with his growing family, much of the spring and early summer were dedicated to consolidating his command and influence over the region, which saw him cultivate amiable relations with local traders and Indigenous representatives, while on May 17th, 1756, England formally declared war on France, at about the same time that the Baron de Dieskau's replacement as Major-General in New France arrived at Quebec with two battalions of reinforcements.

Louis-Joseph, the Marquis de Montcalm, was born in the Château de Candiac, Nimes, France, on February 28th, 1712. From a distinguished military family, he had seen extensive service in the War of Polish Succession (1733 – 35) and the War of Austrian Succession (1740 – 48), over the course of which he had received at least five wounds. Supplementing him in his new command was François-Gaston, the Chevalier, later Duc, de Lévis (1719 – 87), Captain Louis Antoine de Bougainville (1729 – 1811), and Colonel François-Charles de Bourlamaque (1716 – 64), all likewise military veterans.

With their arrival, according to an early 1756 French North American report published at the time, *"We have now on the Continent 1,000 French, 700 Delawares and Chouanons, besides a number of Illonois, as many as 300 French and Indians under the care of Sieur de Villiers, about 250 Miamis and Outagnons, under M. de Belestre, 300 from Detroit and 700 from Michilimackinac, commanded by the Chevalier de Repentigny, d'Anglade [Langlade] and Hebert, Junior [likely Herbin Jr., son of Langlade's friend and patron], amounting in all to 3,250 men."*

The Marquis de Montcalm's first military undertaking in New France was the reduction of Fort Chouaguen, better known and remembered by its English name of Fort Oswego, upon the South-Eastern shore of Lake Ontario, which the English had constructed, in part, to disrupt French lines of communication between Canada and the Mississippi, and from whence they could theoretically launch an attack on Fort Frontenac (modern-day Kingston, Ontario, Canada).

The campaign against said fort was subsequently conveyed in an unsigned letter titled *"Particulars of the Campaign of 1756 in New France, transmitted on the 28th of August of the same year"*, likely intended for the French-Canadian government and French foreign ministers, and is as follows:

"*The Marquis de Montcalm having safely arrived at Quebec in the month of May, with the convoy of troops and munitions sent from France, found the forces of the Colony already very judiciously distributed for its defence; the battalions of La Reine and Languedoc, with a number of Canadians and Indians, forming a camp at Carillon, the most distant of our frontier forts in the direction of Lake St. Sacrament; Guienne at Frontenac and Bearn at Niagara. M. Dumas, Commandant at Fort du Quesne, had collected six or seven hundred Indians; M. de Villiers, with four hundred Indians, was posted at the Bay de Niaouré and seriously harrassed the enemy's convoys to Chouagen, an important post, the reduction of which was meditated, and, finally, M. de Boishebert had gathered the few Acadians the English could not entrap and disperse in their Colonies like the rest, after the capture of Fort Beauséjour, and was maintaining himself with the Indians in the woods and making frequent incursions against the enemy.*

On news that the enemy were making extensive preparations at Albany and at Forts Lydius and William Henry, the last of which places is situated at the head of Lake St. Sacrament, and that they were concentrating the greatest part of their forces, it was apprehended that they designed making an attempt on our frontier at Lake Champlain, for which reason the battalion of the Royal Rousillon, together with a reinforcement of Canadians and Regulars, was sent to the Camp at Carillon shortly after our arrival, and Chevalier de Levis, Brigadier, proceeded to take command of that army, which amounted to three thousand and some hundred men. From the other point, intelligence had been received that the enemy were building sloops at Chouaguen, in sufficient number to assume a decided superiority in Lake Ontario; that they were collecting a prodigious quantity of provisions there, and that, in fine, the strong garrison they had at that place could, in a short time, become an army capable of attacking Frontenac or Niagara, whenever they should think fit. La Sarre proceeded, in consequence, to join Guienne at Frontenac, under the orders of M. Bourlamaque, and the two French Engineers were likewise sent thither to fortify them there. Béarn received orders, at the same time, to complete the fortifications of Niagara, which were commenced last year by Sieur Pouchot, one of the fourth Captains (premiers factionnaires) of that regiment.

These measures being adopted, the Marquis de Montcalm repaired to the camp at Carillon in the month of June, and after assuring himself of the dispositions of the enemy, who might number eight thousand men, arranged with Chevalier de Levis the principal manœuvres of an effective defence, and immediately left for Montreal with the design of trying to cut off the enemy in the direction of Chouaguen, unless they opposed some too serious obstacles thereto, by reducing their army at Lake St. Sacrament, in order to counteract our undertaking; this they could not effect without relieving Chevalier de Levis from uneasiness and embarrassment.

The Marquis de Vaudreuil highly approved of the Chouaguen expedition, which he and the Colony had much at heart, in consequence of the importance of that post, by means whereof the English were trading in every direction with the Indians, whom they attracted by rum, and the high price they have always paid for peltries. In addition to this, its situation at the mouth of the Odondaga river afforded them an easy communication with the Five Nations and with New-York, by means of the Hudson river, and placed them in a position to attack Frontenac and Niagara by Lake Ontario.

The Intendant, coinciding with the Marquis de Vaudreuil's views and the Marquis de Montcalm's designs, issued effectual orders for supplying munitions of war and provisions. M. de Rigaud brought a reinforcement of seven to eight hundred Canadians to M. de Villiers' camp, the command of which he assumed. This officer had, some days before, thrown in great disorder a convoy of five hundred of the enemy's bateaux, which were returning from Chouaguen to Fort Bull, killed between fifty and sixty of their men, wounded a great number and took some prisoners, without any loss than one officer and three militiamen. He had been several *times even under their cannon to kill their people and to make some prisoners, and afforded the means of reconnoitering them quite near.*

The regiment of Bearn was ordered to return from Niagara, to leave only one picket there and to repair to Frontenac, where the Marquis de Montcalm, who arrived at that post on the 29th July, had just given the finishing stroke to the expeditious dispatch of provisions and warlike stores. At length, all being in readiness for the 5th of August, when the first division of the army took its departure with four pieces of cannon, the rest of the artillery, provisions and stores remained for the second division, which, escorted by Bearn, departed on the 7th. The two largest of our sloops were sent on the lake to protect our expedition.

The first division arrived before Chouaguen on the night of the 10th and 11th of August, without having been discovered by the enemy, owing to the precaution taken to advance only by night and to retire into the woods by day, drawing the bateaux ashore and covering them with thick foliage.

That very night the Marquis de Montcalm had his four pieces of cannon posted on the bank; they served, in fact, the next day, to keep off the sloops which the enemy sent to reconnoiter. At the dawn of day Fort Ontario, situated on this side of the river, was examined to determine the attack thereon. This reconnaissance cost the life of Sieur Lombard de Combes, chief of the two French Engineers. The whole of the army was deeply affected by this loss, in consequence of the confidence reposed in his capacity. Sieur de Pouchot received orders, next day, to act as Engineer.

12th. Bearn arrived in the morning with its convoy. It was calculated that the army then amounted to 3,100 men; namely, 1,350 regular infantry; 1,500 Canadians or Colonial troops, and 250 Indians.

On the night of the 12th, everything being ready for opening the trench, 300 pioneers were detailed for that duty, and a parallel of 100 toises [a unit of measurement, with one toises equaling six feet] long was made, during the night, within 90 toises of Fort Ontario.

This was a star fort of eight angles, which was certainly protected from all surprise by a grooved and tongued palisade composed of posts eighteen inches thick, a good ditch, cannon and a garrison of two or three hundred men, but the slope of the elevated plateau, in the middle of which it stood, afforded the facility of approaching it unseen to within 90 toises. At five o'clock of the evening of the 13th the enemy abandoned it and retired to Fort Chouaguen, on the other side of the river, whilst we were engaged in erecting a battery of six guns.

The night of the 13th and 14th was employed in extending the lines and in constructing a barbet battery of nine guns, which was erected on the edge of the declivity at this side of the river; it commanded with considerable advantage [...] around Fort Chouaguen. They had no idea of being thus taken in the rear and had not dreamed or traversing themselves, nor of changing their platforms which were turned in a contrary direction. Therefore, as soon as they discovered, on the morning on the 14th, that M. de Rigaud had crossed the river with the Canadians and Indians in order to surround them, and that there was no part of their camp where they were not exposed, even to the buckle of their shoe, they hoisted the white flag and surrendered prisoners of war. They had abandoned, during the morning, a miserable little fort called Fort George, which they had on a hill beyond [Fort] Chouaguen.

This siege has not cost us more than thirty men killed or wounded. They lost about one hundred and fifty men, among whom was Colonel Mercer, their Commander, who was killed by a cannon ball three hours before the capitulation.

The French troops served at this siege with so much zeal, and dispatched so much business in a brief space of time, that the enemy judged us to exceed six thousand men. The Canadians, likewise, evinced much good will and applied themselves with ardor to whatever was ordered them.

We found, in Chouagen, 1,658 prisoners, 7 brass cannon, 48 of iron, 14 mortars, 5 howitzers, 47 swivels, a quantity of warlike stores, provisions for two or three years, and in the port a bark of

18 guns, a brigantine of 14, a schooner of 8 guns, a sloop of 10, another of 4, and a boat of 12 swivels.

As soon as the enemy had left, we proceeded to evacuate the place, to raze its fortifications, to burn its stores and houses. The whole was finished by the 21st of August, when the three battalions took their departure. Guienne and Bearn had orders to proceed, with dispatch to the camp at Carillon, where they arrived, as well as the Marquis de Montcalm, in the beginning of September. La Sarre remained behind until the entire evacuation of the Bay of Niaouré, the principal depot of the effects captured at Chouaguen; the Canadians went to save their harvests and the Indians returned to their villages, as is their custom when they have struck a blow.

The Marquis de Montcalm found things in a very good condition at the camp at Carillon; the English did not make even a show of coming to attack Chevalier de Levis, and operations were confined, on the one side and the other, to some Indian forays. We had just recently lost Mess's Biville and de Torsac, a Lieutenant in the regiment of La Reine, whom the Mohawks, an Indian Nation, had scalped whilst hunting, in fancied security, within a quarter of a league of the camp. We had ample revenge a few days afterwards; a large party of Canadians and Indians going to see whether the enemy was not forming a post in the islands of St. Sacrament, a hundred or a hundred and ten of the best and most alert among them were detached to strike a blow in the neighborhood of the enemy's camp. They met a detachment of fifty men, all of whom they either took or killed, with the exception of one or two who are supposed to have escaped. We lost two Indians on that occasion.

The season is now too far advanced for anything to occur for the remainder of the campaign except some unimportant forays. Besides, it appears that the number of enemies on one side and the other, the dread they entertain of us and our good arrangement, form obstacles to all expeditions whatsoever. It therefore remains for both sides to make, for the next campaign, the utmost efforts to gain advantage of each other's opponents.

The news from Fort Duquesne and Beautiful [Ohio] river are very favorable. M. Dumas has laid waste, with his Indians, a good part of Pennsylvania, Virginia and Maryland. In vain did these Provinces, which have no Indians to aid them, levy and pay a thousand men, at the opening of this campaign, who dressed and painted themselves in the Indian fashion; in vain did they send these to scour the woods; they have not been the less constrained to abandon more than sixty leagues of country together with the crops and cattle. The English have not abandoned Fort Cumberland, but communication with it has been attended with a thousand difficulties, and Chevalier Villiers, on the 2nd of August, has been very successful in burning another Fort called Fort Grandville, sixty miles from Philadelphia.

Letters from that quarter of the 13th, mention that the prisoners state that the Province of Pennsylvania is making a levy of two thousand men, and Virginia and Maryland another of three thousand, to facilitate the saving of the harvest by the settlers. General Hauke is expected to command them. These preparations have not deterred the Delawares (Loups), Chanousanons and Ilinois going in a body to burn the grain. M. Dumas, the same letters add, has formed the design of going to set fire to Fort Cumberland, with which view he has sent to have it reconnoitred. Finally, it does not appear that this news, whether true or false, excites much uneasiness at Fort Duquesne, and we learn, from all points, that the suffering throughout the whole of the English Colonies cannot be greater. The immense subsidies they have been forced to pay to maintain a force much more numerous than ours, far from having enabled them, up to the present time, to make any attack on us, has not even saved them from all the horrors of a cruel war, and the loss of the Port Mahon of North America; I mean Chouagen.

One observation on the position of the camp of Carillon, five leagues above Fort St. Frederic or Crown Point, on the left shore of Lake Champlain. Our army is encamped on a Point called Carillon, at the junction of the two bays from which Lake Champlain derives its source. The largest of the two, which flows towards the southeast, is about seven to eight leagues deep. It was by this bay that Mr. Dieskaw passed last year, in going to the enemy. It receives Wood creek, with which the English can communicate from Fort Lydius by a road of three leagues.

The smallest of the two bays is only three-quarters of a league in depth towards the southwest. It receives at its head the Fall of Lake St. Sacrament. This fall is full half a league in length, and it is a very easy portage. Lake St. Sacrament lies nearly north and south, and is about twelve to thirteen leagues in length, by one at its widest part.

At the head of this Lake the English have a fort called Williams Henry, or Fort George, where their army has been encamped up to the present time. Another fort, called Lydius, is situated six or seven leagues from Williams Henry, and about ten from the head of the large bay. M. Dieskaw was proceeding against the latter fort, which he supposed to be still open on one side, but having learned from some prisoners that it was beyond insult, and that Colonel Johnson was beginning another at the head of Lake St. Sacrament, he altered his plan and marched against the latter, where he found the enemy in force and fortified. There is a highway between Fort Lydius and Fort Williams Henry, and the communication between Lydius and Albany is by way of the River Orange or Hudson, on which still stands Fort Sarasto.

The enemy was content, this year, with employing his army in perfecting Fort Williams Henry, having merely some strong guards and advanced posts along the shores and in the adjoining islands of Lake St. Sacrament. Our men have likewise been occupied, under the superintendence of our Engineer belonging to the country, in completing a fort commenced at Carillon last year, after the affair of M. Dieskaw, and in advancing two little intrenched camps at the head of the portage, and another camp, also intrenched, beyond the other two. These camps had strong guards and bivouacs in advance, in order to be seasonably advised of the enemy's march. Our design was to give them battle or to stop them at the portage *of the Fall. The immense quantity of timber with which the whole of this country is covered, affords the Canadians and Indians the means of fighting with advantage. This circumstance would allow us to hazard a general engagement with the enemy, although in greater strength, had they come against us."*

That fall, while marauding bands of French-inclined Indigenous bands, usually accompanied by a handful of Frenchmen, continued to terrorize Virginia, Pennsylvania, Maryland, and reduce English outposts, such as Fort Granville, Charles Langlade is believed to have remained at his post on the Grand River, however, he would not remain stationary for long.

In early August, 1756, Captain Jean-Daniel Dumas, who had since inherited command of Fort Duquesne from Claude Pierre Pecaudy de Contrecoeur, and who had previously served alongside Langlade at General Braddock's defeat on the Monongahela, issued him the following order:

"**Dumas, Knight of the Royal and Military Order of St. Louis, Captain of Infantry, Commander of the Belle Riviere [Ohio River] and its dependencies:**

It is ordered to Sieur Langlade, Ensign of the Infantry, to set out at the head of a detachment of French and Indians, to strike Fort Cumberland.

In case the Indians determined to leave the main route, Sieur de Langlade will detach a few reserves with a company of French, to follow them.

The principal object of his mission being to ascertain if the enemy is inaugurating any movements in this quarter.

He will march with precaution and watchfulness in order to avoid all surprise and ambuscade.

If he attacks with the Indians he must do all in his power to prevent them from inflicting any cruelties upon those who may fall into his hands.

Written at Fort Duquesne, Aug. 9, 1756."

As his mission was to perform reconnaissance, utilizing a much smaller force than the one he had previously led at the Monongahela,

Langlade, and his carefully selected band of men, swiftly traversed the same route used by the English in their advance on Fort Duquesne from Fort Cumberland, ultimately confirming the French suspicion that the entire frontier had indeed been abandoned by the English following General Braddock's defeat the previous year.

Upon his return to Fort Duquesne, Captain Dumas retained Langlade as his most capable officer, and that winter, ordered Langlade on a follow-up mission, the object of which was to capture a soldier who could be persuaded to provide information on the designs of the English in the coming year. And it was during this expedition, that one of the few oral histories pertaining to Charles Langlade is recorded. As his grandson, Augustin Grignon, later recalled in his *"Recollections"*:

"Of de Langlade's partisan services, while at Fort du Quesne, I can only mention one incident which he narrated to me.

The Commandant gave him orders to take a party of French and Indians, and go to a certain part of the frontiers, and endeavor to capture a prisoner, from whom to gain information. Reaching a frontier fort, which must have been in Pennsylvania, Maryland, or Virginia, he managed to seized a sentinel in the night; and from him learned that an officer or paymaster was expected to arrive at that fort at a certain time with a large supply of money for public purposes. So, de Langlade took a proper number with him, and among them a French officer who had a little dog along, and they ambuscaded the road upon which the expected prize was to pass.

It was good sleighing in the winter. At length the small English foot guard proceeding the sleigh passed the ambuscade, and soon the sleigh passed by de Langlade who rushed out in the rear of the sleigh, when the French officer was to head the team, but his dog gave the alarm a little too soon, when the English officer, suspecting some trap set for him, instantly about and commenced retracing his trail, when de Langlade dashed behind, seized hold of the back part of the sleigh; but the officer within, used his whip freely upon the horses, and at the same time drew his pistol, when de Langlade snatched it before he could use it, and then the

Englishman used his whip so nimbly and alternatively upon his horses and upon de Langlade, that the latter finally gave up any further attempt, and thus lost the coveted prize. The pistol was his only trophy.

To the premature barking of the little dog, he attributed the miscarriage of his scheme; and he used to repeat, with great pleasantry, the incident of his whipping and the exciting race.

The English foot-guard were captured. My grandfather, after the war, frequently met this English officer in Canada, and they would rehearse the exploit with much good feeling."

On January 21st, 1757, an English scouting party under the command of Captain Robert Rogers (1731 – 95) of Roger's Rangers was ambushed by a group of French, Canadians and Indigenous warriors led by a *"Captain de Basserode"* of Fort Carillion/Ticonderoga (officially) and Charles Langlade (unofficially). Fought in knee-deep snow, the skirmish, popularly known as the *"Battle of the Snowshoes"* due to the combatants' use of the footwear, lasted many hours and only concluded after dark, when neither side could see the other. The French, Canadians and Indigenous warriors suffered approximately ten killed and thirty wounded, while Rogers' Rangers suffered approximately fifteen killed and ten wounded, while between five and eight were reported missing or captured. Several prisoners were indeed interrogated by the French and provided valuable information on the designs and disposition of English in the region.

Encouraged by what he had learned, the Governor-General of New France, the Marquis de Vaudreuil, sought to initiate the campaigning season of 1757 with a renewed offensive against the English on the Lake George frontier, in which previous supreme commander of French regular forces in North America, the Baron de Dieskau, had been seriously wounded and captured by the English. Vaudreuil appointed his younger brother and soon-to-be Governor of Montreal, François-Pierre de Rigaud de Vaudreuil, to the expedition's command (to the annoyance to the Marquis de Montcalm, many of his officers and men), with its main objective being Fort William Henry, however, this initial attack was only partially successful, with the French forces only able to torch buildings outside of the fort itself, which put up a valiant defense, ultimately forcing the French to retreat after suffering significant losses.

However, all was not yet lost, as the French maintained the upper hand with the continued absence of English General, John Campbell, the 4th Earl of Loudon (1705 – 82), who was still preoccupied with an excessively delayed expedition against the French fortress port of Louisbourg, on the Acadian coast (modern-day Nova Scotia), which would ultimately drag on into June, by which time, the French had had ample time to bolstered the garrison of the place to seven thousand men, approximately two-thirds of which were army regulars, in addition to approximately fifteen hundred Indigenous warriors, and amass a fleet of twenty-two ships-of-the-line with numerous lesser vessels inside the port, amounting to approximately fourteen hundred cannon total. So that by time General Loudon finally arrived, he was forced to call a Council of War, the result of which was the abandonment of the expedition altogether, given the bloated size of the French forces defending Louisbourg, while during his extended absence from the Lake George frontier, approximately three thousand French regulars and three thousand Canadians under the Marquis de Montcalm, with approximately eighteen hundred Indigenous warriors from over thirty Indigenous Nations, tribes and/or bands under Charles Langlade, had seized the initiative, and on July 30th, had begun to march on Fort William Henry, news of which Loudon belatedly received on his return to New York, from whence, he and his men had set sail to conquer Louisbourg, several weeks prior.

Situated on the shore of Lake George, Fort William Henry, commanded by Lieutenant-General George Monro (1700 – 57), was not of sufficient size to accommodate the entirety of its garrison within its walls, so a temporary camp had been erected on an earthen high-rise a few hundred yards from the fort itself. Within the walls, were approximately five hundred men, while approximately seventeen hundred others occupied the nearby camp.

The French and their allies advanced on the English positions in two groups. While the vanguard, commanded by the Chevalier de Lévis, and numbering approximately twenty-eight hundred men, including three brigades of Canadians and approximately six hundred Indigenous warriors under French-Canadian partisan leader and one of the wealthiest men in Canada, Luc de la Corne (1711 – 84), proceeded on foot around Lake George, ultimately securing the only route to and from Fort William Henry, on which English reinforcements from near-by Fort Edward, under the command of Lieutenant-General Daniel Webb (circa. 1700 – 73), could theoretically be sent, the Marquis de Montcalm embarked his men, numbering approximately five thousand in total, including French regulars, Canadians and Indigenous warriors, onto approximately two hundred fifty vessels, which proceeded directly across Lake George towards Fort William Henry, with an Indigenous canoe squadron, under the command of Charles Langlade, and constituted primarily of Ottawa warriors, acting as an advanced guard and preliminary landing party. As per an official report of the campaign's transactions, penned by the Marquis de Montcalm shortly after their conclusion and dated July 25th, 1757:

"The Ottawa that I have sent to the lake shore had conceived the project of making an attack on the English barges and de Langlade (in the company of four French officers) were sent with them.

They remained in ambush all day yesterday, and during the night. At break of day the English appeared to the number of twenty-two barges including two skiffs. Their detachment numbered three hundred and fifty men, commanded by Colonel Parker, who was at the head of the Jersey regiment, in place of Colonel Schyler taken prisoner at Oswego."

It was then that Langlade launched his ambush. Continues Montcalm in his report:

"The yells of our [warriors] so filled them with terror, that they made but feeble resistance. Only two barges were saved, all the rest being taken or sunk. The Indians brought away six, which will be

very useful to us. I have here one hundred and fifty-one prisoners, of whom eight are officers, one hundred and sixty killed."

Montcalm's subordinate, Captain Bougainville, the expedition's official diarist, noted the Indigenous warriors' usefulness accordingly:

"Here in the forest of America, we cannot more do without them, than without cavalry on the plains."

With their path now clear, the Marquis de Montcalm and Charles Langlade proceeded inland towards Fort William Henry, which the former dispatched Captain Bougainville to in advance, offering terms of surrender. However, he was refused, with the fort's commander, General Monro, replying that it was his duty to defend the fort to the last extremity before sending Bougainville away.

Thus, the siege commenced with the Marquis de Montcalm ordering the opening of trenches around the fort. Hundreds labored all hours of the day while skirmishers from both sides exchanged a sustained fire on one another. As the battle intensified, the commander of Fort William Henry, General Monro dispatched messengers to request assistance from General Webb at nearby Fort Edward, who had between fifteen hundred and four thousand men under his command, however, instead of mobilizing to march to the former's aid, the latter instead dispatched a return messenger with a recommendation to surrender. But this messenger was intercepted and killed by the French, Canadians and Indigenous warriors under the Chevalier de Lévis and partisan Luc de la Corne, who had occupied the region in between the two forts, with Webb's recommendation to surrender instead being forwarded to Montcalm, who ultimately decided to hand it over to Monro anyway, hoping that it would indeed convince him to surrender the fort.

Captain Bougainville was once again dispatched and conveyed into Fort William Henry under blindfold, where he personally handed General Webb's recommendation to surrender to General Monro, however, the latter's resolve having not wavered in the slightest since their last meeting, Monro once again declined Bougainville's terms of surrender, and the latter departed, at which time the fort and its besiegers resumed fire on one another. However, in the meantime, the whole of the French artillery, approximately thirty cannon and fifteen mortars, had been entrenched at close quarters to the fort, and after a prolonged twenty-four-hour bombardment, had breached its walls, which combined with the fort's own cannons and mortars having been either disabled or running dangerously low on powder and ammunition, as the garrison dwindled in able bodied men, compelled General Monro to finally hoist the white flag, and agree to discuss terms of surrender.

The Marquis de Montcalm permitted General Monro's men be allowed to march out of the fort with the honors of war, including a single cannon, and in possession of their personal effects, while they left all else. They were to be escorted to the vicinity of Fort Edward, where they would then disperse, having agreed to not take up arms against the French for next eighteen months. Prior to their departure, Montcalm called a council with Charles Langlade and the representatives of the over thirty Indigenous Nations, tribes or bands which had accompanied the expedition, to ensure their understanding and conformity to them. All settled, the English began the evacuation of the fort itself on the 9th of August.

All the able-bodied men of the garrison, along with some women and children began to march out at mid-day, leaving behind perhaps a dozen or more sick or wounded as per General Monro's agreed upon terms of surrender with the Marquis de Montcalm. French Colonel de Bourlamaque then proceeded into the fort with a contingent of regular troops to secure the garrison's abandoned weapons, ammunition and powder, while their Indigenous allies were given free rein to plunder everything else. As per usual, under Charles Langlade's orders, and perpetuated by Montcalm's insistence, however, all alcohol discovered was to be either be destroyed or guarded, to prevent any unregulated consumption.

As night began to fall, the approximately two thousand English prisoners, of all ranks, and including women and children, who and marched out of the fort, took shelter within the intrenched earther high-rise camp which neighbored the fort. At dawn they would begin their march to Fort Edward under French protection, as per the terms of surrender. However, at approximately five o'clock in the morning, numerous Indigenous warriors, in the presence of partisan leader Luc de la Corne, arrived at the intrenched camp, and indiscriminately began putting to death the approximately seventeen wounded Englishmen who were being treated by garrison surgeon, Dr. Whitworth. However, the worst was yet to come, as the approximately two thousand prisoners began to file out of the camp, later that same day, and many of the same Indigenous warriors in de la Corne's company begun to demand the prisoners' personal belongings. Those who refused were tomahawked.

General Monro was incandescent with anger and protested vehemently that his terms of surrender with the Marquis de Montcalm were being breached, which prompted the French commander himself, as well as his second in command, the Chevalier de Lévis, Colonel Boulamaque, and numerous other officers, doubtless including Charles Langlade (on account of his influence amongst Natives), to hasten to the scene and attempt to restore order, which, at length they were able to do, however the incident did much to justify the Marquis de Montcalm's growing resentment of all his and France's Indigenous allies equally.

Estimates range, however, approximately one hundred fifty to two hundred fifty English were killed over the course of the siege and subsequent massacre of Fort William Henry, while approximately five hundred and seven hundred were taken prisoner, with approximately three hundred gaining their freedom shortly thereafter at the behest of the Marquis de Montcalm, who remained with a contingent of men at the fort for several days after the massacre of the 9th, destroying all that could not be carried away. French, Canadian and allied Indigenous casualties numbered only about fifty or sixty, although the presence of small-pox in amongst the English garrison with whom they had fought would subsequently result in countless deaths, particularly within the allied-Indigenous community.

While still at the fort, on the 14th of August, Montcalm penned letters to English generals Webb at Fort Edward, and Loudon, who was still at sea, on his return voyage from the failed expedition to capture the French fortress port of Louisbourg on the Acadian coast (modern-day Nova Scotia), apologizing for the conduct of his Indigenous allies who had perpetrated the massacre of Fort William Henry, while also attempting to rationalize it. General Loudon swore vengeance, however, but by the time he and his army finally returned to New York, on August 31st, the French and their allies had long since retired from the Lake George frontier, electing to end the otherwise successful campaigning season early, on account of the growing scarcity of provisions, brought on by over a year's worth of cultivation and harvesting interrupted by warfare.

In the meantime, General Webb, who had remained inactive at Fort Edward the entirety of Fort William Henry's siege, was recalled to England in disgrace, for having failed to aid General Monro in the defense of latter fort, while Monro himself, perhaps on account of the anger he manifested, either against the Webb for having failed to aid him during the siege of his fort, against the French-allied Indigenous warriors for having perpetrated the massacre after the fact, or perhaps both, died of either a stroke or heart attack in November, his former fort having been reduced to little more than rubble, while its wooden components had been extracted and used in a fire which had cremated the dead.

For his services on the campaign, Charles Langlade received the following appointment:

"Pierre Rigaud de Vaudreuil, Governor Lieutenant General for the King, in all his New France lands and territories of Louisiana; we order Sieur Langlade, Ensign of the Troops, detached from the Marine, to leave this city immediately, and to proceed to the post of Michilimackinac, where he will serve in the capacity of second officer, under the orders of Monsieur de Beaujeu, commander of the post.

Done at Montreal, September 8, 1757."

Louis Liénard de Beaujeu de Villemonde (1716 – 1802), former Commandant of French outposts at Kaministiquia (modern-day Thunder Bay, Ontario) and Michipicoton (modern-day Michipicoten River, Ontario) was the younger brother of the late Daniel Hyacinthe

Liénard de Beaujeu, who had been killed during the Battle of the Monongahela while serving alongside Langlade against General Braddock, two-and-a-half years earlier. Charles' new appointment also came with a salary of one thousand francs per annum and the awarded rank of Lieutenant, while after yet another disappointing year, militarily, in order to restore public confidence, the English Ministry welcomed one of (if not) the greatest statesman of the age to its helm.

William Pitt, the 1st Earl of Chatham (1708 – 78), who, despite his credentials, had previously been fired by King George in April, 1757, after his staunch opposition to the court-martialing and subsequent execution of Admiral John Byng (1704 – 57), the latter of whom had been scapegoated for the failure to relieve the besieged English garrison of Minorca, Spain, which had subsequently fallen into French hands. However, as few men proved capable of replacing Pitt, by June, 1757, he was reinstated, as a Minister of War and of Foreign Affairs, and promptly set about developing a new strategy to win the broader Seven Years' War, of which the French & Indian War in North America was a part.

His strategy was simply to tie down as many French troops as possible across central Europe, preventing them from being re-distributed, while the vastly superior Royal Navy launched coordinated attacks on strategic French holdings across the globe, with special attention being afforded to North America, where Pitt decided on three objectives; a second attempt on the fortress port of Louisbourg on the Acadian Coast; with aspirations to then proceed up the Saint Lawrence River to lay siege to the heart of New France itself — Quebec; Fort Ticonderoga/Carillon on Crown Point, and lastly Fort Duquesne, which General Braddock had failed to even reach before being defeated in 1755. To these three principal objectives was added a fourth: Fort Frontenac on Lake Ontario.

To the first principal objective — a second attempt on Louisbourg, Pitt appointed Colonel Jeffery Amherst (1717 – 97), who received the rank of Major-General with his appointment, while General Loudon was recalled and replaced by General James Abercrombie (1706 – 81), who was to lead the expedition against Fort Ticonderoga/Carillon and Brigadier General John Forbes (1707 – 57) was assigned to capture of Fort Duquesne.

Meanwhile, over the winter of 1757-58, bands of French and their Indigenous allies remained active beyond the frontier of New France, terrorizing Anglo-American settlements and fortifications, as described in the following French document, titled "***Bulletin of the Most important Operations during the winter of 1757-8.***"

"Montreal. 18th *April, 1758.*

Although the rigor of the season and the scarcity of provisions, caused by a bad harvest, have forced us to economise, in order to save wherewith to enable us to wait for the supplies expected from France and more abundant crops, and to oppose any attempts of the enemy, should he wish to operate early, we have harassed him all winter by numerous parties which have succeeded each other continually.

M. de Beletre, Captain of the Colonial troops, burnt in the month of November, 17 leagues from Corlac, a village which was very wealthy in consequence of its trade with the Five Nations; those who escaped the fury of our Indians have been brought, women and children, prisoners, to the number of 150. Several parties of our Indians and also of the Five Nations have been to strike a blow towards the same Corlac, and to burn divers settlements.

M. de Langry, an officer of the Colonial troops, surprised, in the month of February, a detachment of 50 men in the neighborhood of Lydius. M. Wolff, a Lieutenant of the troops from France, has been with the Abenakis to burn some settlements near Massachasouet.

*The English have had all winter the design to surprise and bombard Carillon, and have made their appearance before it several times. Captain d'Hebencourt, of the regiment of La Reine, who has been appointed, after the campaign, Commandant of that post, and the garrison have been very alert, and the incursions of the English have always been bootless. Sieur d'Hebencourt being informed that they had a party of 200 men in the field, profited on the 13*th *of March, by the fortunate arrival, on the preceding evening, of 200 Iroquois or Nepissings from Sault St. Louis and the Lake of the Two Mountains, with Sieur Durantaye and several Colonial Cadets, who were joined by Sieur de Langry, a very intelligent officer, some Lieutenants and sergeants of our battalions, whom zeal alone had induced to march thither. The English detachment, composed of picked men and of 12 officers, under the command of Major Roger, their best partizan, has been totally defeated. The Indians have brought back 146 scalps; few prisoners - merely some to furnish their father with live letters - an expression used by the Indians to designate prisoners. The remainder will have perished of want [of food] in the woods. A few, including two officers of Bleknis' regiment, voluntarily surrendered themselves prisoners at our fort at Carillon, at the end of five days, their guide having died the night before. We have lost in that action 8 Indians, and have had 17 wounded; also two Cadets of the Colony and one Canadian. The dead have been covered with great ceremony; presents have been made to the families in the name of the King (the Great Ononthio). The Governor-General will reward the bravery of our Iroquois by a promotion and presentation of some gorgets and medals to those who have distinguished themselves; they will be thereby more encouraged to revenge the loss they have suffered.*

We have at present eight small parties in the field. We shall doubtless learn from the prisoners they will take, what are the enemy's movements, which will determine the others in the forepart of May. We cannot doubt that the English, who received some reinforcements this fall, have in North America, with their Highlanders, 23 battalions from Old England, very complete; our forces are greatly inferior to theirs. The courage of our troops and of the Canadians, the assistance of our Indians will make up for numbers.

M. de Boishebert, a Captain of the Colonials, is about setting out with six or seven hundred Acadians, Canadians or Indians, for the River St. John, thence to proceed to Louisbourg, which the English always seem to menace. We are expecting news from the Beautiful river, where the English leave no stone unturned to detach from our alliance the Delawares (Loups) and Chaouoinons, Indians who are desolating Virginia and Pennsylvania."

Simultaneously, in expectation of a renewed English push on the Lake George frontier, the Marquis de Montcalm had set about reinforcing Fort Ticonderoga/Carillon's outer works, between the conclusion of the 1757 campaigning season, and the beginning of 1758's, while on June 1st, the English fleet under Admiral Edward Boscawen (1711 – 61) finally arrived outside Louisbourg.

He brought with him Major-General Amherst and Brigadier James Wolfe (1727 – 59) at the head of approximately eleven thousand regulars and five hundred colonials, aboard twenty-three ships-of-the-line, eighteen frigates and numerous lesser vessels. They laid siege to the approximately three thousand men of Louisbourg's garrison, and the two to three thousand men that manned the five ships-of-the-line and seven frigates at rest in the harbor.

Bad weather delayed an initial landing by the English to establish beachhead, relegating them to a mere naval bombardment, which had only a minimal effect on the intrenched French defenders, so that when Major General Amherst finally attempted to stage a landing in the second week of June, upon the breaking of the weather, his amphibious force suffered mass casualties against the dug-in French before retreating. However, redirecting the men up a sheltered coastal embankment, Brigadier Wolfe was able to outflank the French intrenchments, which were then abandoned by their men, who regrouped in the fortress, that was then subjected to an intense bombardment. Much infrastructure was destroyed, while the French fleet at rest in the harbor was swept by fire, claiming several ships-of-the-line. Emboldened, the English fleet at sea moved in on the harbor, securing it by June 27th, by which time, French Commandant of Louisbourg, Augustin de Boschenry de Drucourt (1703 – 62) surrendered, after an obstinate and gallant defense. Five thousand, six hundred and thirty-seven fighting men are documented to have been taken prisoner, while two hundred twenty-one cannon, eighteen mortars, many weapons, provisions and ammunition were acquired. However, as Drucourt had intended, it had taken so long for Louisbourg to finally surrender, that General Amherst, Brigadier Wolfe, and their men couldn't aid in the initial advance of General Abercrombie on the Lake George frontier, which had commenced in the first week of June, with Abercrombie arriving on Lake George, with over fifteen thousand men, approximately two-fifths of which were army regulars, and supplemented by Roger's Rangers' colonial militia, led by Robert Rogers.

By the first week of July, Abercrombie landed the main body of his force, unopposed, occupying abandoned French outposts in advance of the fortified position of Fort Ticonderoga/Carillon, commanded by the Marquis de Montcalm, and supplemented by Charles Langlade, at the head of a select few warriors. Although incomplete, Ticonderoga/Carillon's defenses had been reinforced by a carefully crafted series of outer fortifications, constituted of felled trees, which served to be virtually impervious to musket fire, although they could easily enough have been disposed by artillery. But in what would prove a fatal blunder, Abercrombie's artillery was nowhere to be seen, having been left behind at his initial landing area, while believing he should attack at once, less any delay allow for the arrival of French reinforcements, he resolved to attack at once.

While Roger's Rangers made several unsuccessful attempts to dislodge French, Canadian militia and Indigenous warriors under Langlade, held up in the wooded swamp surrounding Fort Ticonderoga/Carillon's outlying fortifications, Abercrombie's men advanced into a hellish quagmire of tangled foliage towards the main French position. Grenadiers, supported by the "*Black Watch*" Highlanders rushed forward bravely, but were mown down en-masse by the French. Era historian Francis Parkman later described their plight as **"*straining for an enemy they could not reach, and firing at an enemy they could not see.*"**

Several attempts were made, however, at length, dissuaded of a quick and easy victory, after suffering approximately two thousand casualties, but with approximately thirteen thousand men plus unused artillery still at his disposal, Abercrombie abruptly called off the attack and reembarked upon Lake George. And so, with scarcely thirty-six hundred men, outnumbered approximately three-to-one by the English, the French under the Marquis de Montcalm, seconded by the Chevalier de Lévis, and assisted by Canadians and Indigenous warriors under Charles de Langlade, had managed to pull off yet another victory, almost three years to the day that General Braddock and his army had met their end on the Monongahela River.

Content with their success, the French, Canadian and Indigenous forces did not immediately pursue the retreating English, who had departed with so much haste as to abandon provisions, ammunition, weapons and baggage, which were later discovered. And although the Marquis de Montcalm afterward contended that "no" Indigenous warriors had assisted him over the course of the struggle for Fort Ticonderoga/Carillon, the reality was combination of factors, chief among them, the growing scarcity of provisions on account of several years of consecutive warfare, the result of which was a great many Indigenous warriors electing to forgo the 1758 campaigning season altogether, in order to hunt, gather or cultivate for themselves and their families, while many more still were dissuaded by the widening smallpox epidemic, which effected Indigenous peoples especially hard, and in many cases had been carried home to family, friends and communities by members of the over thirty Indigenous Nations, tribes or bands, which had been exposed to the disease at Fort William Henry the previous year.

In addition, following the massacre perpetrated by a handful of the numerous Indigenous allies he collectively neither loved nor respected, it is certainly likely that the Marquis de Montcalm was keen to either downplay or relegate the participation of what few Indigenous warriors he actively retained during the battle in order to affirm his own men's capabilities and honor, while simultaneously avoiding a repeat of last campaign's appalling conclusion. However, speculation aside, merely from a militaristic point of view, it would seem unreasonable at best for the services of Charles Langlade to have not been utilized by the French at Fort Ticonderoga/Carillon, for as chronically short of men as they had been since the war's onset,

Langlade was among the most capable and inspiring warriors North America had to offer at the time, and his worth on the battlefield had already been proven many times over.

Yet in contrast to the *"Recollections"* of Augustin Grignon, Charles Langlade's grandson, early Langlade biographer, Canadian, Joseph Tassé (1848 – 95), in his *"Memoir of Charles Langlade"* (1876) asserts that Charles did not participate in the battle of Fort Ticonderoga/Carillon, and uses as his evidence, an entry in the Michilimackinac Register, dated the week of the battle, in which Langlade is listed as a *"Godfather"* to a baptism which took place. That entry is as follows:

"I, the undersigned priest, Miss. [Missionary] of the Society of Jesus, solemnly administered holy baptism to Charles, legitimate son of Antoine Le Tellier and of Charlotte Ouetokis, his father and mother. The Godfather was Mr. De L'Anglade, an officer of the troops and second in command at this post; and the Godmother M. de his wife [Charlotte]. At Michilimakina, July 2, 1758.

[Signed] M. L. LeFranc, Miss. of the Society of Jesus; Langlade; Bourassa Langlade."

However, this "evidence" assumes that for Charles to have been listed as the "Godfather" to the baptized child, he must have been present at the baptism and personally signed the document, which was likely not the case, as Langlade's wife, Charlotte, who was similarly listed as the baptized child's *"Godmother"*, doubtless signed it on her husband's behalf. And were that not enough, it would be simply irrational to contend that such a dedicated and effective warrior-commander as Charles Langlade would neglect a vulnerable frontier, several years into a full-scale war, and at the peak of the campaigning season, to witness a mere baptism, a common enough event in the greater Michilimackinac area.

However, although the English had suffered yet another demoralizing defeat at the battle of Fort Ticonderoga/Carillon, much effort had still yet to be exhausted against Fort Duquesne, the principal objective of Brigadier General John Forbes, who had been delayed through September on account of ill health and the difficulties arising from having to construct a suitable road for his men, horses and artillery, while no sooner was Charles Langlade's assistance on the Lake George frontier no longer required, than he repaired at once to the familiar battlegrounds of Fort Duquesne, where he was supplemented by a few additional warriors, in advance of the looming attack.

While Forbes remained virtually bedridden at the extreme rear of his army, on the morning of September 14th, having sought permission from his superior, Major James Grant, Laird of Ballindalloch (1720 – 1806), proceeded in advance of the main English army with a vanguard of approximately eight hundred men to reconnoiter the French-Indigenous forces, and perhaps lead them into an ambush if they could be coerced out of the fort by a deceptively small scouting party. However, Major Grant had gravely miscalculated the number of French, Canadian and Indigenous forces that Fort Duquesne's Commandant, François-Marie Le Marchand de Lignery had at his disposal, and so when he divided his eight hundred-man force into several, even smaller contingents, he was playing right into their hands, while the silence of the fort itself only encouraged his rashness, convincing him that the French were weak, and therefore reluctant to fight, however they were merely awaiting the opportune moment to strike.

Fully aware of Grant's men's movements, on account of their beating of the drums, the playing of bagpipes and the torching of Fort Duquesne's out buildings, the concealed French, Canadian and Indigenous forces inside the fort at length decided that the time had come to launch their counterattack, and so threw open the gates, through which they poured. Aided by Indigenous sharpshooters in the woods under Charles Langlade, the war whoop was sounded, as the French and their allies then swept Major Grant's scattered English contingents. His Scottish Highlanders fought bravely, however, hopelessly surrounded by a largely invisible enemy and suffering heavy casualties, after approximately three-quarters-of-an-hour, they too were routed. A contingent of the more adapted Virginian militia were able to stage a defense long enough to prevent a total English collapse, however, Major Grant's efforts had been an obvious failure, but far from a fatal one, for General Forbes' main army was still largely intact, while the French, Canadian and Indigenous forces of Fort Duquesne were in a predicament of their own.

Fort Frontenac (modern-day Kingston, Ontario) had been successfully captured by English Lieutenant Colonel John Bradstreet (1714 – 74), whom, at the head of over twenty-five hundred men had forced French Commandant, Pierre-Jacques Payen de Noyan (1695 – 1771), with a garrison of less than two hundred men, to surrender with minimal difficulty, cutting off vast quantities of desperately needed weapons, ammunition, and most importantly, provisions, which had been destined for Fort Duquesne. As a direct result, fort Commandant, Marchand de Lignery, had been forced to disperse most of his Indigenous allies, as he simply did not possess the means to feed them, which greatly reduced his numbers, so that when approximately twenty-five hundred English, in the company of George Washington, dispatched from Forbes' army, renewed their assault on the fort in mid-November, this time, vastly outnumbered (by some accounts, ten-to-one) and starving, de Lignery abandoned it in advance of their approach, retreating to Fort Machault (later Fort Venango - see "Map of the Scene of Operations"; modern day, Franklin, Pennsylvania), leaving the English to capture little more than deliberately destroyed, smoldering ruins.

However, in a stark contrast to the campaigns of the last several years, in 1758, the English had at long last made tangible gains in North America, with three of the projected four expeditions of the year having been ultimately successful; against Louisbourg; Fort Frontenac; and Fort Duquesne, the latter of which had simultaneously deprived New France and its Indigenous allies of their most formidable fortress and their grip on the Ohio River Valley, however, the coming year promised even more daring and desperate endeavors, the likes of which had never before been seen on the continent, while after perhaps his most trying year of active service to date, Charles Langlade returned to his part-time home on the Grand River, where he experienced even greater difficulty in securing provisions for his own family on account of the complete failure of the harvest this year, driving the price of what there was sky high. Per the following letter on the subject, addressed to Langlade from Pierre du Jaunay, Jesuit missionary priest, in reply to an inquiry by the former:

"To Mons. Langlade, officer second in command at Michilimackinac:

Sir,

Your uncle [Kinonchausie] has requested, in starting from here after the Chappelet, to say to you, that he did not think that he could procure any corn for you, first, because there is none — those who used to raise eighty sacks will possibly make up ten; second, because there are at Arbre Croche purchasers who give as much as seven fist-fulls of powder, three hundred balls and [one line here illegible] per sack.

I owe you many thanks, which I hope to make good to you by word of mouth on your passage, for the Indians have told me you were going to winter at Grand Riviere.

My respects, if you please, to your wife and to your parents. This is a year of crisis and desolation for us Michilimackians — the Indians only bringing sorrowful news from the neighborhood of Belle Riviere [Ohio]. A most impetuous wind is now blowing, at ten o'clock in the evening, which is going to finish the ruin of your field. Bless God that it is no worse. I am with much respect, sir,

Your very humble and obedient servant,
P. du Jaunay.

At Pointe St. Ignace, 24th September, 1758."

That winter, the year's military endeavors were summarized in the following English-translated French document, simply titled *"Campaign of 1758"* and are as follows:

"The Marquis de Montcalm having arrived on the 30th of June at Carillon, where the eight battalions were encamped.

2nd July. Seven of them were sent to encamp at the Carrying place and Falls, and the Marquis joined them on the 3rd.

3rd. *M. de Bourlamaque, commanding the battalions of La Reine, Guienne and Béarn, encamped at the head of the Carrying place, learned from scouts that about sixty bateaux were on Lake St. Sacrament. He immediately detached three hundred and fifty men, under the orders of Captain Trepesec, of the Bearn regiment, to go by land to observe the route they should take.*

6th. *In the morning the Marquis de Montcalm, who was encamped at the tail of the Carrying place with the Royal Rousillon battalions and the first Béarn, had advice that the lake was covered with bateau within three leagues of the Carrying place. He immediately sent orders to M. de Bourlamaque to fall back, on whose arrival he joined to the five battalions those of La Sarre and Languedoc, which were encamped on the left bank of the lake falls.*

About two o'clock in the morning a great fire of musketry was heard near the Portage, an eighth of a league beyond the Falls; it proceeded from M. de Trepesec's detachment, which had been surrounded on endeavoring to return to its camp; about one hundred of them escaped, 144 were taken, and the balance remained on the field of battle. Colonel d'How, who commanded the English detachment, was killed in this encounter.

At night the Marquis de Montcalm retired under Fort Carillon, where he bivouacked through the night with his troops.

7th. *In the morning he hastily intrenched himself on the heights of Carillon, where he had abatis formed in advance; this labor was not interruped during that entire day.*

8th. *At day-break, the troops put themselves under arms behind their intrenchments, constructed of timber, piece above piece. The Marquis de Montcalm sent volunteers out to observe the enemy, and ordered each battalion to render the intrenchment it occupied as complete as possible, and to keep its arms at its side, so as not to be surprised.*

The enemy did not delay their appearance; they deployed in four columns at one o'clock in the afternoon. Our main guards and grenadier companies, whilst firing, retired in regular order behind the intrenchments. Thereupon, all the troops took their posts, and the soldiers who happened to be in the fort at Carillon, ran to the intrenchments at the signal of the gun.

The second battalion of Berri had orders to remain in the fort to deliver and to convey all the ammunition necessary for defending the intrenchments. The enemy opened their attack by a most brisk fire of musketry, and immediately advanced to fight with the cold steel, but our fire was so well sustained and directed, that it was impossible for them to approach nearer than 15 or 20 paces. In this way the fight continued until four o'clock, the enemy constantly bringing fresh troops against us, and from four o'clock until seven, they kept up a fire at a greater distance. They finally retreated after a considerable loss.

Waited until next morning to visit the field of battle; the Marquis de Montcalm did not give orders to do so until he was assured that the enemy thought no longer of returning and were hastily embarking to go home. About 1,200 men were buried; the number of wounded carried off has been about 3,000. We have had 14 officers killed and 20 wounded in this action; 92 soldiers or Canadians killed and 248 wounded.

The enemy's army was composed of 15 [or] 16 thousand men of these seven thousand were Regulars. Our's was 3,000 Regulars and 500 Canadians. This brilliant day may be said to have saved the Colony.

The enemy, on arriving at Fort George, detached a body of troops on an expedition against Fort Frontenac, which they reduced on the 26th August, and after demolishing it, and burning the sloops, except two which they employed, returned to Chouéguen. The garrison was sent prisoners of war to Montreal, and exchanged for the same number of men that we had in the Colony.

25th August. The English reduced Louisbourg and made the garrison prisoners of war.

14th September. A force of 800 English was defeated by a detachment of Canadians and Indians, within sight of Fort Duquesne, which they were coming to reconnoiter, thereby checking the march of an army of 6,000 men, who were on their way under General Forbes to besiege it.

Captain de Ligneris, of the Marine troops, who commanded at that fort, having had orders to burn and remove the artillery, warlike stores, and provisions on the approach of the enemy, executed those instructions in the month of October, on learning that they were within at most, two days march of him, and retired to Fort Machault. The enemy contented themselves with building a small fort enclosed with palisades on the River Malengueulée, a short distance from Fort Duquesne." The document then concludes with the sentence, *"Nothing of interest transpired the following winter."*

However, during that time, William Pitt had formed yet another multi-pronged English advance against strategic French holdings in North America for the year 1759, this time, with specially promoted Major-General James Wolfe, targeting the heart of New France itself: Quebec, by fleet, while recently appointed commander-in-chief of the British army in North America, Jeffery Amherst, was to make another attempt on Fort Ticonderoga/Carillon, located on Lake Champlain, before uniting with Wolfe at Quebec, if possible. Lastly, Brigadier General John Prideaux (1718 – 59) was to lay siege to Fort Niagara. While in the meantime, the Langlade family grew, per the following entry in the Michilimackinac Register:

"January 30, 1759, I solemnly administered holy baptism to Louis[e] Domitille, legitimate daughter of Mr. Charles de Langlade and of M. de Charlotte Bourassa, her father and mother. The godfather was Mr. De Beaujeu, Commanding for the King at this post; and the godmother M. de Langlade.

[Signed] M. L. LeFranc, Miss. of the Society of Jesus; Beaujeu; Langlade."

The winter of 1758-59 in Canada had been particularly brutal, and exasperated by a continued lack of provisions, perpetuating unaffordable prices for what little there was, with many French officers simply not making enough money to be able to afford food, while in answer to a repeated request by the Marquis de Montcalm, and supplemented in person by his subordinate, Captain de Bougainville, for more reinforcements, munitions and provisions from Europe, Marshal Charles Louis Auguste Fouquet de Belle Isle (1684 – 1761), French Minister of War, on behalf of the King's Court, addressed the Marquis the following, unsatisfactory reply:

"*Marshal de Belle Isle to M. de Montcalm.*

Versailles, 19th February, 1759.

Sir,

Messrs. de Bougainville and Doreil have handed me the letters you have entrusted to them for me. The former, who is about to depart on his return to Canada, will convey my answers to you. You will have been surprised at not receiving anything from me by the frigate which has been dispatched to you in the month of September last. I was advised of it so late that my packet did not arrive at Brest until after she had set sail. You will find it among those confided to M. de Bougainville.

I shall not repeat what I have already told you of the satisfaction the King entertains of your services. Your promotion to the rank of Lieutenant-General, of which I send you the commission, and the red ribbon that has been accorded to you, will make you more sensible of them than all the assurances I could give you. His Majesty has also had regard to the expenses the command confided to you requires you to incur, and it has never been his intention that a place in which you defend so courageously his interest should be a burden to you.

You will learn that in attending to your interests I have not neglected those of the staff and regimental officers employed under your orders, both in procuring for them an increase of pay and obtaining rewards commensurate with their services. I enclose, herewith, commissions of Major General (Maréchal de Camp), for Chevalier de Levis; of Brigadiers for Messrs. de Bourlamaque and de Senezergues, with the letters of service I have transmitted to them in consequence, and which you will have the goodness to send them. You will find another of Colonel for M. de Bougainville, on whom the King has conferred that rank, in order that he may perform the duties thereof with the troops under your command. The other packets he carries, contain the copies of the particular favors which you will find almost conformable to your propositions. I refer, for the rest, to the letters of detail I write you and with which I hope you will be satisfied.

As regards your duty during this campaign, I am very sorry to have to inform you that you must not expect to receive any Military reinforcements. Besides augmenting the scarcity of provisions which you have only too much experienced up to the present time, it would be much to be feared that they would be intercepted by the English, on the passage; and as the King could never send you assistance proportionate to the forces the English are able to oppose against you, the efforts which would be made here, would have no other effect than to excite the Ministry of London to much greater efforts to preserve the superiority it has acquired in that part of the continent. Although in this conjuncture it is to be expected that the English Generals will desire to profit by their advantage in order to inflict on the Colony severer blows, the recollection of what you have achieved last year makes his Majesty hope that you will still find means to disconcert their projects. M. Berryer will cause to be conveyed to you as much provisions and ammunition as possible; the rest depends on your wisdom and courage, and on the bravery of the troops. His Majesty is convinced that the confidence he reposes in you and in them cannot be better placed. He relies equally on the good understanding he wishes to prevail between the troops of the Marine and those of the Colony, and that the manner you will live with M. de Vaudreuil, will furnish them the example. This is a point whereon M. Berryer must insist, and which I believe it is unnecessary to recommend to you.

I have the honor to be, most perfectly, Sir, & c.

P.S. As it is to be expected that the entire efforts of the English will be directed against Canada, and that they will attack you at different points at once, it will be necessary that you confine your plan of defense to those which are most essential and most *connected, in order that being concentrated on a smaller extent of country, you may be always enabled mutually to help one another, to communicate with and to support each other. However trilling the space you can preserve, it is of the utmost importance to possess always a foothold in Canada, for should we once wholly lose that country, it would be quite impossible to enter it again. To fulfill this object, the King reckons, Sir, on your zeal, your courage and pertinacity. His Majesty expects you will exercise all the industry you are capable of, and that you will communicate the like sentiments to the principal officers and altogether to the troops under your orders. M. Berryer writes to the same effect to M. de Vaudreuil, and directs him to conduct himself with the greatest harmony towards you; you must both feel all its necessity and all its importance. I have become responsible for you to the King. I am well assured that you will not dishonor me, and that for the good of the State, the glory of the Nation and your own preservation, you will have recourse to the greatest extremities rather than ever submit to conditions so disgraceful as those accepted at Louisbourg, the memory of which you will efface. Such are, Sir, substantially, the King's intentions. He has entire confidence in you and all the qualities he recognizes in you. I have fully confirmed his Majesty therein by the testimonies I have rendered. I wish you perfect health, I feel no uneasiness for the rest. Rely also on all the sentiments I entertain for you, Sir, and that I most sincerely desire to find myself in a position to afford you marks thereof."*

If ever there had been a doubt, the Marshal's letter made it abundantly clear that Canada was being left to fend for itself against the ever-growing might of the English.

The following month, the growing disparity in the two armies and the general sad state of affairs was laid out more plainly in a pair of letters addressed to the French Ministry, the first to Louis Hyacinthe Boyer de Crémilles (1700 – 1768), and the second (again) to Marshal de Belle Isle, by the Marquis de Montcalm, the contents of which are as follows:

"M. de Montcalm to M. de Cremille.
                    Montreal, 12th April, 1759.

SIR: I profit by the departure of a vessel which had been dispatched last December and prevented by the ice from proceeding any farther than the Isle aux Coudres.

Our last news announced that the English would force us to abandon Fort Duquesne. Captain de Ligneris, of the Colonists, who was in command there, after having ordered the place to be blown up, retired on the 23rd November, to a pretended fort called Fort Machault.

The English are negotiating with the Delawares and Chasanons, whom they are endeavoring to attract to themselves; whatever people may say about it, 'tis to be feared they will succeed. The Five Nations, on which I, contrary to M. de Vaudreuil's opinion, never placed reliance, appear inclined to the English.

Men have been employed this winter in building two sloops at La Présentation, on Lake Ontario, to repair, as much as possible, the very serious error of the last campaign, the allowing Frontenac to be taken, and the navy we had on Lake Ontario to be burned. 'Twill be very good of the English if they allow us to launch those two vessels, without an effort on their part to burn them.

We have not had anything of interest this winter; some parties on both sides, in the neighborhood of Carillon, to obtain news respectively. Captain d'Hebecourt, of the regiment of La Reine, who has been entrusted with the command of them, has behaved with a great deal of intelligence and application. The accounts we receive of the enemy from all parts, incline us to presume that the new General (Amherst) wishes to take the field early, with a large force. The provincial assemblies met in December to demand of the particular governors their contingents of men and provisions.

They were held the year before, in February. The deliberations were in favor of granting them. Our forces and means are different, but I dare be answerable to you for the good resolution of our troops, for the zeal of Chevalier de Levis and M. de Bourlamaque, and of our principal officers, to second me effectually. M. de Bourlamaque will be able to make the campaign. He is tolerably recovered from his very serious wound.

I cannot tell you precisely how we are off for provisions and warlike stores. Ordinarily, I learn the facts only from the public, which informs me that we are badly off for the one and the other, unless we receive powerful succors from Europe.

The war has changed character in Canada. The vast forces of the English, our example determines them on continuous operations in a country where the Canadians thought they were making war, and were making, so to speak, hunting excursions. Our principles of war, considering our inferiority, ought to be, to contract our defensive, in order to preserve at least, the body of the Colony, and retard its loss; to combine with the system of European tactics the use to be made of the Indians. This is what I am always saying, but the prejudices or councils of quacks are followed. No matter, I serve the King and the State. I shall always express my opinion. I shall execute to the best of my ability; last year I did, indeed, dare to accept battle with an order in my pocket to avoid a general engagement. To retreat would be the ruin of the Colony; to lose the battle, would be to lose both it and myself likewise, who would have been met by the order issued to me. This last did not stop me. I can well sacrifice myself for the [public] good. M. de Vaudreuil, to whom I submitted, on the 20th of March, a Memoir on the campaign, has at length just communicated his plan to me. We do not agree on all points. I shall not the less exert myself, as I have always done, to be successful. I wish, with all my heart, that I may be deceived; that he may be able to sustain himself everywhere, that the English may not come to Quebec, or that the navigation of the River St. Lawrence, often difficult, may afford him time to take those precautions which have been neglected, and might, in my opinion, have been taken beforehand.

M. Bernies, Commissary at War, who has succeeded M. Doreil, and who appears to me qualified to acquit himself well of the duties of his station, will render you an account of the actual strength *and condition of our battalions and of the soldiers, which I shall determine, on reflection, ought to be sent to the Invalides; but 'twill not be by this vessel, not being able to make the review of our battalions until they will enter on the campaign. He will address you, likewise, some representations on the important subject of the high price of provisions, the impossibility of supporting themselves, under which our officers labor, unless you have had the goodness to procure for them an augmentation of pay; and whatever augmentation you grant them, you will never be able to make them live in this country unless sufficient nourishment be allowed them, or at least they be paid in bills of exchange of the first class. I beg you to pay great attention to this Commissary's Memoir, which has passed under my eyes, in order to solicit the Minister of the Marine on the subject. If M. Doreil be in Paris, he will be able to enlighten you, should that Memoir contain anything doubtful or obscure, always observing that every article has doubled since his departure, and is now tripled.*

Perhaps the Marine, on considering the expenses superficially, will think the troops of the Line cost an immense sum in Canada. I proceed to explain that to you. If excessive expenses are incurred, they are placed under the name of 'Depenses pour les troupes de terre', although they regard us not, because in Canada the Intendant's ordinance is the only authority for everything, without being a piece probante. It only remains for me, Sir, to request the continuation of your former kindnesses; you have flattered me with them at all times; the post you occupy enables you to make me sensible of their effects, and I believe I deserve them by my zeal for the service, my attachment to your person, and the respect with which I have the honor to be,

 Sir,

   Your most humble and most obedient servant,

                Montcalm.

 P.S. I annex to this despatch, Sir, an exact return of the English troops which are to be employed on this Continent. I beg of you to have the kindness to lay it before Marshal de Belle Isle; it is exact, as well as the interesting postscript I add in cipher, in support of that article.

According to news we have received, the English are building a fort at Chouaguen, and wish to construct one at the Bay of Cayugas; this proves that the English want to be masters of Lake Ontario, and the fruit of the capture of Chouaguen will be lost by that of Frontenac, which the English effected last year. Should the English ever take Canada, the only means the King will have to secure to the Canadians the preservation of their rights and prevent them being transplanted, as has been the case with the Acadians, is to declare that Hanover and the Hanoverians, and the country of the King of England's allies, will be treated in every respect as the English treat Canada and the Canadians."

And secondly:

"*M. de Montcalm to Marshal de Belle Isle.*
Montreal, 12th April, 1759.

Canada will be taken this campaign, and assuredly during the next, if there be not some unforseen good luck, a powerful diversion by sea against the English Colonies, or some gross blunders on the part of the enemy.

The English have 60,000 men, we at most from 10 to 11,000. Our government is good for nothing; money and provisions will fail. Through want of provisions, the English will begin first; the farms scarcely tilled, cattle lack; the Canadians are dispirited; no confidence in M. de Vaudreuil or in M. Bigot. M. de Vaudreuil is incapable of preparing a plan of operations. He has no activity; he lends his confidence to empirics rather than to the Generals sent by the King. M. Bigot appears occupied only in making a large fortune for himself, his adherents and sycophants. Cupidity has seized officers, store-keepers; the commissaries also who are about the River St. John, or the Ohio, or with the Indians in the Upper country, are amassing astonishing fortunes. It is nothing but forged certificates legally admitted. If the Indians had a fourth of what is supposed to be expended for them, the King would have all those in America; the English none.

This interest has an influence on the war. M. de Vaudreuil, with whom men are equal, led by a knavish secretary and interested associates, would confide a vast operation to his brother, or any other Colonial officer, the same as to Chevalier de Levis. The choice concerns those who divide the cake; therefore has there never been any desire to send M. de Bourlamaque, or M. de Senezergues, commandant of the battalion of La Sarre, to Fort Duquesne. I did propose it; the King had gained by it; but what superintendents in a country, whose humblest cadet, a sergeant, a gunner, return with twenty, thirty thousand livres in certificates, for goods issued for the Indians on account of his Majesty.

This expenditure, which has been paid at Quebec by the Treasurer of the Colony, amounts to twenty-four millions. The year before, the expenses amounted only to twelve or thirteen millions. This year they will run up to thirty-six. Everybody appears to be in a hurry to make his fortune before the Colony is lost, which event many, perhaps, desire, as an impenetrable veil over their conduct. The craving after wealth has an influence on the war, and M. de Vaudreuil does not doubt it. Instead of reducing the expenses of Canada, people wish to retain all; how abandon positions which serve as a pretext to make private fortunes? Transportation is distributed to favorites. The agreement with the contractor is unknown to me as it is to the public. 'Tis reported that those who have invaded commerce participate in it. Has the King need of purchasing goods for the Indians? Instead of buying them directly, a favorite is notified, who purchases at any price whatever; then M. Bigot has then removed to the King's stores, allowing a profit of one hundred and even one hundred and fifty per cent, to those who it is desired to favor. Is artillery to be transported, guncarriages, carts implements to be made? M. Mercier, commandant of the artillery, is the contractor under other people's names. Every thing is done badly and at a high price. This officer, who came out twenty years ago a simple soldier, will be soon worth about six or seven hundred thousand livres, perhaps a million, if these things continue. I have often respectfully spoken to M. de Vaudreuil and M. Bigot of these expenses; each throws the blame on his colleague. The people alarmed at these expenses, fear a depreciation in the paper money of the country; the evil effect is, the Canadians who do not participate in those illicit profits, hate the Government. They repose confidence in the General of the French; accordingly, what consternation on a ridiculous rumor which circulated this winter that he had been poisoned.

We have been driven out of Fort Duquesne at the end of November. One might hope that such an operation would have been deferred by the English until April, but the enemy knew, by their Indians and our deserters, the too public order of M. de Vaudreuil, to evacuate. I have never had communication either of the instructions or news relating to the operations of the war, with which neither I nor Chevalier de Levis have been entrusted. If I have often proffered my advice, even in writing, it has been upon what I learned, the same as the public. Despite of all that will be written, the Indians of the Upper country are beginning to shake and to negotiate with the English. The Five Nations are ill disposed. M. de Vaudreuil alone has wished to persuade the court, that they had pronounced, and that such was his work. In managing in the best manner, neutrality might be expected; I have always written that this would be a great deal.

The loss of Fort Frontenac is a deadly blow, in consequence of the capture of our navy on Lake Ontario. Three months have been spent in deliberating, where new sloops should be constructed. We shall have two within twenty days, if the English do not come and burn them; our Iroquois Indians fear it. M. de Vaudreuil was told and reproached, in full council, that they had notified him three weeks before, respecting Fort Frontenac. They said to him; You are asleep; where is our War Chief? I was then at Quebec. At last Captain Pouchot, of the Bearn battalion, is going to command at Niagara; he ought to have been sent off last fall; he was capable and agreeable to the Indians. Such was promised me, but how resolve to dismiss a Canadian officer, however incapable and disagreeable to the Indians he might be?

All the preparations at Orange and Lydius announce that the English will come early to Carillon with a large force.

The enemy can come to Quebec, if we have not a fleet; and Quebec, once taken, the Colony is lost. Yet is their no precaution; I have written, I have spoken, as also have M. de Pont le Roy, the Engineer, an excellent man, and Sieur Pelegrin, captain of the Port of Quebec, a good seaman, for his part; I have offered to introduce some order, an arrangement to prevent a false maneuver; on the first alarm to repel it; we shall have time.

I know nothing of M. de Vaudreuil's projects, still less how many Canadians he will be able to bring into the field, or how we are off for provisions and ammunition. The public tell me, we are badly off both for the one and the other, and the same public always believe the department of provisions ill governed. I ought to consider myself fortunate, under the circumstances, not to be consulted; but devoted to his Majesty's service, I have given my advice in writing for the best, and we shall act with courage and zeal, Chevalier de Levis, M. de Bourlamaque and I, to retard the imminent loss of Canada. It is foreign to my character to blame M. de Vaudreuil and M. Bigot, depositaries of his Majesty's authority in Canada. I am even attached to M. Bigot, who is an amiable man and a near relative of M. de Pussieux and of Marshall d'Estrées, who honor men with their friendship. But I must write the truth to my Minister, to the Statesman.

I have written it to M. de Moras; I do not write anything to the present Minister of the Marine. 'Tis for my Minister to make use of what I write to him for the good of the state without compromising me. If the war continue[s], Canada will belong to the English, perhaps this very campaign, or the next. If there be peace, the Colony is lost, if the entire government be not changed. The maxims of the book entitled 'L'ami de l'homme', must be followed: to disgrace those who will return from Colonies with wealth, and to reward those who will return from them with the staff and scrip with which they had gone forth.

The general census of Canada has been at last completed. Though it has not been communicated to me, I think I'm correct, that there are not more than 82,000 souls in the Colony; of these, twelve thousand, at most, are men capable of bearing arms; deducting from this number those employed in works, transports, bateaux, in the Upper countries, no more than seven thousand Canadians will ever be collected together, and then it must not be either seed time or harvest, otherwise, by calling all out, the ground would remain uncultivated; famine would follow. Our eight battalions will make three thousand two hundred men; the Colonials, at most, fifteen hundred men in the field. What is that against at least fifty thousand men which the English have!"

Despite so many complaints and the colony's dire circumstances, as the campaigning season approached, at length, the endless feuding between the Marquis de Montcalm and the Governor-General of New France, the Marquis de Vaudreuil — which had reached new lows over the last year, had at length been put aside as the 1759 campaigning season loomed with the two deciding on a defensive plan of action; Colonel Boulamaque was to be dispatched to Fort Ticonderoga/Carillon to keep General Amherst at bay; while French-Canadian partisan, Luc de la Corne, was to be stationed along the St. Lawrence River Rapids, to harass any English advance from Lake Ontario; with General Montcalm himself, his second-in-command, the Chevalier de Lévis, and Captain Bougainville remaining posted around Quebec itself. Every able-bodied man, or young adult boy who could hold a musket was integrated into the ranks, while Charles Langlade once again exerted his influence over numerous local and far-flung Indigenous Nations, tribes and bands to muster a sizeable contingent of warriors to aid in the defense of New France's heartland.

In May 1759, Langlade and his force were noted in the *"Memoirs"* of French Captain Pierre Pouchot, who wrote:

"On the 17th [of May, 1759], a Sauter [warrior] from Saguinan [Michigan] announced that [French] Commandant M. Bellestre

was there and only waiting for M. Pouchot to summon him to come from Detroit. The reinforcements would have arrived late, since they were more than 100 [482km] leagues away. Langlade, a colonial officer resident in that region was due to go down to Montreal with 1,000 Indians. Among that number were the Folles-Avoines [the French name for the Menominee Nation of Green Bay] who, has already been stated, had killed two Frenchman. They brought with them the two men most responsible for the killing and handed them over to [the Governor General of New France] M. de Vaudreuil at a meeting in which they made restitution for the dead [French] men. M. de Vaudreuil gave them [those accused of the murders] back to the Indians to exact justice. They shot them both [...]."

While in an official French government document the following month, it was noted that *"Two hundred [Indigenous warriors] of the Nations around Missilimaquinac, commanded by Sieur Langlade, half-pay officer, established among them, arrived at Montreal June twenty-third, and immediately descended to Quebec."*

On the 26th of June, after successfully navigating the St. Lawrence River thus, the English fleet under Major General James Wolfe, consisting of approximately nine thousand men, came in sight of Quebec, laying anchor off the small river island of Orleans. From here, Wolfe sized up the French, Canadian and Indigenous defenses, which numbered approximately thirty-five hundred men, nearly half Indigenous warriors, plus numerous hunters/trappers and otherwise unofficial soldiers. However, although outnumbered and lacking cohesive experience, the French, Canadian and Indigenous forces defending Quebec did have the benefit of numerous defensive intrenchments, strategically placed around the city and along the adjacent St. Lawrence River, in which their true numbers could be masked from the English, and their men afforded at least some measure of protection from cannon balls or shrapnel.

On June 29th, French Captain Pierre Pouchot additionally noted in his "*Memoirs*" that:

"A courier from Presqu'Isle announced that 100 Frenchmen and 150 Indians were due to arrive from Detroit, plus 6 to 700

Indians with M. Lintot, and 100 Indians with M. Bayeul and then the convoy of M. Aubry from the Illinois with 6 to 700 from the detachments on the Mississippi.

Some Indians from Michilimackinac who arrived the same evening said that M. la Verranderie and Langlade had come down the Grande [Ottawa] Riviere with 1,200 Indians – Christinaux [Cree], Scioux, Sakis [a.k.a., the Sauks], Folles Avoines [the French name for the Menominee Nation of Green Bay], Sauteurs [Chippewa and/or Ojibway] and Renards [a.k.a., the Foxes - whom had historically been enemies of both the French and their allies, the Sakis {or "Sauks"} but were now united against the English under the co-leadership of Charles Langlade]."

After carefully considering the French, Canadian and Indigenous positions around Quebec, on July 9th, English Major General Wolfe resolved to land three battalions, numbering approximately two to three thousand men beneath the Montmorency Falls, which emptied into the Saint Lawrence River, a brisk march upstream from the city of Quebec. He decided that if the rocks surrounding the falls could be scaled successfully, his men could turn the flank and/or rear of the scattered French, Canadian and Indigenous forces, the majority of which faced the river.

The Montmorency Falls were sheltered by a gorge and were surrounded by a thicket of trees and underbrush, and while Major General Wolfe's men affected their landing beneath them, endeavoring to then scale up the rock face, Charles Langlade, after ordering his warriors to lay in ambush for the English, personally hastened with all speed to Lieutenant Louis Legardeur Repentigny, who, at the head of approximately eleven hundred additional French and Canadians, was posted nearby. In one of the few, well-documented testaments to Langlade's personal genius for military observation and strategy, he requested of Repentigny that he march with his approximately eleven hundred French and Canadians to his assistance at once, as so precarious was the English position below the Montmorency Falls, that if they were to be attacked by both his and Repentigny's forces united, they could be annihilated.

Repentigny at once saw the merit in Langlade's proposal, and so immediately forwarded it onto his superior, the Chevalier de Lévis, whom in turn sought out the Governor-General, the Marquis de Vaudreuil's approval, however, here, Langlade's proposal was beset with intolerable delay and indecision, so that when at length, Charles Langlade and his band of warriors ultimately initiated their attack, unassisted, they achieved only minor success against the English, whom had had sufficient time to secure a beachhead, with a golden opportunity to inflict a morale-crushing defeat on them and perhaps drive them back into the Saint Lawrence River, had been irrevocably lost, and would not be forthcoming again.

Scotsman, the Chevalier de Johnstone (circa. 1719 – 91), the Chevalier de Lévis' aid-de-camp during the siege of Quebec, and the attributed author of the subsequent "***Dialogue in Hades between the Marquis de Montcalm and General Wolfe***", later recalled, in a mock dialogue between opposing commanders, Montcalm and Wolfe, of this event:

"***But, Sir,***" Montcalm theoretically addressed himself to Wolfe, "***how do you justify yourself for the imprudence with which you ensconced yourself in the wood, with two thousand men quite opposite to our intrenchments at the ford [of the Montmorency Falls?]; not a single man of your detachment would have been able to escape; nine hundred [Indigenous warriors] in ambuscade, within pistol shot of you, without your having perceived it, would have invested and cut off your retreat. The [warriors] had sent at the instant their officer, M. Langlade, to inform M. Levis of their position, and to beg him with clasped hands to give orders to M. Repentigny, who commanded a corps of eleven hundred men in the intrenchments at the ford, to cross the river with his detachment; and that they would answer with their heads for the success of the attack; adding that you appeared to be about two thousand men, and that they were not strong enough to attack you without reinforcements, which they asked from the Canadians.***

There were a great many officers in the house of M. Levis when Langlade arrived, among others, commanders of battalions.

M. Levis consulted them, but no one officer gave it as his opinion for the detachment of Repentigny to pass the river; they pretended that it was dangerous to attack an enemy in woods, of which it was impossible to know the number, that perhaps this was the whole English army; and that it would be impossible to engage in a general action without being prepared; that if we had the misfortune to be repulsed, M. Levis would be blamed for taking this affair upon himself without waiting for orders; they alleged, besides, many other reasons equally less solid.

Never did anyone see such a blindness! M. Johnstone was the only one who gave an opposite advice, and maintained with spiritedness that there was not the least appearance that this was the whole English army, since the savages, who never failed to exaggerate the number of the enemy, supposed them only two thousand men; that although this should be the whole English army, and that we should engage in a general action in the woods, that was all that we could desire as most fortunate, since one Canadian in the wood was worth much more than three soldiers of regular troops, and that one soldier on the plain was worth more than three Canadians, of whom the greater part of our army was composed; and that it was necessary to suit and make the different kinds of troops, of which our army was composed, available; that, without losing time, it was necessary to send to Beauport to inform M. Montcalm to cause the army to advance at once in echelons, replacing the post of M. Repentigny at the ford by the Royal Regiment Roissillon, which was encamped close to that, and thus to stop the army, always advancing in proportion as they passed the ford; that even supposing that the worst should happen, that we should be repulsed, the English could not reap any advantage from it, since we should have a secure retreat in the thickness of the woods, where the enemy never durst pursue us, at the risk of being cut to pieces by the [Natives] and the Canadians; and he added that in war when fortune presented to us propitious moments, it was necessary to profit by them on the instant.

These reasonings made no impression, and Langlade was sent back without having obtained anything. The ambuscade of the [Natives] was a little more than half a league from the house of M. Levis; in the meantime, Langlade returned once more to give us instant news on the part of the [Natives]. M. Levis did not wish ever to give a positive order to M. Repentigny to pass the river with his detachment, but he charged Langlade with a letter on his part to Repentigny, in which he notified to him the confidence he had in his prudence, and that he could pass the ford with his detachment, to join himself to the [Natives], if he saw a likelihood to succeed. M. Johnstone foreseeing the answer M. Repentigny would make, he said to M. Levis, in sealing his letter, that Repentigny had too much good sense and judgement to take upon himself so delicate an affair. Accordingly, he sent at once to demand from M. Levis an order more positive and more clear. M. Levis in the end determined on it, and mounted his horse to proceed to the ford, in order to give his orders viva voce; but scarcely was he on half the road than he heard a fire of musketry.

The time having slipped away in indecision; the [Natives] impatient at having remained more than an hour in a position so perilous, let go their shots, killing five hundred men, and retiring immediately without having lost a single man. It is evident that had M. Repentigny passed the ford with his detachment, you [Montcalm theoretically referring to Wolfe, or rather, his men] would have been cut in pieces, and accordingly, to all appearance, this action would have determined forever the war in Canada, your army not having anything further to expect after such a loss […]."

Although estimates vary as to the number of men the English lost in their attempt at the Montmorency Falls against Charles Langlade and his band of approximately nine hundred warriors, many sources agree that their losses might have been much, much worse, had only Repentigny and Langlade's forces been permitted to co-ordinate an attack. A document titled "**Operations of the Army, under M. de Montcalm, before Quebec**", barring slight variations in detail, similarly recalls of this event:

"After having lain flat on the ground for five hours in the face of the enemy, without observing the slightest movements among our troops, the Indians, carried away ay last by their impatience, and seeing, moreover, that the enemy was profiting by it, by bringing fresh troops into the woods, decided to make the attack alone. They were so impetuous, as we were subsequently told by a Sargent who had deserted to the enemy, and two Canadians, then prisoners, that the English were obliged to fight retreating more than two hundred paces from the place of combat, before they could rally.

The alarm was communicated even to the main camp, to which Gen. Wolfe had returned. The [Natives] seeing themselves almost entirely surrounded, effected a retreat, after having killed or wounded more than a hundred and fifty men, losing only two or three of their own number.

They met at the ford of the River Montmorency [above the Falls], the detachment coming to their support, which M. de Levis had been unwilling to take the responsibility of sending, until he received orders from the M. de Vaudreuil. The whole army regretted that they had not profited by so fine an opportunity."

The remainder of the summer was spent conversely by General Wolfe endeavoring to coerce the French and their allies into battle, while the latter simply stalled for time, awaiting the arrival of winter within their intrenchments and behind Quebec's walls. However, while the French and their allies were reluctant to engage him in open battle, Wolfe preoccupied himself with dispersing English detachments far and wide to desolate the country surrounding Quebec and to isolate the city from supply. They torched or plundered remaining harvests, houses, barns, and whatever else may have been of use to the French, Canadian and Indigenous forces, while frequently skirmishing with contingents of Charles Langlade's warriors, French-Canadian hunters and armed farmers who constantly stalked the woods.

Simultaneously, the English also moved against Fort Niagara, which was commanded by Captain Pouchot, who documented the lengthy siege as such (referring to himself in the third person) in his "*Memoirs*":

"The garrison [of Fort Niagara] was composed of 149 men detached from the regiments of La Sarre, Royal Rousillon, Guienne and Bearn, under the orders of Captain Pouchot, of the Bearn regiment, Commandant; Captain de Villars of La Sarre; Captain de Cervies of Royal Rousillon; Lieutenant de Morambert of Guienne; Lieutenant Salvignac of Bearn; Lieutenant la Miltière of Languedoc; of 183 Colonials, under the orders of Captain de la Roche, of that service, Lieutenants Cornoyer and Larminac; of 133 Militia and 21 gunners, commanded by Lieutenant Bonnafoux of the Royal Corps. M. Pouchot increased this number to 100 drafted from the troops and from the most adroit of the militiamen; in all 486, and 39 employees, five of whom were women or children, who with two Douville ladies attended the hospital, sewed up gun cartridges and made earth bags.

7th July. Seven barges defiled from beneath the lofty perpendicular shores of the lake to reconnoiter the place. They were allowed to come together and to approach, but when 'twas remarked that they would not come any closer, some cannon were discharged at them, which soon drove them off. M. Pouchot immediately sent a boat to scout, which reported having seen at the mouth of the Little Swamp, 15 [to] 20 barges, each containing 20 men, who were at once considered the van-guard of the English army. He immediately sent off another scout, under the orders of the Lieutenant of the sloop, who reported having seen some barges and a camp on the shore, where there appeared to be a great many people and fires. Another scout, sent out two hours after, stated that he had discovered about 16 barges and a single tent, but a great many people were walking along the bank. The barges had all entered the little swamp, and the army was encamped in the woods.

M. Pouchot dispatched a courier immediately to M. Chabert, the Commandant of the fort at the Carrying place, with orders to fall back by the Chenondac, in case he saw any traces of the enemy near his fort, lest he may be carried off. This courier also carried orders to bring down all the detachments, French and Indians, that may happen to be at Presqu'isle; also, orders to M. de Lignery at Fort Machault, to fall back on Niagara with all the French and Indians he may have, enjoining on them to form a small van-guard to observe if the Little fort was abandoned, and in that case to pass by the Chenondac to Niagara, and leave merely a detachment to protect their bateaux and effects.

At noon he sent out the corvette L'Iroquoise with a month's provisions, to cruise off the Little Swamp. The wind was S. and S.W. She cannonaded the enemy's camp. In the course of the day, some scouts appeared near a copse, 2 [to] 3 feet high, although M. Pouchot had, when he arrived, caused a portion of it to be cut down. Several Indians also appeared, who were looking for a shot. A few cannon balls made them retire.

At night, a Pouteouatamis and Sauteur came from the fort at the Carrying place. M. Pouchot proposed to them to go out on a scout during the night, and gave them a Huron, who was in the fort, as a companion. They went along the perpendicular banks of the lake as far as the large wood at the end of the clearance, and returned by the center of the clearance without having seen anything. An hour before day, the Pouteoutamis, who was very brave, returned thither alone. He left by the precipitous banks of the lake towards the angle which it forms in front of the place; met a canoe with three men in it, and fired on the middle one, who was wounded. The other two discharged their guns at him, without hitting him, and fled. He made the rounds of the clearance, uttering a great many bravadoes to the hostile Indians.

8th. M. Pouchot sent him back in company with two Frenchmen, to M. Chabert with a letter. Being uneasy as to his situation, they dispatched one of their party to him, with word that they had seen the trails of some forty men in the woods. As these trails came from up the river, M. Pouchot feared some of the enemy had crossed over, which rendered him uneasy about those who were to come on that side; he therefore sent out to have those woods searched, but nothing was discovered within the space of a league.

The corvette was signalized at noon to send in her boat. The Lieutenant who came reports that the enemy had formed a camp on a small eminence at this side of the Little swamp, to guard the bateaux; that they appeared to be from 3 to 4 thousand men, and were very busy on the edge of the clearance towards the lake, and were making abatis at which 400 men appeared to be employed. M. Pouchot surmised that this might be the place where they were forming their depot for the trench. The guns of the corvette annoyed them so much that they were obliged to quit their camp and get under cover. They fired some 12's at that vessel. M. Pouchot ordered the corvette to take up a position opposite the mouth of the little swamp, to prevent convoys entering or bateaux going out to carry their artillery to the depot, which was a league and a quarter from the swamp; this would protract their labors. He ordered the Captain of that craft, if overtaken by a squall, to reenter the river, and get close to the shoal which is under the fort. These precautions obliged the enemy to carry on all their operations by land, and protected the place which might be easily insulted from the lake and river sides.

In the afternoon some hundreds of Indians, who came to fire at the fort, made their appearance in the copse of the clearance. They were driven off by artillery loaded with grape [shot]; some of them were killed. At sunset M. Pouchot sent to fetch a Frenchman and two Indians from the other side of the river. The former was the storekeeper's brother that had been sent to raise the Missisakis. He returned accompanied by only one. The rest had gone away on seeing the little fort burnt, which they imagined had been done by the English. The other Indian was an Iroquois whom M. Chabert had sent with a letter announcing that he would come the next day. He had removed to the River Chenondac all the property he could, 20 horses which belonged to him and some oxen he had had brought down on his own account from Detroit. He burned the fort of the Carrying place, as 'twas not tenable. His brother, Joncaire, had arrived on the previous evening, having been brought down by the Iroquois, the bearer of the letter. M. Pouchot made him a present.

About ten o'clock, a white flag was displayed in the clearance. M. Pouchot sent to reconnoiter it with precaution. A Captain of the Royal Americans was conducted to him with eyes blindfolded. He was led through the thickest and densest brushwood, and handed to the Commandant, after the bandage was removed from his eyes, a letter from Brigadier Prideaux, stating that as the King of England had invested him with the government of Niagara, M. Pouchot had to surrender the place to him; if not, he would oblige him to do so by superior force which accompanied him. M. Pouchot answered that he did not understand English; that he had no reply to give. Yet he perfectly understood the letter. The officer insisted on the great force he had. M. Pouchot replied that the King [of France] had confided that place to him; that he was in a position to defend it, and was in hopes that M. Prideaux would never enter it, and that before he became acquainted with them, he should at least assuredly gain their esteem. He had breakfast furnished to the young officer, and had him sent back with eyes blindfolded, to the place whence he had been brought.

In the afternoon, La Force, the commander of the corvette, sent word to M. Pouchot that he saw no more barges nor depots on the strand, and but few people on the banks above. Thereupon M. Pouchot sent a sergeant in a bateau, who went up on the other side of the river, and reported having seen a great many people working at La Belle Famille, from which circumstance 'twas inferred that they designed opening the trench that night. In the evening, some men in their shirt sleeves appeared on the confines of the clearance to the right of the place, who seemed desirous to open a trench. Three or four guns were discharged at them and they withdrew; which showed that it was not the place where they intended opening the trench.

The great quietness of the enemy that day, caused their operations to be distrusted. M. Pouchot, consequently, placed Captain Villars of La Sarre, in the half moon with 60 men; Lieutenant de

Morambert and 30 men in the place d'armes, intrenched by the covert-way on the left; Lieutenant Cornoyer and 30 men in that of the right; Captain de Cervies, with 70 men occupied the salient angle of the covert-way of the lake bastion as far as the salient angle of the covert-way of the half moon; Lieutenant de Larminac and 40 men on the beach under the high bank of the lake bastion, behind the palisade; Captain de la Roche with thirty men at the salient angle of the bastion of the covert-way of the Five Nations bastion; M. Chabert with 60 men on the plateau beneath that salient in the rear of the palisade which ran into the river; 25 men were stationed at each bastion. These different posts furnished all the necessary sentinels. The 100 gunners were distributed among the batteries. There only remained M. Bonnafoux, the officer of Artillery, and Lieutenant de Salvignac of the Bearn regiment, who acted as Major. Such was the arrangement every night throughout the siege. In the day time the soldiers were occasionally relieved, in order that they should get some sleep, or employed in the different jobs which the operations of a siege demanded.

This night M. Pouchot sent out a scouting party of 30 volunteers, among whom were three or four Indians. They passed to the right, the center and the left; fired at some hostile Indians who had crept as far as a cemetery 50 toises [one toises equals six feet] distant from the glacis. A Huron who had strayed from the detachment of the right, was wounded by one of our Indians whilst endeavoring to rejoin his detachment.

10th. At daylight it rained, accompanied by fog, which shut out the field of operations until the day was advanced, when a parallel was discovered at more than 300 toises, which ran from about the center of the front of the fortifications, slanting towards the left, and the lake. It commenced in somewhat low ground which ordinarily was overflown, but was dry on account of the great drought, and thus greatly facilitated the opening of the trench, which, otherwise, the English would have been obliged to commence further off.

Both extremities of this parallel were battered with four pieces of cannon, though it rained heavily. The enemy appeared to work with a will. At night the guns were directed on the left portion, because 'twas thought that they intended advancing on that side. M. Chabert and his brother Joncaire arrived at noon with 70 persons, several women and Indians, three Iroquois; among the rest the chief Kaendaé. The Indians were pretty quiet.

11th. This parallel was perceived in the morning somewhat advanced towards the left; it was briskly battered. They set about perfecting it in the day time, and were remarked throwing up batteries. They were harassed as much as possible by our artillery.

In the afternoon, M. Pouchot, being desirous to remove some stockades which were between the parallel and glacis, to form embrasures, detached some men in order to support those who were to bring back those pickets. They advanced, of their own accord, as far as the elevation at the head of the enemy's trench. They were followed by some sixty men who escaped from the covert way, and fired into [...] the trench. The enemy, who felt confidence on account of our small number, were tolerably off their guard, and abandoned that part. One man ran to advise M. Pouchot that no person was there. Knowing those fellows better, be ordered the man to go and tell M. de la Roche, who allowed himself to be drawn out, to retire with his troops. In that interval all the soldiers and Militia leaped over the palisades of the covert way in spite of the officers, to follow the rest. The garrison was on the point of being engaged with the entire English army, because their Indians, numbering at least 900, and all their troops, came, at the moment, to form themselves in order of battle at the head of the trench. By the officers' precautions we were fortunate enough not to go too far. The enemy were checked by a very brisk fire from the artillery, which prevented them charging our men. The English failed not, in the meantime, to lose some people, as they were under the necessity of remaining exposed. They had also to stand to their arms until night.

This affair gave rise to a very singular adventure. Kaendaé, the Iroquois chief, demanded permission to go and speak to the Indians of his Nation. M. Pouchot did not consider that he ought to refuse him, the rather as he hoped by means of this Indian to prevail on some Senecas at least to abandon the army. The Iroquois agreed to a parley at the edge of the clearance; the result was that the Five Nations would send two deputies to M. Pouchot to ascertain his opinion of them. They asked him for a pass endorsed by M. Joncaire whom they regarded as one of their chiefs. They were brought blindfolded into the Commandant's room, who recognized Tonniac's nephew who had left him 5 [to] 6 days before the arrival of the English. These deputies said they knew not how they became mixed up with this war; that they were ashamed of it. M. Pouchot asked them what cause of war he had given them; that they ought to recollect they had given him the name of Sategariouaen ["the center of good business"] and that he had never deceived them. He expressed his surprise at seeing any Iroquois in the English army, particularly several who had evinced a great deal of affection for him; that they could see, by the way he fought, that he should not spare his enemies, and that his heart was bleeding at the thought of it being possible for him to strike any others than those Whites with whom he was at war. He invited them not to meddle any more in the quarrel and assured them he should not think any more about it. He concluded by notifying them that all the Upper Nations were constantly coming to his aid. Should they find themselves then in the case of shedding their blood, he promised them to interpose his authority to get them to make peace. He gave them a large belt to carry this message to their Nation.

The Missisakis who were present, wished also to speak in their turn. They expressed their pleasure at hearing the Iroquois speak of accommodating matters; that their Nation, which was numerous, would be flattered thereby; invited them not to let go their father's hand anymore; that for themselves their stand was taken; they would die with him, leaving to their Nation the duty of avenging their deaths.

The Pouteotamis said to them: 'Uncles: The Master of Life hath assembled us altogether on this Island. Who hath more sense than our ancestors? Were they not the first to extend the hand to the

French? Why should we not be attached to them? We do not know the English. We are charmed at your intention to stand well with our father. This is the way for us not to let go each other's hands.' These speeches were continued until nine o'clock at night when the deputies were led back blindfolded. They promised to return with an answer on the morrow.

This interview caused the firing to be suspended on both sides. The enemy took advantage thereof to open a casing of about 40 toises which otherwise might perhaps not have been done. This was a lesson for M. Pouchot.

12th. At day-break, a very large pile of earth was discovered within 200 toises, apparently prepared for a battery. 'Twas battered with 11 guns, which did great execution. No sap dared to be advanced outside it, as they were briskly peppered the moment they showed themselves. In the morning, Kaendaé again requested permission to go out and hold a council with the chiefs of his Nation. M. Pouchot had no objection, warning him that he would not listen to a suspension of any of his operations, as the Whites took advantage of these intervals to work. He added that, should his compatriots resolve to come and speak to him, they were to carry a small white flag, when they should not be fired on, but admitted, provided they were few in number.

At 3 o'clock in the afternoon, Kaendaé returned with an Onondaga chief, called 'The Suspended Belt', and two Cayogas, who presented M. Pouchot with a large white Belt in answer to his, saying: 'We have heard thy message; it bore truth; our side is taken; we abandon the English army, and as a proof of it, are going to camp at La Belle Famille.' They thanked him for having given him such good council and for being pleased not to entertain any spite against them. They promised to be quiet in future. Kaendaé's council with the Iroquois had been held in the presence of Johnson, to whom that chief spoke boldly, reproaching him with having plunged his Nation into bad business. Johnson smiled, and took this reproach as a joke.

By another Belt, they asked that Kaendaé, the Iroquois women and children who were in fort, should leave it with Joncaire, whom they regarded as one of their people, so that no kettle (as they called the shells) should break their heads, especially Kaendaé's, who had charge of their transactions with the Indians of the other Nations, all of whose language he spoke.

M. Pouchot answered them, that the women and Kaendaé being present, were at liberty to answer and do as they liked. Kaendaé had assured M. de Chabert that he did not wish to leave us. He made no answer. M. Pouchot performed the ceremony, in presence of the deputies, of covering his body in advance, in case any mishap should overtake him. That ceremony consisted of placing before a person a Belt and outfit, such as is laid in his grave. His death cannot be avenged, as the man is satisfied. The women and children afterwards presented some Strings to M. Pouchot, to assure him they wished to remain with us, who were their fathers, and who had always pity on them.

These deputies also presented some Strings on the part of the Loups, or Moraiguns, who were in the Iroquois council, to induce the Ottawas and other Indians to withdraw to the head of the lake, and to leave the Whites to fight, as they themselves were going away. These two messages seemed to M. Pouchot to be inspired by the English, to disgust those Nations who were attached to us. M. Pouchot answered that he did not know those Nations who sent these Strings, and returned them. He said that, as regarded the Ottaouais and other Nations who were attached to us, they needed no council how to conduct themselves towards their father; that they were at home at Niagara, and he considered it very singular that people with whom they were not connected, should desire to induce them to quit their home. These Outaouais answered the deputies that they had come to die with their father, and told the Iroquois that they were delighted to learn they were leaving the English. M. Pouchot did not wish to return the message of the Loups, which he thought did not come from them.

The same deputies proposed to return at night. M. Pouchot refused; assuring them that all he wanted was, that they should remain quiet. He notified them that at night he did not know anyone, he fired everywhere, but if they came in the day time, few in number, without any condition, that he would receive them. He sent them back each with a loaf [of bread].

To explain these negotiations, it must be observed that the English were employing the Indians at night to cover their workmen. Our fire from the covert way greatly annoyed them; they had lost ten of their men. M. Pouchot, who understood the nature of those people, was not sorry to get rid of 900 men, whose insults he feared more than those of the English, on account of their numbers and the knowledge they possessed of the place. By retaining some of the chiefs, the women and several warriors of the strange Nations, should any mishap occur to them, these same Indians would answer for it to their Nations or to those that they might have offended. They were delighted then to find this excuse for remaining neutral whilst awaiting events. The English on their side, dared not deny the Indians those conferences. They were trying only to turn them to the best advantage.

The Indians being gone, M. Pouchot immediately sent eight volunteers, under M. Conoyer's orders, who went quite close to the battery and heard some pickets planted. Otherwise the trench was pretty quiet. On their return, the artillery opened pretty briskly on the battery, and the musketry, on the right and left where they were to defile. M. Pouchot ordered the corvette to go and reconnoiter Chouegen and to try and learn news of M. de la Corne and of Montreal. This corvette cannonaded the enemy's trench pretty successfully throughout the day and sailed at night.

13th. At day light Messrs. Pouchot and Bonnafoux examined the enemy's works, who had only completed a shell battery of six mortars. It fired all day with little result. We did not fire much this day from our batteries, the enemy's works being too far advanced to be able to ruin them. At night we perceived a white flag and some Indians on the other side of the river. Kaendaé demanded *permission to go in search of them, which was not refused. They were some Indians coming to a council; they asked to pass the night in the fort. This M. Pouchot would not consent to. The fire of our batteries and that of our musketry were pretty brisk, but not so much so as during the previous nights, because there was no further necessity of imposing on the Indians who were covering the workmen. These Indians had told Kaendaé that they had all gone to La Belle Fumille and would remain [neutral]. They told him also that it was reported in the camp of the English that the latter had defeated M. de la Corne at Chouegen.*

14th. In the morning we discovered a work, of 40 [to] 50 toises in prolongation of the trench, slanting towards the lake; its extremity was within 100 toises of the covert way. They immediately set about a mortar battery from which they fired in the afternoon. Kaendaé and Chatacouen asked leave to go and speak to their people. M. Pouchot hesitated about permitting them, but the hope of obtaining some news induced him to grant them leave. They visited the Iroquois and English camps; reported having seen about 1,800 men; one of their camps was at the little swamp and another nearer the trench; they had perceived 10 mortars, two batteries and 15 guns, three of which were of large caliber. Johnson had persuaded the Indians to remain, by offering them the pillage of the place which they were to assault in two or three days; finally, they had but few provisions [but] were expecting a convoy. No more Indians were seen in the trench from this day. The Iroquois asked to go to the other side of the river, through fear of the shells, a hundred of which had been thrown during the day. M. Pouchot had them put across the river with their women, very glad to be rid of them. They had been to the Chenondac to take the M. de Chabert's cows and oxen, saying, 'Twas better they should have them than others. They carried this meat to the English camp. The enemy have been employed perfecting their works. We have kept up a very brisk fire on the place at which we supposed they wanted to commence the continuation of their trench towards the lake.

15th. At day-break they appeared working at the battery. They have thrown, throughout the whole day, a great many shells with 10 mortars. We had several wounded by splinters. In the evening a deserter came in; he was a sort of Frenchman who was with some Iroquois of Kunoagon. He reported that the English army was composed of Halket's, the Royal American, Loudon's, the York and Jersey regiments, and 900 Iroquois or Loups; that they had formed three camps, one at the Little swamp, another near the lake, one in the middle of the woods, and the Indians at La Belle Famille he said the English were to put their guns, consisting of 15 pieces, in battery next day; and added, that they were short of provisions; that the Indians were complaining of being obliged too fast; that they were expecting a convoy from Chouegen where they had a considerable camp, from which M. de la Corne was repulsed when he attempted an attack on it.

16th. Rain all day. Two barges appeared at a great distance in the lake; the 12-pounder [cannon] could scarcely reach them. They wished to reconnoiter the place. The enemy opened a fire of musketry from their trenches. They had crowned the top of their trenches with saucissons in order to cover their sharp shooters.

17th. The fog, which is pretty rare in this country, especially in summer, and rises only very late, prevented us observing that the enemy had made new works. They unmasked their artillery by a cannon shot from Montreal point at the opposite side of the river, which entered the Commandants chimney and rolled beside his bed on which he had just lain down. They had erected, at that place, a battery of two large guns and two howitzers. They unmasked, at the same time, two other batteries, one of five guns, the other of two large pieces and two howitzers. They were all served that day with great industry, and were answered in like manner. The battery on the opposite side of the river obliged the construction of epaulements and blindages, because that part of the place being covered only by an intrenchment, the shots took, in reverse, the bastions and other defenses of the fort. During the night a very brisk fire of musketry was kept up on our side, and the enemy replied as briskly up to midnight, when they ceased. They threw shell and grenades, at intervals, throughout the entire night. M. de Morambert was slightly wounded.

18th. In the morning there was no appearance of the enemy having advanced any works. They appeared busy repairing the damages caused by our batteries. A great smoke was noticed in the evening in their trench. One of our balls had set fire to one of their powder depots. General Prideaux was killed on this day, in the trench. The fire was pretty brisk on both sides, and redoubled at night, with shot, shell and grenades, which gave us great annoyance. Several soldiers were wounded, and some killed. At night, believing that the enemy was to begin on his left to form a zigzag ahead, or to open a parallel, we kept up a very active fire.

19th. The enemy were observed to have made about 30 toises of work in advance, parallel to the bank of the lake, by a double sap, whence they opened a zigzag bayou almost equal to the front between these two batteries. They merely perfected it through the day, and kept up a hot fire from cannon, mortars and howitzers. We answered them very briskly from our artillery.

In the afternoon the corvette made her appearance. She [remained] at a great distance. At sundown M. Pouchot sent off seven men in a bark canoe, which run great risk of being sunk by the volleys of cannon from the enemy, one of whose balls carried away a paddle. As the enemy was expected to advance further, a very active fire was kept up from the covert way and corresponding works.

20th. At daylight we noticed that the enemy had formed the other branch of the zigzag; that they passed from our right to the left, to the edge of the high precipice of the lake, quite near a ravine which lies 30 toises in advance of the left branch of the covert way. They kept up a very hot fire especially of their musketry, until midnight. Ours somewhat slackened towards day break, in consequence of the exhaustion of the troops and the bad condition of our arms. They perfected that trench the whole of this day and posted some sharp shooters in it, who greatly annoyed those who were tending the battery of the lake bastion, where several were killed and wounded. The canoe sent to the corvette came ashore this night. The vessel had brought dispatches from Montreal and Quebec, where they were uneasy about us, but they knew not of our being besieged. They gave intelligence of the operations of the English at Quebec. About ten o'clock in the forenoon, M. Pouchot sent back the canoe with his dispatches for Messrs. de Vaudreuil and de Montcalm.

21st. At daybreak we observed that the enemy had constructed the return of his zigzag from left to right, running towards the salient of the half moon, which they could not reach on account of the sharp fire we made throughout the entire night, to which they replied very briskly until about one o'clock in the morning. This work is about 70 toises long. It appeared this day that they wanted to erect a battery at the extremity of this bayou, towards the salient of the half moon. The enemy's fire was not as lively during this day as during the previous evening, because they were busy finishing their trenches and constructing their batteries. Their musketry nevertheless greatly annoyed our batteries.

About 7 o'clock in the evening, the enemy redoubled their fire from their last parallel. It has been very hot until past midnight. Several men were killed and wounded in the place. We answered very briskly by our fire from the works and covert-way, where three guns have been placed which fired each 50 rounds loaded with grape. A squall, which lasted but too short a time for us and would have flooded their trenches, interrupted this firing.

22nd. At day-break we supposed the enemy had extended a parallel along a ditch which was at the extremity of the glacis; but they only perfected those works and their two batteries, That on the left, of 8 guns, was more advanced than that on the right. Their fire from the trench of their right, on the lake bastion, was very heavy, and from the left, on our works, which they seriously annoyed. They fired few shell.

Towards 9 o'clock in the morning they commenced to send us red hot shot from the battery placed on the opposite side of the river. The battery where their large guns were planted did the same. Owing to M. Pouchot's precautions in keeping barrels full of water in front of the buildings, and squads of carpenters ready with axes to repair to places exposed to the flames, the fire made no ravages although it had commenced at divers places, even in the storehouses; this was by no means astonishing, all those buildings being of wood. The enemy could never understand it. They directed their fire, which was very hot, against the battery of the lake bastion in order to prevent its playing. M. Bonnafoux, the officer of artillery, was slightly wounded and ten men were killed or wounded. The cannon and howitzers dismounted three of the five guns which were on the same bastion; ruined the point of that bastion so that we could not descend on the berm. The shell ploughing into the ground and then exploding, tore away the newly laid sodding, and at each explosion made openings of 6 [to] 8 feet. At night the enemy opened from their parallel a very hot fire on our works and discharged shot and grape at the breach and the attacked bastion. 'Twill be observed that our batteries on the bastions, which were at first formed of barrels filled with earth, having been ruined, they had to be constructed of bags full of earth, which, being laid across each other, formed pretty efficient merlons, easily changed according to the direction of the fire. Unfortunately, these earth bags gave out, being soon torn, worn or burnt in the service. Wadding for the cannon also failed, as well as hay, the supply made by M. Pouchot being exhausted. The beds were stripped of their paillasses, the straw of which, at first, afterwards, the linen, was used.

In the night of the 22nd and 23rd, the enemy pushed their trench forward as far as the hauteur of the salient of the covert-way of the half moon, and kept up all night a hot fire of grape [...] shot against the breach, as well as of musketry, and threw a great many shells. He was answered from the place, but our arms were in so bad a condition, that scarcely one out of ten was serviceable, and in the following morning not a hundred were of any use, notwithstanding all the repairs daily made on them. Seven smiths or armorers were continually employed to repair them. Servants and the wounded were kept washing them; the women attended the sick and wounded, or were busy sewing cartridges or bags for earth. This day M. Pouchot was under the necessity of leaving only a small post of soldiers in the branch of the covert-way of the attacked bastion, as the Canadians did not wish to remain there any longer, on account of the briskness of the enemy's fire. Efforts were made to repair the breach and the palisades of the berm below, but with little success, notwithstanding the willingness of the soldiers to work there. At 10 o'clock in the morning, a white flag appeared on the road from La Belle Famille to the Carrying place. M. Pouchot responded by a like flag. 'Twas four Indians sent by Messrs. Aubry and de Lignery. They were brought in; they handed two letters, one dated the 17th and the other 22nd July, in the former of which, from Presqu'isle, was acknowledged the receipt of those from M. Pouchot of the 7th and 10th stating that they had immediately set out from Fort Machault; that they felt able to engage the enemy with success and to oblige them to raise the siege. In these same letters, they asked M. Pouchot's advice as to the best course to adopt to relieve him. These Indians told M. Pouchot that they had passed through the camp of the enemy's Indians, with whom they had held a council in Johnson's presence; that they had presented the Iroquois with five Belts on the part of the Nations who were accompanying M. de Lignery, requesting them to retire; otherwise, they should strike them the same as the English. The latter assured them that they would not meddle with the quarrel. By the same channel we learned that there were about 600 French and 1,000 Indians, who, when passing the little rapid at the outlet of Lake Erie, resembled a floating island, so black was the river with bateaux and canoes.

    M. Pouchot immediately answered these letters, after having deliberated with all the officers of the garrison, in order to profit by their opinions. We shall repeat here that M. Pouchot had in his letter of the 10th, notified M. de Lignery that the enemy may be 4 [to] 5 thousand, exclusive of Indians; that if he did not feel able to attack them, he ought to pass by the Chenondac in order to arrive at Niagara by the other side of the river, because he would be able to drive off the English who were on that side to the number of only 2,000, and could only with great difficulty be reinforced. He would come from there safely to him, because after defeating that force, bateaux would be sent to bring them to the fort.

M. Pouchot doubted not that the English would read his answer on the return of the Indians; but he was satisfied if it could only reach its destination. He requested M. de Lignery to call to mind what he had already written him; told him that the enemy were in three divisions; one at the Little swamp guarding their bateaux, another about the center of the wood near their trench depot, and the third convenient to La Belle Famille; that there may be at present about 3,900 Indians; that if they felt themselves strong enough to attack any of these divisions, this was at present the best course to pursue, because the enemy, being very near the place, dare not strip its trench. He added, that if they succeeded in defeating one of those posts, 'twas presumable the siege would be raised; that they ought to have scouts ahead, whose reports would enable them to decide on the best course to adopt.

M. Pouchot made four copies of this letter and handed one of them to each of the Indians; one of whom was an Onondaga, the second a Delaware, and the third a Chaouanon, so as to avoid jealousy, and in case the English should retain any to save one, which turned out to be the case.

After having refreshed themselves, those Indians departed with the same ceremony. About two o'clock in the afternoon the Onondaga came back stating that he had lost his wampum, which is tantamount to a European losing his jewels; that he had returned in quest of it, and had entrusted his letter to another Indian. M. Pouchot, thereupon, considered this Indian rather as a spy than a friend, and accordingly distrusted him. The result showed that he was mistaken.

The enemy kept up, the whole day, a tremendous fire, during which their artillery was served in the best style, utterly demolishing *the battery on the flag bastion; only two feet of the upper part of the entire length of its parapet remaining. 'Twill be remarked that the evening previous, we had been obliged to construct our embrasures with bundles of peltry for want of other material, and to use blankets and shirts from the stores for wadding for the cannon. Efforts were made to place two guns in battery on the left side of the curtain, in order to diminish the enemy's fire.*

The Canadians could no longer be persuaded to continue firing into the enemy's embrasures, which would have greatly deranged them. The fire was too hot. Those who were stationed in any quarter, sat down for protection, and went immediately to sleep, notwithstanding all that the officers and sergeants could do to prevail on them to stand to their posts and work. The rest of the garrison, in spite of all possible willingness, was not less harassed. Nobody had been in bed since the 6th, being obliged to be either in the works or employed at indispensable operations. So few people were remaining, that there was neither time or convenience for sleeping.

At night the enemy's fire slackened considerably, especially that of the artillery; they fired only two pieces loaded with ball and grape at the breach, to prevent its being repaired. This diminution was owing, M. Pouchot suspected, either to their desire to raise the siege in order to go and meet a reinforcement, or to arrangements for some serious attack. The greatest possible precaution was taken. We had a great many wounded this night and some killed in our works, which 'twas desirable to repair.

24th. We heard some firing in the direction of La Belle Famille. 'Twas some of M. de Lignery's Indian scouts, who fell in with an English guard that was placed over 22 bateaux which they carried overland to cross the river in, and to communicate with the detachment at the Montreal point. A dozen of them were killed and their heads cut off and stuck on the top of some pickets. This event drew down others. It induced the Indians to ask Messrs. Aubry and de Lignery to wait until the Iroquois had been requested to oblige us to make peace with the English. M. de Lignery dissuaded them from it and wished them to follow him, being on the point of attacking. They refused to do so; some thirty only of the most determined accompanied M. Marin.

M. Pouchot hearing an extraordinary fire of musketry, repaired immediately with M. Bonnafoux to the Five Nations' bastion. He perceived some English who were flying pretty precipitately to their main guards, some troops who were defiling from the center camp to the border of the clearance, to join them at the entrance of the ground at La Belle Famille, where we saw somewhat in reverse an intrenchment of trees. Two guns were directed against it which were discharged two or three times. At this time M. Pouchot noticed some Indians here and there with a white flag. He supposed at first that it might be a piece of bravado on the part of some Iroquois, or a ruse to draw out a sortie. He ordered two guns to be fired between the English and them, to disperse them, or if they were friends, to signify to them that some enemies were yonder, and to prevent them advancing, because seeing them so few, he feared they would fall into an ambuscade. He warned M. Bonnafoux of it. It produced no other effect than the display of a large white flag. A troop was seen at the same time defiling into a path 7 [to] 8 feet wide, with great confidence in very close column in front. It appeared that on perceiving the enemy, very close to which it found itself, that the troop endeavored to place itself in close order of battle without ranks or files. On its right appeared some thirty Indians, fronting the enemy's left flank. This battalion commenced firing one or two volleys when approaching the latter, who appeared making a forward movement beyond their abatis; but having been received with a third volley, retreated pretty precipitately. The battalion then moved forward to enter the abatis, but were checked by a volley from the enemy when it knelt to fire into the intrenchment. In this interval, a considerable quantity of rain fell, which wet their arms. Whilst one half this battalion was firing, the other half appeared retreating somewhat precipitately; the enemy having fired two volleys at those who stood. Very few remained. Some fifty appeared to be firing whilst retreating often kneeling on the ground. Thereupon the English issued from their intrenchment, almost in files, charging with fixed bayonets; but from the little musketry we heard, we judged that the entire battalion had retire. 'Twas in our eyes so trifling, that we concluded in the rain, it might be M. Marin or some other officer, who had come to reconnoiter the enemy and had pushed them to that place.

Whilst this affair was passing, a sergeant who was in the covert-way, judging from the silence in the trench, that it was abandoned, asked of M. Pouchot permission to make a sortie. Although of opinion that the trench was, on the contrary, well reinforced, he (in order to foster emulation among the soldiers and to gratify them), called out 150 volunteers, which was all they mustered, except the officers and sergeants, and ordered M. de Villars to place himself at their head, recommending him to leave the covert-way only with the greatest precaution, and when he should give the signal, but to make a great deal of noise. He enjoined on him to place people on the palisades, as this would not fail to draw the enemy out and enable us to judge of their situation. In fact, the moment the English saw people astride of the palisades, the entire trench seemed immediately to swarm with men stripped to the waist and with companies of grenadiers at the head of the trenches. Some cannon balls were sent at them, which made them get under cover, and our sortie did not take place.

On the arrival of the reinforcement, the Onondaga who had returned, having recognized M. de Lignery's troops, requested M. Pouchot's permission to go out and fight with them, which was granted. He passed freely through the enemy's army, which doubtless paid no attention to him, and joined our troops about noon. He returned towards two o'clock, and recounted the whole of our disaster, which he could scarcely credit, imagining that the English had put the thing in his head. He told us that all had taken to flight; that Messrs. Aubry, de Lignery, de Montigny, and de Repentigny were prisoners, and wounded, and that all the other officers and soldiers had been killed. We hoped this man was not telling the truth.

When M. Pouchot perceived this retreat, he ordered all the batteries that were still effective, to redouble their fire, so as to keep the enemy in check; they returned it to us with great spirit, which again caused the loss of many of our men. At four o'clock in the afternoon, the enemy beat the rappel in his trench, from which an officer came out to parley, who was brought into the fort. He brought a letter from Johnson, who was in command of the army since Prideaux's death.

Johnson said, in his letter, that confidence may be placed in whatever Major Hervey, Lord Bristol's son, might state in his name. The latter gave the names of all the Canadian officers who were taken prisoners. Although M. Pouchot was advised, beforehand, by the Indian, in order to protect himself against any reproach, he pretended ignorance and incredulity, until those officers should be shown to some one of the garrison. Captain de Cervies, of the Royal Rousillon, went to the camp; he saw M. de Lignery wounded, and the others in an arbor, near Colonel Johnson's tent. He could scarcely speak to them, and came to report to M. Pouchot.

This news, which had at first been [relayed] by the Indian, and now confirmed by this officer, had so depressed the courage of the garrison, that M. Pouchot and the other officers had all the trouble in the world to restrain the soldiers and Militia in their posts which they were abandoning on every side, as if all was over. If the enemy could see this disorder, he might assuredly have taken advantage of it. The German recruits, of whom we had a great many in the Colonial troops, and who had arrived this year in Canada, were the most mutinous.

M. Pouchot assembled all the officers of the garrison to deliberate on the situation of the fort, and to adopt the most proper course. He left M. Bonnafoux to describe its condition as the most capable judge thereof. He began at the covert-way, and 'twas agreed that the enemy, considering their proximity, could not fail to be masters of it within two days, either by sap [tunneling] or assault. We had only 110 men to guard the covert-way from the bank in front of the lake bastion to the salient angle of the half moon, and 25 men in the place d'armes of the right, who were guarding as far as the salient of the covert-way of the Five Nations' bastion. There was an interval of more than 8 [to] 10 feet between the men who lined the front attacked. The arms were in so bad a state, that there were not more than 140 muskets fit for service; most of them were without bayonets. The Colonials and Canadians, having none, wood-cutters' knives had been fixed to the end of a stick to serve instead, and these they carried with them to their posts. Of 54 thousand weight of powder, which had been in store, 24 had been consumed. Only very few 4 and 6-pound balls remained; those of 12 were all gone. There was no hope, therefore, of a vigorous defense. The ditches were without any scarp; the earth having crumbled down, the slopes got to be so gentle that a person could run up and down them. To avoid this inconvenience, a palisade had, indeed, been set up at the bottom of the ditch, but the enemy being liberty to descend there everywhere, could kill the entire garrison between the palisade and the covert-way, because by getting mixed up with it, the flanking guns could not protect the men. Besides, there remained, at this time, no more than sixty men in the place, exclusive of gunners. The palisades opposite the breach were all broken, and it was very easy to go down into the breach which occupied two-thirds of the face of the bastion in the ditch. We had hors de service [injured] or lost, 10 men of La Sarre, 9 of Béarn, 8 of Royal Rousillon, 13 of Guienne, 43 of the Colonials, 26 Militia, in all 109 men, killed or wounded, and 37 sick. Independent of these losses, our small force and the superiority of the enemy, the place could be very easily insulted from the river and the high banks of the lake.

    All these considerations induced the officers of the garrison to request M. Pouchot to consent to a capitulation. Up to that time he had not said anything. He requested those gentlemen to examine well whether any resource remained. They represented to him the exhaustion of the garrison, which had not lain down for 19 days, and had been continually under arms or at the works; that the delay of one day, and of even eight days, were that possible, could not save the place and would result only in the useless loss of still more brave fellows, the rather as no help was to be expected from any quarter.

M. Pouchot, sensible of the truth of these reflections, called in the English officer and demanded a capitulation, on condition that the garrison should march out with the honors of war, and be conveyed to Montreal with its property and that of the King, at his Britannic Majesty's expense, in the shortest possible space of time. Negotiations continued the entire night, as M. Pouchot was not willing to recede from his propositions. Colonel Johnson sent him word frankly, that he was not master of those conditions, otherwise he would grant them. At daybreak, M. Pouchot wished to send back the officer, on the ground that being about to be a prisoner, he would risk the event. Thereupon the entire garrison demanded to capitulate. The Germans, who constituted the majority, mutinied, which the English officer unfortunately observed, and therefore became more firm. M. Pouchot was then obliged to be satisfied with the following Articles [of capitulation or surrender]:

Article I.

The garrison shall march out with their arms and baggage, drums beating, and match lighted at both ends, and a small piece of cannon, to embark upon such vessels as the commanders of his Britannic Majesty's forces shall furnish, to convey them to New-York by the shortest route and in the shortest time.

Article II.

The garrison shall lay down their arms when they embark, but shall keep their baggage.

Article III.

The officers shall keep both their arms and their baggage.

Article IV.

The French ladies, with their children, and other women, as well as the chaplain, shall be sent to Montreal, and the commander of his Britannic Majesty's troops shall furnish them with vessels and subsistence necessary for their voyage to the first French post, and this is to be executed as soon as possible; those women who choose to follow their husbands are at liberty to do it. Granted, except with regard to those women who are his Britannic Majesty's subjects.

Article V.

The sick and wounded, who are obliged to remain in the fort, shall have liberty to depart, with everything that belongs to them, and shall be conducted in safety, as soon as they are able to support the fatigues of a voyage, to the place destined for the rest of the garrison; in the meantime, they are to be allowed a guard for their security against Indians, and shall be attended and fed at his Britannic Majesty's expense.

Article VI.

The Commanding officer, all the other officers and private men who are in the service of his Most Christian Majesty, shall quit the fort without being subject to any act of reprisals whatsoever.

Article VII.

An inventory shall be made of all the military stores in the magazine, which, with the artillery, shall be delivered up, bona fide, as well as all other effects, which are the property of his Most Christian Majesty, and which are found in the magazine at the time of the capitulation. The vessels and boats are included in this article.

Article VIII.

The soldiers shall not be plundered nor separated from their officers.

Article IX.

The garrison shall be conducted under a proper escort to the place destined for their reception; the General shall expressly recommend to this escort to hinder the Indians from insulting any persons belonging to the garrison, and shall prevent their being pillaged by them when they quit their arms for embarkation; and the same care is to be taken on every part of the route where Indians may be met with.

Article X.

An exact list shall be made of the names and surnames of the soldiers belonging to the different troops, as well Regulars as Militia, and all others who are employed in his Most Christian Majesty's service; and all those who are so employed, in whatever capacity, shall retain their baggage, and shall be treated in the same manner as the rest of the garrison.

Article XI.

All the Indians, of whatsoever Nation they may be, who are found in the garrison, shall be protected from insult, and be allowed to go where they please. Granted; but it will be advisable for them to depart as privately as possible.

The articles being accepted, the General of his Britannic Majesty's forces shall be put in possession of a gate of the fort, but this cannot be done until to-morrow. To-morrow at seven o'clock in the morning.

[Signed] Pouchot, Captain in the regiment of Bearn, Commanding officer.

Vilar, Captain in the regiment of La Sarre.
Servier, Captain in the regiment of Royal Rouissillon.
Oliver de la Roche Verney, Captain of the Marine.
Bounnaffous, officer in the Royal Artillery.
Cournoyer, Lieutenant of the Marine.
Soluignac, officer in the regiment of Bearn.
Le Chevalier de L'Arminac, Lieutenant of the Marine.
Joncaire, Captain of the Marine.
Morambert, Lieutenant.
Chabert Joncaire, in the regiment of Guienne.

Pouchot, Captain in the regiment of Bearn.
W.M. Johnson."

Meanwhile, by September, both the Marquis de Montcalm's and General Wolfe's armies in and around Quebec were exhausted, but with winter fast approaching, Wolfe was cautioned by the Admiral of the English fleet, which had brought him and his army thence, that their window of opportunity was fast closing, and that if he did not act soon and attempt to take Quebec, the fleet would have to withdraw, and hope that circumstances permit them to return early in the spring, lest they become trapped in the freezing Saint Lawrence River, which could spell disaster. This fact pressed Wolfe to propose a bold and daring venture, similar to the one which he had enacted at the Siege of Louisbourg the previous year, and the one which he had attempted under the Montmorency Falls during the summer, which was to have his men circumvent the more formidable French, Canadian and Indigenous intrenchments altogether, by scaling a much less defended cliff face beyond Quebec, up the Saint Lawrence, which his army then could descend, cross the Abraham Plains which surround the city, and assault it.

After careful preparation, on the night of September 12th, while diversionary English efforts distracted the French and their allies, Wolfe, with a large body of men loaded into boats, and under the cover of darkness paddled their way to shore beneath the Heights of Abraham's rock face, and gradually leapt ashore. Their climb was a perilous one, steep, and undertaken in relative darkness, however, as Wolfe had hoped, in relative silence, so that the sleeping French guard stationed above the Heights were taken by complete surprise and easily overwhelmed. By daybreak, Wolfe had approximately thirty-five hundred of his army's most experienced men formed up between the Heights of Abraham, and the Plains of Abraham, scarcely a mile from the walls of Quebec.

As Wolfe had hoped, the Marquis de Montcalm's attention had been so focused on the distractions of the English fleet throughout the night, so that when he finally realized Wolfe and his men were forming up on the Plains of Abraham in the wee hours of morning on the 13th of September, he was left scrambling to consolidate his own forces, which ultimately amounted to approximately forty-five hundred men, which, although outnumbering Wolfe's army, largely did not consist of the hardened veterans of the latter's.

For approximately an hour, the two opposing armies, separated by slight rise in the plains between them, cannonaded each other with small field pieces, before at approximately ten o'clock in the morning, and without awaiting the arrival of overwhelming reinforcements under the command of Captain Bougainville and the Governor-General of New France, the Marquis de Vaudreuil, Montcalm ordered his men to attack, convinced that if he didn't strike immediately, the English would intrench themselves and/or be reinforced themselves.

While warriors under Charles Langlade ranged themselves to the right of Wolfe's army, behind what foliage, rocks, and other natural forms of cover could be attained and leveled a continuous cover fire upon the English, Montcalm's army advanced, head-on, with their commander leading the charge. Consisting primarily of Canadians, on their advance into the face of the English, Montcalm's army unleashed a volley of musketry into their ranks, which was promptly returned by the English, who then, while the Canadians attempted to reload, charged them with bayonets, which put much of Montcalm's dis-organized army to flight. However, while many accustomed to Indigenous-style guerilla warfare rallied themselves and others to continue skirmishing alongside Langlade and his warriors from under or around cover, there was no disguising that English had the French and the most of their allies on the run, and so Wolfe promptly ordered a pursuit. But as he personally led his men forward, he himself was subjected to the concealed sharpshooting of the Indigenous warriors and Canadians under Langlade, among others, who continued to pick off his men as they advanced.

Langlade's longtime acquaintance and ally, Amable de Gere, would later recall to the former's grandson, Augustin Grignon how, "*He never saw so perfectly cool and fearless a man on the field off battle as my grandfather; and that either here [at Quebec], at the Monongahela, or at Ticonderoga, I have forgotten which, he saw my grandfather, when his gun barrel had got so hot, from repeated and rapid discharges, that he took occasion to stop a little while that it might cool, when he would draw his pipe from his pouch, cut his tobacco, fill his pipe, take a piece of punk-wood, and strike fire with his steel and flint, and light and smoke his pipe, and all with as much sang froid [calmness] as at his own fireside; and having cooled his gun and refreshed himself, would resume his place, and play well his part in the battle.*"

As Wolfe advanced at the head of his men in pursuit of the fleeing French, a musket ball shattered his wrist, but wrapping it in a handkerchief, he pressed on. However, a subsequent shot to the chest dropped him with a mortal wound, from which he would die mere moments later, but so shattered were the French, that even Wolfe's death could not save the battle, for Montcalm, in his retreat from the battlefield, had himself been hit by a musket ball. Conveyed into Quebec, he died early the next day, and was buried in a shell crater under the Ursuline Church, while the remnants of his shattered army regrouped with those under Captain Bougainville, the Governor-General of New France, the Marquis de Vaudreuil, the Chevalier de Lévis and Charles Langlade, in the neighboring Quebec region of Jacques Cartier.

Lieutenant Jean-Baptiste Nicolas Roch de Ramezay (1708 – 1777) had had been left in Quebec's command, however there was little he could do. The city had already been subjected to a prolonged bombardment, and by virtue of the city's positioning along the Saint Lawrence River, it was easily assailable from multiple angles. Ramezey put the fate of the city to popular vote amongst his most senior officers, who overwhelming concluding that resistance was hopeless, and that to avoid the city be carried by bloody English assault, they would instead offer to surrender it — His resolve to do so enforced by the demands of Quebec's every-day citizens, who feared needless violence and looting.

However, Charles Langlade, Captain Bougainville and the Governor-General of New France himself, the Marquis de Vaudreuil, were among those who were openly displeased with Ramezey's decision to capitulate with the English after less than a week, as opposed to holding out, as it had been their intention of immediately regrouping their forces for a counter attack to relieve the city, but with the English promptly occupying it after its capitulation on September 18th, and the campaigning season nearing its inevitable conclusion as winter fast approached, it was ultimately decided that any major counter-offensives would have to wait until the coming spring, of the year 1760. However, the winter was occupied in great preparation and mourning by all parties. All told, the English suffered approximately six hundred and fifty casualties over the course of the siege, mostly injured, while the French suffered approximately seven hundred casualties, with a slightly higher killed/wounded ratio. Among the dead were the two of Charles Langlade's own, unnamed brothers or brothers-in-law, who had decided to join his ranks in the defense of Quebec and had given their lives for it. For his own distinguished services, Langlade was personally honored with a Lieutenant's commission signed by King Louis XV, which was subsequently delivered upon a British blockade-running vessel from France:

"By the King:

His Majesty having made choice of Sieur Langlade to serve in the capacity of half-pay lieutenant in connection with the troops stationed in Canada, he commands the Lieutenant General of New France to receive him, and to cause him to be recognized in the said capacity of half-pay lieutenant by all those and others whom it may concern.

Done at Versailles, February 1st, 1760.

Louis."

Cody Cole

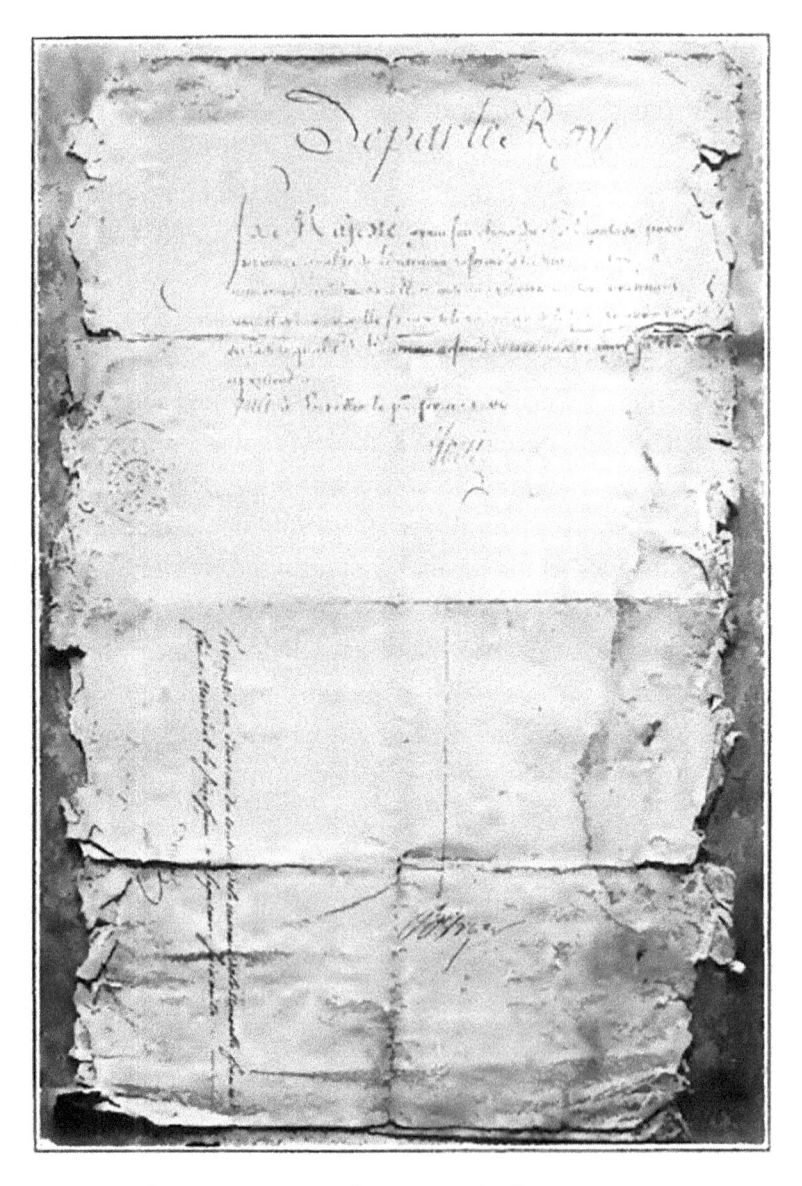

LIEUTENANT DE LANGLADE'S COMMISSION
Signed by King Louis XV at Versailles, given for service in defense of Quebec.
Now in possession of Wisconsin Historical Society.

Black & white, circa. 1900 photograph of Charles Langlade's 1760 lieutenant's commission. From page 166 of "Captain Charles de Langlade: The Bravest of the Brave" (1904), by Publius Lawson.

Auke-wingeke-tawso, or, 'Defender of His Country'

The pommel of the sword (Neville Public Museum, Green Bay, Wisconsin. Photo ID#: L817A) presented to Charles Langlade for his distinguished services rendered to the French cause, leading up to the 1760 campaigning season, by King Louis XV. High quality modern-day photograph courtesy of the Neville Public Museum of Brown County, Green Bay, Wisconsin, who retain the copyright of the photo and possess the weapon. (Image cropped slightly from the left by the compiler/editor.)

Langlade was additionally bestowed an exquisitely crafted sword with his new commission, for services rendered to the French cause thus far, and to ensure his return in the coming campaign, the circumstances of which were the direst of the war and were indeed compelling many of New France's long-standing Indigenous allies to finally abandon the ailing empire.

A highly detailed French-translated account of 1759's military operations in North America, including the siege of Quebec, titled **"Operations of the Army under M. de Montcalm before Quebec. Extract of a Journal Kept at the Army Commanded by the Late Lieutenant General de Montcalm"**, penned over the course the campaigning season and updated with additional observations afterwards by a well-informed and evidently high-raking but unidentified eyewitness, is as follows:

"Canada expected, since the fall of Louisbourg, to be attacked this year simultaneously on all sides. Quebec, the only barrier of this Colony on the river side, being, from the nature of its fortifications, incapable of sustaining a siege, attention was directed, since the beginning of the winter, to putting it at least beyond the danger of a coup de main. The Minister's orders, which came by the first vessels announcing the enemy's designs against this place, urged M. de Vaudreuil to omit nothing to put it in a state of defense. Nevertheless, the work still languished, but the arrival in the river of a fleet of 13 sail, the intelligence of which was received on the 23rd of May, roused men from their languor. M. de Montcalm was already at Quebec, whither M. de Vaudreuil went in a few days after. Several councils were held, at which the defect of the fortifications of the place appeared a new not to admit of the slightest hope of being able to hold out. It was merely resolved:

To close the town either by walls or palisades on the side of the river, where 'twas absolutely open.

To increase the batteries of the Lower town, the communications between which and the Upper, would be intersected and defended by artillery, and to furnish the ramparts with cannon both on the land and river sides.

o form new batteries at the Palace ship yard, for the purpose both of defending the mouth of the River St. Charles and flanking the quarter commonly called the Canoterie.

To line the right bank of that river with intrenchments from its mouth to the General Hospital; to sink two ships in it on which batteries would be erected; finally, to throw an estrade there in order to prevent any surprisal the enemy might attempt in that direction, with a view to occupying the heights commanding the town.

To line the crested bank from the River St. Charles to the Falls of Montmorency with intrenchments, at certain distances whereof should be erected redoubts and redans furnished with batteries, the fire of which might cross each other at different points; and also to take some precautions at L'ance des Mers and Sillery, although that quarter was deemed inaccessible.

To construct a pontoon of a hexagon figure, capable of bearing 12 guns of large caliber, and 6 gunboats, each carrying a 24-pounder; to place four 8-pounders on a gabarre, and arrange 8 flat bateaux so as to receive each a gun of the same caliber: all these vessels were intended as a defense during the night, both to the approaches of the town and the intrenchments, and were themselves to send bark canoes ahead, which patrolling throughout the night would be able to give notice of the slightest movement on the part of the enemy.

Such was the plan I proposed in the Memoir the late Marquis de Montcalm demanded of me on the operations relative to the Marine. It was not followed at first, but was fallen back on towards the middle of the campaign.

To convert eight vessels into fire ships and construct 120 rafts loaded with combustible matter, to be let loose on the enemy's fleet when within reach.

[Italicized sections in this document represent added information and commentary, perhaps by the journal's original author.] These rafts were launched towards the end of July. The current was mistaken and they produced no effect.

Finally, to send the remainder of our ships as far as Three Rivers and even Montreal, and to store there the greatest part of our provisions, one month's supply of which only should be kept in the place for the army.

M. de Montcalm wished, in the beginning, that only fifteen days' supply should be retained; as he did not dare flatter himself with being able to stay the first effort of the enemy, he spoke of abandoning that place at the very moment he was making the fate of all Canada dependent on it, as may be seen by Article 6 of the capitulation, the draft of which he then furnished.

The army consisted of 5 battalions of land troops, (about 1,600 men); about 600 Colonials, 10,400 Canadians and sailors distributed throughout the batteries, 918 Indians of different nations, and a troop of cavalry composed of 200 volunteers taken from the different corps and to be posted promptly wherever the enemy should show themselves, to be attached to the General's suite and to convey orders: in all 13,718 fighting men.

The formation of this corps gave rise, in the beginning, to a great many jokes; M. de Montcalm did not originate it. It has since been universally admitted that vast service was derived from it.

So strong an army was not anticipated, because it was not expected that there would be so large a number of Canadians; the intention was to muster only the men capable of sustaining the fatigues of the war; but such an emulation prevailed among that people, that old men of 80, and children of 12 [to] 13 were seen coming to the camp, who would never consent to take advantage of the exemption granted to their age. Never were subjects more deserving the bounty of their Sovereign; on account either of their constancy at labor, or their patience under the difficulties and wretchedness which, in that country, have been extreme; in the army they were subject to all the corvées.

M. de Montcalm wished to have the Militia incorporated into the battalions, and M. de Vaudreuil consented. All were then subjected to regular service.

No means imaginable were omitted to procure the greatest promptness in the execution of the different arrangements.

Meanwhile the enemy's fleet, favored by a Northeast wind, which has constantly prevailed whilst they needed it, was advancing and becoming daily more numerous in the river.

The vanguard, (13 sail, big and little), found itself at anchor in the beginning of June, under the Isle aux Coudres; the English did not land there however until 3 days after; at first they feared to encounter ambushes there, but finally finding it had been absolutely abandoned, they scattered themselves over the island without any precaution, which the inhabitants of St. Paul's bay remarking from the tops of their mountains, sent word accordingly, and thereupon 'twas resolved to dispatch M. de Niverville, a Colonial officer, thither with detachment of Canadians and Indians, to endeavor to take some prisoners. He proceeded thither, but the sight of the English frightened the Indians who refused to attack, and the expedition had to be abandoned. Among the Canadians was a young man named Desrivières, who, indignant at the cowardice of his companions, declared to them that, not wishing to participate in the disgrace of having abandoned, without cause, a project the execution of which was so easy, he was going to undertake it single handed; thereupon some farmers belonging to the island, who were in the same detachment, offered to accompany him; they set off, to the number of 10, and soon returned with three young midshipmen whom they had captured.

We learned from these young men nothing more than we already knew of the projects England was forming against Canada; they told us nothing respecting either their strength or operations that has not been since verified; they told us that the fleet was bringing 30 thousand men, including troops and seamen, and that was exact, but it appeared to us by their deposition, that Admiral Durel, who commanded that first division, was uneasy for the remainder of the fleet; they added, that at the moment they were taken, more than 600 persons were on the beach unarmed, whom the smallest detachment could have destroyed; that they had remained three days on board, without daring to land, and had not concluded on sending their canoes ashore until by their observations they *were fully convinced that no person remained on the Island; that as for the rest, the Admiral had given the strictest orders to leave everything in the state it may be found, and threatened with the severest punishment those who should commit any disorder.*

June 8th. Eight ships came up as far as Cape Torment, sent to sound the Traverse of the Island of Orleans, where all the marks laid down to designate the channel had been destroyed; experiencing no opposition in their operations, they were on the 14th able to come to an anchor in front of St. Francis, whither they immediately dispatched two boats; they expected to find that place also abandoned, but were mistaken; we had a pretty considerable party of Canadians and Indians, but the impatience of the latter on seeing the English (which is ordinarily the case) did not permit us to derive all the advantage we might gain and expect from the confidence with which those barges made their appearance at the landing. M. de Courtemanche, a Colonial officer, who commanded the corps, had given orders to his troop to allow the English to land and even not to oppose their embarkation, hoping to induce them thereby to return the next day in still greater numbers and still greater security; this ruse might succeed, but the Indians having yelled even before the boats had touched the beach, the latter shoved back after having been exposed to some musket shots, which wounded nobody.

16th. M. Lemercier, Commandant of the artillery, obtained an order from M. de Vaudreuil to have 4 guns conveyed to the Island of Orleans, with which he fired some volleys at the vessels. The latter replied, and that artillery was brought back to town. This will not be the only occasion, 'twill be perceived, where time has been lost.

Some English barges which had advanced to reconnoiter one of the coves of that island, having been discovered by some Indians, were sharply pursued, and one of them overtaken and carried off; 8 men were found on board; these prisoners confirmed what the 3 midshipmen had stated, and added only that the ships were to rendezvous before the town.

The only service rendered by the artillery, which had been conveyed to the Island of Orleans, was to check those barges, whose object was to cut out a schooner armed as a fire-ship, which had been sent thither.

26th. At night the greater part of the feet was anchored at the Island of Orleans.

27th. One ship and two frigates advanced this morning to reconnoiter the town. Mr. Wolf was on board, and we have since learned that as soon as he had taken an exact reconnaissance of the town and our intrenchments, which had been already completed, he did not conceal from some of his principal officers of the army who accompanied him, that he did not flatter himself with success. These three vessels retired in the afternoon, and that same night, in spite of a N. E. wind that was blowing pretty stiff, Mr. Wolf caused a landing to be effected near St. Laurent, where he encountered no resistance. M. Courtemanche's detachment then consisted of 800 men, Canadians and Indians; he was ordered to rejoin the army. Some days before, all the families and cattle belonging to the farmers were removed from the island.

The entire feet having finally come together, 'twas thought proper to bring the fire-ships into operation before the enemy should be masters of both banks of the river, as it was not intended to contest the ground at Point Levy with them; orders were accordingly issued to prepare for starting, and at nightfall, they set sail with a light breeze from the S. W. to the number of 7 only; the 8th had been burnt in the harbor through the imprudence of the men who were preparing it, and the vessel which was to take its place was not yet ready. But two causes militated against the success of this expedition; these fire-ships were not chained two by two, as had been agreed on, and the pilots had the cowardice to set fire to, and abandon them more than a league and a half from the fleet; how indignant soever those in the army were at the conduct of the commanders of those fire-ships, yet, M. de Vaudreuil was unwilling to say anything disagreeable to them, and employed them that very moment at different batteries. This experiment cost the

King about a million, and the life of Sieur Dubois de la Miltière, a young man of promise, who commanded one of these fire-ships; his mate met the same fate.

The Memoir I communicated to the Marquis de Montcalm contained also my opinion on the employment of fire-ships; after discussing the advantage that might be derived from them, I explained, according to the knowledge I may have obtained of the craft and what I have often heard intelligent seamen say, both the precautions to be taken in the preparation of those vessels and the conduct to be observed, to enable them to accomplish the object proposed. I had, above all, insisted on the necessity of chaining them 2 to 2, and I believe that all intelligent seamen will agree that it was hardly possible to derive advantage from them in a stream, the rapidity of which is known to the whole world. My Memoir was read at the Council.

29th. At night the English landed at Beaumont point, on the south shore. M. de Lery, a Colonial officer, who was reconnoitering there with a detachment, thought he should be surprised: He had merely time to escape, after having lost some of his men.

30th. In the morning the enemy following the bank of the river made their appearance at Point Levy to the number of 3 thousand men: A detachment of Indians whom we had sent to that quarter kept up a fire on them the whole night, under cover of the woods; killed two of their men and took one prisoner, according to whose deposition we were to be attacked the next night. That disconcerted the plan which had been formed, to convey a large body of troops across the river to drive the enemy from that quarter before securing a position there, and reduced us to adopt all possible precautions to give them a warm reception on landing.

1st July. It happened at the break of day, by some misunderstanding, the origin of which could not be discovered, that the Militia of the right fired, without any cause, a general discharge of musketry; we thought ourselves attacked in that quarter; the whole army flew to arms and rushed thither.

Nothing else of interest occurred throughout that day; our Indians and some Canadians exchanged shots at Point Levy with the enemy's light infantry, and brought us at night a proclamation of Mr. Wolf, which they had found posted on a church door:

'General Wolf's Proclamations to the Canadians:

By his Excellency, James Wolfe, Esq., Colonel of a Regiment of Infantry, Major General and Commander-in-Chief of his Britannic Majesty's Forces in the River St. Lawrence, &c., &c.

The King, my master, justly irritated against France and resolved to lower her insolence and to revenge the insults offered to the English Colonies, has at length determined to send to Canada the formidable sea and land armament, which the people of Canada now behold in the heart of their country. Its object is totally to deprive the French Crown of its most valuable settlement in North America. For these purposes, he has been pleased to send me here, at the head of the formidable army under my command. The King of Great Britain wages no war against industrious Colonists and peasants, nor against women and children, nor the sacred ministers of religion; he foresees their distressful circumstances, pities their lot and extends to them offers of protection. The people may return with their families to their lands; I promise them my protection; I assure them that they can, without fearing the least molestation, there enjoy their property, attend to their religious worship; in a word, enjoy, in the midst of war, all the sweets of peace, provided they will take no part directly or indirectly in the contest between the two Crowns. But if, on the contrary, a vain obstinacy and misguided valor lead them to appear in arms, they must expect to suffer all the cruelty that war inflicts. Therefore, 'tis for them to imagine to what excesses the fury of an exasperated soldiery can lead; my orders alone can stay their course. 'Tis for the Canadians, by their conduct, to procure for themselves this advantage. They cannot be ignorant of their present situation. A formidable fleet stops the passage of any succors they might expect from Europe; a *numerous army presses on them on the side of the Continent; the choice they have to take does not appear doubtful; what can they expect from a vain and blind opposition? Let themselves judge.*

The unparalleled barbarities perpetrated by the French against our settlements in America, might justify the severest reprisals. But Britons disdain this barbarous method; their religion preaches humanity, and their hearts follow with pleasure its precepts. Should the Canadians be led, by the foolish hope of a successful resistance, to refuse the neutrality I propose to them, and presumptuously appear with arms in their hands, they will only have themselves to blame, when they will groan under the weight of misery to which they will be exposed by this, their own choice. 'Twill be too late to regret the useless efforts of their indiscreet valor, when they behold all they hold most dear, perishing of hunger in the winter. As for me, I shall have nothing to reproach myself with. The laws of war are known; the obstinacy of an enemy justifies the means used to bring him to reason.

The people of Canada may choose: they behold, on the one hand, Britain stretching out to them a powerful and protecting hand; her fidelity to her engagements is known; she is ready to maintain the inhabitants in their rights and possessions: France on the other hand, unable to support these people, deserts their cause at this important crisis, and if during the war she has sent them troops, what have they been good for? only to make the people feel more bitterly the weight of a hand which oppresses, instead of protecting them.

Let the Canadians consult their prudence; their fate depends on their choice.

Jam. Wolf.

Given at our Head Quarters, in the Parish of St. Laurence, on the Island of Orleans, 27th June, 1759.'

The object this General proposed thereby is very palpable; his character is also perfectly perceptible therein. As for the rest, there were at Point Levy only about 3,500 men, who pitched their camp at the foot of the church. The rest of the army was on the Island of Orleans.

2nd [July]. The enemy reconnoitered the entire extent of the right of the river, which faces the town, and employed the following days in tracing the different works they wished to erect there. As for us, always apprehending an attack on our intrenchments, we kept within the bounds of a most strict defensive. Murmurs meanwhile were heard in the army at this inactivity. 'Twas remarked, that it was so much the more easy to annoy the enemy in his works, that supposing even an attack should be repelled, a secure retreat was always to be found in the woods in the rear, where the Canadian and Indian, 'tis known, possess so great an advantage over the Regulars. To this reasoning, it was answered, that being scarcely able to flatter ourselves that we should be strong enough with all our forces (the army was then assembled) to prevent the English landing at Beauport, it would be imprudent, by weakening that quarter, to expose ourselves to open a passage there to the enemy, to whom we should find ourselves, that very instant, obliged to abandon Quebec. The intelligent reader will weigh the pro and con, but certain it is, that the enemy never intended attacking us in front at our camp at Beauport. We have had the misfortune not to be able to perceive the advantage of the position we had taken there; it did not escape Mr. Wolf, who knew how to appreciate the effect which ought to result from the fire of our different batteries, and that of our musketry composed of Canadians, not one of whom, all the world knows, but is a hunter.

M. de Montcalm, according to the talk of some Colonial officers who had navigated, was a long time persuaded that the English had a landing force of 20 thousand men. In vain I endeavored to disabuse him by the plainest demonstrations, referring to the number and size of the vessels which composed the fleet; he did not alter his opinion until he saw my calculation verified by the depositions of divers prisoners and deserters.

6th. *We learned by intelligence received from Carillon, La Présentation and Niagara, that these three forts were threatened. 'Twas then regretted that this last had been too much weakened, the force of which might have been increased about 1,000 men, who were sent to the Beautiful river, without any reasonable view of utility to the King's service.*

7th. *Our boats exchanged shots with the frigates that were approaching Beauport.*

8th. *The batteries which the enemy was erecting opposite the town were, it was noticed, considerably advanced; some volleys of shot and some shells were discharged at them from the place, but M. de Montcalm, considering on the one hand that this fire retarded the enemy's labors but little, and on the other hand, that the state of our magazines required that we should economize our powder, made M. de Vaudreuil consent to order the fire against that quarter to cease.*

This silence excited murmurs, but M. Lemercier the Commandant of the artillery, demonstrated its necessity by submitting a statement of the powder.

Towards the evening of the same day, some forty barges full of troops, supported by a frigate, advanced towards the Falls of Montmorency, whilst a 60-gun ship was cannonading the intrenchments on our left, and a ketch was throwing shell.

This movement created the belief that the enemy might intend landing at Ange Gardien, but, the conviction that the River of the Falls was nowhere fordable, making it to be regarded as very indifferent whether the enemy would proceed thither, no precaution was taken to offer any opposition there, and no attention even was paid to the representations some farmers of Ange Gardien made on this subject, who offered to go thither, assuring, from the knowledge they had of the locality, that with one hundred men the

English could be prevented ascending the hill, which in fact does not fail of being sufficiently steep and wooded.

Finally, about 9 o'clock, the enemy landed some men who, having reported that part to be entirely abandoned, were followed by the detachment the barges were conveying, which, during the remainder of the night, were busy passing troops from the Island of Orleans to the Falls, 80 that next morning, at the break of day, Mr. Wolff was there at the head of 3 [to] 4 thousand men. Then all illusion disappeared. The post of the Falls was no longer considered contemptible, when, on beholding the enemy there, it was admitted that it commanded most advantageously the entire left of our camp, and people were at the same time convinced that the river on which it rested was, as the farmers had announced, fordable at divers places. Chevalier de Levy, who was in command at that quarter, perceived the error our false security had just led us to commit, and undertook to repair it by endeavoring to force the enemy to abandon that post. He marched thither with 600 men, preceded by some Indians; reported to M. de Vaudreuil the course he was taking, and asked that Governor at the same time for orders as to his ulterior operations; no time was lost in giving him an answer, whereupon he thought it his duty to bring his troops to a halt.

M. de Vaudreuil told him positively not to run any risk, and that he was preparing to go in person to the spot. He did not arrive there, however, until two hours after.

Headquarters were at the center, and afterwards a league from the left.

Meanwhile, the Indians, who continued to advance, soon encountered in the woods, after passing the river, a detachment of about 500 men, whom they obliged to fall back on the main army, which they did not fear to attack. They dared not, however, go too far, on observing that they were not supported. They returned, worn out by fatigue, after having killed or wounded a hundred of the enemy, and brought back 36 scalps as a proof of their success. It had been our policy to have had them press very far. We have since been informed by a sergeant who deserted from the enemy's army, that the English had landed in disorder, to which the dread of being every moment attacked by the Indians, did not a little contribute. [This is almost certainly the ambush attributed to Charles Langlade earlier].

Things being in this state, M. de Vaudreuil thought proper to defer the arrangements for a more considerable attack; he contented himself with summoning a Council of War, the result of which was, that we must remain in our intrenchments; neither the real position of the enemy nor his strength was known, it was alleged; the truth is that M. de Montcalm was not of the opinion to attack, and having, previous to the Council, privately spoken to the heads of the corps, it may be said that he had in some sort disposed them to represent matters as impracticable. M. Bigot was the only one who voted for the attack, and it may be said, in support of his opinion against the pretended inconvenience of exposing ourselves to the loss of everything, by hazarding an almost general engagement with troops reported to be already intrenched.

1st. That the enemy was in a very disadvantageous position, inasmuch as the ground 'twas occupying was absolutely commanded by the woods whence we were to make the attack.

2nd. That supposing we should have been repulsed, these same woods would have always assisted our retreat, since they must not only be traversed to reach the fords of the river, but moreover, being very thick and backed by lofty mountains, would certainly not have been liable to be turned.

3rd. That the subject of subsistence also merited serious attention. The country was already suffering from a serious scarcity; it was therefore so much the more essential to make every effort to endeavor to oblige the enemy to raise the siege of Quebec; for, admitting even that he could not carry that place by assault, we, by dragging things to any length, were always exposed to the danger of being forced by the failure of provisions, to open its gates, and consequently those of the entire Colony, to him. Everybody is aware that nothing is more casual than the crops of this country, and those of this year must have been as abundant as they have been (contrary to the usual course of things), to allow us to escape the rigors of famine; besides, we did not require all our forces to attack Mr. Wolf in the disadvantageous post he was occupying; I will add, that never was more ardor visible than was manifested on this occasion by the soldier, the Canadian and Indian, and I owe several of the officers of the different corps the justice to say, that they appeared to despair on seeing such happy arrangements neglected.

10th. The enemy was observed to be fortifying himself at the post he took up the previous evening, where already two field pieces and batteries were in course of erection, destined to batter in reverse the intrenchments which Chevalier de Levy was guarding, whereby that General officer was obliged to change the position of his camp, which continued on the other hand, to be annoyed by the fire from the ship and bomb-ketch. Some shells thrown from a mortar which had been brought from the town, soon obliged those vessels to remove to the offing.

11th. From both sides of the River of the Falls a pretty brisk fire was kept up between our Indians and the enemy's light troops. There were some killed and wounded on both sides; the loss however was much greater on the side of the English.

The enemy's works at Point Levy appearing to be pushed on with very great vigor, the uneasiness of the town augmented and excited some murmurs on the part of the people, because, said they, the enemy was permitted peaceably to erect gun and mortar batteries by which they expected to be crushed. Although several officers pretended, and M. de Montcalm was persuaded himself that those batteries were at too great a distance to do serious injury to the town, yet to avoid discouraging the towns people, M. Dumas, Major-General of the Colonial troops, who volunteered, was permitted to organize a corps of one thousand men, to cross with it to the south shore, in order to endeavor to dislodge the enemy from that quarter and to ruin their works. Men of all ranks, even to the mere scholar, volunteered in crowds for this detachment, which in consequence numbered 1,400 men, including the Indians; M. de Montcalm added to it some fifty volunteers from the Regulars.

To all who saw in this, the attack, only of a mob of Militia, without discipline, on Regular troops in their intrenchments, this expedition will appear imprudent, but 'twill cease to be so considered when it is known that those intrenchments were commanded by woods whence they could be fired on, and that those militia unacquainted with the handling of arms, excel incomparably the regular troops in the affairs which are decided purely by musketry. However that may be, M. Dumas set out at 10 o'clock at night; but having been obliged to go up as far as Sillery, he could not cross the river earlier than the night of the 12th *[to] 13*th*. Then was to be seen all the extravagances a panic is capable of producing. Scarcely did they set foot on the right bank of the river, when they imagined themselves surrounded by the enemy; three times did M. Dumas endeavor to rally his men and three times did his soldiers, mistaking each other for enemies, fire on and fling one another from the top of the bank to the bottom in order to regain their canoes. A retreat became absolutely necessary. The failure of this expedition called forth a great many remarks. Without wishing to endeavor to make known the true causes thereof, I shall simply say, that according to the report of M. Dumas and some other officers of his detachment, the Regulars, the Canadians and even the simple scholars who composed the party, had nothing to reproach each other with; they all equally gave way to their fright. The Indians alone, who formed the vanguard, behaved well, and found everything in disorder, when they returned from their scout with information that the enemy were not making any movement; as for the rest, it may, without fear of hazarding anything, be said, that this misadventure caused us the loss of one of the most favorable opportunities to strike a blow on the enemy, which the singular uneasiness we have since learned they were continually in, might have rendered of so much the greater advantage, as, not only were they unable to make a very vigorous resistance in a position that is commanded, where they* *had as yet only some imperfect intrenchments, but 5 large mortars and three 32-pounders with which they fired very briskly on the town that very night, might have been rendered unserviceable.*

14th. The enemy commenced firing some guns from the batteries they were erecting at the Falls, whereby some of our men were killed and some wounded; they also sent some strong detachments to examine the fords; we thought with the intention of trying to cross at that side. M. de Montcalm accordingly determined to alter his arrangements somewhat; he stripped his center a little, to post at the head of the fords some strong detachments which intrenched themselves there, and he had Chevalier de Levis' lines reinforced towards the river, where epaulements were erected against the enemy's batteries. As these different works could not but be very considerable, they fatigued our men very much; 6 guns more of a small caliber were brought from town to that quarter to annoy the enemy in his works, but 'twas no longer time, his artillery being greatly superior to ours, which had to be removed.

16th. The enemy throwing into the town a great many shell and fire pots, some fell on a house filled with hay, which was not attended to in sufficient season. The fire progressed and the conflagration communicated to 8 neighboring houses, which were completely burnt. The Point Levy batteries opened on the town to increase the disorder, but we did not delay silencing them by the superiority of our fire.

The enemy's works appeared rapidly advancing at the Falls, where some mortars were already in position, from which they threw shell that did not fail to annoy our troops in their camp. Here we undertook to set up a mortar, but this work languished so much for want of arms that it became useless before it could be completed. It was abandoned.

On the same day we received news from Niagara and Carillon, from which we learned that the English were already laying siege to the former fort and that M. de Bourlamaque, despairing of being able to maintain the latter, notwithstanding the new works he had just added to his fortifications, was preparing to fall back on Isle aux Noix so soon as the enemy, who, he knew were marching, should make their appearance to attack him. He was afraid of being turned by St. Frederic, and ' tis pretended that he had received positive orders to retreat; 'tis impossible to avoid one reflection thereupon. If it had been resolved, before the opening of the campaign, to abandon Carillon, why exhaust the troops with fatigue and the King with expense, to increase the defenses of that fort? M. Bourlamaque had, besides, appeared in all his letters previous to that moment, of the opinion that he was able to make a vigorous resistance there.

17ᵗʰ. A small detachment of our Indians having crossed the River of the Falls, took some prisoners, three of whom they brought us, according to whose report we could scarcely determine Mr. Wolf's real intentions; we merely discovered, from the detail they gave us of his forces and movements, that, having only 9 [to] 10 thousand Regulars at most, and estimating our army at 15 [to] 18 thousand, not only did that General not dare to attack us in front, but he was still under a continual apprehension of being attacked himself; they added, that it was generally reported in their army that the General was not sanguine about taking Quebec until he would be joined by General Amherst, whom he was expecting with the greatest impatience, and that, fearful of running short of provisions, the soldier's rations had been reduced to 7 ounces of biscuit and an equal quantity of salt meat. The depositions made by the different prisoners or deserters are pretty uniform as to that reduction.

The same prisoners told us, moreover, that an old man and some women of the North shore were daily carrying refreshments to the English camp, and had also pointed out to General Wolf the fords in the River of the Falls. 'Tis easy to be inferred, from this intercourse, that the enemy was in no wise harassed.

M. de Vaudreuil was fully of the opinion, according to the Canadian custom, to send some detachments to annoy the enemy. M. de Montcalm was always afraid of weakening himself [by doing so].

Some farmers who had been taken by the English, and had been set at liberty, after having received much attention from them and from Mr. Wolf himself, returned to us to-day from the enemy's camp. The above behavior was relative to the contents of the proclamation.

17th. On the same day the Indians, having requested leave to march in detachment, were permitted to do so; they set out to the number of 5 [to] 600, to lie in ambush behind the camp occupied by the enemy at the Falls [Perhaps another attempt by Langlade]. This expedition met with no success.

An English sailor who had been taken prisoner, on being interrogated as to what was thought of our fire-ships in the fleet, told us that great alarm had been felt as to their effects, but much surprise was created by the manner they had been conducted, especially at the precipitancy with which they had been set on fire.

A 60 gun-ship, with 5 frigates or transports, passed in front of the town in the night of the 18th and 19th, on their way to anchor at Sillery. There was not a doubt, but they intended either to cut off our supplies, as they might have been informed that we had stored the greater part of them in our frigates, or to attempt a landing near Sillery; two guns were posted there, and M. Dumas was immediately dispatched thither with 600 men, with orders to follow on the river side the movements of those vessels, but he was unable to prevent the burning of our last fire ship, the fitting out of which was being completed in L'anse des Mers; the English likewise attempted to destroy the rafts we were having prepared there, but were repulsed.

20th. One of General Townshend's servants came to us from the enemy's camp, who assured us that there were at the Falls only about three thousand men; this, agreeing with our observations, M. de Montcalm recalled some troops from the left to reinforce the center. The enemy harassed our left considerably by the continual fire of shot and shell from the batteries at this camp at the Falls.

21st. We learned that 4000 of the enemy's grenadiers had landed at Point aux trembles. M. Dumas received orders to march thither, and a portion of the cavalry was added to his detachment; but the enemy had reembarked, their object having been to obtain exact intelligence of what was passing in the country; they contented themselves with seizing all the women whom they found in that village, about one hundred only of whom, however, they carried away; among these were some ladies belonging to the town, who had taken refuge there; the enemy were harassed and pursued by some Indians, who ran and killed and wounded some of their men; General Wolf had received the idea of this expedition from Stobo, an English officer, who had been taken as a hostage for the affair of Fort Necessity; convicted of having, notwithstanding his character, kept up some correspondence with the English Generals prejudicial to our service, he had been condemned to be hanged, but the Court having ordered the suspension of that sentence, 'twas thought proper to restore him the liberty he had previously enjoyed in his quality of hostage; he took advantage thereof to effect his escape, and was seconded by an individual who had deserted from New England, and had been some years settled at Quebec, who, acquainted with navigation, embarked with him about the middle of last May in a simple canoe, in which they reached Louisbourg.

22nd. The commander of a vessel was sent to propose to the town a suspension of hostilities during 6 hours, in which time the women taken at Point aux trembles were to be delivered up; the proposal was agreed to. All the women, though of different ranks, spoke equally well of the treatment they had received from the English officers; several of them even supped with Mr. Wolf who joked considerably about the circumspection of our Generals; he told these ladies that he had afforded very favorable opportunities for an attack and had been surprised that no advantage had been taken of them.

In the course of the night of the 22nd and 23rd, another conflagration was caused in the town by the vast quantity of fire pots which the enemy continued to throw into it; 18 houses were in consequence reduced to ashes; the Cathedral shared the same fate. The Point Levy batteries did not cease firing all the time; ours replied during the continuance of the conflagration, but when it had been arrested, they discontinued. These troubles were not yet over, when, at 4 o'clock in the morning, one of the enemy's frigates, with a transport, attempted, under favor of a light breeze which sprung up in the N. E., to take advantage of the embarrassment, in which they doubtless thought we were, to pass up to Sillery. They were mistaken; all the gunners had remained at their post; but the wind having changed the very moment when those vessels began to receive the fire of our batteries, they retired without much loss; our fire was this day very well served.

24th. This day was passed in negotiations between the town and the fleet, with which M. Lemercier, the Commandant of the artillery was entrusted, relating to indifferent matters. On the same day we had a very sensible proof of the disorder which prevailed in the army. A great number had gone from it to hunt, who having discovered considerable game towards St. Foy, kept up such a continual fire that the Indians supposing we were attacked at Sillery, proceeded thither; on their return they represented that some inconvenience might result from such practice; M. de Vaudreuil perceived it and forbid the army to hunt any more.

25th. This morning a mistake caused us a pretty serious alarm: a letter came to the camp from St. Michael's cove, informing M. de Vaudreuil that the English had landed there; this news appeared confirmed by the report of cannon which was heard in that direction. The drums were beaten and the army seized their arms; 'twas nothing, however, but the attack of some of our gun boats which, being collected together in that cove, had attracted the attention of the ships and were briskly cannonaded by them, whilst barges were sent to seize them; two were cut out; three went up again to Cap Rouge, and one grounded, which was saved by the fire kept up by some Canadians who had ran thither from the neighboring post. M. Dumas had left M. de St. Martin, a Colonial officer, there with 180 men and had himself marched with a thousand men as far as Jacques Cartier, where 'twas feared the enemy would take up a position; he received orders to have some intrenchments thrown up there. We learned, on the same day *by a new prisoner taken on the left, that the enemy had already a formidable artillery at their camp at the Falls, and were continuing to erect gun and mortar batteries there. From that quarter also came, towards evening, a young Canadian, who is still a child, and had previously been taken by the English and released by them in order to deliver an anonymous note to M. de Vaudreuil, containing injurious reproaches against the Governor on the subject of some scalps taken by the Indians, and of some soldiers killed by the Canadians whom they called assassins. He added that, previous to leaving the English camp he saw notice given to some Canadians who had been taken with arms in their hands, to prepare to die; that he saw them led out by some musketeers, and that he was scarcely out of the camp when he heard several shots fired. Messrs. de Vaudreuil and de Montcalm thought it fitting to come to some explanation on that subject with Mr. Wolf; the tenor of their letter, written in the name of the former, embodied all the dignity, politeness and firmness compatible with the circumstance. M. Lemercier, who was charged with the delivery of that dispatch, added a second to it, which he wrote to Mr. Wolf by order of M. de Vaudreuil, wherein, after having proposed to that General various arrangements respecting parleys, he observed that the use of them appeared to be growing somewhat too frequent. Mr. Wolf on the next day had the following letter communicated by one of his Aids-de-Camp to M. de Vaudreuil:*

   '*Sir,*

   I have the honor, by order of my General, to answer your Excellency's letter brought to him yesterday by Mr. Lemercier respecting some particular articles on the subject of parleys, wherein he complains in your Excellency's name, of the too frequent use of such parleys.

   The General cannot express his astonishment sufficiently at this question: Eh! wherefore have the English demanded a parley? Let the answer be given by those who have received their liberty on the occasion of those parleys.

   General Wolf learns from an intercepted letter written at the Camp of Beauport, that three grenadiers of the Royal American

Regiment, taken some days ago, were destined to be burnt alive in your camp. Mr. Wolf would wish to know what has become of them, so as to regulate his conduct in future accordingly.

The British troops are only too much exasperated; the enormous cruelties already committed, and especially the base infraction of the capitulation of Fort William Henry are yet fresh in their minds.

Such acts deserve and if repeated will certainly meet, in future, the severest reprisals; all distinction will cease between Frenchmen, Canadians and Indians; all will be treated as a cruel and barbarous mob, thirsting for human blood.

I have the honor to be, &.,
Isaac Baarré

Adjutant-General.'

The following is the answer which M. de Vaudreuil ordered M. de Bougainville to make to Mr. Wolf:

'Sir,

By order of the Marquis de Vaudreuil, I reply to the letter written him by Mr. Isaac Baarré, respecting the three grenadiers belonging to the Royal Americans who were taken prisoners. Your Excellency ought to have regarded as soldiers' gossip the tales related in the intercepted letter; the fate of those three prisoners has been the same as that of all the others taken by the Indians; the King has ransomed them out of their hands at considerable expense. The Marquis de Vaudreuil has not instructed me to reply to the menaces, invectives and accusations with which that letter abounds; no doubt you have not read them. Nothing of that sort will make us either cowards or barbarians. Our proceedings are known in Europe and our public papers establish our justification in the matter of the infraction of the capitulation of Fort William Henry.

I have the honor to be, &c.,

Bougainville.'

26th. *At the dawn of day, a strong detachment of English being come to fire at that commanded by M. de Repentigny at the head of one of the fords of the River of the Falls, about 400 Indians were sent across a little further up to turn the enemy, but they applied for a reinforcement which was promised them. They waited, meanwhile, in the woods, lying on their faces in presence of the enemy for 5 hours without noticing any movement among our troops. Finally, carried away by their impatience and moreover seeing the enemy profiting by that time to convey fresh troops into the woods, they determined to make the attack alone; it was so impetuous that, according to what we since learned from a sergeant who deserted from the enemy's camp, and some Canadians who happened to be prisoners there, the English, obliged to fall back, retired more than two hundred paces from the field of battle in order to rally, and the alarm extended as far as the camp, to which Mr. Wolf himself returned for the purpose of ordering up the artillery through roads he had had opened; thereupon the Indians seeing themselves almost surrounded, effected their retreat by the ford, their communication with which they had preserved, after having killed or wounded more than 150 of the enemy and lost only two or three of their own men; they met at the pass of the river, the party which was sent to their aid, and which M. de Levis would never take upon himself to dispatch, without having received an order from M. de Vaudreuil. The entire army regretted the loss of so fine an opportunity.*

27th. *Although Les Anses des Mers, du Foulon, de Sillery and de St. Michel were regarded as inaccessible, nevertheless the Engineers were sent thither for the purpose of having ditches and abatis constructed in the slopes leading thereto; about 400 men were also distributed throughout these different posts. Some Canadians brought us from the South shore three prisoners who were part of a detachment of 7 men which they had defeated; the four others had been killed.*

28th. *The enemy unmasked, opposite the town, a new battery of 5 pieces of cannon.*

29th. *The enemy's ships which were above Quebec were making different movements; they went up, within a few days as far as St. Augustin and afterwards returned to anchor at Sillery. We concluded that they wanted to attract our attention on that side, but what was passing at the camp of the Falls, which we saw bristling with cannon and mortars, appeared to demand our exclusive regard. A detachment of 300 Indians was sent to that quarter; having three days provisions; they were to lie in ambush in the woods in the rear of the enemy whose communication with the country 'twas desirable to cut off.*

30th. *All quiet.*

31st. *Such was not the case to-day. About 10 o'clock in the forenoon, the wind blowing violently from the Southwest, two large transports set sail from the enemy's fleet and advanced towards the Falls of Montmorency; they were soon followed by a 60 gun ship, and all three took up a position opposite Chevalier de Levis' intrenchments, within short cannon range of which the transports grounded full sail sett; the ship kept off, forming with the two former a triangle, whence at the very moment a heavy fire was opened against our lines, which were enfiladed by that from the formidable artillery Mr. Wolf had at the Falls. Whilst our left was exposed to this double cannonade, a great number of barges which were remarked early in the morning to be in motion, after having received troops at Point Levy and from various vessels, were forming themselves into column at the head of the fleet. We could then no longer doubt the enemy's intention to attack us; the army assumed their arms, and the different corps repaired to the intrenchments. The violence of the wind which continued blowing from the S.W., the ebb and the occurrences on our left, not allowing us to fear an attack on any other parts of our lines, M. de Montcalm weakened them somewhat and repaired in person to Chevalier de Levis' camp. Finally, about 5 o'clock in the evening the barges, after having, by divers movements, tried to conceal from us the real point of attack, ranged themselves in three divisions; directed their entire course towards the Falls, and precisely at the moment of low water, touched ground along side two vessels which were high and dry on a very fine shoal. Under cover of their fire all the troops effected a landing without confusion, and formed themselves in order of battle, whilst the force encamped at Ange Gardien was crossing, in column, the River of the Falls, to join them. On account of the distance, we were able to oppose to all those movement, only the fire of a few guns of small calibre, placed in some redoubts that had been thrown up in front of our intrenchments; having fired the whole day on the ships, those redoubts unfortunately ran out of ammunition towards the close of the action; they suffered, besides, considerably from the fire they had been exposed to; both these reasons necessitated their abandonment on the approach of a body of Grenadiers which advanced to the attack and ascended thither; but hardly did these become masters of the place than the brisk fire of musketry they received from our intrenchments, which most advantageously commanded those redoubts, obliged the detachment to retreat; the junction of both the enemy's divisions being effected at this moment, we were expecting a general attack, but a violent storm which supervened, having probably opened Mr. Wolf's eyes to the temerity of his undertaking, that General retreated; it is even probable that he went so far only because he had relied too much on the effects of his artillery; he expected that the Canadians and Indians, frightened by the shell and shot, would not hold out, and that in consequence of their flight, his troops might ascend the bank without encountering any great obstacles; but it is due in justice to all the corps of the army which M. de Montcalm had collected there in succession, to say, that they exhibited, on this occasion, all the firmness that could be expected, and that they manifested the greatest impatience to be engaged; feeling all the advantage of their position, they were full of a confidence from which we could, without presumption, anticipate the total defeat of the English army, had it persisted in advancing. It divided a second time; the greater portion recrossed the River of the Falls to regain the camp at Ange Gardien, and the remainder reembarking set fire* to the two transports, the burning of which put an end to this affair. In the course of it we have had some 60 men killed or wounded by the shot and shell; the enemy's loss, according to the report of prisoners and deserters who have come in since, amounted to about 500 men, almost all grenadiers; a captain of the Royal Americans, and two soldiers were taken prisoners there.

1st *August.* The ship which was at the Falls rejoined the fleet. The provisions reserved at Quebec for the subsistence of the army, being nearly exhausted, it became absolutely necessary to have some brought from Batiscan; but as the transportation by water appeared very hazardous since the enemy had rendered themselves masters of the river, no course was left but to have them brought by land, which still was not unattended by difficulties. There remained in the country only young children, women, or old men whose infirmities did not permit them to bear arms. It was, however, with the aid of such weak hands that 700 barrels of pork or flour were conveyed on 271 carts from Batiscan to the army, 18 leagues. The subsistence of the troops was thereby assured for 12 or 15 days, but from that moment, alarm was felt at the difficulties that service would eventually encounter; a number of carts were already broken; the women and children who guided them, rebuffed by such rude labor, left no hope of their being able to support it long; regret was begun to be felt at having placed the army's stores at so great a distance.

2nd. *A few hours truce, during which M. Lemercier was instructed to go and deliver to General Wolf some letters from M. de Vaudreuil and the Captain of the Royal Americans, who was taken prisoner in the affair of the 31st. This officer, after having spoken in his letter in terms of great praise of the behavior of the French, by whom, he said, he had been rescued with the greatest difficulty out of the hands of the Indians, requested of his General some necessaries which he stood in need of.*

3rd. *The enemy continued to strengthen the artillery at the camp of the Falls; M. Dumas brought back to the army the greatest portion of the troops he had at Jacques Cartier, where he had orders to leave only 200 men.*

4th. Another truce to receive Mr. Wolf's answer to the letters which had been written him on the 2nd. In sending his officer the required baggage, he reproached him, in the answer he sent to his letter, with having, by his imprudent conduct, given M. de Montcalm reason to believe that there was but little discipline in his army, wishing thereby adroitly to convey the impression that bis attack of the 31st had been only an error. As for the letter he addressed to M. de Vaudreuil, he made a long enumeration in it of the grievances of the English Nation against the troops of Canada, and superadded most ferocious expressions to reproaches full of bitterness and spite. 'Twas proposed to continue, for the longest time possible, the sojourn in town of the officer who brought these dispatches, in order to profit by that interval, to remove to the mortar and gun batteries the material necessary to construct merlons there; these batteries being in barbet, the gunners who served them were greatly exposed to the enemy's fire; already, many of the men were killed at them, but the measures that had been adopted in this regard, were disconcerted in consequence of the little order which prevailed in the different parts of our service. Whilst waiting for the English boat at one of the extremities of the Lower town, a merchant officer who was serving at the batteries, left the other end as soon as the boat appeared, and, having received from the English officer the letters and baggage he had to deliver, sent him immediately back. Five new deserters came over to us to day; their depositions contained nothing of interest. We learned this same day the evacuation of Forts Carillon and St. Frederic, which were blown up, the former on the 27th, the latter on the 31st of July; the retreat from Carillon was so precipitate and disorderly, that 20 soldiers were left behind who were prevented by drunkenness from following the troops; they were taken by the enemy, who also found several cannon and 4 mortars in that fort, the fortifications of which had been only slightly damaged.

5th. *The Point Levy batteries continued to keep up a very brisk fire on the town. Three new deserters came over to us.*

In the night of the 5th and 6th several barges passed in front of the town, and went up as far as the ships, whence a pretty large quantity of effects was landed. As these different movements which the enemy was observed making in that quarter, created an impression that it might be with a design to attempt something there, M. de Montcalm determined to send a reinforcement thither, so that we found ourselves then having, between Quebec and St. Augustin, about 1,000 men, whereof M. de Bougainville had the chief command.

7th. Divers vessels which were anchored at Cap Rouge, after having been pretty considerably lightened, went up as far as Point aux écureuils. The King's frigates and the ship Le Fronsac were then at anchor at the foot of the Richelieu; i.e., 3 leagues above Point aux écureuils. The wind did not yet allow of their going any higher up: the intention of the English was probably to capture them, but they took advantage of the north wind which had brought the latter, to ascend the rapid. M. de Bougainville thinned his post somewhat, in order to form a detachment with which he followed the enemy's ships along the river side.

8th. Three sailors who deserted from the enemy's fleet came over to us. The English ships which were at Les Ecureuils dropped down again to Point aux trembles, where they made several attempts to land some men, but were always repulsed by M. de Bougainville; nothing of importance occurred there however. M. de Montcalm sent to the camp some small field pieces and howitzers which had been left in the town.

The large quantity of shell, carcasses and fire-pots which the enemy threw during the night of the 8th and 9th, into the place, occasioned a 3rd fire in the Lower town; 152 houses were reduced to ashes there. We learned on the same day that Niagara had capitulated on the 24th of July, and that the surrender of that fort had been preceded by the defeat of our division which had returned from the Beautiful river. This event increased considerably the dejection which the news of the evacuation of Carillon and St. Frederic had already spread among the people; 'twas feared that the enemy encountering only feeble barriers at the entrance of the Cataracoui river would leap the rapids and suddenly pounce on Montreal, which was at the moment bare of every sort of defense; there were some detachments at La Présentation and Isle au Galo; 'twas thought necessary to reinforce these posts; 1,000 men were detached from the army with orders to proceed thither with all speed, and 'twas considered indispensable to entrust Chevalier de Levy with the command of so delicate a quarter; he set out that very day for that place.

11th. A detachment of 700 men, composed of Canadians and Indians crossed the River of the Falls to attack some of the enemy's workmen who were making fascines. The firing was pretty sharp; 'twas calculated that a hundred men had been killed or wounded; we had only 7 wounded; things would have been pushed farther had the Outaouas been willing to attack. They did not feel, on that day, disposed to fight, and took scarcely any part in that affair; under all circumstances an adverse fortune appeared to disconcert enterprises from which we might expect the most fruit.

12th. On the next day, we had another instance of it. The English, repulsed at Point aux trembles, turned their views to the other side of the river; they were met, on landing by some shots from the farmers who were returning home, but made good their position to the number of 7 [to] 800 men. M. de Montcalm wishing to profit by the circumstance of the passage at Point aux trembles of the troops he was sending to the rapids, to have the enemy attacked in their new camp, by M. de Bougainville's corps, gave orders to that Colonel to cross to the right of the river and to operate there whilst his posts, well guarded, would become a snare into which the enemy might fall if they did not expect him on the other side; nothing was better combined, but the bad weather deranged all, and the fear of delaying too long the relief which was being sent to the rapids, caused the project to be abandoned.

On the same day, four vessels of the enemy's fleet wished to profit by the N. E. wind that was blowing, to go up again above Quebec, but were becalmed opposite the town; they wheeled about and by aid of the ebb, which supervened, regained their anchorage, without having suffered much from the fire of our batteries.

13th. We learned that the enemy's division, encamped opposite Point aux trembles, having spread through the country, burnt all the settlements there. M. de Montcalm apprehending from the movements the enemy were making thereabouts, that they were intending some other considerable enterprise, determined on reinforcing the detachment under the command of M. de Bougainville, which was increased to 1,600 men, and divided among the different posts. Some Canadians released by the English, brought M. de Vaudreuil a third Proclamation published by order of Mr. Wolf, in which after having referred to the two former, that General threatened with the severest reprisals those farmers who would not lay down their arms by the 20th of August.

A courier arrived from St. Paul's bay to inform us that the English, who had not before dared to land in that quarter, where they had encountered a good many musket shots every time they made their appearance had at length, some days ago, landed in consequence of the treachery of a Swiss farmer settled in that Parish, and had already burnt 22 houses.

On the same day, the Indians brought us in two prisoners from the South shore, and a new deserter came over.

15th. We sent a detachment of about 1,200 men into the Parish of Ange Gardien, with a view to surprise the English there, who, 'twas said, were scattered about. No good came of that expedition. The Indians, following the example of the troops, who for some time occupied themselves solely with marauding and pillage, disbanded themselves, and advanced without precaution towards a house, which they supposed abandoned; 'twas full of Englishmen, whose fire they received, which put them to flight; nothing more was to be undertaken in that direction, and a retreat was necessary. Three prisoners were brought in from the South shore; they were taken by some Canadians, but seized by the Indians, who also brought us 4 scalps.

16th. A new fire broke out in the Upper town; its progress was fortunately arrested; one house only was reduced to ashes. We were kept in the greatest state of anxiety by the difficulties experienced in the transportation of provisions, and the dread of seeing them every moment cut off by the enemy. The roads were already become very bad, and water carriage dared still be used as far as St. Augustin and Cap Rouge, only with such caution as rendered all the operations very tedious.

17h. We learned by three new deserters from the enemy's army that a severe dysentery was prevailing there, which had already destroyed a great many people. 5 Canadians arrived from Niagara, who had escaped from the enemy after the surrender of that fort. These men report that the English were busy repairing the fortifications of the fort; that they had detached a large body of troops to conduct their prisoners to New-York, and that there were remaining at Chouaguen, when they passed there, only about 2,000 men, who were making no movement; from this circumstance, 'twas inferred that the English had no intention to come by the Rapids, where Chevalier de Levy then was with 2,500 men.

18th. We received by land a fresh supply of flour, the stock of which the want of carts had caused to become very low.

19th. We learned that a corps of the enemy of about 1,200 men had landed at Deschambeaux M. de Bougainville repaired immediately thither with his men preceded by the cavalry, and M. de Montcalm went in person with the Major-General and some troops as far as Point aux trembles (7 leagues), where, having learned that the enemy had reembarked, after having burnt the house in which the baggage of the army was stored, he returned to the camp, which he did not reenter until the following morning. The English did not lose a man in that expedition; they reembarked on perceiving the approach of our troops, carrying with them a great many cattle which they had collected together in the country.

I must say that no blame can attach to our troops if they were not able to charge the enemy when retreating; they endeavored to do so with much ardor; they used prodigious diligence to get there, but the English Commander, who expected to be attacked, had them closely watched by his ships, according to whose signals he regulated his movements. Two deserters came over to us from that detachment; a third arrived from Mr. Wolf's camp, who informed us that that General, being disposed to reembark in a short time, was sending parties in all directions to burn all the buildings and lay waste the country. He added, that some misunderstanding existed between the land and naval Commanders. We had already heard this, and it is since confirmed.

21st, 22nd, 23rd and 24th were remarkable only for the almost continual rains which, causing us the most lively apprehensions for the harvest, were rendering the transportation of our provisions extremely difficult. The enemy were burning in all directions; houses were seen on fire, simultaneously, at Côte de Beaupré, from the Falls of Montmorency to St. Anne, at the Island of Orleans and all along the right bank of the river.

25th. The enemy was remarked diminishing his artillery at the Falls, and reembarking. Two vessels at Point aux trembles dropped down to St. Michel, whence, after landing some troops on the South shore, they returned to their former station. On the same day we learned that the Abenaquis of St. Francis had stopped two English officers (Messrs. Hamilton and Kennedy) accompanied by 7 Indians whom M. Amherst had dispatched through the woods to Mr. Wolf. It appeared, from the letters that were found on them, that Mr. Amherst's operations were, henceforward, to depend on the success Mr. Wolf should meet with before Quebec. By letters written to different Colonels we learned, also, that singular astonishment prevailed in Mr. Amherst's army at the construction of Carillon; the strength of the fortifications of that place were somewhat exaggerated, and many jokes were uttered at the precipitancy with which we had retired from it. As the enemy's ships, anchored above Quebec, greatly embarrassed the transportation of our provisions, the project was formed to have them carried off by our frigates. M. de Vaudreuil, to whom that proposal was submitted in a favorable point of view, approved of it, and nothing was thought of but its execution. Seamen will decide whether it were easy to carry, by boarding, in a river with a rapid current, well armed vessels, one of which had 50 guns, commanded by men who were daily making us admire the activity of their maneuvers; but a serious inconvenience was experienced at the outset: To complete the crews of the frigates destined to operate, our batteries had to be stripped considerably of the sailors who were there acting as gunners.

26th. Another deserter came to us from the camp at the Falls.

27th. A second, a sergeant in the Royal American Regiment came in, who announced to us the approaching departure of the fleet, and assured us that Mr. Wolf would break up his camp at the Falls within 8 days. He added, that the Abbé de Portneuf, parish priest of St. Joachim, having been taken by the Rangers, together with 9 farmers who were with him, had been massacred after laying down their arms, and that the scalps of these unfortunate men had been carried to the camp. This fact has since been verified by the report of a 10th farmer who was in that detachment and had escaped.

During the night of the 27th and 28th, five new frigates or transports of the enemy went above Quebec; they met from the bateaux of the place, but a feeble fire. These vessels by forming a junction with the former opposite St. Augustin, caused our project to abort, and the sailors were recalled.

29th. Three new deserters came in, who confirmed what the serjeant had told us. They also stated that Mr. Wolf, being attacked by a severe fever, had been confined to bed for the last six days.

In the course of the night of the 29th [to] 30th, the tide being high, the vessels at St. Augustin cannonaded and fired briskly on a small deserted Island near their anchorage, where they had noticed, the day before, at low water, some people pass on foot to save hay, and who had retired on the return of the tide.

30th. The enemy unmasked a new gun battery at Point Levy; 21 pieces were then there.

31st. Considerable movement occurred in the Point Levy camp; also in the fleet, which made us suppose that the enemy was preparing to send some vessels above Quebec; those already above, went up from St. Augustin to Point aux trembles, whence 'twas inferred that they designed attempting the passage of the Richelieu to go and attack our fleet: we had learned, 2 days previously, that a ship, no matter what her draft, could easily ascend that Rapid. This caused us the greater uneasiness, as one of the strongest of the contractors' frigates bad the evening before, run ashore at Grondines. Our little naval force became, by that loss, reduced to the other three of his vessels and the two King's frigates, all which had orders to prepare to oppose the passage of the English.

On the night of the 31st of August and 1st September, five more of the enemy's ships went above Quebec. The movements the English were making near the Falls of Montmorency, left no longer any doubt that they were resolved to abandon that camp. A great quantity of material was observed to be put on board of boats on which our batteries fired, without any answer from those of the enemy, which were already dismounted.

The news we received this same day calmed somewhat the uneasiness we felt for Montreal. We learned on the one hand, by deserters from Mr. Amherst's army, that that General was disposed to confine the operations of this campaign to repairing Forts Carillon and St. Frederic, (the latter had been totally destroyed). And on the other hand, M. Bourlamaque assured that the advantageous post he had taken at Isle aux Noix, the intrenchments he had had thrown up and the formidable artillery he had mounted there, placed him in a position not to fear the enemy, however numerous they might present themselves. That island, 'tis known, is in the River Sorel which it divides into two very narrow arms. The channel was closed to barges by strong stockades (estacades) which 'twas expected the enemy would not attempt to turn by land. Both banks of the river presented only deep swamps covered with timber, a passage across which could not be effected except with extreme difficulty, and 'tis evident that in lengthening the circuit in order to seek more solid ground farther off, the labor would have to be very considerably increased together with the risks of being seriously annoyed.

2nd. The news we received of the return to St. Michel and Sillery of the enemy's fleet which lay at Point aux trembles, dissipated the apprehension we felt that it would go up as far as Batiscan. The enemy continued to evacuate their camp at the Falls, whence two columns crossed in the evening to the Island of Orleans. Further movements in the fleet, which led to the belief that the enemy might intend to attack our intrenchments; what seemed to confirm this opinion was the discovery of six buoys anchored opposite Beauport, which we caused to be removed; a great many people thought 'twas only a feint. 'Twill be seen that they were not wrong.

3rd. At 6 o'clock in the morning we noticed quite a movement in the camps and fleet of the enemy, one hundred barges or canoes full of men started from Point Levy in order to go and lie to in the center of the fleet; 'twas remarked at the same time, that some fifty more of them were going through the same maneuver near the Falls of Montmorency; there was no longer a doubt of the enemy wishing to effectuate the attack which the buoys of the preceding evening appeared to announce. The entire army was ordered under arms. The different corps formed in line of battle each at the head of its camp, and in this position waited for the fleet under cover of which the English were expected to effect their landing. The weather was fine although the wind was from the Northeast. They got off about 10 o'clock and the barges which had gone from Point Levy returned thither. 'Twas thought at first that the roughness of the river had alone obliged them to do so, but the barges of the Falls that had gone into the offing, having taken the same course, opened our eyes by recalling our attention to the camp at Ange Gardien which was completely evacuated. Then those who were heard secretly finding fault with M. de Montcalm because Chevr. de Lévy did not attack the English when they landed at the Falls of Montmorency, although the latter officer could plead the orders he had received not to hazard anything, treated him with the same rigor for not having fallen on their rear guard on the same ground and under circumstances infinitely more favorable. (I have already spoken elsewhere of that ground).

M. de Montcalm and his principal officers, to try to justify themselves for having lost so fine an opportunity, answered that if the enemy had not been attacked when reembarking, 'twas only because more than 2,000 men were perceived lying on their faces behind the intrenchments of their camp, at the moment they were thought to have crossed again over to the Island of Orleans, and there was danger of falling into some snare.

'Tis worthy of remark that people were busy in our camp persuading that there was nothing very [extra] ordinary in Mr. Wolf's maneuvers, and that M. de Montcalm, on the contrary, was comporting himself on that occasion as a consummate General. The reader can judge.

One part of the troops from the camp at Ange Gardien remained at the Island of Orleans, and the other went to take post above the batteries at Point Levy.

Engineers and several other officers who have since been to visit Mr. Wolf's camp, agreed unanimously that no position was more disadvantageous than that which that General had been obliged to take. 'Twas for that reason that he lined his camp with eleven redoubts, almost all intrenched, fraised and palisaded.

4th. M. de Montcalm, regulating his movements by those of the enemy, stripped his left somewhat and removed the principal part of his forces to the right of his camp. He also sent the battalion of Guyenne to encamp on the heights of Quebec, whence it could repair, in case of need, equally either to Sillery or into the town, or towards the River St. Charles. Our misfortune willed, as is soon to be seen, that it should be withdrawn from that post two days afterwards. The Point Levy batteries, increased by the artillery which the enemy had removed from the camp at the Falls, were keeping up a continual fire on the town.

5th. A corps of about three thousand English having marched towards the Etechemin river, M. de Montcalm reinforced M. de Bougainville by pickets from the army, almost all the Indians and the remainder of the volunteers. A frigate belonging to the enemy reascended to Cap Rouge, where it cannonaded one of our schooners which had arrived there the preceding evening from Montreal, with a cargo of flour; we had two gun-boats there which obliged it to sheer off.

The flour was the product of the grain that we had been able to procure within the government of Montreal for cash. Had it not been for this supply, provisions would have certainly failed the army, which would have to be mostly disbanded.

6th. The enemy continued its movements above Quebec, which failed not to cause us uneasiness. One of their schooners passed in open day before the town, towing two long boats, which the fire from our batteries, not very brisk, 'tis true, was unable to check; those of the enemy profited by that moment to cannonade ours, in which we had five men killed or dangerously wounded.

7th. The fleet which lay above Sillery, then consisting of 18 vessels, went up to Cap Rouge accompanied by some sixty barges full of troops, which after having made a show of wishing to land, regained the offing and went to land at the right of the river. M. de Bougainville followed their movements.

The night of the 7th and 8th, four new little vessels passed above Quebec and joined the fleet anchored at Cap Rouge; they encountered a very hot fire from the batteries of the town without being incommoded thereby; 'twas thought in the camp that the enemy would attempt a landing about La Canardière, near the River St. Charles. The entire army, despite of very bad weather, spent the night in bivouac.

The European flour and that made from the purchased grain, as has been stated, being all consumed, the army was, since some days, no longer drawing its subsistence, except from the harvest of the Montreal government, which fortunately turned out extraordinarily fine, but hands were wanting to save it. M. de

Rigaud had already detached two hundred Militia for that purpose. This help not being sufficient, M. de Vaudreuil directed Chevalier de Levy, who had returned from the Rapids to Isle aux Noix, to increase it. That general officer had quit the Rapids without, however, dis-garrisoning them, on the assurance of his scouts who had returned from Chouaguen, that the enemy was quiet in that quarter. The rains continued to render the transportation of our provisions very difficult, and were exciting in us much apprehension for the crops of the governments of Quebec and Three Rivers, which, nevertheless, were not less beautiful than those of the government of Montreal.

9th. The enemy, probably considering the houses of the town sufficiently damaged, directed the most of their fire against the suburbs of St. Roch.

10th. The enemy appeared to build a new intrenchment above their Point Levy batteries; we did not understand what could be the real object of it. Their little fleet extended from Cap Rouge to Point aux trembles.

11th. Throughout the day, on the road leading to the enemy's batteries, a considerable movement of gun carriages was perceptible, and the fleet, anchored above Quebec received all the troops scattered throughout that quarter.

12th. The enemy kept up a very sharp fire the entire day on the town; the fleet, anchored from Cap Rouge as far as Point aux trembles, was continually in motion; towards night some vessels were detached from it, which came to an anchor at Sillery. The movements we saw the enemy making since some time, above Quebec, and the knowledge we had of the character of Mr. Wolf, that impetuous, bold and intrepid warrior, prepared us for a last attack. Such a resolution was really fully adopted in the English army; after breaking up the camp at the Falls, a Council of War, as we have since learned from divers English officers, had been held, at which all the general officers voted unanimously in favor of raising the siege; the naval officers observed that the season, already far advanced, was rendering the navigation of the river every day more dangerous, and the officers of the line, disgusted at the tediousness of a campaign, as fruitless as it was difficult, considered it useless to remain any longer before intrenchments which appeared to them impregnable. Both added, moreover, that their army, always a prey to disease, was melting insensibly away. Then, Mr. Wolf, seeing that he could not gain anything by openly resisting the general opinion, adroitly took things by the other side. He declared to the members of the council that, so far from differing with them, he was, on the contrary, of their opinion in regard to the inutility of prolonging the siege of Quebec; that therefore, in the proposition he was about to submit to them, he wished to divest himself of the quality of General, in order to throw himself entirely on their friendship for him.

'Finally, Gentlemen,' said he to them, 'as the glory of our arms appears to me to require that we should not retire without making one final attempt, I earnestly demand of you to be pleased not to refuse your consent thereto; I feel that, in this instance, it is necessary our first step should place us at the gates of the town. With this view, I am about to try to get a detachment of only one hundred and fifty men to penetrate through the Sillery woods, and the entire army will prepare to follow. Should this first detachment encounter any resistance on the part of the enemy, I pledge you my word of honor that then, regarding our reputation protected against all sort of reproach, I will no longer hesitate to reembark.'

The zeal that animated so brave a general communicated itself to all the officers who heard him, and nothing was any longer thought of in his army but the arrangements necessary for the execution of so noble a plan.

M. de Montcalm, on his side, anxious for the quarter seemingly menaced by the enemy, and fearful, especially, that they intended cutting off our supplies, dispatched additional reinforcements to M. de Bougainville, who then found that he had under his orders, including Indians, about 300 men, scattered in different posts from Sillery as far as Point aux trembles. 'Twas the elite of the army, in which were reunited all the grenadiers, all the pickets, all the volunteers of the army and the cavalry: the order to continue to follow, attentively, all the enemy's movements, was reiterated to him. His center was at Cap Rouge.

Things were in this state, on both sides, when about midnight, between the 12th and 13th, Mr. Wolf after having, by different movements, endeavored to attract our attention on the Saint Augustin side, sent his barges to feel the post adjoining Sillery. Fortune appeared in this emergency to combine with the little order which prevailed among our troops, so as to facilitate the approach of those barges.

A convoy of provisions was to come down that same night by water to Quebec; the rumor was circulated through all the posts in front of which it was to pass, without agreeing, among themselves on any rallying cry; but some unforeseen event having prevented our bateaux taking advantage of the night tide to sail, their departure was postponed to the following day, and no attention had yet been paid to warn those same posts of the fact. The consequence of this twofold neglect was, that when our sentries saw the enemy's barges advancing, they took them for ours, and satisfied with the word 'France', which was returned to the challenge, allowed those barges to pass without giving themselves the trouble to reconnoiter them.

Three captains were in command at those posts: Chevalier de Rumigny of the Regiment of La Sarre; M. Duglas, of Languedoc, and M. de Verger, of the Colony.

The English took advantage of this security, landed between two of our posts, and clambering up the precipice they had to ascend, succeeded, by dint of toil, in gaining its crest, where they did not find a soul.

This combination of misfortune and disorder in our service, prepared the fatal catastrophe which, by a succession of new blunders, in making us lose the fruit of so much fatigue and expense, capped the climax of our humiliation.

So badly established was the communication between each of M. de Bougainville's posts and between the latter and M. de

Montcalm's camp, that the English had turned and dispersed about five o'clock in the morning, the detachments which M. de Vergor commanded at L'ance du Foulon, and were already in order of battle on the heights of Quebec where they even had some field pieces of small calibre, ere any one in our camps was as yet aware that the enemy wished to attack us in that quarter. M. de Bougainville, who was only two leagues off, did not learn the fact, as he says, until eight o'clock in the morning, and M. de Vaudreuil, who was at much less than half that distance, was not exactly informed of it until about half-past six. The army, which had passed the night in bivouac in consequence of a movement perceptible among the enemy's barges at Point Levy, had returned into its tents.

The generale was beat; all the troops resumed their arms and followed, in succession, M. de Montcalm, who repaired to the heights of Quebec where the battalion of Guyenne, which had two days before returned to our extreme right, was already in position between the town and the enemy whom its presence checked.

In consequence of the corps that had been detached from our army at Beauport, the latter found itself since some days reduced to about 6,000 men. The two Montreal battalions composed of about fifteen hundred men were left to guard the camp; they advanced, however, as far as the River St. Charles when M. de Vaudreuil repaired to the army. M. de Montcalm could, therefore, according to this calculation, muster only four thousand five hundred men.

'Twas with such a feeble force, without affording breathing time to the last detachments which had reached him from our left, and which had run nearly two leagues in one single race, that this General resolved, about ten o'clock in the morning, on attacking the enemy, (whose light infantry was since some time engaged with ours,) on a report he had received, which had not a shadow of a foundation, that the English were busy intrenching themselves.

The rash haste with which M. de Montcalm had made his attack originated in jealousy. M. de Vaudreuil had, in a note requesting him to postpone the attack until he had reunited all his forces, previously advised him that he was marching in person with the Montreal battalions. Nothing more was required to determine a General who would have readily been jealous of the part the simple soldier would have taken in his successes. His ambition was that no person but himself should ever be named, and this turn of mind contributed not a little to make him thwart the different enterprises in which he could not appear.

The two armies, separated by a rise of ground, were cannonading one another for about an hour.

Our artillery consisted only of three small field pieces.

The eminence on which our army was ranged in the order of battle commanded, at some points, that occupied by the English where they were defended either by shallow ravines or by the rail fences of the fields; our troops, composed almost entirely of Canadians impetuously rushed on the enemy, but their ill-formed ranks soon broke either in consequence of the precipitancy with which they had been made to march, or by the inequality of the ground. The English received our first fire in good order, without giving way. They afterwards very briskly returned our fire, and the advance movement made from their center by a detachment of about 200 men with fixed bayonets, sufficed to put to flight almost the whole of our army. The rout was total only among the Regulars; the Canadians accustomed to fall back Indian fashion (and like the ancient Parthians) and to turn afterwards on the enemy with more confidence than before, rallied in some places, and under cover of the brushwood, by which they were surrounded, forced divers corps to give way, but at last were obliged to yield to the superiority of numbers. The Indians took scarcely any part in this affair. They kept themselves, for the most part at a distance, until the success of the battle should decide what part they should take. 'Tis well known that they never face the enemy in open field.

These particulars, with the aid of a map, will enable the reader to appreciate the blunders committed by M. de Montcalm on this day. The following are the principal ones with which impartial judges unanimously reproach him:

1st. *He ought, on learning that the enemy had landed, dispatched orders to M. Bougainville, who had, as already stated, the élite of the troops of the army; by combining his movements with those of that Colonel, it had been easy for him to make it quasi-impossible for the enemy to avoid finding himself between two fires.*

2nd. *The fate of Quebec depending on the success of the battle about to be fought, he ought to bring all his forces together. 'Twas useless, therefore, to leave a corps of 1,500 men at our camp, the more especially as being intrenched only on the side of the river, and commanded by ground in the rear covered with timber, it would never become a tenable post for the enemy; besides the batteries which lined it were manned by gunners.*

3rd. *For the same reason, as the army was only 200 toises from the glacis of the town, he ought to draw off the pickets on duty there; this would have been an addition of 7 [to] 800 men. He could in like manner, have ordered up the artillery; there was no lack of field pieces.*

4th. *His army being, in great part, composed only of Canadians, who 'tis known, are not adapted for fighting in a pitched battle, instead of losing the advantage of the post by going to attack an enemy too well arranged, he ought to wait and profit by the nature of the ground to place those Canadians by platoons in the clumps of brush wood by which he was surrounded; arranged in that way, they certainly excel all the troops of the universe by the precision with which they fire.*

5th. *Being determined on attacking, he ought at least, have altered his arrangements. I have already stated in the commencement of this Extract, that the Militia had been incorporated among the Regulars: Could any harmony be expected in the movements of a body, the different parts of which must of necessity, by their constitution, mutually embarrass each other.*

6th. *Finally, he did not dream of forming a corps de reserve.*

As for M. de Bougaineville, he has been blamed for having made it impossible for him to concentrate his troops promptly, by spreading them too much, and for not attending more particularly to Quebec than to any other parts; at noon he was scarcely in the presence of the enemy with half his men. Yet, in these last moments of the fine season, guarding in preference the points included between the River St. Charles and that of Cap Rouge, ought to be regarded as essential; the one and the other, and particularly the latter, forming for the town barriers which the enemy could never pass, except by employing a great deal of time in the work.

But if the errors committed by M. de Montcalm have been fatal to our arms, I will say that these appear to me to have been dishonored by the conduct observed by those who succeeded him in the command.

After the battle, the army mustered in the Horn-work which had been constructed at the head of the bridge thrown over the River St. Charles. Divers officers of the Regular troops hesitated not to say openly, in presence of the soldier, that no other course remained for us than to capitulate promptly for the entire Colony.

All the troops were ordered to go back each to its own camp, and M. de Vaudreuil summoned to a Council of War all the commanders of corps; 'twas there that these gentlemen, exaggerating somewhat the loss we had just suffered, all voted unanimously that the army should retreat to Jacques Cartier (9 leagues). 'Twas decided that advantage should be taken of the darkness of the following night to carry that resolution into effect, and that the troops should leave the tents standing in order to deceive the enemy, who, nevertheless, had killed, taken or wounded only 7 [to] 800 of our men, and it has just been shown that by concentrating M. de Bougainville's corps, the Montreal battalions and the garrison of the town, we should still have remaining about nearly 5 thousand fresh troops, whom we might regard as the elite of the army. M. Bigot was again the only one in the council who voted that we should make a second attack with our entire force. M. de Vaudreuil had indeed been of his opinion, but the plurality of votes carried it.

'Tis to be observed that M. de Bougainville found himself, by his rank, in command of the army under M. de Vaudreuil; the good

fortune of this young Colonel and his talents even had excited jealousies against him.

M. de Montcalm who had, after receiving his wound, returned to Quebec, was applied to for his opinion. That General merely answered that there were three plans to pursue: the first, to make a second attack on the enemy; the second, to retire to Jacques Cartier, and the third, to capitulate for the Colony.

I shall not make any comments on the fright which was manifested lest we should be attacked on the retreat. After our defeat, I admit that we could not, for various reasons, preserve our camp at Beauport, but I will say, that it never appeared to me probable that the enemy would run the risk of crossing rivers and traversing woods for the purpose of coming to disturb us, whilst, by abandoning the country to them, we should allow them quietly to take Quebec, the object of their wishes.

Neither do I ever admit the necessity of the retreat to Jacques Cartier. By renouncing a second general battle, opportunities might still be made good use of, in harassing the enemy during the siege of Quebec; that would be the more easily done, as we should, by proceeding to St. Foy, always have found an assured retreat in the woods in our rear, and, as for subsistence, 'twould reach us there with still less difficulty than at Beauport, since the reverse we had just suffered did not augment the obstacles our transports experienced, and, on the other hand, we approached nearer our stores. Besides, we would thereby be in a position to throw all sorts of supplies at every moment into the town, which the enemy, daring not to spread himself too much abroad, never invested; 'twas not, indeed, until he became certain of our retreat, that he sent, three days afterwards, some detachments to our camp at Beauport; hence, 'tis plain that we might have plenty of time to remove our baggage, and over 8 days' provisions for the entire army, which we left there.

14th. The army having marched all night, halted in the vicinity of St. Augustin. M. de Montcalm died at 4 o'clock in the morning.

15th. *The van-guard of the army arrived about noon at Jacques Cartier. There we received news from Quebec, by which we learned that General Wolf had been killed in the beginning of the engagement; that General, Moncton, his second, had been dangerously wounded, and that the command of the [British] army had devolved on M. Townshend, whose manners were already greatly praised. He had sent a guard of fifteen men to the General Hospital, which continued to be managed as usual.*

16th. We learned that the enemy continued intrenching themselves before Quebec, whence M. de Ramezay sent word that he had only 6 days' provisions; he notified M. de Vaudreuil, at the same time, that he should soon see himself under the necessity of capitulating, should he not receive prompt supplies. Efforts were made to send him some the following night, by land and water, but the bad weather interposed obstacles to our transports.

17th. Chevr. de Lévis, to whom M. de Vaudreuil had dispatched a courier retiring from Beauport, arrived at the army; 'twas immediately resolved to march towards Quebec, and M. de Vaudreuil notified M. Ramezay thereof, whom he exhorted to hold out to the last extremity: he announced to him, at the same time, the departure of supplies of provisions.

18th. The army went to sleep at Point aux trembles; M. de Vaudreuil received there a courier dispatched to him by M. de Ramezay, to inform him that, fearful of a want of provisions, he had sent Adjutant Joannes, of the regiment of Languedoc, to propose to the English General the articles of capitulation drawn up before the opening of the campaign, by the late Marquis de Montcalm, but held out the hope, at the same time, that he would break off the negotiation, should the supply of provisions arrive before its conclusion.

19th. The army went to sleep at St. Augustin, where we found Captain Daubrespie, of the regiment of Bearn, who delivered to M. de Vaudreuil the capitulation accepted by M. de Ramezay. This King's Lieutenant had duly received the supplies of provisions before M. de Joannes' return, but things appeared to him too far advanced to allow him to withdraw. It must be acknowledged that there existed very little good will on the part of any of his garrison, which was exceedingly weak in proportion to the enceinte of the place; to this 'twill be objected, that he had been advised beforehand that the army was marching to his relief.

As the surrender of Quebec did not permit us to undertake anything more thereabouts, the army returned to Jacques Cartier, where 'twas decided to build a fort capable of containing 500 men, to be stationed there during the winter.

According to intelligence received daily from Quebec, the enemy were employed most actively both in strengthening the defenses of the place and in forming magazines for the subsistence of the garrison which was to winter there.

The objections of the English to receive the money of the country, subjected the people who remained there to a very great scarcity, which extended even to the General Hospital, and assistance was finally obtained for it only after having given the English Generals to understand that, rendering themselves, by the capture of the town, masters of the hospitals, which were dependent on it, they were naturally bound to provide for their support. In other respects, the deplorable state to which the rest of the houses of the town had been reduced by shot and shell, rendered accommodations there very scarce. English and French, all experienced the same inconvenience, but the greatest share of it necessarily fell on the latter; people found themselves pell-mell in the houses where this disorder has occasioned considerable pillage.

Towards the fore part of October a detachment of about 200 men of Mr. Amherst's army, headed by Captain Rogers, having had the boldness to traverse a pretty extensive tract of country, covered with timber, succeeded, under cover of the surprise, in burning the Indian village of St. Francis; M. de Bourlamaque was fully advised of his march; he had caused the removal of the canoes which Rogers had been obliged to abandon beyond Isle aux Noix, and expecting him to return by the same route, had him watched, at the passage, by a strong detachment of Canadians and Indians; but

Rogers had anticipated all that, and had, in consequence, resolved to reach Orange by another way; he could not, however, escape the pursuit of a party of 200 Indians who rushed to vengeance. Want of provisions rendered it necessary for him to divide his force in small platoons, in order more easily to find subsistence; the Indians massacred some forty and carried off 10 prisoners to their village, where some of them fell a victim to the fury of the Indian women, notwithstanding the efforts the Canadians could make to save them.

A few days after, we had a very serious alarm in the vicinity of Isle aux Noix. M. de Bourlamaque had dispatched the small fleet we kept on Lake Champlain, towards St. Frederic, to observe the enemy's movements; he was not aware, however, that the one which the enemy had constructed on their side, was very superior to his; what was to happen, happened: whilst Sieur Dolabarats, a man no longer to be employed in any command, who had charge of our Xebecs and other small vessels, was riding at anchor in one of the lake harbors, the English frigates got ready to come in quest of him, but it happened that, having passed him in the night, they found themselves in the morning 5 leagues at this side; whereupon Sieur Dolabarats seeing his retreat in somewise cut off, thought it his duty to call a council, (he had with him a detachment of land troops) which decided that nothing remained for him to do but to sink the vessels and return to Montreal by land. This was accordingly done.

We learn, on closing these dispatches, that the English have already raised one of them.

This adventure, the sight of the English vessels and of some barges which approached Isle aux Noix, caused M. Bourlamaque to suppose that the enemy's army was advancing to attack him. The alarm was great; the farmers, on all sides, who had returned from the army, were assembled; these poor people, fatigued by the campaign which they had just made and being desirous to give the remainder of the late season to their domestic avocations, marched

only with reluctance; our uneasiness unfortunately ceased before all those Militiamen had come in.

Such has been the result of events which, if they have not caused to France the entire loss of a Colony, the preservation whereof costs it so dear, have at least reduced it to the point of no longer being able to find safety except in an early peace, unless it receives in time immense reinforcements from Europe. Those who will peruse these details only superficially, will not fail to place our calamities among the number of those which are attributable only to fortune. Such will not be the case with those, who, animated by an enlightened zeal for the good of the State, will not neglect to probe them, in order to discover their true causes; and as, in making these extracts, my sole object has been to respond on my part to the patriotic views of the latter, and to the confidence they repose in me, in dragging from obscurity facts which it may interest them to know, I shall endeavor, avoiding prolixity however, as much as will be in my power, to make them appreciate their causes.

Instead of seeking them in a fatality which superstition always perceives in whatever calamities overtake men, I think I can, without incurring any risk, flatter myself with finding them in the passions to which we have had the misfortune to be too subject, or rather, in the disorders which are necessarily their consequences.

When the King ordered Regular troops to America, he considered them only in the light of the services they might render there, and it may be said, that his Majesty, instead of exacting such services as a Master, appeared unwilling to look for them except from the gratitude which his favors ought to excite, but these same favors, wherewith the Regular troops were loaded on their arrival in Canada, contributed not a little to disgust those whose lot it was to serve there perpetually, and on whom it cannot be denied, notwithstanding the laxity of their discipline, that more dependence ought to be placed, than on the former. Every country has its own mode of waging war, and that which must be followed in Canada, has, 'tis known, but little in common with the method practiced in Europe.

From this sort of jealousy a misunderstanding soon sprung up between the different corps, for which the division of authority in the command, prepared the way to reascend from grade to grade even to the chiefs, where it produced those ravages, the consequences whereof were to be so fatal.

M. de Montcalm felt it and was the first to allow its fits to be perceptible; full of talent, but ambitious beyond measure; more brilliant in consequence of the advantages of a cultivated memory, than profound in the sciences appertaining to the art of war, the first elements of which he did not possess, that General was ill adapted to the command of armies; he was, besides, subject to transports of passion which had produced a coolness towards him even among those whom he had obliged, and who, by circumstances, ought to have the same interests as he. I will add, that though brave, he was in nowise enterprising; he would, for example, never have attacked Chouaguen, had he not been, as it were, forced thereto by the reproaches of the sort of timidity he exhibited, made by M. de Rigaud, a man, it is true, of limited mind, but full of bravery and boldness, and accustomed to range the woods; and he would have abandoned the siege of Fort George, at the very moment he undertook it, had he not been reassured by the firmness of Chevalier de Lévis. To this mediocrity, in the talents necessary to a military man of his rank, he united a very grave defect in a General; that is, indiscretion. More occupied in the care of giving brilliancy to his eloquence than with the duties his position exacted, he could not prevent himself making his plans public long before they were to be put in execution; and that he had a grudge against any one, was sufficient to make him unceasingly mangle the reputation of such a person in unseemly terms, even in the presence of his domestics, and consequently of the troops. 'Tis by such remarks as these, which at bottom he did not intentionally circulate, that he made M. de Vaudreuil lose the confidence of the soldier, the farmer and even the Indian, to whom that governor would certainly have been dear, had those people been able to penetrate his sentiments in their regard. Good sense, no science (lumières), too facile, a confidence in events which renders circumspection often slow, nobleness and generosity of sentiment, great affability, such are the principal traits that have appeared to me to characterize the Marquis de Vaudreuil; whose goodness carried to excess would, in Europe, certainly have been subject to an infinitude of inconveniences; in Canada, the opposite vice would have assuredly precipitated the ruin of the Colony. Without having lived there, no exact idea can be formed of the patience with which one must be particularly endued in order to support the importunities of the Indians, to which a governor is continually exposed, especially in time of war. Equally ignorant of the maxims of civil or military government, M. de Vaudreuil could, on the other hand, not comprehend how inconvenient it was to push too far the indulgence with which it was proper, notwithstanding, to treat with measure the Militia. That produced two effects equally disastrous: The Canadians, from whose valor, address and docility, properly modified, everything might be expected, fell insensibly into remissness, and M. de Montcalm on his side was sufficiently ignorant of the world (assez peu citoyen ["not very citizen"]) to draw therefrom a sort of right to suffer his regular troops to lose all sort of discipline; the soldier ceased to acknowledge the officer, who, himself, became insubordinate; disorders of every description ensued; there existed no longer, either regularity or exactness in the service; nothing equaled the devastation committed by the troops throughout the rural districts where the army was encamped; complaints thereof were made; the General answered, that everything belonged to the soldier, who informed of these dispositions, roved throughout the settlements, two or three leagues round about. 'Twas on this occasion that a woman, on a day of alarm, reproaching M. de Montcalm the profligacy with which he allowed his soldiers to pillage cattle, fowls, gardens, tobacco plantations and even wheat, told him at M. de Vaudreuil's quarters in presence of twenty officers, that he would have 500 soldiers less to oppose the efforts of the enemy, whose attack was expected every moment, if he did not hasten to send and have the genérale beat at Charlesbourg (about 2 leagues in the interior) where they were busy pillaging even the interior of the houses.

The officers of the Regular troops, in justification of the disorders which the soldiers were committing, made answer to whatever complaints were made them: that the soldiers were dying of hunger. The ration consisted of one pound of very fine bread and one pound of meat.

From the conduct of these two Generals I must pass to that of the Intendant, whose duty it was to concur with them in the arrangements relative to the general operations.

I shall not enter here into an examination of the reproaches cast on M. Bigot by the public; I shall merely say that the advantages, immense indeed, which accrued to him from the funds he had risked in trade, whilst creating for him a great deal of envy, have exposed his reputation to the shafts of the blackest calumny. The resources of a fortunate trade are known in all countries of the world. The most signal good fortune has always constantly accompanied the transactions on this Intendant's account. Starting from these two facts, which, I believe no one can dispute, we shall easily divest ourselves of any astonishment created by his wealth, however extraordinary that may be, when we consider that, owing to the prodigious variation prices of provisions and all sorts of merchandise have experienced in Canada (which is pretty usual in all the Colonies), it has happened that the man who has realized, two years ago, two thousand écus only, may to-day find himself worth 400 thousand francs.

The keg (velie) of brandy which costs, in France, 50 [livres?], now sells here for as much as 110 [livres?], &c., &c., &c. I will add, that he certainly would not have called forth so many remarks, had his generosity not made a great number of ingrates. 'Tis not that I pretend to approve of an Intendant becoming merchant; I am even of opinion, notwithstanding the custom of preceding Ministers tolerating it pretty openly, that infinite inconveniences always will accrue therefrom; but also, when prohibiting it, the

King must allow a man of that rank a salary that would enable him to live decently, &c. This twofold observation must naturally apply, mutatis mutandis, to officers of every grade from whom, private interest, 'tis known, does not now, unfortunately, any longer permit the State to expect any distinguished services.

Neither can I speak, but in very vague terms, of M. Bigot's administration. All the world knows that he has a cunning mind, but no one is ignorant that, to understand exactly the amount of good and the evil an official of that character is capable of doing, one must be a long time in a position to follow the course of his operations, to be able to observe their results. I shall remark, generally, that were he a Colbert, he could not prevent certain abuses arising from the constitution of the service of this Colony. Is it not, for example, grossly irregular for the Comptroller to find himself, from time immemorial, charged with several details of which he is the innate censor? In the infancy of the Colony that might be compatible with the exactitude the service requires, because the Intendant could see to everything; but, for several years that the expenses have become so considerable, is it likely that the man of the most scrupulous probity, the most enlightened and, altogether, the most laborious, could have the capacity to satisfy so many different objects, when his position required from him only the maintenance of regularity, a duty which demands certainly a man's exclusive attention?

He who now fills that office, a man above reproach, has been obliged to admit this to me; he has even of his own accord, made me perceive many consequences of it.

But I will admit, that had the King had at the head of each of these details intelligent persons, who might be induced by a liberal salary to take the good of his service to heart, it would not have been the less impossible for them to satisfy the views of their zeal in consequence of the turn things have taken; I explain.

When the King by his ordinances, has vested a certain authority in the officers to whom the economical department of his government is confided, he has wisely foreseen that such authority was necessary to persons who were to serve as a dam against the pretensions, often unjust, of the military.

Such, I believe, is the system of the Monarchical government.

The laws pronounce penalties on those who will have impeded the humblest constable in the duties of his office; the King's service it seems to me, ought to be the same everywhere; uniformity in all its parts constitutes its solidity.

But in consequence of a deplorable confusion, it has happened that, instead of maintaining these same persons in a respect commensurate with the object of their functions, and which, perhaps, it would have been of advantage further to increase under certain conditions, all the rules both of the service and of decency, have been permitted even in France, to be violated with impunity, in their regard; they have not been able to avoid falling into a contempt, if I dare make use of that expression, which has reduced thein to the necessity of becoming lax, on occasions when it would have been important that they should dare exhibit firmness; but if disorder so deplorable has been seen to prevail in France, under the eyes of the Court, could it be expected that 'twould not reach even to the Colonies, and especially this one, where the long duration of wars and the constitution of things have not only carried the Military to the top- rung of despotism, but moreover where the Intendant's credit has been entirely ruined by the annoyances with which he has been of late publicly overwhelmed? This disorder has, without doubt, penetrated far into it, to produce its most direful effects therein; hence have, necessarily, followed the enormous expenditure occasioned, on the one hand, by the facility afforded detached officers to realize, whilst appearing to turn up a little land, &c., fortunes as considerable as they were rapid, and on the other, by the fraudulent consumptions of all sorts, and particularly of provisions, whereunto that Intendant has been no longer permitted to attempt merely to place a check; he has proofs of the extravagancies M. de Montcalm has been guilty of towards him this year; that General forgot on those occasions, what was due by him to the service and to that Intendant, and what he owed to

himself, and as those pieces related only to unimportant and even contemptible matters, they can serve to explain all the extent of the unjust passion which tormented Mr. de Montcalm.

'Twould be superfluous for me to make any new reflections on what must necessarily result from a government so convulsive. Notwithstanding the precipitancy with which I have been obliged to sketch this picture, I have endeavored to place things in a sufficiently clear order [...]."

In the meantime, with the full blessing of the Governor-General, the Marquis de Vaudreuil, the Chevalier de Lévis had assumed the late Marquis de Montcalm's supreme command of French-allied forces in North America, and had spent the winter of 1759-60 in tireless preparation for an early start to the upcoming campaigning season; stockpiling ammunition, requisitioning butcher's knives to be used as make-shift bayonets, ordering the construction of scaling ladders, procuring enough pairs of snowshoes to accommodate the whole army, and, with continued difficulty, acquiring sufficient provisions.

Inspiring and dauntless, it had been Lévis' initial intention of marching on Quebec as soon as possible, despite the severity of 1759-60's winter in particular, however, he quickly realized that such a venture would be irrational and incredibly dangerous at best, on account of the bitter cold and the enduring fear of insufficient provisions, two factors which, when combined, could theoretically decimate his army before they had even reached their objective, notwithstanding the extreme difficulties that could arise from a mid-winter siege should he and his men even be able to reach Quebec. These facts considered induced Lévis to postpone any attempt on the city until spring, the potential benefits of which were; allowing him additional time to prepare his army; the weather to theoretically improve; and the depletion of Brigadier General James Murray's Quebec garrison from disease and continual harassment by French, Canadian and Indigenous militia.

At length, in April, 1760, the Chevalier de Lévis received his official instructions from the Governor-General, the Marquis de Vaudreuil, which were as follows:

"Memoir to serve as Instructions to Chevalier de Lévis, Maréchal des Camps et Armées of the King.

The winding up of the last campaign, reduced the Colony to the most critical circumstances and most melancholy condition.

1st. By the strong garrison the enemy left in Quebec, and their proximity to our frontiers on Lakes Champlain and Ontario.

2nd. By the exhaustion of our resources, of our other means, and particularly by the extreme scarcity of provisions.

We conceived, nevertheless, the desire of recapturing Quebec during the winter; we arranged, conjointly, with Chevalier de Lévis, the most urgent preparations for such an expedition, the good will of the Canadians seconding perfectly our measures; we had every reason to hope that the first instant would not be lost when the garrison of Quebec would find itself enfeebled by sickness or discouraged by some unfortunate event, such as the firing of its powder magazines, &c.

The knowledge we have had of the enemy's forces, and military arrangements, the obstacles we could not surmount for such a campaign, especially in regard to provisions, the greatest portion of the mills being stopped by the ice; all that being maturely considered and duly reflected on by Chevalier de Lévis and myself induced us, secretly, to postpone the execution of our project until the opening of the navigation; we have, however, made the demonstrations which depended on us to create alarms and prompt annoyances capable of fatiguing the garrison of Quebec, which have not failed to produce the effect we expected.

The moment is now one of the most urgent. We have, after much care, collected together all the resources of the Colony in provisions and munitions of war; the one and the other are very slender, not to say insufficient. Therefore, let us use all the expedients our zeal can suggest to make up for any deficiencies.

We have concerted and concluded with Chevalier de Lévis the plan of the siege of Quebec, and everything relating thereunto; he is convinced, as well as ourselves, that it is the only attempt we have to make to save the Colony.

Our forces consist of about 3,500 Regulars.

3,000 Militia of the districts of Montreal and Three Rivers.

And about 400 Indians of different Nations.

Independent of the Acadians, we expect that the farmers of the district of Quebec, or at least the greater portion of them, will join this army when the place will be invested. We address a circular letter for that purpose to the Parish priests and Captains of Militia in all the parishes of this government.

As the zeal of the Canadians might be susceptible of some abatement, as they are intimidated by General Murray's menaces, Chevalier de Lévis will accompany our circular with a rigid Manifesto, whereby he will relieve these Canadians of their apprehension and compel them to join him on pain of death.

Chevalier de Levis knows that we cannot furnish a larger army, as the Militia that will remain in the governments of Three Rivers and Montreal, are indispensably necessary to put seed into the ground; he also knows that we must, at the same time, provide for the safety of the frontiers on Lakes Champlain and Ontario.

Our presence in this town being required by those two points and to watch the enemy's movements, and to provide for everything in the interior of the Colony.

We hand over to Chevalier de Lévis, with the confidence we repose in his zeal and experience, the command of the army, which we have, jointly with him, destined for the Quebec expedition, and in consequence of our distance and of cases which we cannot now actually foresee, we deposit with him the same powers we would ourselves have were we to command this army in person, authorizing him to act as he shall judge best for the good of the service, the interest of the Colony and State.

Although the success of the siege of Quebec appears doubtful, both in consequence of the small means we possess in ammunition, artillery and provisions, and by reason of our force compared with that of the enemy, which we prudently estimate at about 4,000 fighting men, who will possibly be increased in number by the reinforcements the English are expecting, from one moment to the other, we have, nevertheless, maturely reflected and determined with Chevalier de Lévis, that all these obstacles should not stop us; that the Quebec expedition is the only step to be taken, both for the further preservation of the Colony for the King and to enable us to receive, unimpeded, the reinforcements his Majesty will please to order to be dispatched to us, more especially as the enemy, having taken up a position on the South shore, opposite Quebec, and being erecting batteries there, these reinforcements cannot pass without imminent danger.

According to these powerful motives, it is important that Chevalier de Lévis apply the greatest activity to his operations; whereupon we have nothing to prescribe to him, relying entirely on his zeal, experience and the particular attachment we have always known him to feel towards this Colony.

As there are among the troops that compose the garrison of Quebec, a number of French and Germans who have left the King's service or that of their lawful Sovereigns, his Majesty's allies, to enter that of the King of Great Britain, after mature reflection and seeing that, under existing circumstances, we ought to try all lawful means to increase our forces and weaken those of our enemies, we have considered it, for the good of the King's service, to call on those same soldiers to enjoy the amnesty granted by his Majesty's ordinance of the 29th of December, 1757, and in consequence we have enacted ours, whereof Chevalier de Lévis will make use, agreeably to the conditions inserted therein.

Should Chevalier de Lévis be so fortunate as to succeed in obliging the garrison of Quebec to sue for a capitulation, he will take advantage, as much as he possibly can, of the circumstances and situation in which the enemy may be placed, so as to grant them only the articles mentioned in the draft we have furnished him of an advantageous capitulation for ourselves; far from intending to restrict him on this point, we observe to him that the situation of the Colony, the uncertainty of success and the apprehension of the forces the English may receive by way of the river, do not permit us to be particular. Therefore, we inform Chevalier de Lévis beforehand that we approve, in advance of all the conditions he will consider it his duty to grant that garrison, our principal object being to accelerate the relief of the Colony by the surrender of Quebec, and the placing of ourselves in a condition to oppose the efforts the English will possibly make to penetrate into the interior of the Colony, by Lakes Champlain and Ontario.

Chevalier de Lévis will employ all the means and negotiations imaginable to accelerate the surrender of Quebec; he will grant to that end such sums as he shall judge necessary, to such persons as will contribute thereunto, were he even obliged to give a free and entire course to the expense we are authorized to incur by the Minister's letter, in cipher, of the 10th February, 1759, addressed conjointly to the late Mssr. de Montcalm and us, a copy whereof is in Chevalier de Lévis' possession.

Chevalier de Lévis is instructed that we have established lookouts at St. Barnabé, Bic, and Ile aux Coudres to hail the French ships and to furnish them with practical pilots. We communicate to Chevalier de Lévis copies of the orders we have given on that point, the signals those vessels and the one that has wintered at Gaspé, are to make.

Supposing a French fleet to arrive, Chevalier de Lévis will transmit to the Commander thereof the letter we write requesting him to communicate to Chevalier de Lévis his orders and instructions, he will correspond and cooperate with him in the execution of the King's views towards this Colony, according as circumstances may require, until we regulate his operations.

Chevalier de Lévis will be careful to cause all our dispatches to be delivered to him, he will give, or cause to be given, a receipt for those of the Court, if necessary. He will have those dispatches diligently transmitted to us by a reliable person.

For the rest, Chevalier de Lévis will send us couriers every day, or as often as possible, to inform us of his progress. We shall have no greater desire, on our part, than to communicate to him whatever of interest will occur on our frontiers.

Dated at Montreal, the 16th April, 1760.

Vaudreuil."

That same day, the Governor-General also penned letters to the priests of the parishes within and surrounding the district of Quebec, as well as to the various captains of the peasant militias, encouraging them to support the Chevalier de Lévis' on his impending march to relive Quebec. The latter of which was worded as such:

"Copy of the Circular letter written by the Marquis de Vaudreuil to the Captains of Militia of the parishes, North and South, within the government of Quebec.

Montreal, 16th April, 1760.

Sir,

Since the close of the last campaign, I have been seriously occupied by the situation to which the misfortunes of the war have reduced the Canadians of the government of Quebec.

I have been particularly alive to the threats General Murray has uttered in all his Manifestoes, the vexations he has exercised towards them and the harsh and cruel treatment he has made the greater portion of the Canadians undergo without any legitimate right or reason.

The sad state of these Canadians, the sentiments of zeal, which I know they entertain for the King's service, and their attachment to the country, all that has not a little contributed to increase the desire I have always felt to retake Quebec, and thereby to deliver the Canadians from the tyranny they have only too severely experienced.

'Tis with this view, Sir, that I have reassembled a very powerful army with a considerable train of artillery to besiege Quebec; nothing equals the ardor of the troops, Canadians and different Indian Nations I have destined for that expedition.

My presence being essentially necessary in this town, either to watch over the safety of our frontiers on Lakes Champlain and Ontario, or to reinforce the army, which is going to lay siege to Quebec, should the garrison of that town receive, contrary to my expectation, succors from Europe, I have placed the command of that army in the hands of Chevalier de Lévis, Marshal of the camps and armies of the King, both on account of his love for everything Canadian, and of the confidence the latter, the troops and the Indian Nations equally repose in him.

This army is about to march and the town of Quebec will be soon invested.

'Tis my intention, Sir, that you, your officers, and all the Canadians of your company, march, with arms and baggage, on the receipt of this letter and of Chevalier de Lévis' Manifesto, to join that General and his army. I have authorized him to give you that order on pain of death. I am fully convinced of your zeal to execute it, and that your courage will yield in nothing to that of the troops and Canadians of the army.

You have therein, Sir, as well as your Militia, a very particular interest; you have only too truly experienced the aversion of the English for everything Canadian; you have also had the saddest proofs of the severity of their government; whence you must conclude what will be your lot, should they have entire possession of Canada.

You approach the moment of triumph over that enemy; he cannot but succumb before the efforts of our army.

We, too, approach the moment of receiving powerful succors from France.

At length, brave Canadians, 'tis yours to signalize yourselves; you ought to undertake everything, risk everything for the preservation of your religion and the salvation of your country.

The Canadians of this government and of that of Three Rivers are marching with zeal, and out of attachment and love for you. You ought to imitate them in every point; unite your efforts to theirs and even surpass them.

I guarantee to those among you who will furnish brilliant proofs of their zeal, signal rewards on the part of his Majesty. But, likewise, I cannot conceal from you that those who will have been or shall be traitors to the country, will be punished with the greatest rigor of his Majesty's ordinances.

I am, Sir, your affectionate servant,

Vaudreuil."

The Chevalier de Lévis' army, which gathered at Montreal, numbered approximately seventy-five hundred men, consisting of approximately thirty-six hundred regular troops, three thousand militiamen, predominately Canadians, as well as approximately four hundred Indigenous warriors from numerous Nations, tribes and/or bands, led by Charles Langlade and Luc de la Corne. In addition to these, it was Lévis' and the Governor-General's hope that many more able-bodied men, carried away by patriotic fervor, would join his ranks on their march to Quebec. While to avoid the difficulties of transporting his twelve-piece artillery train through snow, ice and along terrible roads, in lieu of a horse drawn cart convoy, Lévis had elected to load the cannons, in addition to the army's ammunition, provisions and scaling ladders onto several frigates and numerous lesser vessels, which would navigate down the partially thawed Saint Lawrence River, alongside the army's march on shore.

The expedition formally commenced on April 20th, and after a grueling march, through whirling blizzards and violent thunderstorms, Lévis' numerically superior army finally clashed with Brigadier General James Murray's scurvy-depleted English garrison near the village of St. Foye, beneath the walls of Quebec, on April 28th. A brutal slugging match, one of the bloodiest in Canadian history, after an hour-and-three-quarter long struggle, Lévis' army finally secured victory, driving General Murray's men from the advantageous high ground they had occupied, and pursuing them into the city, around which, a traditional siege then commenced, with Lévis immediately ordering the construction of intrenchments and fortifications around Quebec, in anticipation of reinforcements and resupply direct from France, which he hoped would beat the English fleet up the thawing Saint Lawrence River, so soon as safety permitted. Whoever's vessels navigated the river first would decide the fate not only of Quebec, but the entirety of the campaign and New France itself — so mutually desperate were the French and English armies.

During the first week of May, the Governor-General of New France, the Marquis de Vaudreuil wrote French magistrate, politician, and close confidant of the King, Nicolas René Berryer, the Comte de La Ferrière (1703 – 62), detailing the Chevalier de Lévis' campaign to his own knowledge, and to which he subsequently annexed a more detailed journal of the expedition, almost certainly penned by an active participant, and provided after its conclusion, before belatedly sending the pair together to the aforementioned Minister:

"M. de Vaudreuil to M. Berryer.
Montreal, 3rd May, 1760.

My Lord,
Chevalier de Levis' army arrived on the 24th of last month at Point aux trembles with the Kings frigates [,] ships and other vessels having on board the provisions, artillery, munitions of war, implements and field furniture.

Chevalier de Lévis employed the entire of the day of the 25th to collect and regulate the order of march of his army in order to put it in motion on the 26th.

On the news he received [...] that the enemy were fortifying themselves on the heights of Cap Rouge and on the bank of the river at the head of the three slopes (rampes) he determined to march by land, to ascend the River of Cap Rouge so as to deploy by la Suède.

'Twas 6 o'clock in the evening when the army commenced defiling, preceded by our Indians.

From the position of the English, there was reason to suppose that they were ignorant of Chevalier de Lévis' taking that route, and that General Murray, who, with 2,500 men, had repaired to the heights of St. Foy, was waiting for them there, but as soon as he had perceived the head of our army, composed of the Grenadiers and Indians, he made his retreat; abandoned two spiked 16-pounders at St. Foy, burned the church of that place in which was stored some powder, 1,500 muskets and a great quantity of provisions. We were able to overtake only the rear guard of the English which we pressed as far as Dumont's house, a short distance from the town. The English had several wounded; we had, on our side, one Indian killed, one Cavalry officer, one cavalier and three grenadiers wounded.

Were it not for a frightful storm which lasted 24 hours, Chevalier de Lévis would have surprised the enemy, who were expecting us only by the river and Cap Rouge; he allowed our army very little rest; directed his main efforts to hem in the enemy in order not to lose a moment in opening the trench.

28th. Mr. Murray marched forth from Quebec with about 4,000 men, and placed himself in the order of battle at Dumont's house; our grenadiers occupied it and a height on the left, at the opening of the wood above the Foulon cove; our army was cantoned from La Fontaine's house to the St. Foy church. Chevalier de Lévis mounted his horse at day-break with M. de Bourlamaque, to go and reconnoiter the enemy. Seeing them in full march, he directed the genérale to be beaten and gave orders for our army to march with the greatest diligence to support our grenadiers. He left M. de Bourlamaque to command the van-guard and arrange the troops as they came up; he proceeded, in person, to La Fontaine's house to bring the army up in several columns; notwithstanding all his efforts, it could not be formed on the ground designated by M. de Lévis for the field of battle, before the enemy took up a favorable position, and on the spot we proposed to occupy, our right only had time to form; M. de Lévis, seeing that the left was still at a great distance and could not arrive before the enemy would have charged us, determined to make the right of our army fall back and enter the wood. The enemy advanced to fight us, in full battle array, with 22 pieces of artillery in front. Our grenadiers, who were at Dumont's house, were obliged to fall back on the brigade of La Sarre, which had just finished getting out (déboucher). M. de Levis ordered that brigade to march along the high road; to join the grenadiers and attack Dumont's house, which was in possession of the enemy. The grenadiers and that brigade advanced with the greatest courage. M. de Bourlamaque went thither also, and our troops carried that house; Chevalier de Levis followed along the line to move it and get it out of the wood, to attack the enemy in front and on their right; they were then so near that they were firing grape at us and had the advantage of the height, which did not prevent the center and right of our army defiling from the wood with three pieces of cannon, which composed our whole artillery, and to charge the enemy; the right and center brigades marched with the greatest ardor and commenced to force the enemy. The Canadians of the brigade of La Reine; that of Royal Rousillon, and that of the Marine, took the enemy in flank and upset their left, which threw their right into confusion, forced them to retreat and to leave us 19 guns and 3 howitzers.

M. de Repentigny, who was at the head of the center battalion and of the reserve from the town of Montreal, held and occupied with his sole brigade in open field, the center of the army; he had the advantage of arresting the enemy's center which was advancing with rapid strides, and to oblige it to resume its original position. This brigade had also the advantage of twice driving back two bodies of troops which detached themselves from the right to dislodge it, to stay, by its fire and bold bearing, the pursuit of the enemy, who were closely pressing on our left, which had almost entirely fallen back, and finally to procure for it an opportunity of rallying and recovering. In fine, this brigade was the only one on which the enemy did not gain an inch of ground.

Captain de Melois, adjutant of our troops attached to the brigade of the Marine, performed prodigies of valor; he would have carried off two standards from the enemy which they had left behind, had not false information persuaded him that those colors were already in the hands of the regiment of Guyenne.

Our army pursued the enemy up to the walls of Quebec, but was so fatigued that it could not profit by all its advantage, nor even make use of the bayonet.

The battle lasted three hours, and victory was long uncertain, but Chevalier de Lévis, superior on account of his quick-sightedness, determined in the nick of time, to turn the enemy at the head of a column, and decided by that movement the victory in our favor; therefore, I can say, my Lord, that 'twas he alone who has won the battle. M. de Bourlamaque also performed wonders; he was wounded in the calf of the leg and his horse was killed by the same discharge of grape.

The enemy left on the field of battle 3 [to] 400 dead, 20 officers prisoners, Colonel Yonk is among the latter, and 50 [to] 60 soldiers. M. de Lévis estimates their loss at about 12 [to] 1,500 men, killed or wounded. They admit this themselves, and that there are a great many officers.

Ours may consist nearly of an equal number, including 114 officers killed or wounded. I shall annex an exact return of them to the report I shall have the honor of rendering of the opening of the siege [included after this letter].

This day confers infinite honor on our troops and every corps of the army which equally distinguished themselves.

Chevalier de Levis took advantage of the ground the enemy had abandoned, to open the trenches that night.

The right of our army rested on the Butte à Neveu, and the left 40 or 50 toises beyond the Saint Louis road; this section in the progress of things will extend itself farther.

The enemy have lined their entire front with cannon, and are keeping up a great fire of artillery which carries off many of our men.

The Canadians from below Quebec were beginning to arrive. Chevalier de Lévis has handed over the detail of these Militia to M. de Repentigny.

I greatly long, my Lord to have the honor to inform you of the fall of Quebec. The victory which Chévalier de Levis has just gained is a very good omen, provided always that the obstinate defense of the English do not give time to their reinforcements to arrive.

I am, with the most profound respect, My Lord,
 Your most humble and most obedient servant,
   Vaudreuil."

"(Annexed to the letter of Mr. de Vaudreuil, Governor-General of Canada, of the 3rd of May, 1760. General Memoirs.)

Journal of the Battle of Sillery and Siege of Quebec.

Narrative of the Expedition against Quebec, under the orders of Chevalier de Levis, Maréchal des Camps et Armées of the King.

The want of provisions at the close of the last campaign had prevented the cantonment of troops in the neighborhood of Quebec, to blockade the English garrison during the winter, and deprive it of the means of drawing firewood and the necessary supplies from the neighboring parishes. The troops had to be put in quarters at the end of November in order to provide for their subsistence, and Chevalier de Lévis in quitting the frontier of the district of Quebec, had confined himself to stationing a corps of about 400 men in the parish of Point aux trembles, 7 leagues from Quebec, under the command of Captain de Repentigny of the Colonial troops. This officer threw out advanced posts as far as Saint Augustin, one league above the River Cap Rouge on which he sent frequent scouts. Our lines opposite the English garrison have been during the winter at this river which is three leagues from Quebec. The high road from Point aux trembles to Quebec crosses it at its mouth. A league farther, up it has bridges connecting with a road back from the river.

A fort constructed at the close of the campaign, at the mouth of the River Jacques Cartier, ten leagues above Quebec, served as a retreat and a point d'appui to the troops of Point aux trembles and protected the Colony against any efforts the English garrison might make. The command of this fort and of the entire frontier during the winter, was conferred by the Marquis de Vaudreuil on Sieur Dumas, Major-General and Inspector of the troops of the country.

Brigadier-General Murray, [the then newly, British-appointed] Governor of Quebec, posted on his part, 150 men in the church of St. Foix, a league and a half from Quebec on the high road to Point aux trembles. He placed a similar detachment in the church of Ancient Lorette, one league from the St. Foix, back from the River [St. Lawrence] and on the road which goes up the River Cap Rouge. These two churches were intrenched and palisaded.

The English army on Lake Champlain commanded by Major-General Amherst on falling back the 20th November, left a considerable garrison at Saint Frederic, where it had built, since August, a much more extensive fort than the one we had previously there. Garrisons had been left also at Carillon, Fort George, Fort Lydius and in those on the River of Orange. On our side, Brigadier de Bourlamaque in withdrawing the troops on that frontier on the 28th of November, had orders to leave 300 men under the command of Captain de Lusignan of the troops of the Marine, in garrison in a stockaded fort constructed at the close of the campaign in the center of the intrenchments of Isle aux Noix. Fort Saint John, five leagues in the rear, was guarded by 200 men under the orders of Captain Valette of the Royal Rousillon. Lieutenant- Colonel Roquemaure, commanding the battalion of La Reine, who was quartered at Fort Chambly, had the chief command of that frontier during the winter.

Towards Lake Ontario, Sieur Desandrouins was left with 200 men in a fort which Chevalier de Levis had caused to be built in the month of September, on one of the Islands of the Rapids, and which had been called after him.

The English army, commanded by Brigadier Gage, since the capture of Niagara, had quitted the camp of Chouaguen early, and had left a garrison in a fort it had just constructed there, and another in that of Niagara.

Such was the situation of the Colony on the first of December; all the provisions exhausted by a very long campaign, scarcely left means for a daily supply of food to the small garrisons which protected the country; and no new supplies could be expected before the farmers had threshed the grain of the last harvest.

The Marquis de Vaudreuil adopted, in concert with Chevalier de Levis, the resolution to lay siege to Quebec in the spring because he judged there was no other means of preserving Canada, this year, to his Majesty; he calculated, besides, should circumstances prevent his taking Quebec for want of ammunition, that the two ships which the contractor had demanded, and the dispatch whereof M. de Vaudreuil had solicited, would furnish him some supplies in case relief on the part of the King should fail. With this view, he considered it his duty to harass the English garrison during the winter by false alarms, and to that end made all the preparations for a winter campaign. Ladders were constructed at Jacques Cartier; orders issued to the troops to be prepared to march; Colonel de Bougainville and Brigadier Bourlamaque were sent in succession to the frontier, to annoy the English governor who, in fact, made his troops perform the most rigorous service, and kept them excessively alert.

Towards the end of January the Marquis de Vaudreuil, knowing that some grain and cattle were remaining in the lower parishes on the South shore, detached Captain de Saint Martin, of the Colonials, with 200 men, to take up a position at Point Levy, opposite Quebec, and secure the passage of the trains which were to travel by land along the bank of the river until opposite Point aux trembles. But the river becoming frozen over at the moment of his arrival, formed a very solid bridge between the town and Point

Levy, over which the English Governor dispatched a very superior detachment whereby Sieur de Saint Martin was obliged to retire. The English immediately sent to remove from the parishes the provisions intended for us, and took post in the church of Point Levy.

Sieur Saint Martin's detachment having been augmented to the number of 700 men, that officer was ordered to take up a position again at Point Levy, but three thousand English having crossed the river with cannon, he was once more obliged to fall back with the loss of 30 men. Sieur de Bourlamaque, arriving the day after that event at Point aux trembles, considered the project of getting the provisions past impossible of execution, and confined himself to sending into the parishes which the English had not exhausted, 150 men under the orders of Sieur Hertel, an officer of the Colonials, to prevent the English pushing their levies farther, and to secure the provisions until the troops would arrive before Quebec.

The remainder of the winter was spent in different alerts, which the report of an expedition on the ice had given to the English garrison, and in some sorties made by the latter against our advanced posts, in one of which we lost 80 men; the other frontiers were quiet.

'Twas only with incredible difficulty that the troops were finally put in a condition to make the campaign. The Colony, utterly exhausted, was in want not only of provisions, but likewise of every necessary for the equipment and encampment of the troops. Nothing less than the activity and resources of Sieur Bigot, the Intendant of New France, was required to find means to meet such essential wants.

Men were set to work in the very first days of March at Point aux trembles and the adjoining parishes, to make the gabions, fascines and boards necessary for the siege.

In the beginning of April, the Marquis de Vaudreuil detached Sieur de Bougainville to Ile aux Noix to take the command of that frontier, where the enemy, 'twas apprehended, would make some movements, were he to learn what we were projecting. This officer reunited the garrison of Saint John to that of Isle aux Noix, and the necessary orders were issued to furnish him a considerable reinforcement of Militia as soon as he should receive intelligence of the enemy's approach. Sieur Desandrouins, Engineer, was recalled from Fort Lévis and replaced with some reinforcements by Captain Pouchot, of the Béarn regiment.

Chevalier de Lévis had the command of the troops destined to besiege Quebec. The Marquis de Vaudreuil confided that expedition to him, being obliged to remain at Montreal; where his presence was necessary to the dispatching to the various frontiers the succors they might require.

On the 20th of April these troops left their quarters; they consisted of 8 battalions of troops of the Line, 2 battalions of Colonials, amounting in all to 5 brigades and about 3,000 Canadians, both from the town of Montreal and the country. The former composed a separate battalion, destined to be in reserve, and the others were attached to the brigades of the regular troops. The King's frigates La Tulante and La Pomone, commanded by Messrs. Vauquelin and Sauvage, had orders to drop down the river in a line with the army; they had under their escort two flyboats and several schooners, loaded with artillery, provisions and fascines.

The most of the streams having not yet broken up, 'twas the 24th before the troops were able to arrive at Point aux trembles, which was the rendezvous of the little army; they were even obliged to disembark on the ice, which had as yet left only the middle of the river free.

Chevalier de Lévis learned there that the English continued to occupy the churches of Ancient Lorette and Saint Foix; that they were intrenching themselves at the River Cap Rouge, the banks of which, being very steep on the enemy's side, afforded the means of defending with advantage the high road from Point aux trembles to Quebec, which crosses that river at its mouth.

He learned, also, that the inhabitants of Quebec had within two days been driven out of that place; that those of St. Foix, adjoining

Cap Rouge, had also been driven from their houses, which the English were [...] transporting artillery into.

This intelligence led him to understand that the English had been informed of the departure of the troops, and induced him to abandon the project he entertained up to that time, of landing in the night at Sillery, which is only a league and a half from Quebec. This maneuver would have afforded him the means of cutting off the posts at Lorette and St. Foix, but it became impracticable as soon as the enemy had cognizance of our movement. It was impossible also to land in the River Cap Rouge, as the English were occupying the heights commanding its mouth.

He therefore determined to disembark all the troops at St. Augustin, one league above Cap Rouge, and then to march to the left to reach the upper bridges of the Cap Rouge River, and to turn the enemy by following the road leading to the church of Ancient Lorette, and thence to that of St. Foix across some almost impassable woods and marshes.

The 25th was employed in concentrating the troops and putting the Canadians in order.

26th. Ten companies of grenadiers, some volunteers and 300 Indians, commanded by Captain Saint Luc, of the Colonials, were detached to form the van-guard under the orders of Sieur de Bourlamaque. That officer was instructed to reconnoiter the bridges on the River Cap Rouge; the enemy having destroyed the two principal ones, he had had two others higher up repaired and crossed the river with the van-guard.

Chevalier de Lévis immediately arrived with the head of the army, and learned that the English had abandoned the church of Lorette and neglected to tear up a corduroy road across part of a very deep marsh, between that church and the one of St. Foix, and had postponed that operation until next night.

He immediately dispatched the Indians to occupy the head of that road, and having given orders to the van-guard to support them, commenced crossing the army over the two bridges.

Sieur de Bourlamaque arrived in the beginning of the night at the entrance of the marsh, which the Indians had already crossed, and having traversed it despite a severe storm, placed the entire van-guard in some houses beyond, being separated from the enemy only by a wood of about half a league in depth. Chevalier de Lévis having pushed the van-guard at day-break as far as the edge of this wood, within sight of the enemy, set about reconnoitering their position, with Sieur de Bourlamaque. He had given orders at the same time to the remainder of the troops, who had marched the whole night, to cross the marsh and to form in the rear of the wood.

At about 200 toises from, and almost parallel with the river of this wood is a ridge bordered by settlements; it terminates on one side at the height over the mouth of the River Cap Rouge, and extends on the other, to Quebec, where it takes the name of Côte d'Abraham.

At six o'clock in the morning, the English appeared in order of battle, to the number of about 300 men, on the top of this hill, facing the road on which we were marching, the right on the church of St. Foix, several houses on their left and some in front of their lines; they had lodged some troops in the one and the other and some pieces of cannon in their front.

The wood that covered us, being swampy and impassable, we could defile only by the main road, and not having room enough to form between the wood and the English, 'twas not possible to march against them in front, without being exposed to a disadvantageous fight.

Chevalier de Lévis thereupon adopted the resolution to wait until night to defile and gain the enemy's left flank, by marching to his own right and following the edge of the wood until past his front. This maneuver enabled him to attack the English with advantage at day break and to cut off the Light Infantry that were thrown into the houses towards Cap Rouge; he calculated on taking with him three field pieces, which had accompanied the troops with incredible difficulty.

The morning passed in some firing and volleys of artillery discharged by the enemy at the van-guard.

At one o'clock in the afternoon, the English having collected in the church of St. Foix, all the provisions, ammunition, arms and tools they had brought with them for the defense of that quarter, set fire to the church, and retired towards Quebec, having, however, left a corps in the order of battle on the height to mask their movements; they abandoned some guns which they could not carry off.

The storm that had prevailed through the whole of the preceding night, had retarded, some hours, the march of the troops and rendered it impossible for Chevalier de Lévis to defile on the church of St. Foix at daylight, as he intended. This mischance gave the English time to come in force to mask the high road and saved their detachments towards Cap Rouge.

Another accident had furnished them complete knowledge of our movement. A part of the ice that lined the river having broken loose on the morning of the 26th, carried away some bateaux loaded with artillery, a few of which were submerged; some of the gunners perished and one of them floated on a cake of ice as far as Quebec; the English Governor having learned from him our movements at the marsh, made his arrangements against being surprised.

As soon as the retreat of the English had been ascertained, the troops advanced; the van guard was in close pursuit of the fugitives; Sieur de la Roche Beaucourt at the head of one hundred mounted volunteers, having overtaken their rear, skirmished with them until night fall, and one officer and several volunteers were wounded.

The enemy made a stand at Dumont's house and on the adjoining heights about half a league from Quebec, where they left a strong detachment; the remainder of the garrison returned to town, our van-guard occupied the houses on this side, and the brigades placed themselves in the succeeding houses as far as the church of Saint Foix, Chevalier de Lévis having judged it indispensable to give some repose to the troops after two days' very fatiguing march, the ground, moreover, being covered with snow and overflown.

In Canada, the houses in most of the country parishes, do not stand together as in Europe; they are built along rivers or high roads, at a distance of one hundred to three hundred toises, one from the other; unenclosed, without hedges or groves. Each house is isolated, having near it only the barn, equally isolated; thus, from the Church of Saint Foix to the houses occupied by the van-guard, the little army covered a space of a league and a quarter.

The English detachment abandoned, during the night, Dumont's house and the heights where it had halted on the preceding evening, and fell back on the Butte à Neveu, about 250 toises [a toise equaling six feet] from the walls of Quebec, which that Butte entirely covers, and set about intrenching themselves there. The van-guard was posted in Dumont's house, and on the heights in front of the Butte à Nereu. These heights incline somewhat towards the right and communicate with some open woods bordering on the River Saint Lawrence at that place. A redoubt touching the wood, supported our right and covered Foulon cove, where we were to have brought the vessels, loaded with provisions and artillery, as well as the baggage of the troops.

Chevalier de Lévis had determined on employing the day of the 28th in landing the provisions which were due, some field pieces which could not come by land and in resting the troops, having resolved to attack the heights next morning and to drive the English into the town.

But, at 8 o'clock in the morning, they were seen issuing from Quebec; they appeared disposed to march against us, and formed in front of the heights which they occupied.

Chevalier de Lévis, who was occupied with Sieur de Bourlamaque since the break of day, in reconnoitering their position, immediately gave orders to Chevalier de Montreuil, Adjutant General, to make all the troops advance; the van-guard continued, meanwhile, to occupy the redoubt on the right, the heights in the center and Dumont's house, which is on the slope of Côte d'Abraham and *supported the left of the line that, the troops were to form. The open woods on our right happened to be in the rear of the center, a short distance from our line, whence they extended, retiring very precipitously nearly to La Fontaine's house, where the troops were to defile. This house, situate near the declivity of Côte d'Abraham, was separated from Dumont's by a plain, 250 toises in length.*

The brigades formed into line according as they came up, and the three on the right were already formed, when Chevalier de Lévis, seeing that the right of the English was moving, and that their artillery was beginning a heavy cannonade, concluded he would not have time to put his left in order to receive them; he resolved on throwing the troops who were in line a little in the rear, so as to place them under cover of the wood, and to have Dumont's house abandoned; he calculated on putting the left in La Fontaine's, and in that position allow the troops time to breathe, and to dispose them for marching afterwards against the enemy. But the courage of the troops did not allow him time to do so; he had stationed Sieur de Bourlamaque on the left to execute that movement, who, on countermarching the grenadier companies that were occupying Dumont's house, was wounded, and obliged to retire. The brigades of the left, having been a few moments without receiving any orders, took upon themselves to go and join the grenadiers, and to carry the house they had abandoned; they moved under the most murderous fire of artillery and musketry, and without being formed. Chevalier de Lévis who, from the heights of the center, perceived their movements, judged it necessary to take advantage of this ardor, and hastened to order the brigadier on the right to march against the enemy with fixed bayonets. He returned then to give the same order to the left. The maneuver on the right turned the enemy's left, and perfectly seconded the effect of ours, who, notwithstanding the fire of twenty pieces of cannon and two howitzers directed almost exclusively on that quarter, maintained themselves first at Dumont's house and afterwards by favor of the movements on the right, pressed the enemy in front of them, who were driven inside the walls of Quebec, and lost the ground they occupied in the morning and the entire of their artillery.

The bravery of the troops and the movements of the right, which Chevalier de Lévis ordered at the proper time, have repaired the prodigious disadvantages of having arrived too late, and of being obliged to form under a very superior fire of artillery.

Lieutenant-Colonel d'Alquier, commanding the brigade of La Sarre, composed of that and the Bearn battalions, and Lieutenant-Colonel Poularies, commanding the Royal Rousillon brigade, which was composed of that and the Guienne battalions, have greatly contributed to this success, the former by taking the resolution to march on Dumont's house, although in great disorder and wounded in that movement, and the second, by charging the enemy's left with signal bravery and intelligence.

The brigade of Berry and that of the Colonials, which joined that of La Sarre, seconded with the greatest courage the decisive movement of that brigade. The former was under the orders of Lieutenant-Colonel Trivio, who was slightly wounded on that occasion; the second, under Sieur Dumas' orders. Lieutenant-Colonel Trecesson, commanding the second battalion of the regiment of Berri, was mortally wounded there. Chevalier de la Corne and Sieur de Vassan, each commanding a battalion of Colonials, have distinguished themselves, and were both slightly wounded.

An order incorrectly delivered by an officer who has been afterwards killed, was the cause of the Brigade of La Reine, composed of that and of the Languedoc battalions, not having had as great a share in that movement as it ought.

The battalion of the Town of Montreal, under the orders of Sieur de Repentigny displayed equal courage with the Regulars. The same eulogium is due to the greater part of the Canadians, particularly those attached to the brigade of La Reine. Sieur de Roquemaure had thrown Sieur Deläas, who commanded them, into the redoubt and wood on the right; the superior fire of the enemy dislodged him after awhile, but he soon recovered his ground and *afterwards successfully charged the enemy's left flank, being seconded in that maneuver by Sieur de Saint Luc who could induce only a small number of Indians to follow him.*

The three little field pieces which had accompanied the army, under the orders of Captain de Lovicourt and Lieutenant Duverny of the Royal corps of artillery, did not cease firing on the English troops during the action, and have been a great assistance. Our loss has been considerable, especially in officers. The battalions of La Sarre and Bearn, who were on the left, as well as those of Berri and of the Marine, have suffered considerably. The grenadiers have been reduced to a very small number, chiefly the five companies of the left, commanded by Captain d'Aiguebelle of those of Languedoc, as they remained exposed to the hottest fire, whilst waiting the arrival of the troops.

Chevalier de Lévis has been sufficiently fortunate to escape without a wound, although on horseback throughout the entire of the action, between the fire of the enemy and that of our troops. He has been very well aided in the movements he ordered the latter to make, by Chevalier de Montreuil, Adjutant-General, and by Adjutant Delapause of the regiment of Guienne, acting assistant Quartermaster-General of the army.

The loss of the enemy, notwithstanding the advantage of their position and that of their artillery, has been more considerable than ours; we took twenty pieces of cannon from them, 2 howitzers and a great number of tools. It appears that in coming to form in front of the heights which they were occupying, their intention was only to work under cover of their lines and guns, in intrenching themselves on the heights before Quebec, in order to keep us at a distance from the heart of the place; but when they saw the grenadiers and the first brigades fall back some steps, they looked on the movement which was ordered as involuntary and believed they ought to advance so as to profit by the disorder in which they supposed we had fallen.

The siege of Quebec, which appeared almost impossible before the battle, owing to our situation and resources, commenced to appear probable when the enemy was pent up in the place.

Quebec forms a species of triangle, which occupies a very high point of land on the left bank of the river Saint Lawrence. The river defends one of its two sides which run inland; that following the escarpment of the Côte d'Abraham commands with great superiority a low flat, through which the River St. Charles winds. This Côte d'Abraham runs almost parallel with the River St. Lawrence and rejoins it at the mouth of the River Cap Rouge. The Quebec side which is bounded by that Côte and by the escarpment of the river, is alone accessible; it is defended by an enceinte of six bastions, faced (rerêtus) and almost on a straight line. A shallow ditch, the depth of which in some places is only 5 or 6 feet, some earth collected on the counterscarp, and 6 or 7 wooden redoubts constructed by the English, protected that enceinte, the extent of which, from the River [St. Lawrence] to the Côte d'Abraham, is only about 6 or 700 toises. The ground is solid rock, which becomes almost bare in approaching the body of the place.

The ramparts of Quebec are visible from the heights which the English abandoned. Chevalier de Levis hastened to occupy them, and Sieur de Pontleroy, engineer in chief of New France, having reconnoitered the place with Captain de Montbeillard, of the Royal Artillery and commanding that of Canada, 'twas decided to begin by a parallel [from] the heights which are in front of the bastions of Saint Louis, of the Glaciére and of Cape Diamond, and to erect batteries there, which, 'twas hoped, were capable of making a breach, although the distance was 250 toises. The revetement was badly constructed at that point.

Up to the 11th of May, day and night were employed in perfecting the parallel and building 3 batteries. One of six guns battered somewhat slantingly the face and right flank of the bastion of the Glacière, another of 4 guns placed to the left, battered directly that same spot and crossed with the first: the 3rd of three guns was directed against the flank of the Saint Louis bastion, opposite the Glacière bastion; to these were added a battery of 2 mortars.

A battery of 4 guns was erected also on the left bank of the Little River Saint Charles, whence the fronts attacked would be seen in reverse; 'twas expected to annoy the besieged on their ramparts from that point, although the distance was very considerable.

The parallels and batteries could not be finished except after incredible difficulties; the work was all rock. The earth had to be brought a very great distance in sacks. The enemy soon had 60 cannon unmasked on the attacked fronts. This artillery, served with the greatest activity, not only retarded the construction of the batteries, but also prevented the workmen transporting material; the balls plunging behind the heights, left no spot protected. The troops were even obliged several times to decamp.

Finally, on the 11th of May, the batteries opened, and notwithstanding the great superiority of those of the English, would have been successful in their fire had our little artillery been of a better quality. 'Twas composed of 6 iron 18 and 12-pounders, only one 24, and although the best in the Colony had been selected, the most of the guns were, on the second day unfit for service, and the remainder soon threatened to be in the same state.

Chevalier de Lévis, under these circumstances and in order not to find himself uselessly deprived of ammunition, resolved to reduce the fire of the batteries to 20 shots each in 24 hours, and to remain in that situation until the arrival of the ships, hoping that the Court would, before long, send by the river some succors in artillery and provisions, which would enable him to terminate the siege of Quebec in a few days, as their passage, besides, was rendered quite easy in consequence of the position assumed in front of that place.

An English frigate arrived on the 9th before Quebec and brought the Governor [Murray] some London newspapers which he took occasion to communicate to Chevalier de Lévis, who found only vague and uninteresting news in them.

of the two frigates which had wintered at Quebec, one had got ready to sail on the first of May, and dropped down the river without her destination being ascertained; 'twas conjectured however, that she had left for Europe; the second had her guns on board and appeared soon ready to join the one that had just arrived.

15th. At ten o'clock at night, Chevalier de Lévis learned that two men-of-war, suspected to be English, had just anchored at the end of the Island of Orleans. He did not hesitate to bethink him of retreating, being well assured that [his French vessels] 'L'Attalante' and 'La Pomone' ill equipped, without guns and men, were not in a condition to resist the enemy's vessels and protect our transports having our provisions on board.

He immediately sent orders to these vessels to reascend the river to a place of safety. This order was conveyed and executed too late in consequence of bad weather, the river having been agitated in an extraordinary manner the whole night; he also ordered the removal of all the guns from the batteries and their transportation to the Cóte du Foulon, where they arrived at 7 o'clock in the morning.

At day-break an English ship of the line and two frigates got under way and fell in the twinkling of an eye on our frigates, which were obliged to retreat. 'La Pomone' ran aground in front of Sillery. Sieur Vauquelin, commanding 'L'Attalante', seeing that the transports were going to be overhauled, signaled to them to run ashore at the mouth of the River Cap Rouge. He was himself obliged to do the same 4 leagues higher up, opposite Point aux trembles, where he was exposed, during two hours, to the fire of the two English frigates, and having expended all his ammunition and seriously damaged the enemy's ships, was taken prisoner without having removed the King's flag; almost all his officers were killed or wounded, as well as a great number of his men.

The vessel that sailed from Quebec with the two frigates anchored before the Foulon cove, and cannonaded our bateaux so vigorously, that 'twas impossible to put our siege train on board; only our ammunition could be saved; some officers were obliged to abandon their baggage.

16th. The troops remained in the same position the whole day; at 9 o'clock at night, Chevalier de Lévis ordered the trenches to be evacuated, and fell back in good order with the light artillery as far as the River Cap Rouge, which he crossed on the morning of the 17th. He employed that and the following days in discharging the fly-boats and vessels that were stranded, and getting the provisions and ammunition out of them. The fly-boat 'La Marie', commanded by Sieur Cornille, being found serviceable, went up the river, having passed under the English frigates in the night; all the other craft were burned.

19th. News received of the arrival of 8 or 10 vessels in the port of Quebec, determined him to retire behind the River Jacques Cartier, which the troops crossed on the morning of the 20th, a corps of 400 men being left at Point aux trembles.

The wind from the northeast, which prevailed since the 10th of May, became so violent during the 4 days employed in getting back the provisions and ammunition, that a great number of bateaux were lost; several of those which were conveying the baggage of the troops shared the same fate. One of the frigates that fought 'L'Attulante', having dragged her anchors the day after the engagement, was also lost in an instant.

'Twas never expected, when leaving Montreal, that we could take Quebec with the mere resources the country was able to furnish, as that town was provided with an immense artillery and guarded by a numerous garrison, composed of good troops, under an active and experienced chief. The plan was to confine that garrison within the walls of the town sufficiently early, to deprive it of the power of constructing external works before the fronts which have been attacked, and to wait under cover of the first approaches until the arrival of the reinforcements demanded from France should enable us to continue the siege. One single French flag would have been sufficient to produce that effect.

The victory of the 28th might have afforded hopes of more prompt success, had the artillery been in a condition to produce the effect expected; the bad quality of the guns has prevented *us profiting by the good dispositions of the troops, which were impatiently waiting the opening of the breach; and the want of all reinforcements from Europe has at length forced Chevalier de Lévis to retire [...]."*

Before retreating in the direction of Montreal, however, the Chevalier de Lévis ordered all that which his men could not carry off to be destroyed, leaving small garrisons stationed at Point-aux-Trembles, Jacques Cartier, Isle-aux-Noir, and along the upper Saint Lawrence, including in the recently constructed Fort Lévis, in amongst the Thousand Islands. In command of these were; Captain Dumas (under whom Charles Langlade had served as second-in-command at Fort Duquesne); Captain Bougainville; Luc de la Corne; and Captain Pierre Pouchot, who had since been reassigned since his capture and release after the fall of Fort Niagara.

Brigadier Bourlamaque oversaw the fortification of Montreal in preparation of an English siege, however, the complete and utter lack of virtually everything an army requires to function prompted many to desert the French cause, drastically decreasing its army's size to only a few thousand men, who, by fall, were beleaguered by nearly twenty thousand English, approaching from every direction.

In early, August, having since returned to Montreal after what was initially a successful campaign, the Chevalier de Lévis documented the rapidly deteriorating state of affairs to French Minister, the Marshal de Belle Isle, in the following terms:

"Chevalier de Lévis to Marshal de Belle Isle.
Montreal, 7th August, 1760.

My Lord,
The courier being unable to leave since my last letter of the 14th ult [last month]., I have the honor to report to you hereby, that the enemy are on the march from Quebec since the 14th of last month, with forty sail and a landing force of two thousand five hundred men; they have since received a reinforcement from Quebec, of about one thousand troops. They are at this moment at Three Rivers. The detachment which was at Des Chambeau, follows

them along the north shore, their plan is, apparently, to come to Montreal or Sorel in order to facilitate their junction with M. Amherst. We possess no means of stopping them; we are making a mere defensive demonstration to retard their march.

The principal point with us is to defend Montreal and the North shore as long as we shall be able; the Canadians are frightened by the fleet; they are afraid their houses will be burned. We are on the eve of a crisis. M. Amherst has reassembled fifteen thousand at Fort Frederick; there is another considerable force collected at Fort Chouaguen to penetrate by the Rapids; there is no doubt that they are about to move with a view to simultaneous action. If they have delayed until this moment, 'tis probably with the design to wait until the season of harvest, to deprive us of the farmers, in the expectation that we shall find it difficult to collect them together at that time.

We shall act as I have had the honor to inform you in my preceding letter. We shall try every means to save the Colony, but that will require miracles our situation is so deplorable. Our armies will have nothing but bread to subsist on.

Being in want of flour, as the discredit of the contractor's notes and bills of exchange prevents his being able to procure any, I have been induced to make strong representations on that subject to the Marquis de Vaudreuil and the Intendant, offering to pledge myself personally to persuade the troops to give the little cash they might possess, and to employ in that levy, officers capable of acquitting themselves perfectly of that duty. This has produced the effect I anticipated, and has supplied us with means to procure bread for this month. The Marquis de Vaudreuil and the Intendant have also pledged themselves for this purchase.

I do not cease moving so as to be everywhere to introduce order and prepare all possible means of defense. I start this moment for Lake St. Peter.

I am with profound respect, My Lord,
    Your most humble and most obedient servant,
        Chev. de Lévis.

[P.S.] I have returned from the Islands of Lake St. Peter, where there is an English fleet which has been augmented by twenty sail. There are no means of stopping them at the Islands nor between that and Montreal. There is reason to believe that they are about trying to establish themselves at the mouth of the River Sorrel or that they will come to Montreal. We have just learned that a reinforcement of three of the enemy's battalions has arrived from Quebec; a fourth is expected from the garrison of Isle Royale. They are blowing up that place. The armies of Lake Ontario and Lake Champlain are in motion; the Quebec fleet coming up to Montreal will force us to abandon the frontiers. The armies will then form a junction without any obstacle; all united, they will then have at least forty thousand men in the heart of the Colony; you are aware of our strength and abilities. From that judge of what may be expected. If we do not save the Colony, we will sustain the honor of the King's arms."

Eleven days after the Chevalier de Lévis' letter of August 7th, Pierre Pouchot, the former Commandant of Fort Niagara, who now commanded the minimally manned Fort Lévis, in amongst the Thousand Islands of the St. Lawrence River, commenced a stalling campaign against the English forces which were amassing around him, and whose intention it was to jointly proceed against Montreal. Per Pouchot's "*Memoirs*":

"*On the 18th [of August, 1760], the enemy left La Presentation with a fresh breeze. Their whole army remained about four hours in battle array in their bateaux [flat bottomed boats] at the beginning of the rapids, forming a very fine spectacle. M. Pouchot then thought that they intended to attack with a strong force, and make an entry upon the Island [on which Fort Levis was situated in the St. Laurence River]. He had accordingly so placed nine cannon to fight up the river and had placed the others in the epaulement, so that they could make eleven rebounds upon the water. It is thought that the enemy would have lost heavily before they could have secured a landing, if they had entertained such a thought. They determined to file along the north shore with a considerable interval between one bateau and another, to escape the fire of artillery from the fort. They caused the Outaouaise [an English vessel] which they had taken, to approach to within half cannon shot to cover them.*

M. Pouchot only sought to retard their passage by four pieces which he could bring to bear upon them. We fired a hundred and fifty cannon shot with very little damage, which appeared to us to be occasioned by the wind being strong, and the currents made them quickly loose the point of aim. As M. Pouchot knew many of the officers of this army, several of them bade him good day in passing; and others thought from our allowing them to pass that they were his friends, but did not stop to pay any compliments. The greater part of the army encamped at Point d'Ivrogne. They also threw quite a force upon La Cuisse, la Magdelaine and Les Galots Islands.

On the 19th, their regiment of artillery left Old Gallette, with all their field artillery, and defiled past as the former had done, to go and encamp at Point d'Ivrogne. The vessel kept up the heaviest fire possible to cover them. We fired but little at the bateaux, because it was attended with but little success, but rather directed our attention to the vessel. Of fifty shots that we fired, at least forty-eight went through the body of the vessel, which obliged them to get a little further away. Their captain named 'Smul', behaved with the greatest bravery, walking continually on the deck in his shirt sleeves. He had many men disabled.

The two other vessels, one of twenty-two cannon, eights and sixes, named the Seneca, and the other of eighteen pieces of sixes, named the Oneida, came in the evening, and took position by the side of the former.

On the 20th, there was quite a movement of the enemy's army, and a great number of bateaux went and came from their camp at La Presentation. They also encamped two regiments at Point de Ganataragoin, who began to throw up earth works on that side, as also on the island La Cuisse and la Magdelaine. We tried some volleys of cannon at them to disturb the laborers, but had to be extremely saving in our powder, not having more than five thousand pounds when the enemy arrived.

On the 21st, everything remained quiet, as the enemy were working with their full force on their batteries. Their vessels withdrew also beyond can non range. We fired on the laborers, but without much result, as they were already covered, and their ground was some twenty-four feet higher than that of the island.

By noon we discovered their embrasures, and in the evening their bateaux made a general movement, and we counted as many as thirty-six barges carrying each at least twenty men, who threw themselves into the three vessels, from which we judged that they were going to attack the next morning. We consequently worked to make epaulements of wood to cover the parties that we thought would be the most exposed in the direction of the enemy's batteries. All the artillery was loaded with shot and grape, and everyone was ordered to pass the night at his post.

On the 22nd, at five in the morning, the three vessels approached to within about two hundred toises [one toise equaling six feet] of the fort, and occupied the whole range of the river above, from the Island La Cuisse to Point Ganataragoin, from which we thought they intended to cannonade us vigorously from the vessels and land batteries. They formed together a half circle around the fort. Consequently M. Pouchot ordered the artillery officer to collect his pieces of artillery, and put them under cover of merlons, so that they should not be dismounted. He also masked his embrasures with the ends of great logs of wood to represent cannon. We were only clear and in condition to resist from above.

As soon as the vessels were placed, they began a very brisk and continuous fire, from twenty-five cannon and at the same time the enemy unmasked the battery at Ganataragoin, consisting of two twenty fours, and four twelves, as also that on the Island of La Cuisse, of fourteen pieces of twelves and eighteens, and a third one on the Isle la Magdelaine, of two pieces of twenty-four, and six of twelve. At the first volley, M. Bertrand, artillery officer, was instantly killed by a cannon ball through his loins, as he stood pointing out to M. Pouchot the caliber of their guns.

A quarter of an hour later, they began to throw bombs from the Island la Magdelaine, where they had two twelve-inch bomb mortars, six mortars for royal grenades, and two howitzers. On the Island La Cuisse six mortars for royal grenades, and on Point Ganataragoin two twelve-inch mortars, two for royal grenades and two howitzers, making in all seventy-five mouths of fire.

M. Pouchot received quite a bruise from a piece of wood ten feet long, and fourteen inches square which a twelve-inch bomb knocked over, injuring his back, but this did not prevent him from being wherever he was needed.

All these batteries were served with the greatest vigor and without ceasing till noon, and made the fort fly into pieces and splinters. Our men remained under cover, each one at his post, and the sentinels only observed the movements of the enemy. Thinking from our silence that we were perhaps disconcerted, they advanced their vessels to within pistol shot of the fort. They were filled with troops, even to the rigging, and were supported by the fire of all the land batteries.

Fortunately they could only come before the fort one by one, from the manner in which the first vessel came up, and which saw as far to the entrance of the fort, which was also enfiladed by the battery of La Magdelaine. M. Pouchot had in advance covered this with heavy blindages, leaving only a passage sufficient for one man.

He thought that the enemy intended to attack with a heavy force. At least three thousand men, volunteers, grenadiers and light troops, were embarked in bateaux, and placed behind the point of La Cuisse Island, from whence they could emerge under the aid of the fire of the three vessels and the land batteries.

The movements of the vessels soon induced M. Pouchot to place 150 men, and four officers on the side opposite the epaulement. He fought the vessels one after another with five guns, the only ones that were mounted, charged with balls and grape, without replying to the land batteries.

Notwithstanding the superiority of the enemy's fire with our five pieces and our musketry, we forced the Outaouaise and then the Oneida [English vessels], to run aground half a league from the fort, near the Galot Islands. One of the two was not in further condition to serve. The Seneca of 22 guns, in trying to come nearer the fort grounded also, and was so cut to pieces that she struck her flag, having then on board three hundred and fifty men. The side of the vessel towards the fort was in very bad condition, her battery touched the water and her port holes made only one opening. The water she had taken in made her lean towards the fort. M. Pouchot gave orders to discontinue the fire as he wished to save his powder. The second captain, and some sailors came to surrender. M. Pouchot retained them as hostages, but could not receive the whole, as they were more numerous than his garrison.

In the intervals between these combats, the enemy attempted to land two or three times, to make an attack from the point opposite the Isle la Cuisse. Two guns that were pointed in that direction re strained them, and made them retire behind that point. It is probable that the bad condition in which they found their vessels, took away their desire of advancing. This action lasted from five in the morning, to half past seven in the evening, without the fire ceasing. We had forty men killed or wounded. We cannot too much praise the firmness which the officers, colonial soldiers, militia and especially the cannoneers, who were sailors, displayed on the occasion. Three or four of the latter could never be rewarded for their address and activity in serving their pieces. The enemy, like ourselves, fired ball and grape constantly. M. Pouchot directed a blacksmith to cut up some old irons with which he filled sacks and put into the bore of his guns, adding a ball, which did terrible execution upon the vessels, on account of the height of the ramparts which placed them under our fire, so that we could see upon their decks.

One thing which amused the garrison at the most serious moments of the battle was, that the Indians, who were perched upon their trenches and batteries, to watch the contest with the vessels, which they regarded as on their side, on account of the names that had been given them, and because they carried an Indian painted upon their flags, made furious cries at seeing them so mal-treated. The English had assured them that with these vessels alone, they would make the place surrender. When these Indians saw them drift off and ground, they redoubled their cries, and sung out railing names at the English, saying: — "You did not want to kill our father at Niagara; see how you are taking him! If you had listened to us, you would not have been here! A Frenchman's fist has made you cringe!" This action had, however, dismantled all the tops of the parapets around half of the fort, thrown down the fascines that were placed on the side of La Cuisse Island, and in front of the two demi-bastions.

At night, M. Pouchot endeavored to repair with sacks of earth, the batteries of the bastion opposite the island so that they could be served. This bastion was ready to tumble down, and we could have walked upon the slope formed by the earth that had fallen down.

The enemy continued through the night to bombard us, and fired volleys of cannon from each battery, loaded with shot and grape, at intervals, to prevent us from making repairs. We had two men killed and several wounded.

On the 23rd, the enemy continued to bombard and cannonade vigorously all day. At night we tried the same bombardment and volleys of cannon at intervals as on the night previous.

On the 24th, they unmasked a new battery to break down the wooden redoubt at the end of the island, and to enfilade our intrenchments on the side opposite the islands. Their batteries continued as violently as on the preceding days, and fires caught in the ruins of the magazine, and in the quarters of the commandant, but these were happily extinguished without the enemy observing our difficulty. We had but little trouble to take care of what little powder and balls we had left. The enemy's batteries dismounted all the cannon of the bastion opposite the islands. *The coffers of the parapets were razed down to within two feet of the terreplein, greatly exposing the powder magazine, which was only made of some large beams.*

On the 25th, at day break, M. Pouchot fired vigorously three pieces upon the batteries which troubled us the most, and which were the only ones left on the side attacked. Even one of these three pieces and the most important one, wanted a third of its length, having broken twice. Notwithstanding its caliber, we put in two or three small balls. We had perceived by the enemy's movements, that this kind of firing troubled them much in their trenches, but we found it out of our power to ruin or even to materially injure their batteries.

The activity of our fire put the English in bad humor, and in the afternoon they redoubled theirs from all their batteries, and fired red-hot balls, fire-pots and carcases. This was too much for this miserable fort, which was now only a litter of carpenter's wood and fascines. The hot shot set fire to the saucissons of the interior revetment of the bastion, already down, but we extinguished it. From this we may see how the rampart was ruined. Some fire-pots also kindled twice in the debris of the fort, and we also extinguished these flames with water found in the holes made by bursting bombs.

This determined M. Pouchot, with the advice of all the officers of the garrison, to write to [English commander,] General Amherst, complaining against this kind of warfare never used but against rebels, and which should not be practiced against a brave garrison which deserved not such treatment. In reply he sent his aid-de-camp with a kind of capitulation for us to surrender as prisoners of war, with the threat that if we did not accept within half an hour, he would resume hostilities.

M. Pouchot received the officer, and read what Amherst demanded before all the officers and the garrison. The latter made the most urgent entreaties for him to accept them, in view of the impossibility of escaping a general conflagration in case of a fire, on account of the small capacity of the fort and the incumbrance of the ruins.

There remained at this time on the front attacked, only two cannon in condition to fire, and no more balls. The outer batteries of the fort were all ruined, as they were commanded by the islands, as were also the epaulements of the intrenchments, which were no cover against an assault.

On the 26th, in the morning, when the enemy entered, they were greatly surprised at seeing only a few soldiers scattered around their posts which they left, and some sixty militia, with handkerchiefs on their heads, in their shirt sleeves, and with necks bare as is the Canadian fashion. They asked M. Pouchot where was his garrison? He replied that they saw the whole. We had more than sixty men killed or wounded. All the officers had been more or less wounded."

On September 3rd, in advance of the English army's impending arrival outside Montreal, his warriors starving and exhausted, Charles Langlade granted leave to those in his company from the more far-flung French-aligned Indigenous Nations, tribes and/or bands of Canada to return home to prepare for the coming winter, while he and a select few fulfilled the following orders (among the last) from the Governor-General of New France, the Marquis de Vaudreuil:

"To Sieur Langdale, half-pay Lieutenant of the Colonial troops, whom we have intrusted with charge of the Indian Nations of the Upper Countries, who are returning to their villages:

It is ordered to use the utmost diligence to report with them at Michilimackinac; to keep watch that they commit no theft nor insult upon those canoes of voyagers, which they may meet on their route; to encourage them always in their attachment to the French nation, giving them to understand that if we have the misfortune to be taken by the enemy, the Colony will remain but a few months, at most, in his power, for peace, if not already declared, is most certainly on the point of being so.

We notify Sieur de Langlade that he will, by our orders, pass two companies of deserters from the English army through the

Upper Country, on their way to Louisiana. They are commanded by two sergeants, one of whom is Irish, the other German, both very intelligent men, and capable of maintaining discipline among their troops; the Sieur de Langlade will, therefore, give attention that his Indians stir up no quarrel with these deserters, and that they do not rob nor insult them while of the party; he will also procure for them the facilities they may need along the route, and when they separate; he will besides enjoin upon the Canadians destined to act as their guides, not on any account to abandon them.
   Done at Montreal, the 3rd Sept., 1760.

Vaudreuil."

On September 7th, with the arrival of the English army, Vaudreuil offered to begin negotiations with their commander, General Jeffery Amherst, for the capitulation of the colony. All the terms were quickly agreed to except one on which Amherst insisted — that the French regular troops be barred from active service in Europe during the present war. A demand which the victor of St. Foye, the Chevalier de Lévis, openly resented, and made clear of in a letter of protest, addressed to the Marquis de Vaudreuil. However, the Governor-ordered Lévis to obey the demand and to disarm his men, which Lévis did, albeit begrudgingly, and only after burning his army's regimental standards to avoid their capture by the English. The surrender was formalized the following day, September the 8th. On September the 9th, the now *former* Governor-General of the *late* colony of New France, issued a final letter to Charles Langlade:

   "*Montreal, 9th September, 1760.*

   I inform you, Sir, that I have to-day been obliged to capitulate with the army of General Amherst. This city is, as you know, without defenses. Our troops were considerably diminished, our means and resources exhausted. We were surrounded by three armies, amounting in all to twenty thousand and eighty men. General Amherst was, on the sixth of this month in sight of the walls of this city, General Murray within reach of one of our suburbs, and the army of Lake Champlain was at La Prairie and Loungueil.

Under these circumstances, with nothing to hope from our efforts, not even from the sacrifice of our troops, I have advisedly decided to capitulate with General Amherst upon conditions very advantageous for the colonists, and particularly for the inhabitants of Michilimackinac. Indeed, they retain the free exercise of their religion; they are maintained in the possession of their goods, real and personal, and of their peltries. They have also free trade just the same as the proper subjects of the King of Great Britain.

The same conditions are accorded to the military. They can appoint persons to act for them in their absence. They, and all citizens in general, can sell to the English or French their goods, sending the proceeds thereof to France, or taking them with them if they choose to return to that country after the peace. They retain their negroe and Pawnee Indian slaves, but will be obliged to restore those which have been taken from the English. The English General has declared that the Canadians have become the subjects of His Britannic Majesty, and consequently the people will not continue to be governed as heretofore by the French code.

In regard to the troops, the condition has been imposed upon them not to serve during the present war [which would continue to rage in Europe for over a year], and to lay down their arms before being sent back to France. You will therefore, sir, assemble all the officers and soldiers who are at your post. You will cause them to lay down their arms, and you will proceed with them to such sea-port as you think best, to pass thence to France. The citizens and inhabitants of Michilimackinac will consequently be under command of the officer whom General Amherst shall appoint to that post.

You will forward a copy of my letter to St. Joseph, and to the neighboring posts, in order that if any soldiers remain there, they and the inhabitants may conform thereto.

I count upon the pleasure of seeing you in France with all your officers.

I have the honor to be, very sincerely, Sir, your very humble and very obedient servant

Vaudreuil."

The two would never confer again. As with many French officers, after the war, Vaudreuil returned to France, where he would live quietly until his death in 1778.

Among other officers that returned to France after the war were; the Chevalier de Lévis, who would subsequently serve in one last, glorious campaign in Europe, before retiring from active service in 1763. He was honored for his services with a Marshal's Baton in 1783 and was made a Duke a year later. He died in 1787; Jean-Daniel Dumas, who commanded alongside Charles Langlade at Fort Duquesne and on the Monongahela against General Braddock. After returning to France, he was briefly appointed Governor General of Mascarene (a series of islands in the Indian Ocean, east of Madagascar) in 1766 and in 1780 was promoted to Field Marshal. He died in 1794; Pierre Pouchot, former Commandant of Fort Niagara and Fort Lévis. After returning to France, he penned his memoirs before being redeployed to the island of Napoleon Bonaparte's birth: Corsica, in the year of Napoleon's birth: 1769, to assist in putting down that island's ongoing Revolutionary War, but was killed in action before the year was out; François-Charles de Bourlamaque, who frequently served in the company of Charles Langlade and was primarily stationed in the greater Michilimackinac/Green Bay region. After the war, returning to France, he was promoted Major-General and served briefly as Governor of Guadeloupe before his death in 1764; Louis Antoine de Bougainville. Following his return to France, among his many, many accolades was his circumnavigation of the globe, for which he won world-wide acclaim. Rewarded lavishly for his services by First Consul, and later, the Emperor, Napoleon, he died in 1811.

It is worth noting that as an epilogue to the French and Indian War and in acknowledgment of Charles Langlade's distinguished services during it, that official documents of English General Jeffery Amherst's note that in his army's advance on Montreal in late-August/early-September 1760, via the La Chine Rapids of the Saint Lawrence River, without having encountered scarcely a single French, Canadian or Indigenous contingent, his army lost eighty-four men, while twenty troops transports and seven artillery boats were smashed to pieces. This fact led the aforementioned, Chevalier de Johnstone, the Chevalier de Lévis' aid-de-camps during the latter stages of the war, to observe that, "*If 900 Indians had been there, as they should have been, scattered in the woods upon the boarders of the river, with 1,200 Canadians, which they had solicited earnestly from M. de Vaudreuil, to defend those difficult passes of the Rapids, but which this officer obstinately refused, what would have become of General Amherst? How could he have got out of the scrape? As it happened to Braddock, Amherst and his army must have perished there; his expedition would have been fruitless […].*"

However, as per the famous quote, invariably attributed to Napoleon or Frederick the Great, "*To be effective, an army relies on good and plentiful food.*" And as Charles Langlade's grandson, Augustin Grignon later vividly recalled in his "*Recollections*", neither good, nor plentiful food were to be had: "*I remember he told me, that on one occasion, when he and his party were nearly starved, they discovered some live […] snakes, and by means of forked sticks placed on their necks, severed their heads from their bodies, dressed the meat and made a most savory meal.*" Such was just one of the many hardships Langlade, among countless others, endured during the latter stages of the war.

Charles Langlade's British scarlet red Officer's coat (Neville Public Museum, Green Bay, Wisconsin. Photo ID#: L817). Modern photograph courtesy of the Neville Public Museum of Brown County, Green Bay, Wisconsin, who retain the copyright of the photo and possess the item.

Chapter III

1761-63: The English Occupation of Green Bay to Pontiac's War

Following the capitulation of Montreal on September 8th, 1760, which effectively saw the dissolution of New France as a colony, the English did not immediately take possession of the former's more remote outposts, such as Michilimackinac, on account of the coming winter. But with the French promptly evacuating it, through the winter of 1760, until the English finally arrived, on September 28th, 1761, in the form of a detachment commanded by Captain Henry Balfour and supplemented by Lieutenant William Leslie, Charles Langlade, a King Louis personally appointed Lieutenant, was amongst the highest local authority, who exerted equal influence over Michilimackinac and its neighboring outposts.

In 1762, Captain George Etherington (circa. 1730 – 87), a veteran of the 1758-60 campaigns, was formally appointed to Michilimackinac's permanent command by General Jeffery Amherst, relieving Langlade of that temporary duty, with the captain shortly thereafter requesting an oath of allegiance to the English Crown be taken personally from every prominent person in the vicinity of the post. And among those who heeded this call was Charles Langlade, who stood to benefit greatly by doing so.

To ensure continuity and as smooth as possible an administrative transition, Etherington thought it wise to retain Langlade in his French-appointed roles of local Superintendent of Indian Affairs, as well as head of the greater Green Bay militia, and therefore, on the government's payroll. His invaluable frontier military experience, combined with his profound influence amongst numerous north and central North American Indigenous Nations, tribes and bands were priceless assets which would be virtually impossible to replace, and as a result, in large part due to Michilimackinac' remoteness, the infantile English colonial government was rather circumspect in their administration, treatment and dealings with the outpost and with Langlade personally. This led to a period of rapid growth and prosperity in the greater Green Bay area, as its inhabitants, for the first time in nearly a decade, could focus exclusively on cultivation and trade in the absence of war. But all was not as idyllic as it appeared.

On the 10th of February 1763, the Treaty of Paris was signed by the courts of Great Britain, France, Spain and Portugal, which formally brought an end to the global event which was the Seven Years' War, of which, the French & Indian War had been the North American theatre. This treaty handed over to the English "***Canada, with all its dependencies***", as well as all of the country to the left side of the "***Mississippi, from its source, to the River Iberville***", which included the entirety of the Allegheny Mountain region, so that now, the Mississippi was the boundary between the English colonies and "*Indian Country*", not the Alleghenies as before. And in consequence of this treaty, the English Crown also considered all individuals within these newly acquired territories summarily as "subjects" and demanded their allegiance, an indiscriminate measure which incensed many within previously French-aligned Indigenous communities, who, until late, had been sworn enemies of the English, and in many cases, had been so for decades and generations. Such was also the disposition of Charles Langlade's longtime ally and acquaintance, the great warrior, Pontiac.

On the 13th of September, 1760, just three days after the Governor-General of New France, the Marquis de Vaudreuil had surrendered the colony, General Amherst dispatched Major Robert Rogers of Roger's Rangers on a most important mission, which was to take possession on behalf of the English, the isolated French outposts of Detroit, Michilimackinac and St. Joseph's, inform them of the French capitulation, and ensure their allegiance to the country's new masters. And although as previously stated, Michilimackinac was not formally occupied until September 28th of the following year, on November 7th, 1760, while traversing the country on this mission, Major Rogers encountered an Indigenous deputation of Pontiac's, with the two shortly thereafter meeting in person. Respectful but assertive, Pontiac demanded to know on what pretense Rogers was entering his country and to where he was proceeding, to which, Rogers replied that Canada had been surrendered to the English by the French, and that he and his men were relieving the French at the outposts on the frontier, whom he described to Pontiac as "*an obstacle to peace between the Indians and the English.*" Satisfied with these answers, Pontiac replied that if Rogers required anything on his mission, he would be all too glad to put his warriors at Rogers' disposal but requested that he postpone proceeding until a more formal council could be held between the two the next day. Rogers accepted, and on the morning of November 8th, Rogers and Pontiac smoked the peace pipe, with the latter ultimately agreeing to grant Rogers unmolested travel through Indigenous country in pursuance of his objective, with Rogers eventually reaching Detroit in late November, but unable to proceed thence to Michilimackinac, etc., due to the onset of winter.

In the meantime, the friendly disposition that Pontiac had initially manifested towards Robert Rogers began to drastically alter, as it became apparent to him that the English, whom Rogers represented, had little interest in bonding and conducting business with their Indigenous neighbors as intimately as the French had endeavored to do so over the previous century. While the French had often intermarried with and adopted Indigenous customs while living amongst allied Indigenous Nations, tribes and bands, traded on relatively equal terms and bestowed generous amounts of presents to them in exchange for friendship and loyalty, the English newcomers, in addition to incorrectly viewing all their newly acquired Indigenous neighbors as "conquered" peoples, were also keen to line their pockets in Indigenous trade and sales. This combination, facilitated by greed and arrogance, perpetuated the storm that was brewing.

Indeed, the precarity of Anglo-Indigenous relations during this period are best summarized in a speech, delivered at Michilimackinac and attributed to none other than Pontiac himself, who addressed it to a group which included a newly arrived English trader named Alexander Henry (1739 – 1824), who documented it:

"*Englishmen*", began Pontiac. "*You know that the French king is our father. He promised to be such, and we in return promised to be his children. This promise we have kept.*

Englishmen, it is you who have made war with our father. You are his enemy; and how then could you have the boldness to venture among us, his children? You know that his enemies are ours.

Englishmen, we are informed that our father, the King of France, is old and infirm; and that, being fatigued with making war upon your nation, he has fallen asleep. During this sleep, you have taken advantage of him, and possessed yourself of Canada. But his nap is almost at an end. I think I hear him already stirring and inquiring for his children the Indians; and when he does awake, what must become of you? He will destroy you utterly.

Englishmen, although you have conquered the French, you have not yet conquered us. We are not your slaves. These lakes, these woods and mountains, are left to us by our ancestors. They are our inheritance, and we will part with them to none. Your nation supposes that we, like the white people, cannot live without bread, and pork, and beef; but you ought to know that He, the Great Spirit and Master of Life, has provided food for us in these spacious lakes and on these woody mountains.

Englishmen, our father, the King of France, employed our young men to make war upon your nation. In this warfare many of them have been killed, and it is our custom to retaliate until such time as the spirits of the slain are to be satisfied in either two ways: the first is, by the spilling [of] the blood of the nation by which they fell; the other, by covering the bodies of the dead, and thus allaying the resentment of their relatives. This is done by making presents.

Englishmen, your King has never sent us any presents, nor entered into any treaty with us; wherefore he and we are still at war; and until he does these things, we must consider that we have no other father or friend among the white men than the king of France. But for you, we have taken into consideration that you have ventured among us in the expectation that we should not molest you. You do not come armed, with an intention to make war. You come in peace to trade with us, and supply us with necessaries of which we are in much want. We shall regard you, therefore, as a brother; and you may sleep tranquilly, without fear [...]. As a token of our friendship, we present you with this pipe to smoke."

However, with Anglo-Indigenous relations scarcely improving over a two-year period, and the latter incessantly encouraged to revolt against English rule by French sympathizers, at length, in early 1763, Pontiac concluded that the time for diplomacy and negotiation had passed, that the English clearly had interest only in profit and servitude, and that only through a coordinated uprising could such a state of affairs be remedied.

In early April, 1763, utilizing his own vast influence, Pontiac called a supreme council of Indigenous Nations, tribes and bands on the River-aux-Ecores, a tributary of the Detroit River, a few miles below the settlement itself. Among those in attendance were representatives of his own Nation, the Ottawa, as well as the Chippewa, the Potawatomie, the Miami, the Shawnee, the Outagamie, the Winnebago, the Massasauga, the Mingo, the Wyandot, the Kickapoo, among others, to whom, Pontiac proposed his stratagem, which called for a series of well-organized, simultaneous Indigenous attacks on colonialist outposts, among them; Fort Pitt (which had replaced the French built Fort Duquesne), at the confluence of the Allegheny and Monongahela Rivers (modern-day Pittsburg, Pennsylvania); Fort Venango (which replaced the French built Fort Machault), at the confluence of French Creek and the Allegheny River (modern-day Franklin, Penn.); Fort Le Boeuf, also on French

Creek (modern-day Waterford, Penn.); Fort Presque Isle, on the bay of the same name (modern-day Erie, Penn.); Fort Sandusky, on the bay of the same name (modern-day Erie County, Penn.); Fort Detroit, on the Detroit River (modern-day Detroit City); Fort Miami, situated where the St. Joseph's River and St. Mary's River form the greater Maumee River; Fort St. Joseph, on Lake Huron (modern-day Jocelyn, Ontario, Canada); and Fort Michilimackinac, which controlled the Michilimackinac Straits between lakes Michigan and Huron.

Pontiac's plan called for these forts and others to be attacked as simultaneously as possible so that each post would be too preoccupied with its own defense to render assistance to any of the others, while every precaution was to be taken to lure the intended targets into a false sense of security beforehand, giving the attackers an added element of surprise for when the attack finally came. If executed properly, this scheme would see the English presence eradicated in interior America, with any attempt at reentry rendered extremely difficult without the periodic safety and reinforcements of such forts as previously named. Pontiac scheduled this uprising to occur ***"at a coming change of the moon in the month of May"*** and found its aims well-received by the supreme council he had called, whom he assured of his odds of success on account of his distinguished service during the French Regime, particularly against General Braddock on the Monongahela alongside Charles Langlade in 1755.

Pontiac was to personally lead the attack on Fort Detroit, which was in the vicinity of several Ottawa, Wyandot and Pottowattomie villages, and which he and his band of warriors intended to gain admittance to by gestures of friendship to the fort's commander, Major Henry Gladwin (circa. 1729 – 91), before brandishing concealed weapons and dispensing with his unsuspecting garrison. In preparation for this, files and saws were borrowed from French forgers to be used in shortening musket barrels for easier concealment under draped blankets, while peaceful Indigenous envoys continued to routinely present themselves to the fort to maintain outward appearances. However, Major Gladwin and his Detroit garrison were not as unsuspecting as Pontiac had hoped.

Several oral traditions attempt to account for the Major's knowledge of the impending attack, however none are concrete in their conclusions. Jonathan Carver (1710 – 80), who later visited Detroit in 1766, just three years after the incident, provides the following: That while Pontiac was busy making his final preparations to assail the fort, Major Gladwin had hired a local Ojibway girl, invariably referred to as "*Catherine*", to fashion him a pair of moccasins, and so pleased with the first pair that she delivered, that he endeavored to employ her to make a second pair, perhaps for his wife, whom he had just married within the last year (1762), however, appearing hesitant to accept the additional work, Gladwin inquired of her what was the matter, to which, under the pretense of absolute secrecy, she revealed to him Pontiac's impending plot. Yet, as plausible as this theory sounds, two others are worth mention;

The first suggests that a "*Madame Guoin*", a French woman who went to trade at an Ottawa encampment returned and reported to her husband that the Ottawa were up to something, as while in their encampment, she noted a great many Ottawa warriors shortening the barrels of muskets despite their efforts to conceal their work, with either she, or her husband subsequently reporting this strange behavior to the fort, who were then put on alert.

The second is based on a 18th century French manuscript, which was found hidden in the attic of a Canadian homestead on the eve of its demolition. In this document, which was unsigned, but alleged to have been penned by a priest of St. Anne's, "*Mohiacan*", a disillusioned Ottawa warrior, appears before the gates of Fort Detroit, the very night before Pontiac's intended assault and informs an English officer on duty that, the next day, Pontiac, with sixty warriors, would arrive outside the fort, request admittance to discuss a treaty, and upon entry, at a given signal, would brandish concealed weapons and massacre the garrison. He was noted as being so fearful of retribution that he would not trust in the fort's French interpreter, Monsieur la Butte to be present to translate his warning, instead delivering it himself, one-on-one, through the gate in broken English before leaving. Beyond these three theories, are increasingly unsubstantiated conjectures, among them that it was an Indigenous mistress of Major Gladwin who revealed to him Pontiac's scheme. The reality is that we will likely never know exactly how Gladwin came to know of Pontiac's intentions, as historian Charles Moore thoroughly examined all of Gladwin's official papers during the 19th century and could find no trace of his informant's identity within them.

Nonetheless, the night of May 7th, 1763, was one of busied preparation inside Fort Detroit. The sentinels were put on high alert, while the inhabitants were ordered to stay indoors through the coming day in anticipation of Pontiac's arrival, which occurred at about 10 o'clock the next morning. Prior to arriving, Pontiac had decided that if the situation proved *favorable* for a massacre, he would present Major Gladwin with a wampum (diplomatic or ceremonially beaded) belt in a *reversed* position, while if the situation was *unfavorable* for a massacre, he would present the belt in the *usual* manner. Based on this, Pontiac's brethren would know whether to be on alert or at ease.

Having been granted entry into the fort upon his arrival, Pontiac and his brethren were ushered into the local assembly hall, where Major Gladwin and a heavily armed bodyguard were awaiting them. Pontiac sat on the floor before the Major, as was the custom, and after exchanging opening remarks, Pontiac addressed the obvious precautions that the Major had taken:

"**Why does my English brother keep his young men armed and on parade as if for battle?**" asked he. "**Does my brother expect the soldiers of the French?**" Gladwin considered shortly.

"**I keep my soldiers armed that they may be perfect in their exercise of arms, so that they may be ready to fight well if a war should come**," replied he.

The tension in the hall must have been palpable. Pontiac and his brethren desired nothing more than the massacre of Major Gladwin and his garrison, but Gladwin knew it and Pontiac certainly knew Gladwin knew it by this stage. So, he began to address the latter in friendlier terms, assuring the Major of his allegiance and his high esteem of the English, before slowly rising, and approaching him.

He then began to unfasten the belt of wampum tied to his waist to present to Gladwin, as his brethren looked on — the manner in which Pontiac handed this belt to the Major would decide the fate of all those present, not only in the assembly hall, but the fort itself. Casually, he handed it to Gladwin in the *usual* fashion, conveying to his brethren that the situation was not optimal for a massacre. The Major accepted the belt, but in replying to Pontiac, angrily reproached him and his brethren for their true intentions:

"Look! False chief, you have thought to deceive me with lies and to slay me by treachery, but I know the treachery and hate that your lying tongue would hide. You are armed, every man of you with a shortened gun like this chief by my side." And accosting the nearest of Pontiac's brethren, lifted his blanket cloak, revealing a concealed sawed-off musket.

As Jonathan Carver later described, **"*Pontiac endeavored to contradict the accusation, and to make excuses for his suspicious conduct; but the governor [Gladwin], satisfied of the falsity of his protestations, would not listen to them [and] advised them [Pontiac and his brethren] to make the best of their way out of the fort lest his young men, on being acquainted with their treacherous purposes, should cut every one of them to pieces.*"** And so leave Pontiac and his brethren did, but not for long. The next day (May 9th, 1763) they launched their first attack on the fort from the exterior, but it was repulsed, though the fort was positively surrounded and put to a regular siege. Many other outposts were not as fortunate, however.

On May 16th, several Indigenous representatives appeared at the gates of Fort Sandusky and requested a council with the outpost's commander, an *"Ensign Paully,"* who unsuspectingly granted their request and admitted them entrance. No sooner had they entered, that at given signal they brandished concealed weapons and promptly massacred the fort's entire twenty-seven-man garrison, although sparing Ensign Paully, who was carried off into captivity and pressured into marrying a widowed Indigenous woman.

Nine days later, a large deputation of Pottawotamies appeared before the gates of Fort St. Joseph, and similarly requested a council with its commanding officer, an *"Ensign Schlosser,"* who, similarly, unsuspectingly granted their request and admitted them entrance. By one account it took less than two minutes for Ensign Schlosser's entire fourteen-man garrison to be massacred, with he carried off into captivity.

Finally, on May 27th, Fort Miami commander, an *"Ensign Holmes"* was lured out of his outpost by an Indigenous deputation and promptly assassinated, with his tiny garrison afterwards surrendering. Fort Ouatanon, on the Wabash (modern-day Lafayette) was also captured by Indigenous stratagem, as was Fort Venango, with the lives of former's garrison and commander, a *"Lieutenant Jenkins"* being spared at the behest of local French merchants and traders, who's opinions the Natives respected, but the garrison and commander of the latter, a *"Lieutenant Gordon"*, being massacred by representatives of the Seneca. The worse slaughter of the uprising, however, occurred at Michilimackinac during the month of June 1763.

Since the previous year, Charles Langlade, and his father, Augustin, had become friendly with Fort Michilimackinac's commander, Captain George Etherington, who, in April of 1763, had given the pair permission to expand their enterprises in the following terms:

"Michilimackinac, April 13, 1763.

I have this date given permission to Messrs. Langlade, father and son, to live at the Post of La Baye, and do hereby order that no person may interrupt them in their voyage thither with their wives, children, servants and baggage.

Geo. Etherington, Commandant."

But although Charles Langlade and his father had sought permission to expand into La Baye, Charles in particular continued to frequent Michilimackinac, the local population of whom he was deeply ingratiated with on account of his and his father's trading there. And it was this friendly disposition of Charles' towards the inhabitants of the post, as well as his sense of duty and honor that compelled him to inform Captain Etherington of the impending storm that was Pontiac's Rebellion, of which Charles possessed considerable knowledge on account of his affiliation with Ottawa Nation, of whom he (to a lesser extent) and Pontiac (to a greater extent) were a part.

However, although a veteran of the French & Indian War and well versed in Indigenous guerilla-style warfare, in part due to his association with Charles Langlade, his family, friends and associates, who manifested a more-or-less friendly disposition towards him, as well as Michilimackinac's remoteness, Captain Etherington had become blind to the Indigenous discontent beyond his fort's own walls and deaf to his ablest subordinate's warning that he was not as safe from the brewing Indigenous wrath as he so firmly believed.

On numerous occasions leading up to June 1763, Charles Langlade approached Captain Etherington with dire warnings that Indigenous Nations, tribes and bands in allegiance with Pontiac were plotting Michilimackinac's demise, however, Etherington, taking these warnings none too seriously to begin with, but to satisfy his own convictions, at length summoned local Indigenous chiefs to a conference, to personally ask them if they were indeed plotting with Pontiac against Mackinac, to which they lied, telling Etherington exactly what he wanted to hear — that they manifested nothing but friendship towards him and his outpost and that no plotting was going on. Wholly satisfied and deceived, Captain Etherington then sent the chiefs away, before continuing as usual in complete ignorance of Charles Langlade's continued warnings. He even went so far as to chastise Langlade, telling him, as the latter's grandson, Augustin Grignon, later recalled in his *"Recollections"*:

"Mr. De Langlade, I am weary of hearing the stories you so often bring me; they are the foolish twaddle of old women, and unworthy of belief; the Indians have nothing against the English, and cherish no evil designs; I hope, therefore, that you will not trouble me with any more such stuff."

"Captain Etherington," [replied] Langlade, *"I will not trouble you with any more of these 'women's stories', as you call them, but I beg you will remember my faithful warnings."*

However, Charles Langlade was not the only bearer of dire warnings which Captain Etherington had ignored and chastised leading up to June 1763. Some months before, a Frenchman by the name of Laurent Ducharm is also recorded as having sought out the captain to inform him of the brewing storm, but Etherington is said to have threatened Ducharm with arrest and conveyance to Fort Detroit as a prisoner for peddling such falsehoods. This ignorance would cost him and his garrison dearly.

The 2nd of June was an English holiday — the King's birthday. Early that morning a small fleet of canoes carrying Indigenous men and women paddled out to Michilimackinac Island and proposed staging a game of *"baaga'adowe"*, better known by the French name of *"lacrosse"*, outside the fort for all to enjoy. After all, it was a beautiful summer day. Enamored with the idea, Captain Etherington not only granted the Indigenous deputation's request but is said to have placed bets as the game commenced.

The Indigenous women, wrapped in blanket shrouds, spectated and mingled with the fort's English garrison, who were immensely interested in the game, during which the Indigenous men displayed their athletic prowess. They played naked, save for a loincloth, and were arrayed in two teams of large numbers (by one account up to one hundred players each). The game was an enthusiastic affair, with the crowd cheering as the opposing teams struggled with one another over control of the ball, which eventually found itself hurled up and over the fort's wall in an apparent accident. And naturally, the Indigenous players of the game pursued the ball into the fort through its ajar gates, however, once inside the fort, the killing started.

The Indigenous women, brandishing concealed weapons from under their blankets, armed the men, who then began massacring all within the fort itself and within its immediate vicinity. The English trader, Alexander Henry, was in his residence near to the fort when the slaughter started. As it happened, his next-door neighbor was one of Michilimackinac's most prominent citizens, Charles Langlade, who, like him, had been home, tending to business affairs instead of out watching the baaga'adowe game which had developed earlier in the morning. Their houses were separated by a low picket fence, which Henry jumped after fleeing his own residence. He hammered at Langlade's door, which Charles promptly answered, and when he did, Henry pleaded for concealment within his home. Langlade, in his ignorance of what was transpiring, so busied with business as he had been that morning, is documented as having replied "**Why do you wish to be concealed?**", unaware that the massacre he, among others, had foreseen, was now taking place.

Screaming and the firing of rifles then reached Langlade's ears. He strode across his residence to the nearest window for a better view, with Henry being beckoned into the home by one of the Langlade residence's servants. She led him up to the attic and locked him inside. Feeling secure, he peered out of a window to see what was happening and beheld a horrifying field of view. According to Henry's own eyewitness account, later reprinted in the "*Boys' Own Magazine*" (1893), under the title of "*The Fall of Mackinaw*":

"While the trader [Henry himself, referred to by his profession and in the third person] was watching these heart-sickening scenes, he heard a number of Indians enter the room below. Through the crevices of the boards, he could see them and hear every word they uttered.

The first inquiry of the Indians was whether there were any Englishmen concealed in the building. Langlade replied that he did not know of any being there, but he could not answer positively. This was literally true, as he had not observed the act of his servant. The Canadian [Langlade] [...] suggested that the Indians should examine for themselves.

Acting upon this [...] they ascended the stairs, and a moment later the trader heard them trying the door of the place in which he was concealed. [...] A momentary delay was occasioned by the absence of the key, during which he glanced about him, and saw in one corner a number of vessels of birch bark, such as are used in maple-sugar.

Beneath these, the trader crept at the very moment the door was opened, and four Indians in their war-paint, and their tomahawks smeared with blood, entered the apartment.

They passed around the room, which was dimly lighted, and finally departed, without discovering the fugitive. […] There was a feathered bed upon the floor, upon which the trader threw himself, and slept until the dusk of evening, when he was aroused a second time by someone entering the room.

Upon looking up, he saw Mr. Langlade's wife [Charlotte] before him. She was greatly surprised, but advised him not to be uneasy, as there was hope of his being saved. The massacre was over, and it appeared as if the greatest danger had passed.

The trader lay for a long time meditating on his condition and prospects of escape, when, as before, he fell in a slumber which continued until the morning light entered the apartment. He was aroused by the sound of voices of Indians, who stated that they had found nothing of Henry, the trader, and they concluded that he must be concealed somewhere in the [Langlade] house.

It seemed from the appearance of things, that Langlade had learned of the fugitive being concealed in his dwelling. The moment that the [Indians] inquired for him, his wife told him that they must not attempt to hide him away any longer, as they would be punished for it.

Langlade at first resisted, but finally coincided with his wife, and stated to the [Indians] that the trader they sought was secreted in a room above, but that he had come without their knowledge. A moment later the party began ascending the stairs.

All hope had now departed, and rising to his feet, Henry appeared before his enemies, as they entered the room, and surrendered himself their prisoner. They were all drunk, and surveyed him a moment with maudlin indecision.

One of them caught him by the hair, and held a large carving-knife brandished for a moment above his head. Finally he dropped it, saying: "I won't kill you"; adding, in explanation, that he had *lost a brother in battle, a short time previous, and that he would adopt him as his brother.*

Hope once again dawned in the miserable man's breast, and he obeyed the [Indian] when he ordered him down the stairs, and across the parade-ground to his cabin.

Henry was about to obey when he reflected that all the [Indians] were intoxicated, and if he should expose himself to their gaze, certain death would be the result. Through Langlade, he represented this view of the case, and the Indian consented that he should remain where he was until he chose to remove him.

Henry had enjoyed about an hour's rest, when a strange Indian appeared, saying that the Englishman's master had sent for him, and he must accompany him at once. It is needless to say that he obeyed this command with misgivings, almost certain that it was a stratagem to take his life, and yet not daring to refuse the order.

He passed out [of the Langlade residence], the [Indian] following close behind him, until they had gone beyond the gate of the fort, when the trader discovered he was leading him towards some bushes.

Stopping short, Henry told him [the Indian] that he knew he meant to take his life, and that in his opinion it was not necessary to proceed any further to carry out his intention. The [Indian] replied very coolly that his supposition was right, and immediately raised his knife to dispatch him.

Naturally enough, the trader caught his arm, and threw him back, and started on a full run for the fort, his enemy following close behind. Entering the fort, he ran up to his adopted Indian brother and master, and appealed to him for protection. The [pursuing Indian], however, continued striking at him with his knife, until [he] darted into the house of Mr. Langlade, and was again given a few hours of respite.

[...] In the morning, when he was summoned to descend [again], he encountered, with unspeakable joy, [Captain] Etherington, [...] and Lieutenant Leslie."

But as Charles Langlade's grandson, Augustin Grignon later recalled in his *"Recollections"*: ***"Captain Etherington and Lieutenant Leslie, who were among the survivors, and [were] now in the hands of the Indians, came near [to] being burned at the stake [a tradition amongst the Indians and applied to specific prisoners]; the wood was all ready, [...] the prisoners [were] pinioned, and the torch would soon have been applied, when M. de Langlade arrived with a party of friendly Indians, and he at once stepped up to the prisoners and cut the cords from their arms, and then, in a firm, determined manner, told the hostile Indians, "If you are not pleased with what I have done, I am ready to meet you [in hand-to-hand combat]"; but none came forward; they saw too plainly that he and his friends were well prepared to fight, and they knew that Charles Langlade was a stranger to fear.***

Now that he had saved [Captain] Etherington and [Lieutenant] Leslie from the stake, he turned to the former and said, "Now, Captain Etherington, if you had listened to the 'old women's stories', of which I timely warned you, you would not now be in your present humiliating situation, with all your men nearly slain."

Members of the Chippewa had been the principal attackers on that otherwise beautiful June morning, a fact which greatly displeased the local Ottawa, who had not subscribed to Pontiac's scheme (if not at all, then certainly not as wholly), thus causing much resentment between the two. Tense negotiations then took place between representatives of both parties, which mostly focused on the fate of the survivors of the massacre. During this uncertain period, deposed Michilimackinac Commandant, Captain Etherington made two decisions; the first was to pen the following letter to Charles Langlade, in which he appointed the Canadian as his successor to Michilimackinac's command, given his detainment by the Chippewa:

"To Monsieur Langlade [...]

Sir — As I am oblig'd to leave this, and have a great confidence in you, I hereby impower you to take upon you the Command of this Post, and I order all the Inhabitants as well those that are within

the Fort, as those that may arrive from different places, to obey you as such, as they shall answer the Contrary at their peril.

You will prevent as much as within your power, the [Natives] from committing any more outrages against any of His Majesty's Subjects that may arrive here in my absence, either French or English.

You will immediately collect all the provisions that was taken out of the Kings store since the second Instant [of this month — June], and take it under your charge to be dispos'd of as hereafter may be directed.

You will please advise me from time to time, of what Batteaux or canoes may arrive here and when the vessel arrives, you will send of the letter to the Captain which I gave you for that purpose, and endeavor to furnish him with a pilot to come up to the mission or L'Arbre Croche [a Michilimackinac village] or where we may at that time be.

Geo. Etherington, Capt.
1st. B.R.A. Regiment, late Commandant at Michilimackinac

This is to certify that I thoroughly believe Monsieur Langlade was entirely ignorant of the design of the Chippewas to surprise this post on the second instant [this month — June], and since that time he has us'd his utmost endeavors to accommodate matters with [them], and that he was very instrumental in saving Lieutenant Leslie's, mine, and the lives of the soldiers that were taken prisoners, and without doubt will be rewarded accordingly.

Geo. Etherington, Capt.
1st. B.R.A. Regiment

10th June, Michilimackinac, 1763."

Captain Etherington's second decision was to pen a letter to his superior, Major Gladwin, whom he entrusted to Michilimackinac's Jesuit missionary priest, Pierre-Luc du Jaunay (1705 – 80), to deliver, uncertain of what had transpired at Fort Detroit:

"Michilimackinac, 12 June, 1763.

Sir: — *Notwithstanding that I wrote you in my last [letter], that all the [Natives had] arrived, and that everything seemed in perfect tranquility, yet, on the 2nd instant [of this month], the Chippewas, who live in a plain near this fort, assembled to play ball, as they had done almost every day since their arrival. They played from morning till noon; then throwing their ball close to the gate, and observing that Lieutenant Leslie and me a few paces out of it, they came behind us, seized and carried us into the woods.*

In the meantime, the rest rushed into the fort, where they found their [women], whom they had previously planted their, with their hatchets hid under their blankets, which they took, and in an instant killed Lieutenant Jamet and fifteen rank and file [soldiers], and a trader named Tracy. They wounded two, and took the rest of the garrison prisoners, five of whom they have since killed.

They made prisoners [of] all the English traders, and robbed them of everything they had; but they offered no violence to the persons or property of any of the Frenchmen.

When the massacre was over, Messrs. Langlade and [Jaques] Farlie, the [Indigenous] interpreter, came down to the to the place where Lieutenant Leslie and me were prisoners; and on their giving themselves as security to return us when demanded, they obtained leave for us to go to the fort, under a guard of [friendly Natives], which gave time, by the assistance of the gentlemen above mentioned, to send for the Outaways [Ottawa], who came down on the first notice, and were very much displeased at what the Chippewas had done.

Since the arrival of the Outaways, they have done everything in their power to serve us; and with what prisoners the Chippewas had given them, and what they have bought, I have now with me Lieutenant Leslie, and eleven privates; and the other four of the garrison, who are yet living, remain in the hands of Chippewas.

The Chippewas, who are superior in numbers to the Ottaways, have declared in council to them that if they do not remove us out of the fort, they will cut off all communication to this post, by which means all the convoys of merchants from Montreal, La

Baye, St. Joseph, and the upper posts, would perish. But if the news of your posts being attacked (which they say was the reason why they took up the hatchet) be false, and you can, send up a string reinforcement with provisions, &c., accompanied by some of your [Indigenous warriors], I believe the post might be reestablished again.

Since this affair happened, two canoes arrived from Montreal, which put it in my power to make a present to the Ottaway Nation, who are very well deserve anything that can be done for them.

I have been very much obliged to Messrs. Langlade and Farli, the interpreter, as likewise to the Jesuit, for the many good offices they have done us on this occasion. The Priest seems inclinable to go down to your post for a day or two, which I am very glad of, as he is a very good man, and had a great deal to say with the [Natives], hereabout, who will believe everything he tells them, on his return, which I hope will be soon. The Outaways say they will take Lieutenant Leslie, me, and the eleven men which I mentioned before were in their hands, up to their village, and there keep us, till they hear of what is doing at your post. They have sent this canoe for that purpose. I refer you to the Priest for the particulars of this melancholy affair, and am, dear sir,

    Yours, very sincerely,

        Geo. Etherington.

To Major Gladwyn.

P.S. — The Indians that are to carry the Priest to Detroit, will not undertake to land him at the fort, but at some of the Indian villages near it; so you must not take it amiss that he does not pay you the first visit. And once more I beg that nothing may stop your sending him back, the next day after his arrival, if possible, as we shall be at a great loss for the want of him; and I make no doubt, that you will do all in your power to make peace, as you see the situation we are in, and send up provisions as soon as possible, and ammunition, as what we had was pillaged by the [attackers].

    Adieu.

Geo. Etherington."

Father du Jaunay accomplished his task with tact and diplomacy, successfully speaking with Major Gladwin, informing him of what had transpired at Michilimackinac, and bringing news of Fort Detroit's ongoing siege back to Captain Etherington, who, through the intercession of Charles Langlade, among others, was shortly thereafter transferred to Montreal, from whence, Thomas Gage, who had previous been defeated by forces under Langlade's command alongside General Braddock on the Monongahela in 1755, and was now the Military Governor of Montreal under General Jeffery Amherst, wrote to the thirty-four-year-old thanking him for his services rendered to the English cause:

"*From Montreal, this 17^h of July, 1763.*

Mr. Langlade.
Sir: — The services which you have rendered to the king after the unfortunate surprise of the Fort Michilimackinac deserve my greatest thanks, [and] I cannot allow the Indians to depart, without [testifying] to you how much I am obliged to you for all you have done to save the lives of so many persons, by treating to have them delivered from out of the hands of the [attackers] and for having saved the peltry of several traders, who without this help would to-day be reduced to beggary.

I hope that the fort will soon be re-occupied by the King's [troops]. Until such time, all trading on the [Grand] River will be forbidden, and I pray you to put affairs in the best order which shall be possible for you in the confusion you must be in at present, and please prevent as far as may depend upon you, that the Soteux have no powder. It is important for all nations to join you, to draw reason out of the perfidy and [treason] which the Soteux have been guilty of. They will be sustained by sufficient military force and by this means the war will be short, otherwise it might draw out lengthily, and in this case I am afraid other nations might take part in it for want of abundant treaty. I send to you inclosed, a note which Monsieur Leslie has left with me. If it shall be possible for you to regain the papers in question, you will render a great service to a family of distinction.

Mr. Etherington has left here a few days ago to render account to General Amherst of all that has happened, and will not fail to render the justice which is due to you and the Rev. Father Du Jaunay. I have the honor to be with much esteem, sir,

Your very humble and very obedient servant,

Thos. Gage."

And a month later, deposed Captain Etherington formally manifested his thanks to Langlade in the following terms:

"Montreal. 15th August 1763.

Monsieur Langlade, Michilimackinac.

Sir — I have just time to thank you for all your favors and to tell you that I have acquainted the General [Amherst] of your good behavior, who will write you himself by the [friendly Natives] who have been very well received.

For further particulars, I refer you to the General's letter, my compliments to Mr. Farley and all your family and am, Sir,

Your most obedient, humble servant,

Geo. Etherington."

In the meantime, Pontiac's Rebellion dragged on. It would not be fully resolved until July 26th, 1766, when Pontiac personally concluded a peace treaty with English Superintendent of Indian Affairs, Sir William Johnson in Fort Ontario, New York, having the previous year began negotiations with Johnson's subordinate, George Croghan (1718 – 82). Although he had been unable to achieve his stated goal of driving the English from interior North America, Pontiac's uprising had been far from a complete failure, as it had brought about a much-needed change in Anglo-Indigenous policy, namely, the recall of General Jeffery Amherst, who's deeply unpopular (even amongst his own colleagues) and inflammatory Indigenous policies had been a prime motivator of Pontiac's Rebellion/Revolt/War to begin with, and who was replaced as Commander-in-Chief in America by Thomas Gage. Returning to London, Amherst expected to be lauded and rewarded for his services in America, instead, he was compelled to answer for his conduct, which was openly ridiculed by Sir William Johnson and George Croghan, among others.

In contrast, Charles Langlade's conduct during the crisis not only secured him the admiration and appreciation of English high-command, but further engrained his name (and aliases) into local Wisconsin Indigenous oral history. As Wisconsinite, Louis B. Porlier, the descendant of James Porlier — one of Green Bay's earliest settlers, whom arrived in 1781, documented, eighty-five years later, in a paper titled *"The Capture of Mackinaw, 1763 — A Menomonee Tradition"* (subsequently annotated by Lyman Copeland Draper, published and re-published by the Wisconsin Historical Society):

"On the 14th of October, 1848, Hon. William Medill, Commissioner of Indian Affairs, called a council at Poygan, Wisconsin, to negotiate a treaty with the Menomonee tribe of Indians. H. S. Baird was appointed Secretary to the Commissioner. On the morning of the day of the meeting, Osh-kosh came to our tent and said to Augustin Grignon, Sr., "I have been notified to attend the council; will you go with me?" Mr. Grignon replied that he would, and they both started towards the council-house. Immediately after I told Augustin Grignon, Jr. to call our men to put up our shanty so as to be in readiness for the annuity payment, which was to take place immediately after the treaty should be concluded. As soon as the shanty was up so they could get along without me, I told the younger Grignon that I was going over to listen to the council, and started towards the council house.

Just before reaching the place of assembly, I saw Sho-no-nee, or 'Silver' — one of the principal Menomonee chiefs, coming out of the council-house, and walking towards a group of Indians who were gathered at a short distance away. I followed him thither, as I knew that he would relate what had been said in the council. He seated himself on a log and they all thronged close around him, anxious to ascertain what was the business of the Commissioner.

[...]

Sho-no-nee then made running remarks about different tribes of Indians who had been removed from their country to distant lands, referring especially to the Winnebagoes and the Pottowattamies; and in winding up his remarks, said: "We know by those who have come back from the country whither they have been removed, to what dangers they are exposed;" and, after a pause, he added: "It is but the result of what Pontiac had foreseen and foretold." The by-standers inquired who Pontiac was, and what he had foreseen. Sho-no-nee then resumed by saying: "Pontiac lived before my time; but I will simply state to you what my ancestors have related to me in regard to him. He was, they told me, a noble-minded Indian; he had come to Milwaukee at one time, and then and there had assembled different tribes of Indians, and addressed them as follows:

"My Friends! I have come here to consult you in behalf of our common cause. When the white man came across the ocean and landed on our shores, he spoke with a sweet and silver-tongued mouth, saying that we had large possessions of land, and that he had none, and asked to be permitted to settle in a corner, and live with us like brothers. We received and admitted them as such; and they lived true to their proposition and promise until they had gained strength. They then commenced to encroach upon us more and more. Their purpose is clear to me — that they will continue to encroach upon us, until they discover that they have sufficient power to remove us from our country to a distant land, where we will be confronted with all kinds of danger, and perhaps be annihilated. The time is not far distant when we shall be placed in a critical position. It is now in our power to force the whites back to their original settlements. We must all join in one common cause, and sweep the white men from our country, and then we shall live happy, and we shall have nothing more to do with the hated race. We shall have no unsatisfied desires, as we have an abundance of *game in our forests our rivers and lakes are teeming with all kinds of fish, fowl and wild rice we shall live as did our forefathers; we shall with our furs and skins obtain all necessary supplies, and be, happy."*

The inquiry was then made, what answer did Pontiac receive from the assembled nations. "Well," said Sho-no-nee, "with the exception of the Menomonees, they all joined with him, and placed themselves in readiness to take the war-path at the first warning. Mackinaw was the first point to be attacked; and after its capture, messengers were to be sent eastward, and the successive attacks would have been like a large prairie set on fire, with a strong wind spreading the flames in every direction, making the whole one solid mass of fire, destroying everything before it as it rushes along! And this would have been the result; but you are familiar with our customs in regard to incantations. The spirit that gave the power to the war-chief, required of him to make a sacrifice of the officers captured at Mackinaw, before taking any further step. The Chippewa war-chief succeeded in capturing the post of Mackinaw; but before he could make the sacrifice, the 'Bravest of the Brave' came and snatched the officers out of his hands and the war-chief squatted down, foiled in his purpose." It was then asked, who was this Bravest of the Brave? — and why did the war-chief not stand his ground, and prevent him from rescuing the officers? "The Bravest of the Brave," said Sho-no-nee, "was Au-ke-win-ge-ke-taw-so, or 'Defender of his Country', Charles Langlade, the grand-father of Augustin Grignon — and he was too well known all over the western world for anyone to dare oppose him."

As for Pontiac himself, he would outlive the event which carries his name by only three years. On April 20th, 1769, he was stabbed to death under mysterious circumstances near Cahokia (modern-day St. Clair County, Illinois). Thus ended the life of one of 18th century North America's most enigmatic warriors. His exact resting place is disputed.

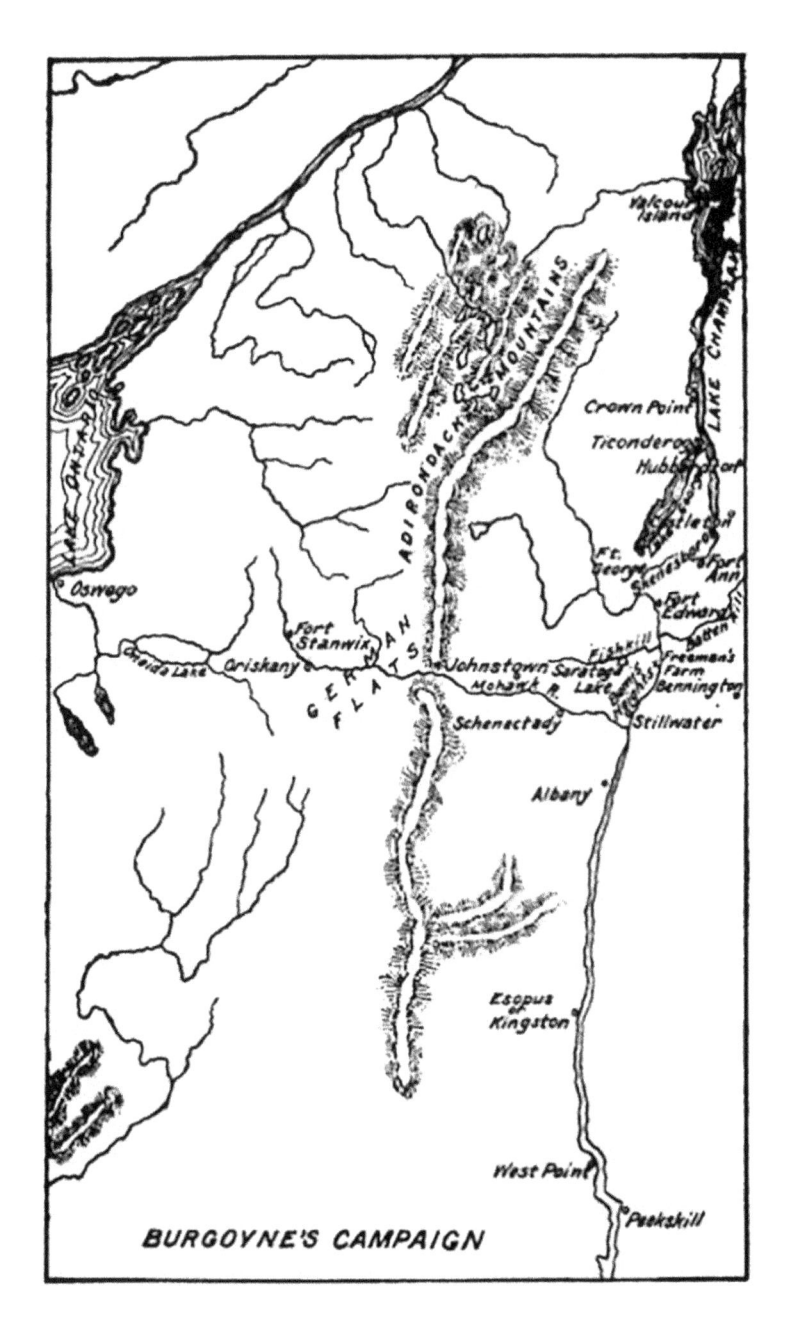

The region in which English General John Burgoyne's army campaigned in 1777. From "The American Revolution", by John Fiske (1891).

Chapter VI

1764 – '81: Charles Langlade, the Brewing Storm & the American Revolutionary War

With peace more-or-less restored, the most pressing issue for the English crown and government was attempting to pay off the enormous debt accumulated by the waging of the last two wars (The French & Indian War, and Pontiac's War/Rebellion). In England, the national debt had sky-rocketed, with the crown and government making clear its opinion that the American colonies should bear a responsibility in repaying this debt, as England had incurred it whilst defending and expanding American interests. However, few colonies shared this sentiment, on account of their having funded their own militias, which had suffered considerable losses during the French & Indian War in particular. But this didn't stop the English crown and government from levying new taxes, such as the 1764 Sugar Act, the 1765 Stamp Act, the 1767-68 Townshend Act, and the 1773 Tea Act, or renewing old ones, such as the 1733 Molasses Act, in a bid to lessen the country's debt at America's expense. This, combined with the violence of the 1770 Boston Massacre, and the implementation of the 1774 Intolerable Act, in response to the Boston Tea Party of the previous year, prompted the meeting of the First Continental Congress in September 1774, in which twelve of the thirteen colonies partook, and the result of which was a petition sent to King George III (1738 - 1820) of England, requesting a repeal of the Intolerable Act, and the addressing of other colonial grievances.

However, this petition went unheeded, and in April 1775, American-based English Commander-in-Chief, Thomas Gage, received orders from London to take preemptive action against Patriotic forces. He chose as his first operation the seizure of stockpiled weapon and ammunition that the Patriots had amassed, the scramble for which resulted in some of the earliest shots of the American Revolutionary War being fired, at the battles of Concord and Lexington.

No sooner had these engagements occurred, that the English colonial government redoubled its efforts to ensure the allegiance of the Canadian and Indigenous populous of the Northwest, and to induce them to join their cause against the rebelling American Patriots. Early in 1776, English Captain Abraham De Peyster (1753 – 98), who had officially assumed Michilimackinac's command following Captain Etherington's resignation in favor of Charles Langlade during Pontiac's Rebellion, enlisted the amiably disposed forty-seven-year-old Canadian to exert his considerable influence in raising and leading a supplementary force of Indigenous warriors and Canadian militia, which were to aid the English regular forces in defending or advancing beyond the Canadian frontier. Through the spring and early summer, Langlade succeeded in raising a large contingent of warriors and militia which amassed at Michilimackinac, where, on the 4th of July 1776, the very day American independence was formally declared, he received his marching orders from De Peyster:

"To Monsieur Langlade, Orders.

Monsieur — You will take command of the [militia] of this post that consists of People of several [Indigenous] Nations and some Canadian volunteers, with these you will undertake your journey in order to join the Superintendent of Indian Affairs in the neighborhood of Montreal or the officer that commands the troops of the King in that Quarter from whom you will receive your orders.

You will do your best to harass the Rebels wherever you may encounter them, and in all matters you will conduct yourself with your customary prudence and Humanity.

At Michilimaquenac, July 4, 1776."

Arriving at Montreal, Langlade and his men joined General Sir Guy Carleton (1724 – 1808), the Commander-in-Chief of English forces, his second in command, General John Burgoyne (1722 – 92) and their army, from whence, they advanced on the American army commanded by Benedict Arnold (1741 – 1801), which had encamped at Sorel, southwest Quebec. The English army successfully pursued Arnold onto Lake Champlain but were unable to promptly continue the chase as they lacked a sufficient number of vessels to accommodate their own army. Carleton promptly set about remedying the situation, and by early October, had improvised a small fleet consisting of approximately one ship-of-the-line, two schooners, and over twenty smaller vessels, carrying a total of approximately eighty-seven guns. Boarding his men, Carleton, resumed the pursuit of Arnold's army, sailing from Sorel, past Ilse-aux-Noir and onto Lake Champlain.

On the morning of October 11th, 1776, supplemented by a large contingent of Indigenous warriors and Canadian militia in their birchbark canoes, some of which were immense in size, spacious enough to fit thirty men, Carleton seized upon the Benedict Arnold's fleet, which had drawn its vessels into a crescent shape between Valcour Island, and the shore. A fierce engagement then commenced, which lasted until nightfall, after which the American fleet thought it prudent to withdraw, being in no condition to effectively resume the fight on the morrow. Accordingly, the majority withdrew by moonlight to the fortress of Crown Point, the guns of which the American fleet hoped to supplement themselves with. On the morning of the 12th of October, Carleton's English fleet dispersed the remnants of Arnold's and pushed on Crown Point, which the Americans ultimately chose to abandon without a fight, preferring to make their stand at Fort Ticonderoga, which had been considerably reinforced leading up to the campaign. Thus, concluded military operations in that quarter for the year, as it was seen as too late in the season for Carleton to attack Fort Ticonderoga, and with the traditional departure of the Indigenous warriors and Canadian militia to return home and prepare for winter, his army's numbers would be significantly reduced should he continue. However, the campaign, overall, had been a commendable success, with Charles Langlade's service warranting much praise, firstly, in a letter to English Colonel Caldwell:

"Off Point-au-Fer, 6th Octr. 1776.

To Lieut. Col. Caldwell.
Sir, Mr. Langlade being on his return to Michilimackinac to pass by your post, I recommend him to your notice as [a] man I have had reason to be very satisfied with and who from his influence amongst the Indians of that district may be of very much use to His Majesty's affairs — I have authorized him to bring down 200 of them early next Spring.

I am just now upon the point of proceeding upon the Lake with our armed Vessels and boats in order to clear that place of the Rebels who are upon it with considerable naval force. I fear the season is far too advanced for anything further this year. I should be glad you gave directions that all which can be spared of the 8th Regiment & all the Indians of your neighborhood be prepared to take the field early in the spring.

I beg to have all the Intelligence you procure from time to time.
I am & c.,"

And secondly, in an unsigned letter addressed to Michilimackinac's Commandant:

"Off Point-au-Fer, 6th October, 1776.

To Captain Depeyster.
Sir, I think it necessary to acquaint you that I have been very much satisfied with the conduct of Mr. Langlade, but quite the contrary with that of Anis & Gauthier, who have shown nothing but deceit & have been attentive only to their own concerns, and personal interests. I have commissioned Langlade to bring me down 200 chosen Indians in the Spring, in which I beg you to give him every assistance in your power and to dispatch him as early as possible. I send you two medals and a Gorget [neck/chest armor

plate] for chiefs whom Mr. Langlade will inform you of. I am just going with the armed Vessels and boars to endeavor to clear the Lake of the Rebels who are upon it with a considerable naval force; but I do not expect to be able to accomplish more this season.
I am & c.,"

His military duties for the year accordingly fulfilled, Langlade, his Indigenous warriors and Canadian militia began homeward, with Captain William Potts of 8th Regiment, aiding Langlade in procuring transportation thus:

"Fort Erie, 16th Novr., 1776.

To Mr. Langlade, on H.M. Service, Little Niagara.
Sir, in compliance with an order from Capt. Potts, [I] have sent you, a Corporal and Party, with a Batteau, to expedite you in your Intended Journey. I have the Honor to be,
Sir, your very hum. Serv.,
Walter Butler,
C. King's Regt."

Early the next year, Langlade's report on the late campaign reached the attention of Michilimackinac's commander, who manifested his sentiments in regard to it accordingly:

"From Mr. De Peyster, dated Michilimackinac, February, 1777.

Sir, I am just honored with Your Excellency's Letter of the 6th October by Monsieur Langlade.
You may depend upon it that nothing shall be wanting on my part to dispatch the Indians as soon as the nature of the service will admit.
I have already engaged such as wintered here with the small pox; and shall advise him to take such only as have had it.
The last fall I had deputies from several nations to assure me they will be ready at call; I wish I may be able to subsist them all. The Five [Six] Nations have sent a large belt inviting those of this

part to meet them at Niagara to settle an alliance in favor of His Majesty's arms; such as choose it shall have my leave to go, but it shall not interfere with Langlade's Expedition."

And as per the summons for him to repair to the frontier with a stated "***200 chosen***" Indigenous warriors and Canadian militia come spring, in April 1777, Langlade once again began amassing his forces, which were supplied with provisions from Michilimackinac, as per a report, dated early in the month, from Michilimackinac's commander:

"*From Ar. S. De Peyster.*

*Michilimackinac, 12*th *April 1777.*

Sir, I have the pleasure to inform your Excellency that the season affords me an early opportunity of sending of provisions to meet Monsr. Langlad's Indians at La Baye.

I have seen many Indians during the course of the winter who are all well inclined; the only fear I have now is the not being able to prevent the whole country from going down. Such as are prevented will take it ill, they must however be diverted from it.

Ar. S. De Peyster."

Eight days later, Captain de Peyster addressed the following letter to Langlade, urging him to repair at once to Michilimackinac with however many men he could immediately muster, without waiting for greater numbers which may not be necessary:

"*To Capt. Langlade.*

*Michilimackinac, 18*th *April, 1777.*

Sir, this is the first moment we can avail of. If I had been able [I] would have sent sooner, for I flatter myself that Capt. Langlade on his part will not fail to seize the first opportunity. […] If these, my children [referring to Langlade's assembled Indigenous warriors and Canadian militia], wish to be of the party [the army for this year], they must not stand on ceremony; but come at once to Mackinac. I pray you not to wait for a great number, for I believe we will have too many volunteers here.

I send you eighty pounds of tobacco, a sack of corn — ground, in order that the gentlemen may not compel their wives to grind it — two barrels of sco-ta-wa-bo [whisky], that they may not drive you wild. Besides, I send my best respects to Madame Langlade, and, beg her to accept two kegs of brandy, one barrel of salt, a small barrel of rice, and twenty pounds of tobacco, if necessary. I also send for Madame, a sack of one hundred and twenty-three pounds of flour, as a present. It is necessary to await the boat. Tell Carron [the great warrior and friend of Charles Langlade] that I shake him by the hand, as I do all my children at the Bay. […]
        Your very humble and obedient servant,
                A. S. De Peyster."

After collecting at La Baye, with Langlade at their head, in early May, the assembled Indigenous warriors and Canadian militia proceeded to Detroit, where they were received, personally, by the Governor:
"*From Governor Henry Hamilton.*
                Detroit, May 11th, 1777.

Sir, several bands of [Indigenous warriors and Canadian militia] have lately arrived at this place from their wintering. They all have behaved very quietly and give me the strongest assurances of their being determined to act as I shall require them. Your Excellency's orders will order my conduct, in expectation of which, I shall detain them from the time of their meeting in council, which may be about the 25th of this month, till letters arrive from Canada respecting their management.

As some of the Delawares appear wavering I have given one of their Chiefs a [wampum] belt, with a present to induce them to come to the Council, when I make no doubt they will be influenced as I would wish.

The King's vessels on these lakes, are put in the best repair possible, and the timber for the new one is all cut, but naval stores *and iron are yet wanting to proceed with the building of her. On arrival of these articles no time shall be lost in the building and equipping [of] her.*

I am &c.,

Henry Hamilton."

In accordance with the Governor's letter, Langlade's force remained at Detroit until council was held later in the month and their first marching orders of the year were received. Through June, although falling ill, and amidst unfriendly overtures from the Spanish, Langlade worked tirelessly to coordinate affairs with his English superiors, as evidenced by the following letters. Firstly;

"From Captain De Peyster.

Michilimackinac, 4 June 1777.

Sir, Mr. Langlade arrived here with sixty Indians from La Baye. He says he expects more but I fear they will come too late. I have completed him with the number required from this post. The Nations here have accounts that Spanish Agents have been amongst their Neighbors; If it be true, I suppose it is to draw off the Trade during these Troubles. The News however has made the Indians rather more difficult to move than I expected, such is their curiosity and fear, for I think I may affirm they are all well inclined. The embarkation is now ready and will take place immediately. I must beg leave to refer you to Mr. Langlade for further particulars.

I have the Honor to be with great respect, Your Excellency's most Hum. Servant,

A. S. De Peyster."

Secondly;
"From Captain De Peyster.

Michilimackinac, 6 June 1777.

Sir, since Mr. Langlade's departure for the Island, I have received an Express from Monsr. Laurent Ducharmes at Milwaukee, informing that the Chief Siginakee or Letourneau has received a Parole from the Spanish Commandant, to raise all the Indians between the Mississippi and the little Detroit of La Baye.

I am sensible we can undersell the Spaniards, but still I am led to believe they can only have Views of Trade flattering themselves with gaining that advantage during our Troubles.

The enclosed Letter from a Trader, will at least confirm that the Spaniards rather favor the English Traders. I must however observe that my intelligence from Milwaukee is dated the 15th May, Mr. Ducharme answers me, that he will be on the lookout, and come off to me immediately, should anything happen to require it [...].

Monsr. Langlade has left me his Papers, when they can be digested into a regular account, I will forward them.

The 2776 Livres, refer'd to me by your Excellency's order, I have caused a Merchant to pay him, as he said he cou'd not do without it. I begin to perceive that he wants some looking after, I believe him to be strictly honest, and quite disinterested, but I see he retains all the French Customs — nothing so easy given as a bon au Compt du Roy. In short, he can refuse the Indians nothing they can ask, and they will lose nothing for want of asking.

The presents Mr. Langlade brought up for the Minomunies, he tells me have been Pillaged, and, believes before they left Montreal, whilst he was sick. I shall take the first opportunity to have them examined, and shall transmit him the Bill of Parcels, whether they have been rob'd or not, by the Bulk they appear to be more than they deserve, at present after so many of them shamefully leaving Langlade yesterday [...].

I am with the Greatest respect Your Excellency's most Humble and obedient Servant,

A. S. De Peyster."

And thirdly;
"*From Captain De Peyster.*

Michilimackinac, 13th of June 1777.

Sir, Since the departure of Mr. Langlade, the Pottawatamies arriv'd here from St Joseph's fifteen in number who are all either chiefs or chief's sons totally ignorant of Bark Canoes. I am therefore oblig'd to send them in a Return Canoe, I hire for that purpose as Mr. Langlade assured me you [were] very desirous of seeing some of that nation. Their behavior here has been Remarkably good they came under the conduct of Monsr. Le Chevallier, a man spoken very ill of at Detroit. I however perceive by the great attachment those Indians have to him that he had better be caressed at present than otherwise. Charlot Lassossissay, the Iroquois, came also with them and conducts them to Montreal. This Indian speaks good French and is a good subject. Mr. Langlade sent him with Therry to St. Josephs to raise the Pottawatamies where he fell sick, but nevertheless was indefatigable in bringing over those Indians […].

Gautier is this instant arriving with the Sauks and Raynards. I must therefore hurry them off before they see each other, as a meeting will be rather inconvenient at Present and may greatly protract this Voyage.

Gautier it seems has been employ'd by Mr. Langlade to bring those Indians in here. I can count in the Canoes to the number of thirty-two.

I am &c.,

A. S. De Peyster."

Two days after this letter, the additional Indigenous warriors and Canadian militia Langlade had earlier promised arrived at Detroit:

"**From Lieut. Gov. Hamilton.**

Detroit, 15th June 1777.

I have the honor to inform your Excellency, that the Ottawas, Chippewas, Pouteowattamis, Hurons, Miamis, [have] come to this place and are to meet in Council on Tuesday next. There are also some Shawanese, Delawares, Quashtanows, but a few in Number.

I shall keep them together as long as possible in expectation of your Excellency's orders. Tho' the Majority should return home, I make no doubt of being able to assemble a Thousand Warriors in three weeks, should your Excellency have occasion for their services.

I have the honor to be, most respectfully, Your Excellency's most devoted & most humble servant.

Henry Hamilton."

However, the campaign of 1777 had already commenced by this time, with the embarkation of the English army, numbering upwards of ten thousand men, three days before, on the 12th of June. With General Burgoyne in command, the English fleet proceeded across Lake Champlain once more, with the objective of reducing Fort Ticonderoga, which the American army had selected for their last stand late the previous year, and the capture of which circumstances had dictated be postponed until the present.

As eyewitness volunteer, Thomas Anburney (circa. 1759 – 1840) later recalled of the fleet's voyage, in his "*Travels Through the Interior Parts of America*" (1789):

"*All things being in readiness, Burgoyne, in the early summer of 1777, sailed up Lake Champlain; and, on the 17th of June encamped on the western shore of that lake at the falls of the little river Bouquet, now Willsborough. At this place he was joined by about four hundred Indians, under the Chevalier St. Luc and Charles De Langlade, whom, in a council and war feast called and given specially for the purpose, he addressed in a speech designedly couched in their own figurative language, and intended both to excite their ardor in the approaching campaign, and 'to inculcate those humane principles of civilized warfare which to them must have been incomprehensible'.*"

Auburney later added:

"*I cannot forbear portraying to your imagination one of the most pleasing spectacles I ever beheld. When we were in the widest part of the lake, whose beauty and extent I have already described, it was remarkably fine and clear, not a breeze was stirring, when the whole army appeared at one view in such perfect regularity as to form the most complete and splendid regatta you can possibly conceive. In the front, the Indians went in their birch bark canoes, containing twenty or thirty each; then the advanced corps in regular line with the gun boats; then followed the 'Royal George' and 'Inflexible', towing large booms — which were thrown across two points of land — with the two brigs and sloops following; after them, Generals Burgoyne, Philips and Riedesel in their pinnaces; next to them the second battalion, and the rear was brought up with the settlers and followers of the army.*"

On June 24th, General Burgoyne addressed the Indigenous contingent of his army, in which Charles Langlade and Luc de la Corne commanded, thus:

"**Chiefs and Warriors,**

The great King, our common father, and the patron of all who seek and deserve his protection, has confided with satisfaction the general conduct of the Indian tribes, from the beginning of the troubles in America. Too sagacious and too faithful to be deluded or corrupted, they have observed the violated rights of the parental power they love, and burned to vindicate them. A few individuals alone, the refuge of a small tribe, at the first were led astray; and the misrepresentations, the specious allurements, the insidious promises, and diversified plots in which the rebels are exercised, and all of which they employed for that effect, have served only in the end to enhance the honor of the tribes in general, by demonstrating to the world how few and how contemptible are the apostates! It is a truth known to you all, these pitiful examples excepted — and they have probably before this day hid their faces in shame — the collective voices and hands of the Indian tribes over this vast continent, are on the side of justice, of law, and the King.

The restraint you have put upon your resentment in waiting the King, your father's call to arms, the hardest proof, I am persuaded, to which your affection could have been put, is another manifest and affecting mark of your adherence to that principle of connection to which you were always fond to allude, and which is the mutual joy and the duty of the parent to cherish.

The clemency of your father has been abused, the offers of his mercy have been despised, and his farther patience would, in his eyes, become culpable, in as much as it would with-hold redress from the most grievous oppressions in the provinces, that ever disgraced the history of mankind. It therefore remains for me, the General of one of his Majesty's armies, and in this council his representative, to release you from those bonds which your obedience imposed. Warriors you are free — go forth in might and valor of your cause — strike at the common enemies of Great Britain and America — disturbers of public order, peace and happiness, destroyers of commerce, parricides of state." Burgoyne then pointed out the officers of his army's German allies. Before continuing: "*The circle round you, the chiefs of his Majesty's European forces, and of the Princes [of] his allies, esteem you as brothers in the war; emulous in glory and in friendship, we will endeavor reciprocally to give and to receive examples; we know how to value, and we will strive to imitate your perseverance in enterprise and your constancy, to resist hunger, weariness and pain. Be it our task, from the dictates of our religion, the laws of our warfare, and the principles and interest of our policy,* "*to regulate your passions when they overbear, to point out where it is nobler to spare than to revenge, to discriminate degrees of guilt, to suspend the uplifted stroke, to chastise and not to destroy.*

This war to you my friends is new; upon all former occasions, in taking the field, you held yourselves authorized to destroy wherever you came, because everywhere you found an enemy. The case is now very different.

The King has many faithful subjects dispersed in the provinces, consequently you have many brothers there, and these people are more to be pitied, that they are persecuted or imprisoned wherever they are discovered or suspected, and to dissemble, to a generous mind, is a yet more grievous punishment.

Persuaded that your magnanimity of character, joined to your principles of affection to the King, will give me fuller control over your minds, than the military rank with which I am invested. I enjoin your most serious attention to the rules which I hereby proclaim for your invariable observation during the campaign.

I positively forbid blood-shed, when you are not opposed in arms. Aged men, women, children and prisoners, must be held sacred from the knife or hatchet, even in the time of actual conflict. You shall receive compensation for the prisoners you take [...].

He then concluded by saying, "*bear immoveable in your hearts this solid maxim, (it cannot be too deeply impressed) that the great essential reward, the worthy service of your alliance, the sincerity of your zeal to the King, your father, and never-failing protector, will be examined and judged upon the test only of your steady and uniform adherence to the orders and counsels of those to whom his Majesty has entrusted the direction and honor of his arms.*"

On June 29th, the English fleet came within sight of Crown Point, and on July 1st, it appeared before Ticonderoga. The fort was commanded by General Arthur St. Clair (circa. 1736/37 – 1818), former President of the Continental Congress, who had assumed command of the post only three weeks before, and who's own army was outnumbered by General Burgoyne's, approximately four-to-one, a fact unknown to St. Clair at the onset of the siege. The next day, on the morning of July 2nd, a detachment of Burgoyne's army, under the command of Brigadier General Simon Fraser (1729 – 77), screened by Indigenous warriors and Canadian militia, seized an unutilized hilltop then called "*Sugar Loaf*" (modern-day Mount Defiance), cutting St. Clair's line of communication with nearby Mount Hope and with Lake George, while generals Friedrich Adolf Riedesel (1738 – 1800) and William Phillips (circa. 1731 – 81) pushed on Ticonderoga.

It was on the morning of July 5th that General St. Clair awoke to the gravity of his situation, when he and his sentinels beheld sight of the English establishing artillery batteries on the nearby earthen high rise called "Sugar Loaf", and from which their generals were eyeing their every movement through telescopes. St. Clair at once called a war council with his officers to decide the fate of the fort, the result of which was the immediate abandonment of the whole position, in which so much confidence had hitherto been placed. Accordingly, on the night of the 6th, a retreat commenced, with vast quantities of guns, ammunition and provisions being abandoned to the enemy. However, Burgoyne's army caught up with St. Clair's retreat in the dual battles of Hubbardton, on July 7th and Fort Anne, on July 8th, both of which resulted in further American withdrawals.

Before advancing further, on July 11th, while awaiting the consolidation of his widespread Indigenous allies, General Burgoyne wrote Lord George Germain (1716 – 85), the Secretary of State for the Colonies of the United Kingdom (a.k.a., the Secretary of State for the American Department) from Skenesborough (modern-day Whitehall, New York), informing him of the campaigns progress thus far. This letter, in part, reads:

"I am informed that the Ottawas and other Indian tribes, who are two days' march from us, are brave and faithful, and that they practice war and not pillage. They are under the orders of M. Saint Luc [de la Corne], a Canadian of merit, and one of the best partisans of the French cause in the last war, and of M. de Langlade, the very man who with these tribes projected and executed Braddock's defeat."

In early August, in a bid to seize more desperately needed supplies and provisions that were being stored there by the American army, General Burgoyne ordered Lieutenant Colonel Friedrich Baum (1727 – 77), at the head of a detachment, consisting of approximately eight hundred regular troops, supplemented by Canadian militia, Indigenous warriors, etc., under the command of Luc de la Corne, to capture the town of Bennington, Vermont, which he believed to be lightly defended, while in reality, it was garrisoned by approximately fifteen hundred men under the command of General John Stark (1728 – 1822). From August 11th to 15th frequent skirmishing occurred as the opposing armies probed one another's lines, with the battle itself formally commencing in the afternoon the 16th, following heavy rainfall, near a farm in Walloomsac, New York, approximately ten miles (16 km) from Bennington, Vermont, the result of which was not only the decisive defeat of Lieutenant Colonel Baum's outnumbered mixed detachment, but the death of Baum himself, who was mortally wounded during the engagement.

The dismal result of the battle, combined with the death of Jane McCrea (b. 1752), at the hands of at least one Indigenous warrior theoretically under his command, also compelled Luc de la Corne to depart Burgoyne's army (after stinging criticisms from General Burgoyne himself concerning his leadership), taking with him a great many of the Indigenous warriors and Canadian militia that had accompanied the expedition hither, however, a select few remained, among them, Charles Langlade, who commanded, but Burgoyne's army was now seriously short on reconnaissance runners, skirmishers and foragers, while its provisions and supplies continued to dwindle, hundreds of casualties had been incurred with no tangible gains, and the steady approach of winter meant that Burgoyne's army would soon need to establish winter quarters — his options either a retreat to Ticonderoga or an advance on Albany, which would take his army deeper into American territory. With calls to retreat dismissed as dishonorable, Burgoyne elected to push on Albany.

In doing so, on September 19th, the vanguard of his army encountered an American defensive line, commanded by General Horatio Gates and Benedict Arnold, in the vicinity of Saratoga, with skirmishing quickly graduating into a desperate struggle which persisted until sundown, with the Americans ultimately effecting another withdrawal during the night. However, Burgoyne hesitated in pursuing, electing instead to await a diversionary attack on Fort Montgomery on the New York frontier by General Henry Clinton (1730 – 95), which was then delayed until October 6th. During the intervening period, the situation of Burgoyne's army had further deteriorated, with the traditional departure of his remaining Indigenous warriors and Canadian militia under Charles Langlade for home in advance of winter, while provisions and ammunition became critically short. By October 13th, Burgoyne's army was not only vastly outnumbered, but hopelessly surrounded, and on the 17th, in acknowledgement of his impossible position, he surrendered the remainder of his army, numbering approximately six thousand men, to General Horatio Gates, a decision which would drastically altered the course of the war, as Burgoyne's surrender marked American's biggest victory yet and encouraged England's old enemy, France, to formally enter into allegiance with the Americans against them, while the Spanish became all the bolder. Yet the war was far from over.

In the spring of 1778, Charles Langlade was once again called upon to raise and lead a contingent of Indigenous warriors and Canadian militia to aid the English cause, with his nephew, Claude-Charles Germaine Gautier de Vierville (circa. 1737 – 1803), having spent the fall of 1777, through the subsequent spring, visiting the many western Indigenous Nations, tribes, bands, etc., attempting to induce them to join the upcoming campaign on his uncle's behalf.

The latter's official "*Journal*" of his efforts, reads, in part:

"To His Excellency, de Carletonne, General for his Britannic Majesty in Canada.

Having found myself able and indeed designed to go and induce the Nations of the Mississippi to come and take your orders, I left two mountains the 28th [October, 1777], to carry out my mission and accidents have so detained me that I was not able to go to Missilimakinac with my Indians until the 31st where after presenting my orders to the Commandant and receiving his I set out again the 6th [November] for La Baye and arrived there the 25th where I began to announce your plans which I supported and confirmed in Indian fashion by wampum belts and presents.

[...]

While I remained at this post [La Baye], I sent runners to the winter quarters of the Indians in the vicinity with belts and presents both to several Folles Avoines and to Puants seeing that M. de Langlade did not come into this region this year.

[...]

The 3rd of January, 1778, I continued my journey to the River La Roche, carrying out my orders on the way up to the 14th of it [January] and I fell upon a lake near 2 villages, whose inhabitants, one to the number of 100 Puants, the other 200 Sakis, had left for winter quarters, and the 15th I arrived at the River La Roche where there was no one. I was compelled to seek them taking the road as well as I could to Prairie du Chien, and at all the little lodges I met with I announced your plans, as far as the Prairie du Chien where I was awaited by a part of each nation who were meanwhile in winter quarters and who had very little to eat.

[...]

The 17th I had a runner leave to go and seek Sabache, a great Scioux chief, and another to go among the Sauteux of Manominikara with belts and the customary presents. For them I made use of the name of 'Mr Pehster, their father at Missil.' [Captain de Peyster, Commandant of Michilimackinac.] I invited them to come and see me promising them peace with the Scioux.

[...]

7th April, I arrived at River St. Pierre where I found St. Berty and several other workmen with De Sarpeton. I spoke to them and talked about war, with a belt and ordinary presents.

[...]

20th. I took the Road to prairie du Chien gathering on the way the most Indians it was possible.

26th. Arrived at Prairie du Chien where I expected the nations and prepared to receive them.

I bought food, drink and some merchandise that I thought necessary, Indians arrived every moment from winter quarters.

[...]

I received a letter from Sr. de Langlade through Siskomsin in which he commanded me to speak to all the chiefs and warriors and not to others, that he himself was a warrior and not a chief, that he invited his comrades the warriors to come & see him at La Baye and to succeed in this they had only to take this tomahawk by one end because he held it by the other.

[...]

The 13th May, left the prairie and took the road for the Village of the Renards [Foxes] with seven Scioux families and arrived there the 15th and waited till they came.

The 17th, I talked war [...].

18[th.] Left for the Sakies [Sauk] and on the way I spoke to [the] different [Indigenous Nations, bands, tribes, etc.,] that I met.

22nd. I arrived at the Village of the Sakies and the next day I talked war.

26th. Stopped at the Village of Nibakoa [...].

27th. Arrived at the portage with my Scioux and the Folles Avoines [Menomonee] [...].

29th. I sent a runner to see if the Renards and Sakies were coming, the Puants of the River La Roche came to join me there.

[...]

2nd June. Arrived at La Bay where I found Sr. de Langlade waiting for me, he was anxious on account of my delay and after telling him a part of my troubles I gave him an account of my mission.

3rd. I remitted to Sr. de Langlade recruits, comprising men women and children:

- 37 Scioux and families.
- 20 Renards and families.
- 20 Sakies and families.
- 20 Puants [of] River La Roche.
- 6 Nabakoa and families.
- 80 Puans and families. &
- 7 Agos and families.

4th. Sr. de Lincot, the younger, arrived from the Village of the Agosoin and in giving the account of his mission, he said to Sr. de Langlade, his friend, that the Spaniards had sent word to the

Agosoin not to heed the 'venimous and empoisoned mouths' which should come or which had already spoken to them that those bad men had no other end in view than to destroy them [...].

[...]

After handing over my recruits of two hundred and ten men to Sr. de Langlade, not including women and children, the Folles Avoines, to whom I had spoken, came to join the number of men in camp, and all together, we departed and de Langlade and I [set out] from the Bay [...] the 6th of June 1778 for Missilimakinac, with the aim of so well pleasing the Indians that we could make them go to Montreal, so let it be.

[signed] C. GAUTIER,
VRETENEQUE [a Renard/Fox chief],
TESKINAWA [a Sakie/Sauk chief],
ORESHKATÉ [a Scioux chief].

[Indorsed:] From the best information I can get it appears to me that Mr. Gautier has met with the many difficultys set forth in the body of this his Journal, and that he was absolutely under the necessity of putting the Government to some extraordinary expense. Given under my hand at Fort Machilimackinac this 22nd day of June 1778.

A. R. S. De Peyster, Major to the Kings Commanding."

In the meantime, Michilimackinac-based Irish fur trader and merchant, John Askin (1739 – 1815) noted the movements of Charles Langlade and Gautier's assembled Indigenous force in a letter addressed to a business associate earlier that month:

"*Michilimackinac, June 17, 1778.*

[To] Mr. John Hay, Esq., Detroit.
As a true Irishman I want to tell you that at this present time I have nothing to say, or rather that it worth your hearing, all the spring news from Montreal you must have had. Your last canoes from Montreal left about the 16th of May, at which time there was

not any vessels arrived from London, or any part of Europe at Quebec.

Messrs. Langlade and Goties [Gautier, Langlade's nephew] are on their way from La Bay here with above two hundred warriors who are going down the country.

[...] This is my busy time, I shall therefore conclude by presenting Mrs. Hay & Family with Mrs. Askin & my compliments. I am, etc.,"

Through the summer, Langlade's force was employed in defending the Canadian frontier, while detachments periodically raided American possessions. This continued until the fall, when American Colonel George Rogers Clark (1752 – 1818), commanding Virginian forces, captured several minimally defended English outposts in Illinois Country, among them, Fort Sackville and Fort Vincennes (modern-day Knox County, Indiana). In response, the Governor of Quebec, Henry Hamilton (circa. 1724 – 96), plotted an expedition to retake all that had been lost and drive Clark back. To aid in this venture, the Commandant of Michilimackinac issued Langlade and his nephew the following orders:

"*To Monsr. Captain Langlade and Lieut. Gautier.*
　　　　Given at Michilimaquenac, this 26 October, 1778.

Monsieurs — In accordance with the power that has been given me by his Excellency, General Haldimand, Commandant-in-Chief of the Armies of his Majesty, the King of Great Britain, in Canada, etc., etc., to do all in my power to assist Lieutenant Governor Hamilton in all his enterprises against the Rebels, and as I have learned by letter from the Lieutenant Governor that he has gone to dislodge the Rebels of the Illinois and asks me to give him assistance — You are ordered by these presents to depart and try to arouse the [Indigenous] Nations. Monsieur Langlade from the Grand River as far as St. Joseph, where are the Court Oreilles and the Sauteur, causing them to assemble without loss of time at St. Joseph.

Monsieur Gautier will go direct to St. Joseph, there addressing himself to Mons. Chevalier, in order to require him to assist Mons. Ainse in assembling the Pottawatomies, while Gautier does his best to obtain Intelligence of the situation of Monsieur Hamilton, making his report thereof to Monsieur Langlade. They will do their best to join him by the shortest route, or descend the Illinois River if possible and better calculated, to second the operations of Monsieur Hamilton.

As one cannot arrange for operations in case Monsieur Hamilton has given up [his expedition] and returned to Detroit, in such an event, if you do not consider yourselves strong enough to make a stroke on the Caskakias, or at the Cahokias, you will send back the [Indigenous warriors] to their wintering-grounds and you will regain your different posts by the shortest possible route.

Monsieur Langlade will go by La Bay, and Monsieur Gautier to the Mississippi, and there try to keep the [Indigenous] Nations well disposed for the service until the arrival of new orders.

In this enterprise, I recommend to you to exhort the warriors to use Humanity towards the prisoners, and others who are found without arms since there are English traders retained by force among [the Rebels].

The prisoners will be ransomed. As the Nations have already had, in general, many presents from His Majesty, you are recommended top incur as little expense as the nature of the service will permit in giving them nothing that is not absolutely necessary.

A. S. De Peyster,
Major of the Reg. Of the King and Commandant
at the said post and dependencies."

The very next day, de Peyster wrote to General Haldimand, informing him of Langlade and Gautier's employment in Governor Hamilton's Illinois expedition thus:

"*To His Excellency, the Commander in Chief [General Haldimand].*

Michilimackinac, 27th Oct., 1778.

Sir, — Soon after my letter of the 24th instant [of this month] was dispatched by a light canoe, Messrs. Langlade and Gautier arrived here and informed me that they were sent up to attend my order. I was surprised they [brought] me no letters, but they tell me Your Excellency was at Chamblée and that Lieutenant Colonel Campbell sent them off lest the weather should set in so as to prevent them getting up. I have come to the resolution to send these Gentlemen off to give every assistance in their power to Lieutenant Governor Hamilton.

I have provided them with some Goods, which I believe with their presence amongst the Indians will do more good than I could have expected by sending my Belts by the hands of Indians.

Mr. Langlade is to undertake the Grand River, near which the Ottawa's and Chippewa's from the place winter. And Mr. Gautier is to proceed straight to St. Joseph's, where he will give orders for the Indians in that neighborhood to assemble whilst he endeavors to get intelligence of the route Mr. Hamilton has taken, so as to be able to join him with all [haste].

Mr. Hamilton by this means will not meet with any impediments from want of such assistance as [is] in my power to give him.

Should they find that he is returned to Detroit, they then have orders to cross the country to their old stations, to keep the La Baye and Mississippi Indians in temper and there wait further orders.

I also sent off my Interpreter to St. Joseph's to bring me back necessary intelligence.

At this present juncture, I should have found the benefit of having the sloop, Welcome, as I have been obliged to press from some of the inhabitants […] to make out a canoe to transport them to St. Joseph's, and the winds are rather high.

I have the honor to be, with the greatest respect, Your Excellency's most humble and obedient servant,

A. S. De Peyster."

As per their instructions, Langlade, Gautier and a contingent of Indigenous warriors whom they had raised and led, joined Governor

Hamilton on his army's march into Illinois against Colonel George Rogers Clark, through November 1778, with the entirely of the Governor's army arriving outside Fort Vincennes on December 14th. According to Clark's own intelligence, Governor Hamilton's army consisted of "**thirty regulars [troops], fifty French volunteers, and four hundred Indians**" led by Langlade and seconded by Gautier. Against such a force, the local populous made no resistance, while the "garrison" of the fort itself, which consisted of only two men, Captain Leonard Helm (circa. 1720 – 82), and a private soldier named "*Henry*", made a commendable effort to appear more formidable than they actually were, by loading and firing a cannon at Governor Hamilton's approaching army, but which had no effect. Before they could reload and fire again, Governor Hamilton called out to the men, requesting their surrender. Captain Helm initially declined, replying that "***No man enters here until I know the terms [of the surrender which was requested].***"

To this, Governor Hamilton replied that, "***You shall have the honors of war.***"

Satisfied with this answer, Captain Helm surrendered himself, the private soldier named "Henry" and Fort Vincennes to Hamilton. Helm even invited the Governor to share in some whisky while they discussed further matters, and whether that offer had any sway on his decision or not, Hamilton nonetheless decided to winter in the fort, before resuming his pursuit of Clark in the spring.

In the meantime, Charles Langlade's nephew, Gautier, returned to the Mississippi to exert himself in securing more Indigenous warriors for the coming spring, while Charles Langlade himself, personally reported to the Commandant of Michilimackinac, who, in turn reported to his superior, General Haldimand, thus:

"***To His Excellency, the Commander in Chief.***
                                Michilimackinac, 29th Januy 1779.

Sir, — I did myself the honor to write to your Excellency on the 27th of October acquainting you with the steps I had taken towards giving assistance to Lt. Gov. Hamilton, having sent Messrs.

Langlade, Gautier & Ains [Interpreter at Michilimackinac]. [They have] returned with the following report, […] that they did not reach the mouth of the Grand River till the thirteenth day of November, where Mr. Langlade landed agreeable to his [intentions]. That on their way to St. Joseph's, they spoke with the Ottawa chiefs, who declined the expedition for want of previous notice, but declared themselves ready in the Spring. That detained by a continuation of bad weather, he, Ains and Gautier did not arrive at St. Joseph's until the second day of December, where they found Mr. Louis Chevalier, who had been twenty-two days from Mr. Hamilton's little army, which passed near the pays plat [flat lands] before he left it, that he, le Chevalier, was informed there that Gibault, the Priest [that] had been at the Post [of] Vincennes & at Ouia [Fort Ouatenon], with a party of rebels [had] obliged six hundred inhabitants to swear allegiance to the Congress [of America] & that by the best accounts he could get, the rebels [in] Illinois did not exceed three hundred men, who are ill provided [for].

The Above news of Mr. Hamilton's having got so far, the start being told to the Indians at the Grand River, where Langlade had raised about eighty, they declined to follow at so great a distance, on which Mr. Langlade set out for his post at La Baye and Gautier, finding that Mr. Chevalier had already taken the few Pottawatamies, which could be raised at that advanced season [for] Mr. Hamilton, set out for his post on the Mississippi, carrying with them Belts [of wampum] and [giving] speeches to exhort the Indians to be ready in the Spring if called upon. Your Excellency's answer to my letter of the 21[st. of] September (through Lt. Col. Bolton) [has] just come to [my] hand.

I have the honor &c.,

A. S. De Peyster."

The description of George Rogers Clark's Illinois forces as **"not exceeding three hundred men, who are ill provided [for]"** during this period is indeed highly accurate — Clark's situation was perilous. His army was too small to withstand a prolonged siege at either Cahokia of Kaskaskia, while so remote and barren was the surrounding country that, even as small as his army was, it could not sustain itself off the land. This set of circumstances prompted Clark to take preemptive action against Governor Hamilton, who, after passing the winter at Fort Vincennes, would march to annihilate him come spring. After receiving intelligence from Colonel Francesco Vigo (1747 – 1836) that Charles Langlade and his nephew, Gautier, had taken leave of Hamilton's army and returned to Green Bay to report on the campaign's progress, while a large portion of the Indigenous warriors they had brought on the expedition had departed, either to raid American territory, or to return home for the winter, Clark began preparations to attack the fort, the garrison of which was much reduced to approximately eighty men, including Governor Hamilton, but was armed with three cannons total and several swivels (smaller caliber mounted cannon).

On February 7th, 1779, Clarke commenced his march against Fort Vincennes with approximately one hundred and seventy-five men, while approximately forty-five others, armed with two four-pound cannon were dispatched to blockade the White River on the Wabash, by which provisions and supplies occasionally found their way to Governor Hamilton's men in the fort. For nearly a week, Clark and his men marched towards their objective, across severely inundated country, while starvation began to set in. Fortunately for them, on February 22nd, an Indigenous canoe of provisions and supplies, intended for Fort Vincennes, was captured by Clark's men stationed on the White River on the Wabash, the contents of which; buffalo beef; corn; kettles; etc., were eagerly distributed to his starving men. Thus refreshed, the next day, just before sundown, Clark and his men began their final push against the fort.

Their movements obstructed from view by a steep bank, they approached to within thirty yards of the walls, before they opened fire on the English sentries posted topside by Governor Hamilton. Their first volley was actually mistaken for the firing of some of Hamilton's allied Indigenous warriors, who had previously saluted the fort and the Governor by the discharging of a musket volley into the sky, however, when an English sentry fell dead from a subsequent shot, Hamilton and his men realized that they were in fact under siege.

The next morning, the 24th of February, at about 9 o'clock, Clark dispatched a letter to Governor Hamilton under a flag of truce, it read:

"*To Gov. Hamilton.*

Sir, — In order to save yourself from the impending storm that now threatens you, I order you immediately to surrender yourself, with all your garrison, stores, &c., For if I am obliged to storm [the fort], you may depend upon such treatment as is justly due to a murderer. Beware of destroying stores of any kind, or any papers or letters that are in your possession, or hurting one house in town. For, by heavens, if you do, there shall be no mercy shown you,

G.R. Clark."

The English commander, however, replied thus:

"*Governor Hamilton begs leave to acquaint Colonel Clark, that he and his garrison are not disposed to be awed into any action unworthy of British subjects.*"

And so, the siege continued. But by the following day, his men's spirits waning, Governor Hamilton at last resolved to surrender the fort. He and his men were made prisoners, while Clark reinstated Captain Leonard Helm to the fort's command. Meanwhile, unaware of these developments, under Major de Peyster's supervision, Charles Langlade and his nephew, Gautier, continued their efforts to solicit additional Indigenous aid, with which they had hoped to reinforce Governor Hamilton in the spring. As per a report to General Haldimand:

"*To His Excellency, the Commander in Chief.*

Michilimackinac, 29th March, 1779.

Sir, — I did myself the honor to write Your Excellency the 29th [of] January, when I informed you that Langlade had failed in his attempt to move the Indians from their hunting grounds, as they heard that Lt. Gov. Hamilton had got so much the start [on] them [in his campaign of 1778]. Since [then] I received a letter from Mr. Louis Chevalier of St. Joseph's, informing [me] that the Pottawatamie [had] returned home to pass the winter, that they brought him a letter from the Lt. Gov. informing him that he intended not to leave Post Vincent [Vincennes] till the spring. I should have been glad to have had a line at the same time. However, in compliance with Your Excellency's orders to give every assistance in my power, I again ordered the Ottawas & Chippewas to march and send off express to Mr. Gautier, requiring him to move down with a body of Sabres, Toyes [Sauk, Fox warriors] and Wernippigoes [Winnebagoes], and he by this time, should be on the march, joined by some active Canadians.

I have the honor, &c.,

A.S. De Peyster."

It was not until April that news arrived that Governor Hamilton, his garrison, and Fort Vincennes, had fallen into the hands of George Rogers Clark, with Charles Langlade's nephew, Gautier, noting it in an April 19th report on his progress, addressed to Major De Peyster at Michilimackinac, which read in part:

"At the very moment of this parley, the news arrived that Governor Hamilton was taken [prisoner]."

As he was occupied elsewhere, Charles Langlade himself did not receive the news until later still, a fact alluded to in another report of de Peyster's to General Haldimand:

"To His Excellency, the Commander in Chief.

Michilimackinac, 13th May 1779.

Sir, — I did myself the honor to write to Your Excellency on the 2nd instant [of this month — May] a copy of which letter I now enclose.

The Chippewas of the Island of Michilimackinac arrived here [on] the 8th from the Grand River, and reports that the Ottawas and Grand River Traders are on their way, they declare that the news of the Virginians building boats on the Lake Mitchig [Michigan] was the invention of some evil minded Indians, and that neither themselves, nor the Ottawas would listen to the Rebels' belt [of friendship].

Mr. Langlade arrived last night and informed me that on his arrival at La Baye [during the winter], he received an order from Lt. Gov. Hamilton, acquainting him that he wintered at Post Vincent [Vincennes, and] therefore required of him and Gautier to join him early in the spring by the Illinois River. That he accordingly out with some Indians and reached Milwaukee, [where] he received accounts of Mr. Hamilton's being taken [prisoner and] the Indians, disheartened, would proceed no further.

The enclosed letter from Gautier [the one previously referenced] will give Your Excellency an account of his expedition. Mr. Langlade assures me that a Canadian named Benclo, at the head of twenty horsemen, is travelling […] to purchase horses […] telling the Indians that they will be with three hundred men at La Baye soon. But Mr. Langlade rather believes that they mean to transport themselves to Detroit. The Indians were so much divided that it was not possible to take Benclo and his party […].

I have the honor to, &c.,

A.S. De Peyster."

On the 12th of January, 1779, George Washington had addressed a letter to Congress in which he set forth the importance of an American expedition to capture Detroit from the English, with George Rogers Clark envisioned to lead it. News of this intention belatedly reached de Peyster in late June, who responded by ordering Charles Langlade to raise a body of Indigenous warriors and Canadian militia to unite forces with a *"Lieutenant Thomas Bennett"* in defending the frontier:

"*Instructions for Mr. Langlade.*

Sir, — You are required, for the good of His Majesty's service, to start from here, and do your best to levy the peoples of la Fourche, Milwaukee, the Puants and others along the shore of Lake Michigan, and with them, hasten to join Mr. Bennett at

Chicagou; and, if Mr. Bennett has passed on, to follow him by rapid marches so as to catch up to him before he arrives at the Pée [Peoria, Illinois], and work with him for the good of the service in accordance with the orders he has received from me.

A. S. De Peyster.
Given at Fort Michilimackinac, the 1st of July, 1779."

Bennett's orders had been to proceed to St. Joseph's, where he arrived on July 23rd, and promptly set about raising a contingent of Indigenous warriors from the local Pottawatomie, erecting fortification and intrenchments, in anticipation of an American advance on that post, in conjunction with that of Detroit. But as it happened, neither American expedition took place and in August of that year, Abraham de Peyster was granted leave of Michilimackinac and was replaced in his command of the post by Captain Patrick Sinclair (1736 – 1820), who arrived in late September/early October. However, in a stark contrast to de Peyster, Sinclair had no faith in, nor respect for Charles Langlade or his nephew, Gautier, and openly spoke ill of them in at least one letter addressed to General Haldimand:

"Sir, — A supply of Indian presents is wanted very early. In that department, a Monsr. Langlade, with a Captain's commission from Gen. Carleton, a Mr. Gautier, Interpreter in the room of Mr. Ains, a man of abilities, allowed to retire by Major de Peyster, are men of no understanding, application or steadiness, though I believe well disposed to undertake services which I cannot confide in either […].

I have the honor to be with respect, Sir, Your Excellency's most obedient, humble servant,

Pat. Sinclair.
Lt. Gov. of Michilimackinac."

Indeed, Sinclair's open disdain for Langlade at length compelled Charles' dearly beloved wife, Charlotte, to begin writing letters in her husband's defense. The first of these was addressed to an unrecorded priest (perhaps Father Pierre du Jaunay, Michilimackinac's missionary for thirty years, who had educated a young Charles Langlade, was well acquainted with his family, and in early 1780, despite entering the last months of his life, was still highly influential in the greater Green Bay area). It was as follows:

"Montreal, January 16th, 1780.

Reverend Father — You have always manifested so much friendship for Mr. Langlade, my husband, that I have no hesitation in asking you to recommend me to His Excellency [General Haldimand], and remind him of the services that rendered by my husband during the twenty years he has been employed in the service, to the detriment of his private interests and of his family's welfare. In one of his letters written last autumn and dated at Michilimackinac, he tells me that the Commandant [Captain Sinclair], influenced either by his enemies or by caprice, has given him much annoyance by making use of his own pupils instead of him. He does not deserve such a reward, as you know. I also fear that some of those same enemies may turn his Excellency against him. A few words from you might prevent this and have justice done him, as is his due.

If His Excellency would grant me a permit for a canoe […] this spring, I would go and join him [Langlade, her husband], and I could thus take my things and minor necessaries. I therefore beg you, reverend father, to be good enough to speak to him [His Excellency, General Haldimand] about it, […] you will be doing a good action, as is your custom.

I remain with respect, Reverend Father,

Dourana [Bourassa] Langlade."

Charlotte's second letter in defense of her husband was addressed to His Excellency, General Haldimand himself, in which, while requesting transportation to join her husband at his new post, reminded the General of Langlade's service thus far:

"Montreal, 22nd May 1780.

My General, — It is to you alone that I can apply for permission, to have a canoe to go to M. de Langlade, my Husband, who desires me, and who has been for several years in the service of his Majesty, at the upper posts, and is now at Michilimackinac; The zeal of his service and his disinterestedness have made his fortune so small that I have no other resource than to entreat you to command Mons. Campbell to pay me the six months of his salary, which will fall due next month, in order that I may make some small provision for this hard journey.

The uprightness and the devotion with which M. de Langlade has served his Majesty for twenty years on different occasions, make me hope that His Excellency will not refuse me this favor. He can see a sketch of his services in the most gracious letter of His Excellency, General [Thomas] Gage, at the time of the defeat of the fort at Michilimackinac [during Pontiac's War — June 2nd, 1763], a copy of which I add here [See previous chapter for said letter], not daring to entrust the original to the post office.

I am with the most profound respect, My General, the most humble & most obedient servant of Your Excellency,

Dourna [Bourassa] Langlade."

Meanwhile, on June 16th, 1779, Spain formally declared war on Great Britain, after having previously entered an alliance with France, America's ally, the month before. For Spain, the goal in doing so was the acquisition of the Mississippi Valley, in which the British profited greatly from trade. The day after the declaration was announced, Lord George Germain wrote General Haldimand from London, ordering him to immediately commence with a military campaign against the Spanish posts along the Mississippi, while an army and naval fleet under Major General John Campbell (circa. 1727 – 1806) was to proceed against Natchez, where the latter would then rendezvous with the army from the north, which, en-route, was intended to capture St. Louis. The Spanish, however, acted first.

In spite of his council's recommendation to focus exclusively on defensive preparations, Don Bernardo de Galvez (1746 – 86), the

Spanish Governor of New Orleans took it upon himself to organize a preemptive campaign against the British, targeting their posts in the Mississippi Valley. He personally assembled an army of approximately fourteen hundred men, consisting of regulars, local militia, volunteers and several Americans, among them, Oliver Pollock (1737 – 1823) of Virgina — the inventor of the dollar ("$") sign, and despite being poorly equipped, Galvez's army marched against the British post of Fort Manchac, located on the strategic confluence of the Manchac Bayou and the Mississippi River (modern-day East Baton Rouge Parish, Louisiana), capturing it on September 8th, 1779, before moving against Baton Rouge, which was taken by stratagem and surrendered on September 21st. With this success, Galvez's army not only took five hundred prisoners and acquired thirteen pieces of heavy artillery, but as per the terms of Baton Rouge's capitulation, possession of the neighboring post of Natchez, one hundred and thirty miles up the Mississippi, was also seceded to Spain. Afterwards, Galvez returned to New Orleans, where he began immediate preparations to continue the campaign the next year, which commenced in February 1780, with he leading an army of approximately two thousand men upon the Mississippi, to lay siege to Mobile, which surrendered later that month without significant bloodshed. However, the British, at length, were commencing their own campaigns.

With assistance from Captain Abraham de Peyster, in his new role of Commandant of Detroit, and under the watchful eye of General Haldimand, Captain Sinclair of Michilimackinac entrusted the command of the Anglo-Indigenous expedition against the Spanish and the neighboring Illinois country to local trader, Captain Emanuel Hesse, who, on February 15th, repaired with a large contingent of allied Menominee, Sac, Fox, Puant and other Indigenous warriors to the confluence of the Fox and Wisconsin rivers, from whence, well-provisioned, they began a five hundred mile journey down to the Mississippi. Along the way, they were joined by notable Ottawa warrior, *"Matchikuis"*, whose extensive service under the British banner, like Charles Langlade, had permitted him to wear the scarlet coat, awards and accolades of an officer.

In addition to this main body, three complementary forces were also raised, similarly consisting of predominately Indigenous warriors, which were intended to facilitate the success of Captain Hesse's expedition. Charles Langlade, who personally commanded one, received his orders thus:

"To M. Capt. Langlade, Commandant of the Troops of His British Majesty, ordered to make war upon all rebels, all subjects of Spain, or any other alien or domestic power allied with the said rebels.

Sir: You are commanded to put your detachment on land as near Milwaukee as the circumstances will permit and without losing time to get across the land, in order to gain the first village of Illinois, which is named Peoria. You will send by canoes as much provisions as you will find necessary by the River Chicago, taking good care not to overload your canoes, and that they are sufficient in number to carry your detachment to Cahokia, the village opposite of St. Louis.

Hasten to set out quickly in order to inform M. Louison Hamelin to follow you by the same route and keep him informed of your march from time to time […]."

And while Langlade's force was to occupy the Illinois River, the second was ordered to *"watch the plains between the Wabash and the Mississippi"*, with the third, the largest, ordered by de Peyster from Detroit, and under the command of Captain Henry Bird (circa. 1740 – 1801), to keep Colonel George Rogers Clark, who manifested a friendly disposition towards the Spanish, in the form of St. Louis' Governor, Captain Don Fernando de Leyba (1734 – 80), from potentially interfering by rendering military assistance.

St. Louis, or *"Pencour"*, as it was known in 1780, was a settlement of approximately one hundred and twenty residences, the majority of them stone, with a total population of approximately eight hundred, the majority of whom were French. It was the administrative capital of the Upper Louisianna and had grown prosperous on account of the booming fur trade, with the neighboring settlements of Carondelet, St. Ferdinand and St. Charles, among others, all having sprung up as a result of its success. The settlement was garrisoned of less than fifty men, under the command of Captain de Leyba, and was in no shape to withstand an assault, the likes of which the British were projecting against it. However, when it was learned from a trader that an attack on their home was imminent, the citizens of St. Louis rallied to the settlement's defense, with nearly three hundred villagers volunteering to fight, while dozens more volunteered their labor to dig intrenchments and build fortifications, including a raised platform, upon which five cannon were placed, giving them a commanding view of the surrounding countryside.

"*Captain Don Fernando de Leyba, of the infantry regiment of Luisiana, was commandant of the post of San Luis de Ylinoises; and having received information that a body of one thousand two hundred men, composed partly of [Indigenous warriors] and partly of troops, was being drawn up for an attack upon the town, under the orders of Captain Hesse, he fortified it as well as its open situation permitted,*" later read a Spanish account of the battle, penned by Martin Antonio Navarro (1738 – 93), the Spanish Superintendent of Louisiana, dated August 18th, 1780 and addressed to the President of the Council of the Indies, Don José de Galvez (1720 – 87), the uncle of New Orleans Governor, Don Bernado. "*He built at the expense of the inhabitants, a wooden tower at one of the ends of town, overlooking it, and placed therein five cannon. In addition to these, he had some cannon with which he defended the two intrenchments that he threw up at the other two extreme points. These were manned by twenty-nine veteran soldiers and two hundred and eighty-one countrymen. The enemy arrived May 26th, at one o'clock in the afternoon, and begun the attack upon the post from the north side., expecting to meet no opposition; but they found themselves unexpectedly repulsed by the militia which guarded it. A vigorous fire was kept up on both sides, so that by the service done by the cannon on the tower where the aforesaid commander was, the defenders at least succeeded in keeping off a band of villains, who, if they had not opportunely been met by this bold opposition on our part, would not have left a trace of our settlements. [...] The enemy, at last seeing that their force was useless against such a resistance, scattered about over the country [...].*" Navarro concluded his report with a tally of the dead and wounded, which numbered twenty-nine and twenty-four respectively.

Generally speaking, Navarro's report is consistent with other eyewitness accounts of the battle, although Captain de Leyba's conduct during the engagement has been repeatedly called into question by others, with accusations of drunkenness and cowardice being levelled against him, although both may have been misinterpreted results of his rapidly failing health. Nonetheless, St. Louis had been saved. The main Anglo-Indigenous force under Captain Hesse rapidly retreated from Louisianna in two divisions — one via. the Mississippi River, the other, overland to Michilimackinac, while the smaller force under Charles Langlade narrowly escaped an attack by two-hundred-man strong Illinois cavalry contingent, which arrived in the vicinity of Chicago a mere five days after his departure from the region upon two vessels and several canoes. Their retreat of four hundred miles was affected with many hardships, most prominent among them, an almost total lack of provisions.

No sooner had George Rogers Clark received word of the Anglo-Indigenous retreat, that he mustered an expeditionary force to pursue them, numbering approximately three hundred and fifty men and consisting of regular troops, French Illinois volunteers and St. Louis Spaniards. These, under the command of Colonel Montgomery, he first ordered against the Sauks and Foxes, before they proceeded upon the Mississippi and Illinois rivers as far as Peoria, from whence, they continued on foot against the Indigenous villages on the Rock River, which were already abandoned.

Meanwhile, Captain Bird, in command of one hundred and fifty soldiers, militia and one thousand Indigenous warriors, supplemented by two pieces of light artillery, had begun his march from Detroit. Although his instructions had been to attack George Rogers Clark at the Ohio Falls, the arrival of American reinforcements from Virgina, under the command of Colonel George Slaughter (1736 or '39 – 1818), news of Captain Hesse's and Langlade's retreats, plus the movements of Clark's, compelled him to alter his course. He instead targeted the stockaded forts of Ruddle (Cynthiana, Kentucky) and Martin (Bourbon County, Virginia) on the Licking River, which surrendered after short successive sieges. Content with these minor successes, Captain Bird retreated to Detroit upon the route he had come, along the way, abandoning his cannon and shot, which were buried, to avoid their capture by Clark, who had once again organized a retaliatory pursuit force, although, like the previous under Colonel Montgomery, was soon terminated without giving battle.

In a letter addressed to General Haldimand and dated the 8th of July, Captain Sinclair of Michilimackinac attributed the failure of the Anglo-Indigenous campaigns against Louisiana and the Illinois country to; the "treachery" of Joesph Calvé, an interpreter who had been appointed to a commanding role in the campaign; Laurent Ducharme, a trader who had similarly been invested with an important role for the campaign, and had also acted as the guide for Charles Langlade's expeditionary force; while noting that a complete and utter lack of secrecy had doomed the expeditions before they had even commenced — with the Spanish having received intelligence of the Anglo-Indigenous designs upon the Louisiana and Illinois countries as early as March, upwards of two months before the campaigns against them had even begun. This fact was confirmed in the statement by one William Brown, who had been captured by the Anglo-Indigenous attackers of St. Louis on May 26th and carried back to Michilimackinac as a prisoner when the latter's army retreated.

Brown had actually served the English as a hunter for the Lieutenant Governor of Detroit, Henry Hamilton, until the latter and Fort Vincennes were captured by George Rogers Clark in 1778, after which, Brown volunteered to join Clark's expedition against the Shawnee, but deserted soon thereafter. In March 1780, he found himself in St. Louis or "Pencour" at the time, where his account begins:

"About the end of March, John Conn, a trader, went down the Mississippi with a report of an attack against the Illinois by that route. Upon the arrival of Conn, the Spaniards began to fortify Pencour [St. Louis]. The report was afterwards confirmed by

a French woman who went down the Mississippi. The woman mentioned was the wife of Monsieur Honroe. The post at the entrance of the Missouri was evacuated and the fort blown up, all the outposts called in, and the videttes of the cavalry (for all are mounted except the garrison) were placed around the village of Pencour. Platform cannon with a parapet were placed over a stone house. An intrenchment was thrown up and scouts sent out. Two days before the British detachment appeared before Pencour, Colonel Clark [George Rogers] and another rebel colonel, we believe named Montgomery, arrived at Pencour, it was said, with a design to concert an attack upon Michilimackinac, but whether with that design or to repel the expected attack by the Mississippi, it was agreed that one hundred [men] from the west side and two hundred [men] from the east side [of the Mississippi] should be equipped and in readiness to march when ordered. We believe Clark and Montgomery to have been in the village of Cahokia when the Indians were beaten off. Colonel Montgomery, or some rebel officer, was killed with a private of the rebel troops, who wore a bayonet marked "42nd Regiment". They imagined that no others were killed at the Cahokias, as they filed off early to a rising ground lower down the river than the village where all of the rebels were concealed in a stone house and could not be drawn out. Indeed, few stratagems were used, owing to Canadian treachery.

In the Spanish intrenchments numbers were killed, as the Indians occupied a ground which commanded the greatest part of it and made several feints to enter it in order to draw the Spanish from such part of the works as afforded them cover […]."

As evidenced by William Brown's testimony, recorded immediately upon his arrival at Michilimackinac and presented to Captain Sinclair, who later forwarded it to General Haldimand, an additional factor which ultimately contributed to the failure of the Louisiana and Illinois campaigns which Sinclair, and subsequently Haldimand, scarcely acknowledged at the time, was the inopportune movements of George Rogers Clark, who had been supposed to be beyond intercession distance — at the Falls of Ohio, but who like the Spanish, as Brown's testimony confirms, had been well-informed of the Anglo-Indigenous advance, and had prepared for it with much vigor. Nonetheless, the conduct of Calvé and Ducharme during the campaign remained inexcusable to Sinclair, who detailed it, among other proceedings, in the aforementioned letter of July 8th to General Haldimand:

"Sir, — I have the honor to inform Your Excellency that the two vessels sent into Lake Michigan have returned [carrying Charles Langlade's force]. They fortunately carried from this [place] a force sufficient to enable the Party retiring from the Illinois by Chicago to pass with safety through a band of Indians in the rebel interest and to embark in security. Some in canoes and some on board the vessels. The others retired in two divisions, one by the Mississippi with Monsieur Calvé, who allowed the prisoners taken by the Sacks and Outagamies, to fall into the hands of the enemy. The other division penetrated the country between Lake Michigan and the Mississippi and [have] arrived here with their prisoners. Two hundred Illinois Cavalry arrived at Chicago five days after the vessels left it. On the 26th of May, Mr. Hesse, with the Winnebagos, Sioux, Ottawa, Ochipwa, Iowa, and a few of the Outagamies, Sacks, Mascoutins, Kickapoos and Pottawatomies [...].

Twenty of the volunteer Canadians sent from this, and a very few of the traders and the servants made their attack against Pencour [St. Louis] and the Cahokias. The first two mentioned Indian nations would have stormed the Spanish lines if the Sacks and Outagamies, under their treacherous leader, Mons. Calvé, had not fallen back so early, as to give them but too well grounded suspicions that they were between two fires. A Mons. Ducharme, and others who traded in the country of the Sacks, kept pace with Mons. Calvé in his perfidy [deceitfulness or untrustworthiness]. They have long shared the profits arising from the lead mines, and from a commerce with the Illinois. The attack, unsuccessful as it was, from misconduct and unsupported I believe, by any other against New Orleans, with the advances made by the Enemy on the Mississippi, will still have its good consequences. Many of the Indians are entered, and many are riveted in our interest. [...].

The Winnebagos had a chief and three men killed, and four wounded, I fear one of them mortally. They are the only sufferers.

The rebels lost an officer and three men killed at the Cahokias and five prisoners.

At Pencour, sixty-eight were killed and eighteen black and white people made prisoners. Amongst who [were] several good artificers [skilled artisan or craftsmen], many hundreds of cattle were destroyed [...]. There is no doubt [that] can remain from the con-current testimony of the prisoners, that the enemy received intelligence of the meditated attack against the Illinois, about the time I received a copy of Lord George Germain's circular letter. A like disaster cannot happen next year, and I venture to assure Your Excellency that one thousand Sioux [warriors], without any mixture from neighboring tribes, will be in the field in April under Wabasha. His interpreter, Monsieur Rocque, is a thorough, honest man, and both have conceived the necessity for a profound secrecy, as well as the design, and manner of executing it. In order to avoid the bruited reports of couriers, and the curiosity and suspicion they always excite in traversing such an extent of country, everything was settled with Wabash here, and his wants were supplied principally by the timely arrival of the King's canoes. Sixty Winnebagos and a party of Indians from the west side of Lake Michigan are sent to cross the roads leading from the rebel posts — on the Ohio and the Wabash — to the Illinois, to cover Capt. Bird of the 8th [Regiment], who may be encumbered by artillery [which was abandoned], and to intercept convoys of provisions, or parties of the rebels occasionally in motion from either quarter.

From this to the close of harvest, small parties will be sent from here in that direction. I have hired for a year, three men who undertake to carry expresses from Niagara to this post, in ten or twelve days, which Your Excellency may think a preferable route to that of Detroit, for such matters as may require secrecy or dispatch. I have the honor to be, sir, Your Excellency's most obedient and most humble servant,

Pat. Sinclair, 84th Reg.

P.S. No accident happened to any of the Indians or others in retiring. Mons. Ducharme permitted two profligate Frenchman, who were in his charge as prisoners, to go to the Illinois. Numbers of that stamp are brought in from the Indians with their consent and approbation, and the whole are ordered in. Mr. Aines, [our] interpreter here, is sent to bring in the crew from St. Joseph's, Mons. Chevallier is his uncle, and will come in, I believe, through favor and compulsion, if he is not encouraged to stay here."

General Haldimand's reply was thus:

"Quebec, 10th August, 1780.

Sir, — I have received you letter of the 8th [of July], covering [William] Brown's information and reporting the return of the vessels [carrying Charles Langlade's force] sent into Lake Michigan and the service rendered by them to the party retiring from the Illinois, and likewise, the attacks made upon Pencour [St. Louis] and Cahokia and the cause of their being unsuccessful. It is very mortifying that the protection Mons. Calvé and others have received should meet so perfidious [a deceitful or untrustworthy] and so ungrateful a return. The circumstances of his and Mon. Ducharmes' conduct, you are best acquainted with and to you I leave to dispose of them as they deserve. If you have evident proof of their counteracting or retarding the operations committed to their direction, or in which they were to assist, I would have them sent prisoners to Montreal, in all events, they are improper persons to remain amongst the Indians, and I imagine you will think it necessary to remove them. Their influence with the Natives, unless employed for the King's interests, must be dispensed with, and there is no doubt that the Indians will soon be reconciled to whoever may be appointed to supply their wants.

I am glad to find that although our attempts proved unsuccessful, they were attended with no inconsiderable loss to the enemy.

You will find that captive artificers [skilled artisan or craftsmen] very useful at present, my letter of this date will authorize you to employ them.

After the removal of the two interested or disaffected traders, I hope you will find the management of the Indians less troublesome and more satisfactory. I hope no accident will happen to Wabasha, his and the conduct of his nation merit distinction.

Your intention of discriminating, I am persuaded, will have a good effect, and I hope the operations of the ensuing campaign will discover it.

I approve much of you having engaged the three men as couriers between your post and Niagara — It will open an expeditious communication between those posts and this part of Canada. When the men are not out, you can employ them otherwise.

I am, Sir, &c.,

Fred. Hamilton."

Considering the less than stellar conclusion of the previous year's campaign, the English and their allies, despite initial planning, ultimately undertook no large scale operations, such as those they had attempted between 1777 and 1780, during the campaigning season of 1781, which was instead limited to little more than raiding and counter-raiding excursions, as the western theatre of the war wound down, with the entirety concluding upon the defeat of Lord Charles Cornwallis (1738 – 1805) at Yorktown, in the fall of that year, October 19th — although peace would not be formalized until 1783.

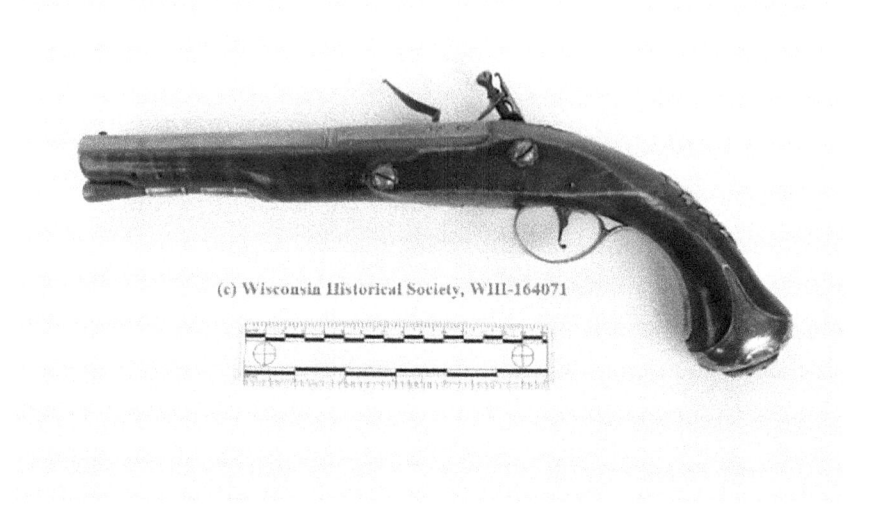

A silver-mounted flint-lock pistol (Wisconsin Historical Society, WHI-164071), owned by Charles Langlade. Modern-day photograph courtesy of the Wisconsin Historical Society, who retain the copyright of the photo and possess the weapon.

Chapter V

1782 – 1800: The Later Life & Career of Charles Langlade; His Death, etc.,

Following the conclusion of the American Revolutionary War, Charles Langlade would never again serve in a military campaign (to the knowledge of this work's compiler anyways), although the last twenty years of his life, following the conclusion of the 1780 campaigning season, would be far from an idle existence.

Over the course of the war (approximately 1777), Charles' father, Augustin, died at approximately seventy-five years of age. Upon her husband's death, Domitilde, Charles' mother, had removed to Michilimackinac. Various reasons may have induced her to do so, among them; that she herself was advanced in age by the 1770s, and in moving to Michilimackinac, she would be closer to her extended family; also, the fact that, during the war, her preferred residence of La Baye had been a potential target for American and/or Spanish forces. However, with the western theatre of the war winding down by 1781, Domitilde sought to return to her previous abode, and sought permission to do so from Captain Sinclair, who granted it in the following terms:

"By the Honorable Patrick Sinclair, Esq., Captain in the 84th Regiment, Lieutenant Governor, Superintendent and Commander of the Post Michilimackinac and dependencies, etc., etc.

Madame Langlade has permission to go to the Baye and repossess herself of her houses, gardens, farms and property; she may take a hired man with her.

Given under my hand and the Post seal, the 14th Sept., 1782.

Patrick Sinclair,
Lieutenant Governor."

Domitilde's great grandson, Augustin Grignon, asserts in his "*Recollections*", that his great grandmother likely died soon after her return to La Baye in 1782, for he was born in 1780, and later recalled that he had no memories of her from his youth.

Although no longer active, militarily, Charles Langlade nonetheless remained head of the Green Bay militia, as well as the local Superintendent of Indian Affairs, administering Indigenous relations and conflicts, while keeping the colonial British Government up to date on any developments either within or between local Indigenous Nations, tribes and/or bands, via. occasional reports. One such example is as follows and is addressed from Langlade to Captain Daniel Robertson (circa. 1733 – 1810) of the 84th Foot Regiment, who, in 1782, replaced Patrick Sinclair as the Governor of Michilimackinac — a post Robertson would hold until his death, the result of an accidental fall, in 1787. Originally written in French, the English translation suffers numerous spelling and punctuation errors, which are corrected for clarity:

"*To Captain Robinson, Governor of Michilimackinac, at Michilimackinac.*

La Baye, March 5, 1783.

Governor, — These presents are to assure you of my most humble respect, and to inform you that, according to what some Puants report, when the traders crossed the portage of the Ouisconsin, their nation wanted to plunder them, that in the confusion, there was a Puant called "Boeuf Blanc" killed, and that to be revenged, they took from Sieur Reilh, the worth of five or six pieces of money in drink [liquor] and in other things, and as they were still drunk when Monsieur Blondeau passed, he was obliged to give them also a great deal of spoil, in order to save his life [...]. Carron, Chief of the Folles-Avoines, died on the third of November, and a man named "Marcotte", a trader, was killed, we don't know whether by the Sauteux or the Sioux, but his three men were saved, although two were wounded.

I hope to have soon, the honor to go and offer you my most humble respect, and, if you have need of my service, command me wherever you please, you will find me always ready to receive your orders, for I am always, with the greatest respect, Governor, the faithful servant of the King,

Langlade,
Captain of the Indian Department."

For his services during the American Revolutionary War, Charles Langlade received an annuity of eight hundred dollars from the British Government, as well as a grant for three thousand acres of land along the (La) Trenche River in Quebec. And although he spent the majority of his time in Green Bay, his role of as "Indian Agent" often required him to travel considerable distances, including upon the Great Lakes, to Prairie du Chien and to Toronto. Following the war, he resided on the east side of the Fox River, with long-time acquaintance and fellow trader, Amable Roy, whose service alongside Langlade during war-time dated back to the French and Indian period, and Pierre Grignon Sr., another trader — among the region's most prominent, and who, by his marriage to Charles and Charlotte Langlade's second daughter, Louise Domitilde, in 1776, was his son-in-law, as neighbors.

Pierre's grandfather, François Adhémar de Monteil, the Comte de Grignan (a.k.a., simply *"Count Grignan"*) [1632 – 1714], had been an administrative Governor of Provence, France for forty-four years and was a distinguished military commander, while his grandmother, Francoise-Marguerite de Sevigne, the Comtesse de Grignan (1646 – 1705), a noblewoman, was the daughter of Marie de Rabutin-Chantal, the Marquise de Sévigné (1626 – 96), one of 17th century France's most celebrated literary figures, renowned for her letters to and from her daughter.

Pierre himself was born on November 16th, 1740 in Deschbault, Quebec, and later moved to Green Bay, sometime prior to Pontiac's War (1763) to pursue a career in trade. His marriage to Charles and Charlotte Langlade's second daughter, Louise Domitilde, was a happy one, and produced nine children; Pierre Antonie, born October 21st, 1777; Charles, born June 14th, 1779; Augustin, born June 27th, 1780; Louis, born September 21st, 1783; Jean Baptiste, born July 23rd, 1785; Domitilde, born March 21st, 1787; Marguerite, born March 23rd, 1789; Hippolyte, born September 14th, 1790; and Amable, born on an unspecified date in December, 1795.

By his first son, the self-styled Charles Langlade Jr., born to an Ottawa woman prior to his 1754 marriage to Charlotte Bourassa, Charles Langlade Sr. also had numerous descendants. Among them; Charles Langlade III; Dea or Dedier Langlade; Louise Langlade, who later married Joseph Restoul; Pierre Langlade, whose own descendants lived in Penetanguishene, Ontario, Canada; Adelaide Langlade, who later married and outlived Joseph Precourt, dying at an advanced age in Penetanguishene with many descendants; Marguerite Langlade, later the second wife of George Gordon and who died in Toronto, Ontario, Canada; Marguerite (the 2nd) Langlade, who died in Penetanguishene, unmarried; Angelique Langlade, who died in Penetanguishene at an advanced age; Charlotte Langlade, who died young in Penetanguishene; and Katrine Langlade, who similarly died young in Penetanguishene. There was also a Marguerite (the 3rd) Langlade, a cousin, who later married Charles Vasseur and died in Ontonagon, Michigan; and Jean Baptiste Langlois, who was distantly related to the Langlades.

Up until 1788, Green Bay was home to no more than seven non-Indigenous families, who, including domestic and indentured servants, numbered no more than fifty-four persons. These families were; Charles & Charlotte Langlade, plus two Pawnee indentured servants and three domestic servants; Pierre Grignon Sr., his wife, Louise Domitilde, their (then) six (and later nine) children, two Pawnee indentured servants plus twelve domestic servants; a man named "*Lagral*", and his wife; Jean Baptiste Brunet, his wife, three children and a domestic servant; Amable Roy, his wife, Agate Langlade — Charles Langlade's elder sister, two Pawnee indentured servants, a domestic servant, plus Jean Baptiste Leduc, an elder trader whom lived with them; Amable's brother, Joseph Roy, his wife, their five children, plus a domestic servant, and lastly; Marchand, a Michilimackinac Trading Company agent with four domestic servants.

In 1790, trader-explorer Hugh Heward (sometimes recorded as "*Howard*") encountered Charles Langlade conducting business upon Lake Michigan and described the then sixty or sixty-one-year-old in his "*Journal*" as a "**smart and obliging man**". The 1790s also saw the steady growth of Green Bay, with the arrival of additional settlers. Among the earliest was James Porlier, who came from Montreal in 1791. A well-educated man, he was promptly employed in the teaching of Pierre Grignon and Louis Domitilde Langlade's nine children, before briefly entering the fur trade, and later becoming Justice of the Peace, Captain of the Green Bay militia, Chief Justice of Brown County and a Judge of Probate. He was followed by Charles Reaume in 1792, after which a great many others began to arrive as well, so that, leading up to the War of 1812, Augustin Grignon figured that the population of Green Bay had grown to approximately two-hundred and fifty.

From this period, the following letter, penned on behalf of the Lieutenant Governor of Upper Canada, John Graves Simcoe (1752 – 1806), is of note:

"***To Captain Doyle, 24*th *Regiment, Commanding at Michilimackinac.***

Navy Hall, 22*nd *June, 1793.

Sir, — His Excellency, Lieutenant-Governor Simcoe directs me to acquaint you that he has been pleased to appoint you a magistrate, and has ordered the Secretary of this Province to transmit you a commission for that purpose. I am to request you to be so kind

as to send by the first convenient opportunity, to the Attorney General of this Province, residing at Niagara, the best evidence and depositions possible respecting M.M. Langdale [Langlade] and Gautiere [Gautier] of the Indian Department.
I am etc., etc.,

E.R. Littlehales."

What, if any part, Charles Langlade played in the ongoing Northwestern Indian War, which commenced in 1786 with George Rogers Clark leading approximately one thousand, two hundred men up the Wabash River in September of that year, and persisted with yearly campaigns until the defeat of the Northwestern Indigenous Confederacy, at the "*Battle of the Fallen Timbers*" in August, 1794, is unknown. Many Indigenous Nations, tribes and bands with whom Langlade associated took part, nonetheless, no documentation exists for his personal involvement. However, the following letter, addressed to Langlade in 1794, shows that he continued to manifest a desire to serve during the period:

"*To Captain Langlade, Captain of the Indian Department at La Baye.*
Michilimackinac, July 26th*, 1794.*

Sir, — I have received you letter dated 23rd *of June, and note, with pleasure, the good dispositions you seem to manifest for serving the Government. I have just written to Colonel England, commanding His Majesty's troops at Detroit, and have told him you attachment to the service, and I have no doubt that you will not be forgotten if the Government needs good men.*

I am much pleased to learn that peace is restored between the Folles and the Puants, which cannot but be most advantageous for the trade of this part of the country.

Our Court Oreilles and Sauteux warriors have returned to this post after assisting in the defeat of an American party of two hundred men as they came out of Fort Recovery, whither they had conveyed provisions. Several prisoners were taken together with three hundred and twenty-five horses and thirty oxen. The loss of our warriors was twenty-five persons, among all the Nations who numbered fifteen hundred. But three-fourths of them arrived after the action and attacked the fort when they lost a portion of the number of twenty-five already mentioned.

The warriors of this post were too precipitate in the return. This has not pleased their brothers, the Chauounons [Shawnee], Loupe [Delawares] and [the Miami], who had asked them to remain and help them repel the Americans, who are to advance towards La Glaize, where a portion of the Nations are still assembled.

Mr. Le Claire has just arrived from St. Joseph, and he tells me that all the Poux of the neighborhood had started ten days before for La Glaize, where the other Nations had asked them to go.

There is every appearance that I shall receive news of another engagement before long, as I expect a King's barque [bark canoe] to arrive at this post at any moment. I shall inform you of the same by the first suitable opportunity, so that you may communicate it, with this news, to my children, the Folles [Menominee].

I have the honor to be, Sir, your servant,
      William Doyle, Capt. Commanding."

 Despite his advancing age, through the 1790s, Langlade remained active in Green Bay's affairs, although he eventually turned stewardship of his vast farming lands over to his son-in-law, Pierre Grignon, who would manage them until his sudden death at age fifty-five in early November, 1795, after which his sons (Langlade's grandsons) took control.

 In the later years of his life, grandson, Augustin Grignon, described Charles Langlade as: "*A man of medium height, about five feet, nine inches, a square built man, rather heavy, but never corpulent. His head was bald, and in his old age, the hair on the sides of his head had a silvery whiteness; his eyes were large and deep black, with very heavy eyebrows grown together. His face was round and full, and he presented altogether a fine appearance.*

When dressed, as I have often seen him, in his British scarlet uniform, his military chapeau, his sword and red Morocco belt, he exhibited as fine a martial appearance as any officer I ever beheld." He goes on to described how, every year, on the 1st of May, a holiday was celebrated amongst the Canadians of Green Bay, with the raising of a flag and a volley of musket fire, which, in his words, "*were designed as complimentary to their militia Commandant; and thus was Charles de Langlade most affectionately reverenced and honored by the simple-hearted people of the settlement.*"

In 1796, the British military post of Michilimackinac was ceded to the United States by mutual consent, with the English regular troops, French-Canadians and most of the local Indigenous population relocating to the neighboring post of St. Joseph's, where in 1797, a fort and several storehouses were subsequently erected, with reference to such in the following letter:

"*To Captain James Green.*

Island of St. Joseph, 4th, Nov., 1797.

Sir,

I have the honor of receiving your letter dated the 28th [of] August and the 27th [of] Oct. with the sketch of the point where the new Block House is erected, which shall be particularly observed if the lots were regularly laid out, it might prevent some confusion hereafter. Mr. Lacy will inform you of every circumstance respecting the work carried on here, and what is intended to be done during the winter.

Them who have proposed to erect houses are the Interpreter, Storekeeper and if Capt. McKee is ordered here, he will also build. A council room will also be necessary, and a Storehouse for the Indian Presents, unless it is intended to have them in the lower part of the Block House. The only traders who have built are Messrs. Langlade and Culbertson. The North West Company inform me they intend to build next summer [...].

I have the honor to be, Sir, your most obt. & hum. srvt.,

Peter Drummond,

Capt. 2ⁿᵈ Batt. R. C. V."

The following document from 1798 also exists, baring Langlade's name:

"A List of Persons Building & Preparing to Build near the New Blockhouse, on the Island of St. Joseph, September 28ᵗʰ, 1798:

- *Captain LaMothe }*
- *Mr. Duggan }*
- *Mr. Langlade }*
- *Mr. Birkett }*
- *Mr. Chaubine } - Building.*
- *North West Company }*
- *Mr. Ogilvie }*
- *Mr. Gillespie }*
- *Mr. Mitchell }*
- *Mr. Pathier }*
- *Mr. Chiset }*
- *Mr. Frerot } - Preparing to build."*

As does the following document from 1799:

"Report of a Board of Survey held at St. Joseph's, the 31ˢᵗ of July, 1799, on Articles remaining in the Indian Store by order of Capt. Peter Drummond, 2ⁿᵈ Batt., R.C. Volunteers, Commanding.

Present:

- *W.M. [Wisconsin Militia] Fraser, Lieut.*
- *W.M. [Wisconsin Milita] Dean, Ensign*
- *Chas. Langlade, Merchant."*

After listing twenty-nine items, such as; *"Common hats: twenty"*; *"Russian sheeting: thirteen yards"*; and *"Irish linen: twenty-five yards"*, etc., the document is then signed:

"W.M. Fraser, Lieut., 2nd Batt., R. C. V.
W.M. Dean, Ensign, 2nd Batt., R. C. V.
C. Langlade, M't."

On February 25th, 1800, Langlade wrote Peter Drummond, the now former Commandant of Michilimackinac, now commanding the neighboring post of St. Joseph, informing him of his success in negotiating a peace agreement between at least two warring Indigenous Nations over the winter, with Drummond replying early the following month thus:

"Isle St. Joseph, March 11, 1800.

Monsieur: — It is with much pleasure that I learn from your letter of the 25th [of] February, that you have succeeded in arresting the quarrels among the [Indigenous] nations who have been at war. I hope it will be the means of securing a general peace among them, and at the same time, convince them of the attention and regard bestowed upon them by the Britannic Government.

I hope that you will continue your efforts in ensuring this peace, which is so much desired by the whole world.

I will take care to inform them at Quebec by the first opportunity of your success. The two Indians have received presents for their trouble and provisions, to take back with them for their nourishment. The [Natives] will bring the gun you sent for.

Awaiting the pleasure of seeing you this spring, I am,
Yr. very humble servant,

Peter Drummond,
Commanding."

According to his grandson, Augustin Grignon, it was after a prolonged illness of two weeks that Charles Langlade died. And it was perhaps while suffering from that illness that Langlade penned the following letter, which delt with his business affairs:

"Michilimackinac, July 26th, 1800.

Messrs. Rocheblave and Porlier.

Gentlemen — As in my power of attorney of this date, I refer you to notice for the disposal of the [money] that may be derived from the sale of my lands. My intention is that you being by keeping one hundred and twenty livres for the costs that may be incurred here. After retaining that sum, the first debt to be paid will be that due Mr. Grayson for six thousand one hundred and eighty-three livres, two sols; and after the above payments are made, to Mr. Frank, three hundred and eighty livres, and to Mr. Bouthiller, the [a]mount of my note. If there be any balance, it will remain with you on account.

I remain, Gentlemen, you[r] very humble servant,
Langlade, Captain.

Adhemar St. Martin, witness."

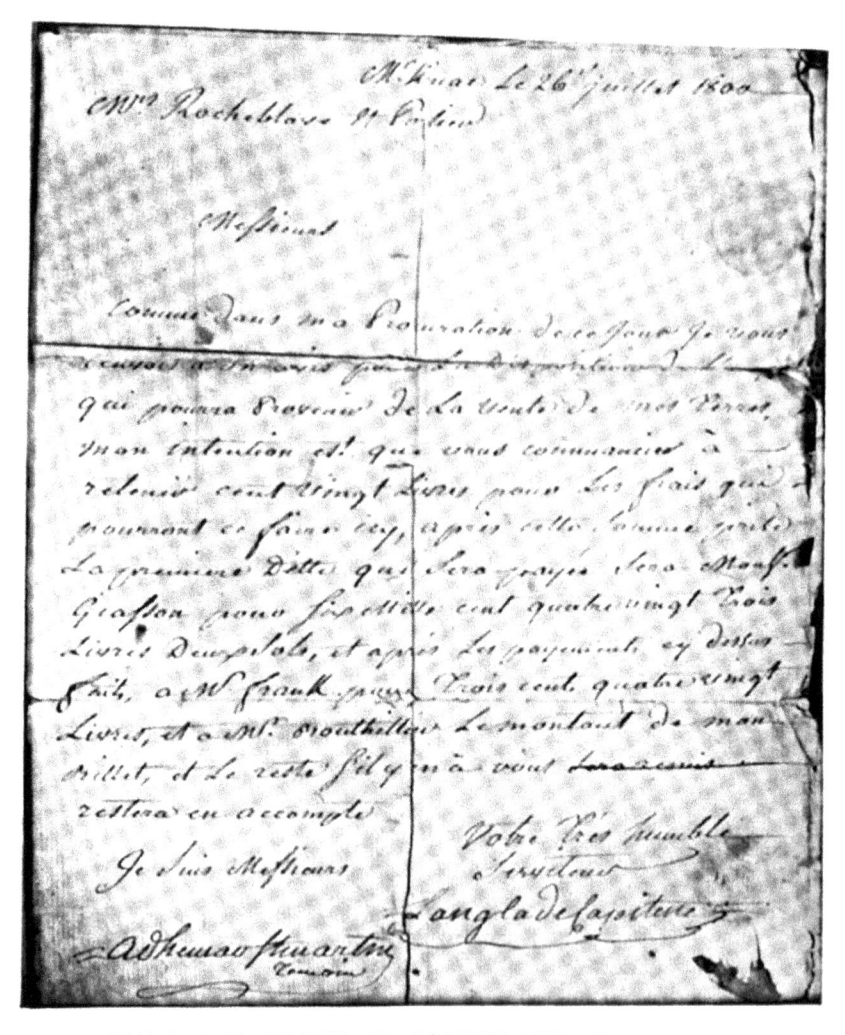

LANGLADE'S LETTER TO ROCHEBLAVE AND PORLIER
Dated, July 26, 1800. Reduced facsimile of original

Circa. 1900 black and white photograph of Charles Langlade's letter of July 26th, 1800, to Messrs. Rocheblave and Porlier. From "The French Regime in Wisconsin, 1634-1760: 1748-1760", by Reuben Gold Thwaites (1908).

No later document than the one above, penned by Charles Langlade, is known to exist (to the compiler of this work, anyways), and therefore it is highly likely that he died shortly thereafter, with the following document from spring, 1802, referring to his then recent death:

"*La Baye, 8 May, 1802.*

[To] Mr. Adhemar St, Martin, Esquire.

Sir – I have charged Mr. Rocheblave to deposit my inventory in the record office, thus signing in my name the renunciation that I make to the community of goods that I had with Mr. De Langlade for maintaining my rights. I hope that you will be good enough to receive this in my stead.

I beg you to present my respects to the ladies and believe me with consideration, Sir, your very humble servant,

The Widow Langlade [Charlotte Bourassa]."

"***Thus passed away the Sieur Charles de Langlade,***" eulogized the former's grandson, Augustin Grignon, in his "*Recollections*", "*whose long life was one of varied excitement, replete with martial deeds, and scenes of deepest interest in the forest and among the [Natives].*" Langlade, "*had, as he often stated, been in ninety-nine battles, skirmishes, and boarder forays, and used to express a desire in his old age that he could share in another, so as to make the number one hundred. He was mild and patient, but could never brook an insult; friendly and benevolent in his feelings, and was devotedly loved by all classes of his acquaintances. He was very industrious, and always employed in some useful occupation, often chopping his own woods, and hewing timber for houses. His integrity was proverbial; [...] and [he] died as he had lived, an honest man. The name given him by the Indians, is expressive of their idea of the leading trait of his character — A-ke-wau-ge-ke-tau-so, or, He-who-is-fierce-for-the-land, that is, a military conqueror. Like his father before him, he was un-bon Catholique.*"

Charles Langlade was buried next to his father in Green Bay. He was pre-deceased by his and his wife, Charlotte's first daughter, Charlotte Catherine, affectionately known as *"Lalotte"* (born 1756), who had died young and childless, shortly after her marriage to a gentleman named *"Barcellou"*. Evidently, Langlade's own death was a private, discreet and confidential affair, as no documentation pertaining to its exact date are known to exist (once again, to the compiler of this work, anyways), while British North America's enemies continued to operate in fear of him, such was the case of Spanish South American administrator, Sebastian de la Puerta Y O'Farrill, Marquis de Case Calvo (1751 – 1820), who, in 1799, arrived from Cuba to serve as military Governor of Louisiana. On October 19th, 1800, he wrote to Count Don Mariano Luis de Urquijo (1769 – 1817) from New Orleans, explaining the preparations that he and his subordinates were undertaking to oppose a suspected, renewed Anglo-Indigenous campaign down the Mississippi, twenty years after the failed attempt in 1780:

"You Excellency — After having informed Your Excellency of occurrences to the 8th of the current month, yesterday I received a letter from the Lieutenant-Governor of the settlements of Ylinoa, Don Carlos Dehault Delassus, Lieutenant-Colonel by brevet in the regular regiment of Luisiana. He informs me in that letter, dated August 20th, last, that he had had advices that the English of Canada are making efforts to get together an expedition with the various Indian tribes of the upper Mississippi and attack our possessions under the direction of the famous interpreter and leader, Langlade, as Captain. The latter, on May 26th, 1780, covered the invasion made by the Englishmen, Hesse, against the said posts where a terrible massacre was made, although the English were driven out.

[…] The Lieutenant-Governor, Lassus, was very confident of obtaining the success of his preparations, their own defenses and that of their possessions and families being an incentive to those inhabitants, which has made them show generally in the review, the most ready and effective determination so that all the citizens

of the capital city of San Luis [St. Louis], even those past sixty years [of age] have presented themselves with their carabines, thus giving a good example to the young men. It is believed that, if the crisis comes, the greatest difficulty will be to restrain these, so that they may not exhibit too great rashness. The latter concludes by assuring me that, although he counts only on the forces which he has there, I may rest assured of his zeal, which assuredly, will not allow him to neglect any effort which he believes suitable for the defense and honor of our arms, in order that the settlements under his command many be conserved.

The inclement season of the winter and the distance of five hundred leagues do not permit the prompt sending of any reinforcements to him, for they would arrive late, as it is not possible to penetrate by water, for the river, from forty leagues below those settlements, is frozen from November until March. However, the great valor of the Lieutenant-Governor, seven hundred militiamen, and the many Indians, who can be mustered in the eleven villages under his command, remove all fear from me. Meanwhile, for my part, I am doing my best to arouse the [local] Indian tribes to resist or destroy the premeditated invasion of Langlade. [...] May God preserve Your Excellency many years.

Nueva Orleans, October 19th, 1800."

The following year, Charles Langlade's elder sister, Agate, Madame Roy (formerly Madam Souligny) died. Having been born in 1722, she'd have been seventy-seven or seventy-eight years of age at the time of her death.

Langlade's dearly beloved wife, Charlotte Bourassa, would outlive her husband by nearly twenty years, dying in 1818 at an undocumented, but advanced age. She never remarried, as many of her extended family and neighbors had when pre-deceased by their spouse, instead, she lived out the remainder of her days in the shared company of her daughter, Louise Domitilde, who, after the death of her first husband, Pierre Grignon Sr., in 1795, had married her second, John Baptiste Longevin (or "*Langevin*") in 1806, but by which time, Louise had already been largely bedridden for many years by an unspecified ailment. As her granddaughter, Ursula M. Grignon, Louis Grignon's daughter, later recalled of her ancestors:

"Grandmother [Louise Domitilde] Langevin [widow Grignon] and her mother, Madame [Charlotte Bourassa] de Langlade, lived together in their old age. These benevolent old ladies were mothers to all of the inhabitants. The voyageurs were always kindly entertained by them, for there were no taverns in those days. Hospitality was their proverb and they were looked upon by the Natives as queens. Madame Langevin was an invalid and confined to her bed for over thirty years proceeding her death, but during that time she was always foremost in all good works. She boarded my uncles and their families and always kept an open table for all that chose to visit them. During Advent, it was the custom of the people to meet once a week at some house to sing hymns and praise the Lord. The first meeting was always held at her house, and after services, a sumptuous supper was served. On Christmas, everybody visited her, at which time, her tables were loaded with the best provisions that the land afforded. On that day, my father and his children always made her a call to pay their respects and receive her blessing and that of her mother. If there was anyone sick, grandmother was always the first to know it, and her Pawnee servants were sent to his aid. If there was to be a funeral, the remains were brought to her house for prayer, and after the burial, the mourners would repair thither to sup. She was a great reader and always found words of consolation for them. Madame de Langlade died in 1818, and in November, 1823, my grandmother also passed away.

The children of [Louise] Domitilde and Pierre Grignon [Sr.] were nine in number, seven boys and two girls. Pierre and Charles went to college in Montreal and returned in 1795. The parents were preparing to send Augustine, Louis, Baptiste, Domitelle, and Marguirite, and a second cousin, Catishe Cardin, when, in November, 1797 ['95], the father [Pierre Grignon Sr.] died. Thus, the remaining children were deprived of a collective education, excepting Louis, who went [to college] the next year. Pierre

[Jr.], being the eldest, necessarily took the charge of his father's business. He became in time, quite a prominent man. He was agent for several [fur trade] companies, Judge of Probate, etc. He married a Native, who bore him two sons and one daughter. In 1823, he died. His son, Robert, settled at Butts de Mort, but Bernard remained at Green Bay, where he has filled several offices of trust, such as Clerk of Court, Sheriff, etc. He married Judge Lawe's oldest daughter, and they had five children, three sons (only one of whom survives — Justice David Grignon of Green Bay,) and two daughters. Augustine Grignon settled at Kaukauna and carried on the Indian trade as long as he lived. His daughter, Marguirite married Ebenzer Childs, from whom she was afterwards divorced; and Sophia espoused L.B. Porlier. Charles went to Canada and engaged in trade for some compony there, but afterwards returned and settled at Oshkosh. Baptiste and Paul followed trading, being equipped by their brothers. Amable traded several years in British America. He married a Miss Bourassa of Mackinaw [relatives of Charles Langlade's wife, Charlotte Bourassa]. Domitelle married D. Brunette, a farmer; her descendants still reside at Howard, Duck Creek and Bay Settlement. Marguirite became Madame Corbielle. She died in 1823. Her Husband, who still survives her, resides in Bay Settlement.

My father, Louis Grignon, commenced his career as trader, in company with Augustine Grignon, in 1801. They bought of Rochbleve & Porlier; the Southwest Company; Crawford, Franks & Co., Oliver, Berthold & Co. In the war of 1812, he was commissioned as lieutenant in the Indian Department, under Col. Dickson; and on his return, he continued his trading business without interruption till the time of his death. In the pursuit of Redbird, he served as lieutenant under Captain Smith in the Indian Department, and later, he held many positions of trust in the country. He was married, in 1802, to Miss Theresa Rankin, the daughter of a trader. His children by this marriage were Charlotte (Mrs. Harteau) and Agate (Mrs. Brese). Three children were the fruits of this marriage, Elizabeth (Mrs. Mitchell) myself and Peter.

My father was an advocate of education, and procured all the educational advantages possible for his children. He was also, at various times, trustee, or director of the school.

[...] Regarding the disputed question of who built the first mill [in Green Bay], I will say that my grandfather, Pierre Grignon Sr., commenced a mill shortly before his death, which occurred in 1797 ['95], its site being where Madison Street crosses the ravine. Pierre Grignon Jr., moved the same mill to Dutchman's Creek, on the west side of [the] Fox River. Years after, he tore it down and had the iron taken to Kaukauna.

My father was actively engaged in business enterprises from 1801 until his death, which occurred in 1839, built a mill near his residence in 1818. He had the first bolting mill ever used in the northwest, and which cost him quite a handsome sum of money. He afterwards gave it to his nephew, P.B. Grignon, and it was transferred to a mill at Kaukauna. The first wharf on [the] Fox River was also built by my father, in 1818, at Grignon's Point, and he kept a ferry about the same time."

The Grignons would remain highly influential and productive in business through the nineteeth century, with many distinguished branches. Businessman, Napoleon Grignon (1842 – 1922), for example, was widely known in the Great Lakes region to ship builders during the late 19th and early 20th centuries and would later serve as the Vice-President of the Deluth Superior Dredging Company. His son, Peter Grignon Jr. would later oversee the amalgamation of the Marine Iron Company and the Deluth Dry Dock Company into the Marine Iron & Shipbuilding Company in approximately 1912.

Ursule Grignon herself was later described by historian Ella Hoes Neville as "*a part of the best of the old French régime. Of gentle courtly manner, modest and retiring, with a fine command of language, her presence was always a delight. As one passed her on the street, in her black garb, with a shawl drawn tightly about her sloping shoulders, one instinctively felt her birth and breeding. It was a pleasure to receive her recognition, and the personality of her bow was a benediction. Miss Grignon's last appearance at a* social gathering — in early years was one of the [...] most eagerly sought dancers of them all — was in the old colonial home of one whom we of today love and respect, as a part of the last of the old garrison days. She stood beside her hostess in a drawing room filled with spindle-legged furniture and old pictures, a charming presence, cheerfully, benignly receiving the greetings of a newer, younger, — I can not say better,— Green Bay; a link between the dreamy, peaceful life of the past, and the pushing, commercial existence of today."

As noted in the "*Proceedings of the Wisconsin Historical Society*", Vol. 60 (1913), "**Pierre Grignon [Sr.]'s old house stood near the intersection of Stuart and Washington streets [Green Bay, Wisconsin], about two-hundred feet south of the slough, and the same distance from [the] Fox River [on which he was a neighbor to his father-in-law, Charles Langlade, beginning as early as approximately 1760-62, as previously noted]. It [faced] the west, was fifty feet square and one-and-a-half stories high, with its gables north and south. It was built of pine logs, hewn and dressed with the plane, until they lay flat 10x12 inches. In laying up this timber, the workmen had nicely dovetailed each corner, making a very close joint — in fact, this was the case throughout the building, great pains having apparently been taken to do the work well.**

The roof was very steep, covered with cedar bark, [...] nearly six inches thick. There were many layers of the cedar covering, showing that it had frequently been repaired without removing the old bark.

The upper floor was supported by heavy beams, 12x14 inches in size, crossing the building east and west, four feet apart, and dressed with an inch [of] bead worked on the lower corners. The floors were all made of two-inch pine plank, dressed plowed, and grooved. All of the partitions were dressed in the same way, but on both sides. There were two chimneys, one on each gable, built of limestone and flush with the outside of the timbers, showing the stone from top to base. The fireplaced were high and broad,

projecting well into the room, and could easily take in a four-foot log.

The first floor of the house was divided into four rooms, besides a vestibule, in the following manner: A 25x30 feet room was in the southwest corner; on the east side of this large room were two bedrooms, 15x15 feet square, opening into it. The kitchen was a large room in the northeast corner, with a door opening to the east, also an inner door entering the vestibule on the west side. The main entrance to the house was through this vestibule, in the northwest corner, where also was the stairway and a door leading into the large front room. In this latter room was one of the fireplaces, also two triangular closets, one in its northeast, and the other in the southwest corner, made of pine; each with four doors, two below and two above. The two upper doors of each closet were ornamented with a carving in demi-relief, representing the royal insignia of France — the fleur-des-lis. How meritorious the carving was when first made [...].

Over the main entrance of the house was a portico, which showed considerable artistic taste and skill. The windows were few and small. The upper story was without divisions, save the supports of each rafter; there were two windows in the north gable, on each side of the chimney.

This old house, with its surroundings and the farm on which it stood, plainly showed the intelligence and enterprise of the man who planned and built it [...]. Could [its] walls have spoken, they would have told of deliberate councils held within, debating the chances of peace or war, of trade and commerce. They would have told of festive scenes, the table loaded with fish, flesh and fowl, gathered by the hunters' skill from the river, lake, and forest. They would have told, too, of music and the dance, so dear to the gay and festive Frenchmen. Thither came Native chiefs and warriors; white men also, for trade and profit; others for the mere love of exploration — men wise in council, strong in war, who led that host of [warriors] who surprised and defeated Braddock."

Charles Langlade's colored porcupine quill decorated buckskin travelling sack (Wisconsin Historical Society, WHI-164070). Used to carry weapons, attire, documents and so forth. Modern photograph courtesy of the Wisconsin Historical Society, who retain the copyright of the photo and possess the item.

Epilogue

The breed of people to whom Charles Langlade belonged (The "*Coureurs de bois*" and their offspring, the "*Bois brulés*", or "*Métis*" — individuals born of European and Indigenous North American communion) are highly romanticized figures in North American history, in novels such as James Fennimore Cooper (1789 - 1851)'s "*The Last of the Mohicans*" (1826) and Publius Lawson (1853 - 1920)'s "*Bravest of the Brave: Captain Charles de Langlade*" (1904; which introduced the compiler of this work to Charles Langlade in the first place), among countless others. Indeed, as author Jacob Piatt Dunn observed in his 1888 work, '*Indiana: A Redemption from Slavery*', "***Their every movement attracts the rosiest coloring of imagination. We see them gliding along the streams in their long canoes, shapely and serviceable as any water-craft that man has ever designed, and yet buoyant and fragile as the wind-whirled autumn leaf. We catch afar off the thrilling cadence of their choruses, floating over prairie and marsh, echoing from forest and hill. Starling the buffalo from his haunt in the reeds, telling the drowsy denizens of the posts of the approach of revelry, and whispering to the Indian village of gaudy fabrics, or trinkets, and of fire-water [alcohol]. We feel the genial warmth of the camp-fire that breaks the chill of the night wind, and dissipates the fog which rises from stream, bayou, and marsh, as the men gather about it and whiff the narcotic incense from their stumpy pipes***", before going on to observe that, "***what a rollicking life was this! And yet it takes but little experience in the wild [...] to satisfy one that there is far more romance in imagining*** *all this in an easy-chair than there is in living it.*" - A sentiment which the compiler of this work wholeheartedly believes could be universally applied.

In short, Charles Langlade's life and career were perhaps best summed up in the following poem, titled: '*De Langlade: The Pioneer Settler of Wisconsin*' (1876), by Bella French (edited by the compiler) from "*The American Sketch Book, Vol. III — History of Brown County, Wisconsin: A Collection of Historical Incidents with Descriptions of Corresponding Localities*", and is as follows:

"*MICHILIMACKINAC, the lake-girt isle,*
Where first the morning sun is wont to smile,
Before it drops its rays upon the lower earth;
On which they linger last at close of day,
As though a benediction they would say,
Is where our loved Wisconsin's pioneer had birth.

His father had a noble lineage,
Of many ancestors, both proud and sage,
Who were at rest beneath the smiling skies of France,
A younger son, whose fortune was his name,
Come hither, hoping that by wealth and fame,
He might the honor of that noble house enhance.

The mother was an untaught forest child
A creature, who was daring, proud and wild,
With lineage as noble as her husband's own;
For here within the land of her nativity,
Related to Nis-so-wa-quet was she,
Who had an undisputed title to a throne.

Young Charles De Langlade in his boyhood proved,
A brilliant leader where so e'er he moved.
He learned to scale the rocks and glide upon the waves.
His trusty bow and arrow brought down game,
So speedily, that the young hero's name,

Auke-wingeke-tawso, or, 'Defender of His Country'

Became a talisman of triumph to the braves.

For on a day when stern defeat had met,
Full twice the force of King Nis-so-wa-quet,
A chieftain's spirit sought him in a dream.
Take with you, King," said he, "De Langlade's boy,
His face shall lead to victory and joy.
Try once again. You're nearer triumph than you seem."

Uprose the king, next morn, and marched to war,
Bearing the child although from danger far;
Yet full of faith he made the third and last attack,
On the resisting village, and so well
That almost instantly it yielded - fell;
And full of honors proud the Ottawas came back.

Back to Michilimacinac, which rung,
With gayest notes of triumph ever sung,
While Charles De Langlade, crowned the hero of the day,
Had the assurance that in every fight
His youthful voice should counsel them aright,
His tiny feet should lead them in the better way.

Thence forth upon the war-path marched the lad,
And many victories the chieftains had,
For Fate looked smiling down where the young hero went.
Even his father's daring countrymen,
Believed in him so much, that always, when
He bore them company, they moved to war content.

And so the years sped by, and manhood came,
Adding new luster to De Langlade's name;
When that sweet, lake - girt island home to him grew small,
As he bethought him of a broader land,
Where he could look around, on every hand,

As far as eye could reach, and say he owned it all.

For, in his wanderings he oft had seen,
A bay encircled by a frame of green;
A swift clear river mingled with the waves of foam;
Beyond, a broad expanse of wood and glade,
Where beaver, mink and deer roamed unafraid,
There he would found a colony and make a home.

Till now no one had harbored such a thought.
The "fathers," it is true, the [Native] mind had taught,
And traders here had plied their money-making schemes;
But none had journeyed hither who had not
The hope that future time would cast his lot,
At least his grave, upon the land of childhood's dreams.

A hundred years since white men's feet had trod,
For the first time upon the virgin sod,
Yet fair Ouisconsin's founder yet must thither roam,
And by unwearying years of patient toil,
Must clear the lands and cultivate the soil,
And pioneer a mighty people to their home.

But after all the island of his birth,
Was dear to him, though it had lesser worth
Yes, dearer far than was the land beyond the bay.
Upon those rocks had rested first his sight;
His feet pressed first the beach, wave-washed and white;
There first his infant lips were taught to sing and pray.

The friends who clustered round him in his youth,
And all that loved him still were there forsooth;
Even the maiden who had warmed his youthful heart,
Whom, clinging to her friends and forest life,
He could not take with him and make his wife,

Auke-wingeke-tawso, or, 'Defender of His Country'

From all of these with few exceptions he must part.

His parents and their other children, too,
Would follow in the path he was to hew,
And at La Baye des Puants live and leave their graves.
The hour for their departure now was nigh.
Friends gathered on the shore to say good bye,
And their canoes were tossing on the restless waves.

Farewell! Michilimackinac, farewell!
Loved is each rock-bound cliff and shady dell!
Upon the high arched precipice, vine- wreathed,
And crowned with evergreens, De Langlade knelt.
Emotions both of joy and woe he felt,
While to his Native isle, a low farewell he breathed.

The grape-vines twined their tendrils o'er his head.
Below, the wild sweet-briar fragrance shed,
Upon the balmy air; and shimmering down,
All broken into spangles by the trees,
That waved their foliage in the summer breeze,
The sunbeams came and rested on his brow — a crown.

Then on the waves where that same sunlight fell,
Through crystal waters, lighting every shell,
Which at the bottom lay, and gilding every fish,
The party went that bonny summer day;
And as the isle in distance sank away,
A bright dissolving view, they breathed a silent wish.

That they might make, upon La Baye's fair shore,
A name and fame to last forever more,
A wish that had fulfillment in the after time;
For on those rice-grown plains, a city rose,
In wealth and numbers matching some of those,

Of the far-distant French imperial clime.

Green Bay! as it in after years was known,
Because of banks by trees and shrubs o'ergrown,
Which o'er transparent waters hung their leaves of green,
Reflected by those waters till the bay
Became distinguishable miles away,
A picturesque as well as most enticing scene!

Green Bay, a city of the coming years,
A land of promise to the pioneers,
Was ever after that De Langlade's dwelling place.
He tilled the soil and largely dealt in trade,
And many were the brilliant schemes he laid,
That might distinguish yet his noble house and race.

He built his home upon the river side,
Where he could watch the changing of the tide,
Which ebbed and flowed as regularly as the sea;
Where he could fish, mayhap, and trap his game,
Or with his stores could barter for the same;
And live a life of work, yet one bondage free.

Surrounded by the [Native] bands, he yet
Was ever free from fear and vain regret;
For, knowing of his prowess and his bravery,
The Sauks and Foxes did not dare attack,
One who would hurl such speedy vengeance back;
And for this cause, he made friends with the Menominee.

And yet the warlike Foxes tribute asked,
From each and all who by their village passed,
Which was some thirty-seven miles above the bay,
Upon the river which now bears their name.
The traders paid it with a flush of shame,

Auke-wingeke-tawso, or, 'Defender of His Country'

Until Morand resolved to do the fraud away.

His trading house was farther to the south,
Not far from the Ouisconsin River's mouth;
By lakes, and bay, and rivers, with the hardest toil,
His goods were carried from on eastern place;
Therefore he would no more submit with grace,
And so resolved to drive the Foxes from the soil.

He took De Langlade and a trusty crew,
Those who the labyrinths of forests knew;
All going out in bark canoes a glorious fleet,
They turned their faces to the river's head.
Over each canoe, a covering was spread,
Like tradesmen's goods preserved from rain and heat.

Dividing near the place, the gallant band,
In part proceeded to attack on land;
While, in the boats, the other forces hidden lay,
Save two, in each, that rowed straight to the shore,
As if to pay their dues, as heretofore,
Then pass, as tradesmen always did, upon their way.

Well planned was the surprise. They took the place,
And gave the Foxes chase, instead of
tribute, till they made a stand,
With rallied forces, and a battle fought;
Which for the Foxes only came to naught.
They were defeated and lost many of their band.

As "Hill of Death" from thence the spot was known,
Because of bodies which in heaps were thrown,
And left to decay in the autumn sun and air.
The Indians made retreat from Butte des Mor's,
And built on the Ouisconsin River's shores.

But Morand considered it unsafe to leave them there.

Two hundred miles through cold, and drifted snow,
The traders marched, and, laying many low,
Made prisoners of those who were as yet alive.
But pity swelled the captors' bosoms then,
They gave the Foxes freedom once again,
And bade them over the Mississippi to thrive.

The French and Indian war next gave a chance,
To test the scion of the house of France.
Commissioned by the Government, he sought the field,
Commandant of a force, which he had led,
From forest homes, his heart content to shed,
Its bright life-tide, before he would the country yield.

To Fort Du Quesne, he and his soldiers went,
And, urging an attack, from thence was sent.
To where the Braddock army were in camp,
All little thinking that a stern defeat,
Would very soon their mighty forces meet,
And many fall, an Indian arrow in each breast.

Toward the Fort Du Quesne, twelve hundred strong,
Had Braddock's well drilled forces moved along,
So sure of victory, that seven miles away,
All unconcerned, they stopped to rest and dine;
And while as yet they lingered over their wine,
They found how fatal to their hopes was their delay.

Now rang the Indian war-whoop through the air,
That told the French and Indian troops were there.
That shrill war-whoop that struck the stoutest hearts with awe;
Beaujeu, commander, his French forces led:
The Indians had De Langlade at their head;

Auke-wingeke-tawso, or, 'Defender of His Country'

And neither knew or followed British battle law.

Fast flew the arrows; bullets fell like hail;
And hearts that were not known to shrink or quail,
Grew cold and silent with Beaujeu's surprised attack.
He fell amid the battle's heated toil;
But, loaded with rich stores of British spoil,
De Langlade led the most triumphant army back.

Back through the sweetness of a summer time,
In beauty bursting on that northern clime;
When, like a paradise, the forests were in bloom;
When crystal brooklets murmured all day long,
In keeping with the birds' unceasing song,
And all the air was redolent with rich perfume!

But to admire De Langlade could not pause.
He was demanded by his country's cause,
Again to take the field. Thence forth, in thickest strife.
Through Canada, he led his dauntless braves;
And though while there so many found their graves,
He seemed to have a Providence-protected life.

The story of his prowess crossed the sea,
And so much pleased the king of France, that he,
An ensign's full commission to De Langlade sent.
This gave the soldier new and added zeal,
Such as ambitious bosoms love to feel,
And which a brilliant luster to his daring lent.

Privations often to De Langlade fell;
And of his weary marches, who can tell?
Sometimes his meals were made of roots, or rattlesnakes;
And oft, with stormy skies above his head,
Worn out and hungry, he would seek his bed,

In some unhealthy swamp upon the crispy brakes.

Still on he marched, and bravely met the foe,
Laid many of the valiant leaders low.
With that blind worship for his far-off father-land,
Which Frenchmen have, he felt not want or pain,
But, living in the triumphs he might gain,
He nerved to reckless deeds his savage band.

Crown Point, also Ticonderoga stood,
Both monuments to his brave hardihood.
But, later on the fatal plains of Abraham,
He met the British forces and defeated fled,
With many wounded and a thousand dead.
The victims of a fearless British leader's sham.

Quebec thus fell; with it the Province too.
Since thus it was, what could De Langlade do?
But lead his now despondent army home once more?
He loved the cause of his own father-land,
And felt more deeply than his [Native] band,
Who only loss of gain and plunder could deplore.

But, while he had within Quebec sojourned,
A lesson far more pleasant he had learned,
The one of love. A maiden with such soft- brown eyes,
Had looked upon his life and warmed his heart,
Becoming of that life a very part,
Before he dreamed it, as he found to his surprise.

Just in his prime was Charles De Langlade then.
Like a commanding spirit, among men,
He moved and worked, though not in statue large or tall.
His eyes were bright and piercing as the eagle's own,
And black as midnight when upon her throne;

Auke-wingeke-tawso, or, 'Defender of His Country'

While grace and swiftness marked his motions one and all.

Charlotte was charmed; yet could but grieve,
Her childhood's happy home and friends to leave,
And others seek among the children of the west,
Of whose wild lives she had so often read,
Those feelings only of misfaith and dread,
As of a most blood-thirsty clan, had filled her breast.

Yet, womanlike, to be her hero's wife,
She would imperil, as she thought, her life,
Consenting at La Baye to cast her future lot;
And with her coming hitherward, must date,
The first of women settlers in the State,
In whose patrician veins some Indian blood flowed not.

The British were in rule, and British law.
Extended to Michilimackinac;
And, from that fortress, the commandant sent abroad,
An order that the French should all report,
By an appearance at the fort;
Which surely was so that all might laud.

With right good will, he shook the captain's hand;
Then chose an escort from his trusty band,
And well supplied with stores sent Etherington away.
Then for a time, at least, no British law
Ruled o'er the isle Michilimackinac,
Although it was resumed at some not-too distant day.

As years sped by, increasing stores of gain,
De Langlade liked the more the British reign,
And yielded most implicitly to all their laws;
And, when the colonies a war declared,
The British neither work nor trouble sparred,

To win the influential hero to their cause.

No wonder he, a Native of the west,
So far removed from eastern interest,
Should fail to give the colonies his sympathy.
He surely did not realize that they,
With almost hopeless toil, would pave the way,
Toward a mighty nation's future liberty.

We sorrow that Wisconsin's pioneer,
By better foresight, did not help to rear,
The everlasting monument to Freedom's name,
To the inquiring world a guiding light,
And thereupon in shining glory write,
The matchless story of his deeds and fame.

But so it was. True to the British sway,
With rallied troops, he quickly made his way,
To join the forces, stationed on Canadian ground.
And through the many, long, eventful years,
Through triumphs and defeats, hopes and fears,
Was never a dereliction of truth or duty to be found.

Though in that war no records gave his name,
Within an everlasting wreath of fame,
Since those of the defeated do not thus descend,
He was rewarded by the Government,
Of Britain, by a pension yearly sent,
And by a gift of lands when war was at an end.

Nor did the new-fledged nation quite forget,
How influential was De Langlade yet,
Not more in times of war than he would be in peace.
The forest sons, through battles, he had led;
And now that peace again its luster shed,

Auke-wingeke-tawso, or, 'Defender of His Country'

It was not fitting that his work and rule should cease.

He took command of Indian affairs,
Sharing with them their pleasures and their cares,
And working always for their best and highest good.
Slowly did trade and commerce take the place,
Of battle triumph and exciting chase,
And of the weary marches through the pathless wood.

The years sped on. Around him at La Baye,
The colony grew larger, day by day.
His daughter's children often clustered at his knee.
To listen to the story of his life,
Which had been so eventful, so full of strife.
And of privation upon privation, yet dishonor free.

He lived again the battles of the past,
Yet was regretful to the very last,
That he had not participated in just one more,
So, a total of a hundred, could then have been made.
Engagements they had been of every grade,
From forays up to conflicts, of unspeakable gore.

He was by rich and poor alike revered;
Loved by the good and by the evil feared.
And as a mark of honor, every first of May,
Canadian custom was a flag-pole raised,
And many of his deeds rehearsed and praised,
All with salutes of musketry throughout the day.

So peacefully his moments glided on,
That there were signs of the approaching dawn,
Before he really knew that night had yet appeared.
But faith in his religion gave him strength,
To meet the mighty conqueror, at length,

Fearlessly, his hundredth battlefield he neared.

The bell of eighteen-hundred had just been rung;
The requiem of a dying century thus sung;
The world was ushering a bright successor in,
When Charles De Langlade took his last breath on earth,
And in another sphere experienced re-birth,
Where it is hoped there is no strife or battling.

They laid the casket where the leafy trees,
Bowed their proud heads in answer to the breeze;
And set wreathed flowers all o'er the place.
Today a big city's eager people do tread,
Where lay there lay the sacred ashes of the dead,
Though on the surface there remains not a trace.

The relics of the past are in decay;
Another people own these lands today;
And everywhere the word "Progression" is engraved;
But still a name, most dear to memory,
De Langlade's is and forever will be,
A noble name in History's bright annals to be saved.

Bibliography

(In Approximate Order of Appearance)

- *"Astoria; or, Anecdotes of an Enterprise Beyond the Rocky Mountains"*, Washington Irving, George Bell & Sons (1882 Ed.)
- *"Manitoba"*, George Bryce, Sampson Low, Marston, Searle & Rivington (1882).
- *"Seventy-Two Years' Recollections of Wisconsin"*, Augustin Grignon, Wisconsin Historical Society (1857).
- *"The Northwest Under Three Flags: 1635-1796"*, Charles Moore, Harper (1900).
- *"Charles Langlade: First Settler of Wisconsin"*, Montgomery Eduard McIntosh, Francis Parkman Club Publications (1896).
- *"Complete History of the Present War, From its Commencement in 1756, to the End of the Campaign in 1760"*, 'Printed for W. Owen' (1761).
- *"History of Canada: From its Discovery till the Union Year"*, Francois Xavier Garneau (translated by Andrew Bell), John Lovell (1860).
- *"Appendiculae Historicae, Or, Shreds of History Hung on a Horn"*, Frederic William Lucas, Henry Stevens & Son (1891).
- *"The Canadian Magazine: Of Politics, Science, Art & Literature"*, Vol. XXIII, The Ontario Publishing Company (1904).
- *"Two Missionary Priests at Mackinac"*, Edward Osgood Brown, Barnard & Gunthrop Printers (1889).

- *"Pioneer Collections: Report of the Pioneer & Historical Society of the State of Michigan"*, Vol. VIII, W.S. George & Co. Printers and Binders (1886).
- *"History of Wisconsin Under the Dominion of France"*, Stephen Southric Hebberd, Midland Publishing Company (1890).
- *"The Discovery and Conquests of the Northwest: Including the Early History of Chicago, Detroit, Vincennes, St. Louis, Ft. Wayne, Prairie Du Chien, Marietta, Cincinnati, Cleveland, Etc., Etc., and Incidents of Pioneer Life in the Region of the Great Lakes and the Mississippi Valley"*, Rufus Blanchard, Cushing, Thomas & Company (1880).
- *"Landmarks of Wayne County and Detroit"*, Robert B. Ross & George B. Catlin, Revised by Clarence W. Burton, Higginson Book Company (1898).
- *"Leading Events of Wisconsin History: The Story of the State"*, Henry Eduard Legler, Sentinel Publishing Company (1898).
- *"Magazine of Western History Illustrated"*, Vol. III, William Williams (1885-86).
- *"Journal of Captain William Trent from Logstown to Pickawillany, A.D. 1752. Now Published for the First Time from a Copy in the Archives of the Western Reserve Historical Society, Cleveland, Ohio, Together with Letters of Governor Robert Dinwiddie; an Historical Notice of the Miami Confederacy of Indians; a Sketch of the English Poet at Pickawillany, with a Short Biography of Captain Trent, and Other Papers Never Before Printed"*, Alfred Goodman (editor), Robert Clarke & Co. (1871).
- *"The British Invasion from the North: The Campaigns of Generals Carleton and Burgoyne, from Canada, 1776-1777, with the Journal of Lieut. William Digby, of the 53d, Or Shropshire Regiment of Foot"*, James Phinney Baxter, James Munsell's Sons (1887).
- *"The Southern Magazine"*, Vol. XVII, Southern Magazine Co. (1875).

- *"Ohio Archaeological and Historical Quarterly"*, Vol. XII (1903).
- *"A Popular History of the United States: From the First Discovery of the Western Hemisphere by the Northmen to the End of the First Century of the Union of the States: Preceded by a Sketch of the Pre-historic Period and the Age of the Mound Builders"*, Vol. III, William Cullen Bryant and Sydney Howard Gay. Scribner, Armstrong & Company (1881).
- *"Michigan Historical Commission Bulletin No. 5: Names of Places of Interest on Mackinac Island, Michigan"*, Illinois State Historical Society (1916).
- *"Boys' Own Magazine: The Fall of Mackinaw"*, S.O. Beeton (1873).
- *"Pioneer Collections: Report of the Pioneer Society of the State of Michigan"*, Vol. III, Thorp & Godfrey, State Printers and Binders (1881).
- *"Memoirs on the Late War in North America Between France and England"*, Pierre Pouchot (translated and edited by Franklin Hough), W. Elliot Woodward (1866).
- *"Collections and Researches Made by the Pioneer and Historical Society of the State of Michigan"*, Vol. X, Thorp & Godfrey, State Printers and Binders (1888).
- *"Collections of the State Historical Society of Wisconsin"*, Reuben Gold Thwaites & Lyman Copeland Draper, 'Published by the Society' (1876 – 1920).
- *"Proceedings of the State Historical Society of Wisconsin"*, various contributors, 'Published by the Society' (1876 – 1920).
- *"Travels Through the Interior Parts of America"*, Thomas Anburney, William Lane (1789).
- *"The History of Illinois, from Its Earliest Settlement to the Present Time"*, W. H. Carpenter and T. S. Arthur, Lippincott, Grambo & Company (1854).
- *"History of Lieutenant-Colonel George Rogers Clark's Conquest of the Illinois and the Wabash Towns 1778 and 1779"*, Consul Willshire Butterfield, F.J. Heer Press (1904).

- "*Historical Collections of Ohio: An Encyclopedia of the State; History Both General and Local, Geography with Descriptions of its Counties, Cities and Villages, its Agricultural, Manufacturing, Mining and Business Development; Sketches of Eminent and Interesting Characters, Etc., with Notes of a Tour Over it in 1886*", Vol. III, Henry Howe, Henry Howe & Sons (1891).
- "*Narrative and Critical History of America*", Vol. VI, Part II, Justin Winsor, Houghton, Mifflin & Company (1887).
- "*Some Chapters in the History of Missouri*", Eugene Morrow Violette, Journal Printing Co. (1914).
- "*Record of Testimony and Proof Taken Before Commissioners Appointed to Take Testimony in Said Cause*", Gunthrop Warren Printing Company (1914).
- "*Missouri, the Center State: 1821 - 1915*", Vol. II, Walter B. Stevens, S.J. Clarke (1915)
- "*The Settlement of Illinois: 1778 – 1830*", Arthur Clinton Boggess, The Chicago Historical Society (1908).
- "*Chicago and the Old Northwest, 1673-1835: A Study of the Evolution of the Northwestern Frontier, Together with a History of Fort Dearborn*", Milo Milton Quaife, University of Chicago Press (1913).
- "*The American Sketch Book: A Collection of Historical Incidents with Descriptions of Corresponding Localities*", Vol. III, Bella French, The American Sketch Book Company, Publishers (1876).
- "*Collections and Researches made by the Michigan Pioneer and Historical Society*", Vol. XVI, Joseph Greusel, Wynkoop Hallenbeck Crawford Co., State Printers (1910).
- "*Collections and Researches made by the Pioneer and Historical Society of the State of Michigan*", Vol. XII, Thorp & Godfrey, State Printers and Binders (1888).
- "*Proceedings of the Mississippi Valley Historical Association for the year 1908-09*", Vol. II, Benjamin F. Shambaugh, Torch Press (1910).

- *"Pennsylvania Archives: Second Series"*, Matthew S. Quay, John B. Lynn and W. M. H. Egle, M. D. (1877).
- *"The Campaign of 1760 in Canada: A Narrative Attributed to Chevalier Johnstone"*, Chevalier James Johnstone, Printed at the 'Morning Chronical' Office (1770s; published 1887).
- *"Dialogue in Hades Between the Marquis de Montcalm and General Wolfe"*, attributed to Chevalier Johnstone, Literary and Historical Society of Quebec (1770s; publishes 1887).
- *"Illinois on the Eve of the Seven Years' War, 1747-1755"*, Theodore Calvin Pease and Ernestine Jenison, Trustees of the State Historical Library (1940).
- *"Indiana: A Redemption from Slavery"*, Jacob Piatt Dunn, Houghton, Mifflin & Company (1888).
- *"Montcalm and Wolfe"*, Francis Parkman, Little, Brown & Company (1884).
- *"Half Century of Conflict"*, Francis Parkman, Little Brown & Company (1892).
- *"The American Revolution"*, John Fiske, Houghton, Mifflin & Company (1891).
- *"Beeson's Inland Marine Directory"* (1912).
- *"Minnesota: Special Limited Edition"*, Lewis Publishing Company (1915)

Milton Keynes UK
Ingram Content Group UK Ltd.
UKHW020741221124
451186UK00024B/273